BROKEN HIERARCHIES

CHOSEN HIERARCHIES

GEOFFREY HILL

Broken Hierarchies

POEMS 1952–2012

EDITED BY
Kenneth Haynes

OXFORD
UNIVERSITY PRESS

OXFORD
UNIVERSITY PRESS

Great Clarendon Street, OX2 6DP,
United Kingdom

Oxford University Press is a department of the University of Oxford.
It furthers the University's objective of excellence in research, scholarship,
and education by publishing worldwide. Oxford is a registered trademark of
Oxford University Press in the UK and in certain other countries

First edition published in 2013

Impression: 4

Published in the United States of America by Oxford University Press
198 Madison Avenue, New York, NY 10016, United States of America

British Library Cataloguing in Publication Data
Data available

ISBN 978-0-19-960589-7

Typeset in Ehrhardt
by Peter Kahrel Ltd, Lancaster

As printed and bound by
CPI Group (UK) Ltd,
Croydon, CR0 4YY

Or if there were a simpathie in choise,
Warre, death, or sicknesse, did lay siege to it;
Making it momentarie, as a sound:
Swift as a shadow, short as any dreame,
Briefe as the lightning in the collied night,
That (in a spleene) vnfolds both heauen and earth;
And ere a man hath power to say, behold,
The iawes of darknesse do deuoure it vp:
So quicke bright things come to confusion.

A Midsummer Night's Dream

If the rulers of states think only of amassing riches, they will be surrounded, surrounded ineluctably, by mean men, and the depraved. And these mean men will make the ruler think they are great ministers, and the depraved men will manage the state, and moreover calamities will descend out of heaven, and vengeance rise from the people. And if, when things have come to such pass, there be a just man come to rule, he will be helpless against the evil; for private gain is not prosperity, and equity is the treasure of states.

EZRA POUND, *Ta Hio*

necesse est enim omnem animam ad originis suae sedem reverti, sed quae corpus tamquam peregrinae incolunt cito post corpus velut ad patriam revertuntur, quae vero corporum illecebris ut suis sedibus inhaerent, quanto ab illis violentius separantur, tanto ad supera serius revertuntur.

MACROBIUS, *Commentarii in Somnium Scipionis*

CONTENTS

For the Unfallen

To Nancy

Genesis

I

Against the burly air I strode
Crying the miracles of God.

And first I brought the sea to bear
Upon the dead weight of the land;
And the waves flourished at my prayer,
The rivers spawned their sand.

And where the streams were salt and full
The tough pig-headed salmon strove,
Ramming the ebb, in the tide's pull,
To reach the steady hills above.

II

The second day I stood and saw
The osprey plunge with triggered claw,
Feathering blood along the shore,
To lay the living sinew bare.

And the third day I cried: 'Beware
The soft-voiced owl, the ferret's smile,
The hawk's deliberate stoop in air,
Cold eyes, and bodies hooped in steel,
Forever bent upon the kill'.

III

And I renounced, on the fourth day,
This fierce and unregenerate clay,

Building as a huge myth for man
The watery Leviathan,

And made the glove-winged albatross
Scour the ashes of the sea
Where Capricorn and Zero cross,
A brooding immortality—
Such as the charmed phoenix has
In the unwithering tree.

IV

The phoenix burns as cold as frost;
And, like a legendary ghost,
The phantom-bird goes wild and lost,
Upon a pointless ocean tossed.

So, the fifth day, I turned again
To flesh and blood and the blood's pain.

V

On the sixth day, as I rode
In haste about the works of God,
With spurs I plucked the horse's blood.

By blood we live, the hot, the cold,
To ravage and redeem the world:
There is no bloodless myth will hold.

And by Christ's blood are men made free
Though in close shrouds their bodies lie
Under the rough pelt of the sea;

Though Earth has rolled beneath her weight
The bones that cannot bear the light.

God's Little Mountain

Below, the river scrambled like a goat
Dislodging stones. The mountain stamped its foot,
Shaking, as from a trance. And I was shut
With wads of sound into a sudden quiet.

I thought the thunder had unsettled heaven,
All was so still. And yet the sky was cloven
By flame that left the air cold and engraven.
I waited for the word that was not given,

Pent up into a region of pure force,
Made subject to the pressure of the stars;
I saw the angels lifted like pale straws;
I could not stand before those winnowing eyes

And fell, until I found the world again.
Now I lack grace to tell what I have seen;
For though the head frames words the tongue has none.
And who will prove the surgeon to this stone?

Holy Thursday

Naked, he climbed to the wolf's lair;
He beheld Eden without fear,
Finding no ambush offered there
But sleep under the harbouring fur.

He said: 'They are decoyed by love
Who, tarrying through the hollow grove,
Neglect the seasons' sad remove.
Child and nurse walk hand in glove

As unaware of Time's betrayal,
Weaving their innocence with guile.
But they must cleave the fire's peril
And suffer innocence to fall.

I have been touched with that fire,
And have fronted the she-wolf's lair.
Lo, she lies gentle and innocent of desire
Who was my constant myth and terror.'

Merlin

I will consider the outnumbering dead:
For they are the husks of what was rich seed.
Now, should they come together to be fed,
They would outstrip the locusts' covering tide.

Arthur, Elaine, Mordred; they are all gone
Among the raftered galleries of bone.
By the long barrows of Logres they are made one,
And over their city stands the pinnacled corn.

The Bidden Guest

The starched unbending candles stir
As though a wind had caught their hair,
As though the surging of a host
Had charged the air of Pentecost.
And I believe in the spurred flame,
Those racing tongues, but cannot come
Out of my heart's unbroken room;
Nor feel the lips of fire among
The cold light and the chilling song,
The broken mouths that spill their hoard
Of prayer like beads on to a board.
There, at the rail, each muffled head
Swings sombrely. O quiet deed.
This is the breaking of the bread;
On this the leanest heart may feed
When by the stiffly-linened priest
All wounds of light are newly dressed,
Healed by the pouring-in of wine
From bitter as from sweet grapes bled.
But one man lay beneath his vine
And, waking, found that it was dead.
And so my heart has ceased to breathe
(Though there God's worm blunted its head
And stayed.) And still I seem to smile.
Wounds have proud lips and cannot tell
If there is blackness couched beneath.
'Yet there are wounds, unquenched with oil,
And blazing eyes that would compel
Evil to turn, though like a mole
It dug blind alleys down the soil.'
So I heard once. But now I hear,
Like shifted blows at my numb back,
A grinding heel; a scraped chair.
The heart's tough shell is still to crack
When, spent of all its wine and bread,
Unwinkingly the altar lies
Wreathed in its sour breath, cold and dead.
A server has put out its eyes.

In Memory of Jane Fraser

When snow like sheep lay in the fold
And winds went begging at each door,
And the far hills were blue with cold,
And a cold shroud lay on the moor,

She kept the siege. And every day
We watched her brooding over death
Like a strong bird above its prey.
The room filled with the kettle's breath.

Damp curtains glued against the pane
Sealed time away. Her body froze
As if to freeze us all, and chain
Creation to a stunned repose.

She died before the world could stir.
In March the ice unloosed the brook
And water ruffled the sun's hair.
Dead cones upon the alder shook.

The Turtle Dove

Love that drained her drained him she'd loved, though each
For the other's sake forged passion upon speech,
Bore their close days through sufferance towards night
Where she at length grasped sleep and he lay quiet

As though needing no questions, now, to guess
What her secreting heart could not well hide.
Her caught face flinched in half-sleep at his side.
Yet she, by day, modelled her real distress,

Poised, turned her cheek to the attending world
Of children and intriguers and the old;
Conversed freely, exercised, was admired,
Being strong to dazzle. All this she endured

To affront him. He watched her rough grief work
Under the formed surface of habit. She spoke
Like one long undeceived but she was hurt.
She denied more love, yet her starved eyes caught

His, devouring, at times. Then, as one self-dared,
She went to him, plied there; like a furious dove
Bore down with visitations of such love
As his lithe, fathoming heart absorbed and buried.

The Troublesome Reign

So much he had from fashion and no more:
Her trained hard gaze, brief lips whose laughter spat
Concession to desire. She suffered that,
Feeding a certain green-fuel to his fire.

Reluctant heat! This burning of the dead
Could consume her also. She moved apart
As if, through such denial, he might be made
Himself again familiar and unscarred,

Contained, even wary, though not too much
To take pleasure considering her flesh shone,
Her salt-worn summer dress. But he had gone
Thirty days through such a dream of taste and touch

When the sun stood for him and the violent larks
Stabbed up into the sun. She was his, then;
Her limbs grasped him, satisfied, while his brain
Judged every move and cry from its separate dark.

Darkly distinguished now, in common stead,
Their mouths being drawn to public and private speech—
Though there was too much care in all he said,
A hard kind of no-feeling in her touch—

By such rites they saved love's face, and such laws
As prescribe mutual tolerance, charity
To neighbours, strangers, those by nature
Subdued among famines and difficult wars.

Solomon's Mines

To Bonamy Dobrée

Anything to have done!
(The eagle flagged to the sun)
To have discovered and disclosed
The buried thrones, the means used;

Spadework and symbol; each deed
Resurrecting those best dead
Priests, soldiers and kings;
Blazed-out, stripped-out things;

Anything to get up and go
(Let the hewn gates clash to)
Without looking round
Out of that strong land.

The Distant Fury of Battle

Grass resurrects to mask, to strangle,
Words glossed on stone, lopped stone-angel;
But the dead maintain their ground—
That there's no getting round—

Who in places vitally rest,
Named, anonymous; who test
Alike the endurance of yews
Laurels, moonshine, stone, all tissues;

With whom, under licence and duress,
There are pacts made, if not peace.
Union with the stone-wearing dead
Claims the born leader, the prepared

Leader, the devourers and all lean men.
Some, finally, learn to begin.
Some keep to the arrangement of love
(Or similar trust) under whose auspices move

Most subjects, toward the profits of this
Combine of doves and witnesses.
Some, dug out of hot-beds, are brought bare,
Not past conceiving but past care.

Asmodeus

1

They, after the slow building of the house,
Furnished it; brought warmth under the skin.
Tiles, that a year's rough wind could rattle loose,
Being close-pressed still kept storms out and storms in.
(Of all primed and vain citadels, to choose
This, to choose this of all times to begin!)
Acknowledging, they said, one who pursues
Hobbies of serious lust and indoor sin,
Clearly they both stood, lovers without fear,
Might toy with fire brought dangerously to hand
To tame, not exorcize, spirits; though the air
Whistled abstracted menace, could confound
Strength by device, by music reaching the ear,
Lightning conducted forcibly to the ground.

2

The night, then; bravely stiffen; you are one
Whom stars could burn more deeply than the sun,
Guide-book martyr. You, doubtless, hear wings,
Too sheer for cover, swift; the scattered noise
Of darkness looming with propitious things;
And nests of rumour clustered in the world.
So drummed, so shadowed, your mere trudging voice
Might rave at large while easy truths were told,
Bad perjurable stuff, to be forgiven
Because of this lame journey out of mind.
A tax on men to seventy-times-seven,
A busy vigilance of goose and hound,
Keeps up all guards. Since you are outside, go,
Closing the doors of the house and the head also.

Requiem for the Plantagenet Kings

For whom the possessed sea littered, on both shores,
Ruinous arms; being fired, and for good,
To sound the constitution of just wars,
Men, in their eloquent fashion, understood.

Relieved of soul, the dropping-back of dust,
Their usage, pride, admitted within doors;
At home, under caved chantries, set in trust,
With well-dressed alabaster and proved spurs
They lie; they lie; secure in the decay
Of blood, blood-marks, crowns hacked and coveted,
Before the scouring fires of trial-day
Alight on men; before sleeked groin, gored head,
Budge through the clay and gravel, and the sea
Across daubed rock evacuates its dead.

Two Formal Elegies

For the Jews in Europe

I

Knowing the dead, and how some are disposed:
Subdued under rubble, water, in sand graves,
In clenched cinders not yielding their abused
Bodies and bonds to those whom war's chance saves
Without the law: we grasp, roughly, the song.
Arrogant acceptance from which song derives
Is bedded with their blood, makes flourish young
Roots in ashes. The wilderness revives,

Deceives with sweetness harshness. Still beneath
Live skin stone breathes, about which fires but play,
Fierce heart that is the iced brain's to command
To judgement— studied reflex, contained breath—
Their best of worlds since, on the ordained day,
This world came spinning from Jehovah's hand.

2

For all that must be gone through, their long death
Documented and safe, we have enough
Witnesses (our world being witness-proof).
The sea flickers, roars, in its wide hearth.
Here, yearly, the pushing midlanders stand
To warm themselves; men brawny with life,
Women who expect life. They relieve
Their thickening bodies, settle on scraped sand.

Is it good to remind them, on a brief screen,
Of what they have witnessed and not seen?
(Deaths of the city that persistently dies . . . ?)
(To put up stones ensures some sacrifice.)
(Sufficient men confer, carry their weight.)
(At whose door does the sacrifice stand or start?)

Metamorphoses

1 The Fear

No manner of address will do;
Eloquence is not in that look,
But fear of a furred kind. You
Display the stiff face of shock.

Hate is not in it, nor that
Which has presence, a character
In civil intercourse— deceit
Of a tough weathering-nature.

This fear strikes hard and is gone
And is recognized when found
Not only between dark and dawn,
The summit and the ground.

2

Through scant pride to be so put out!
But feed, feed, unlyrical scapegoat;
Plague shrines where each fissure blows
Odour of laurel clouding yours.

Exercise, loftily, your visions
Where the mountainous distance
Echoes its unfaltering speech
To mere outcry and harrowing search.

Possessed of agility and passion,
Energy (out-of-town-fashion)
Attack every obstacle
And height; make the sun your pedestal.

Settle all that bad blood;
Be visited, touched, understood;
Be graced, groomed, returned to favour
With admirable restraint and fervour.

3 The Re-birth of Venus

And now the sea-scoured temptress, having failed
To scoop out of horizons what birds herald:
Tufts of fresh soil: shakes off an entire sea,
Though not as the dove, harried. Rather, she,

A shark hurricaned to estuary-water,
(The lesser hunter almost by a greater
Devoured) but unflurried, lies, approaches all
Stayers, and searchers of the fanged pool.

4 Drake's Drum

Those varied dead. The undiscerning sea
Shelves and dissolves their flesh as it burns spray

Who do not shriek like gulls nor dolphins ride
Crouched under spume to England's erect side

Though there a soaked sleeve lolls or shoe patrols
Tide-padded thick shallows, squats in choked pools

Neither our designed wreaths nor used words
Sink to their melted ears and melted hearts.

5

Doubtless he saw some path clear, having found
His love now fenced him off from the one ground
Where, as he owned, no temperate squalls could move
Either from the profession of their love.

Storm-bound, now she'd outweather him, though he,
Between sun-clouded marshworld and strewn sea
Pitched to extremities, in the rock's vein
Gripped for the winds to roughen and tide stain.

But when he tore his flesh-root and was gone,
Leaving no track, no blood gritting the stone,
Drawn freely to the darkness he had fought
Driven by sulphurous blood and a clenched heart,

Grant the detached, pierced spirit could plunge, soar,
Seeking that love flesh dared not answer for,
Nor suffers now, hammocked in salt tagged cloth
That to be bleached or burned the sea casts out.

Picture of a Nativity

Sea-preserved, heaped with sea-spoils,
Ribs, keels, coral sores,
Detached faces, ephemeral oils,
Discharged on the world's outer shores,

A dumb child-king
Arrives at his right place; rests,
Undisturbed, among slack serpents; beasts
With claws flesh-buttered. In the gathering

Of bestial and common hardship
Artistic men appear to worship
And fall down; to recognize
Familiar tokens; believe their own eyes.

Above the marvel, each rigid head,
Angels, their unnatural wings displayed,
Freeze into an attitude
Recalling the dead.

Canticle for Good Friday

The cross staggered him. At the cliff-top
Thomas, beneath its burden, stood
While the dulled wood
Spat on the stones each drop
Of deliberate blood.

A clamping, cold-figured day
Thomas (not transfigured) stamped, crouched,
Watched
Smelt vinegar and blood. He,
As yet unsearched, unscratched,

And suffered to remain
At such near distance
(A slight miracle might cleanse
His brain
Of all attachments, claw-roots of sense)

In unaccountable darkness moved away,
The strange flesh untouched, carrion-sustenance
Of staunchest love, choicest defiance,
Creation's issue congealing (and one woman's).

The Guardians

The young, having risen early, had gone,
Some with excursions beyond the bay-mouth,
Some toward lakes, a fragile reflected sun.
Thunder-heads drift, awkwardly, from the south;

The old watch them. They have watched the safe
Packed harbours topple under sudden gales,
Great tides irrupt, yachts burn at the wharf
That on clean seas pitched their effective sails.

There are silences. These, too, they endure:
Soft comings-on; soft after-shocks of calm.
Quietly they wade the disturbed shore;
Gather the dead as the first dead scrape home.

The White Ship

Where the living at hazard go,
And with expense, the drowned wan-
der their while; are spun
In harp-surges, St-Lô;

Submerge to reappear.
It does not much matter
How artless grief is. Water
Silences cries that distrained the ear;

Withholds, still, what it might give
As casually as it took away:
Creatures passed through the wet sieve
Without enrichment or decay.

Wreaths

1

Each day the tide withdraws; chills us; pastes
The sand with dead gulls, oranges, dead men.
Uttering love, that outlasts or outwastes
Time's attrition, exiles appear again,
But faintly altered in eyes and skin.

2

Into what understanding all have grown!
(Setting aside a few things, the still faces,
Climbing the phosphorous tide, that none will own)
What paradises and watering-places,
What hurts appeased by the sea's handsomeness!

Elegiac Stanzas

ON A VISIT TO DOVE COTTAGE

To Peter Mann

Mountains, monuments, all forms
Inured to processes and storms
(And they are many); the fashions
Of intercourse between nations:

Customs through which many come
To sink their eyes into a room
Filled with the unused and unworn;
To bite nothings to the bone:

And the daylight between facts;
And the daylight between acts;
Groping of custom towards love;
Past loving, the custom to approve:

A use of words; a rhetoric
As plain as spitting on a stick;
Speech from the ice, the clear-obscure;
The tongue broody in the jaw:

Greatly-aloof, alert, rare
Spirit, conditioned to appear
At the authentic stone or seat:
O near-human spouse and poet,

Mountains, rivers, and grand storms,
Continuous profit, grand customs
(And many of them): O Lakes, Lakes!
O Sentiment upon the rocks!

After Cumae

The sun again unearthed, colours come up fresh,
The perennials; and the laurels'
Washable leaves, that seem never to perish,
Obscure the mouthy cave, the dumb grottoes.

From the beginning, in the known world, slide
Drawn echoing hulls, axes grate, and waves
Deposit in their shallow margins varied
Fragments of marine decay and waftage;

And the sometimes-abandoned gods confuse
With immortal essences men's brief lives,
Frequenting the exposed and pious: those
Who stray, as designed, under applied perils,

Whose doom is easy, venturing so far
Without need, other than to freeze or burn,
Their wake, on spread-out oceans, a healed scar
Fingered, themselves the curios of voyage.

Little Apocalypse

Hölderlin: 1770–1843

Abrupt tempter; close enough to survive
The sun's primitive renewing fury;
Scorched vistas where crawl the injured and brave:
This man stands sealed against their injury:

Hermetic radiance of great suns kept in:
Man's common nature suddenly too rare:
See, for the brilliant coldness of his skin,
The god cast, perfected, among fire.

The Bibliographers

Lucifer blazing in superb effigies
Among the world's ambitious tragedies,
Heaven-sent gift to the dark ages,

Now, in the finest-possible light,
We approach you; can estimate
Your not unnatural height.

Though the discrete progeny,
Out of their swim, go deflated and dry,
We know the feel of you, archaic beauty,

Between the tombs, where the tombs still extrude,
Overshadowing the sun-struck world:
(The shadow-god envisaged in no cloud).

Of Commerce and Society

VARIATIONS ON A THEME

1 The Apostles: Versailles, 1919

They sat. They stood about.
They were estranged. The air,
As water curdles from clear,
Fleshed the silence. They sat.

They were appalled. The bells
In hollowed Europe spilt
To the gods of coin and salt.
The sea creaked with worked vessels.

2 The Lowlands of Holland

Europe, the much-scarred, much-scoured terrain,
Its attested liberties, home-produce,
Labelled and looking up, invites use,
Stuffed with artistry and substantial gain:

Shrunken, magnified (nest, holocaust)
Not half innocent and not half undone;
Profiting from custom: its replete strewn
Cities such ample monuments to lost

Nations and generations: its cultural
Or trade skeletons such hand-picked bone:
Flaws in the best, revised science marks down:
Witness many devices; the few natural

Corruptions, graftings; witness classic falls
(The dead subtracted; the greatest resigned);
Witness earth fertilized, decently drained,
The sea decent again behind walls.

3 The Death of Shelley

i

Slime; the residues of refined tears;
And, salt-bristled, blown on a drying sea,
The sunned and risen faces.

There's Andromeda
Depicted in relief, after the fashion.

'His guarded eyes under his shielded brow'
Through poisonous baked sea-things Perseus
Goes— clogged sword, clear, aimless mirror—
With nothing to strike at or blind

in the frothed shallows.

ii

Rivers bring down. The sea
Brings away;
Voids, sucks back, its pearls and auguries.
Eagles or vultures churn the fresh-made skies.

Over the statues, unchanging features
Of commerce and quaint love, soot lies.
Earth steams. The bull and the great mute swan
Strain into life with their notorious cries.

4

Statesmen have known visions. And, not alone,
Artistic men prod dead men from their stone:
Some of us have heard the dead speak:
The dead are my obsession this week

But may be lifted away. In summer
Thunder may strike, or, as a tremor
Of remote adjustment, pass on the far side
From us: however deified and defied

By those it does strike. Many have died. Auschwitz,
Its furnace chambers and lime pits
Half-erased, is half-dead; a fable
Unbelievable in fatted marble.

There is, at times, some need to demonstrate
Jehovah's touchy methods that create
The connoisseur of blood, the smitten man.
At times it seems not common to explain.

5 Ode on the Loss of the 'Titanic'

Thriving against façades the ignorant sea
Souses our public baths, statues, waste ground:
Archaic earth-shaker, fresh enemy
('The tables of exchange being overturned');

Drowns Babel in upheaval and display;
Unswerving, as were the admired multitudes
Silenced from time to time under its sway.
By all means let us appease the terse gods.

6 The Martyrdom of Saint Sebastian

Homage to Henry James

'But then face to face'

Naked, as if for swimming, the martyr
Catches his death in a little flutter
Of plain arrows. A grotesque situation,
But priceless, and harmless to the nation.

Consider such pains 'crystalline': then fine art
Persists where most crystals accumulate.
History can be scraped clean of its old price.
Engrossed in the cold blood of sacrifice

The provident and self-healing gods
Destroy only to save. Well-stocked with foods,
Enlarged and deep-oiled, America
Detects music, apprehends the day-star

Where, sensitive and half-under a cloud,
Europe muddles her dreaming, is loud
And critical beneath the varied domes
Resonant with tribute and with commerce.

Doctor Faustus

For it must needs be that offences come; but woe to that man by whom the offence cometh.

1 The Emperor's Clothes

A way of many ways: a god
Spirals in the pure steam of blood.
And gods— as men— rise from shut tombs
To a disturbance of small drums;

Immaculate plumage of the swan
The common wear. There is no-one
Afraid or overheard, no loud
Voice (though innocently loud).

2 The Harpies

Having stood hungrily apart
From the gods' politic banquet,
Of all possible false gods
I fall to these gristled shades

That show everything, without lust;
And stumble upon their dead feast
By the torn *Warning To Bathers*
By the torn waters.

3 Another Part of the Fable

The Innocents have not flown;
Too legendary, they laugh;
The lewd uproarious wolf
Brings their house down.

A beast is slain, a beast thrives.
Fat blood squeaks on the sand.
A blinded god believes
That he is not blind.

A Pastoral

Mobile, immaculate and austere,
The Pities, their fingers in every wound,
Assess the injured on the obscured frontier;
Cleanse with a kind of artistry the ground
Shared by War. Consultants in new tongues
Prove synonymous our separated wrongs.

We celebrate, fluently and at ease.
Traditional Furies, having thrust, hovered,
Now decently enough sustain Peace.
The unedifying nude dead are soon covered.
Survivors, still given to wandering, find
Their old loves, painted and realigned—

Queer, familiar, fostered by superb graft
On treasured foundations, these ideal features.
Men can move with purpose again, or drift,
According to direction. Here are statues
Darkened by laurel; and evergreen names;
Evidently-veiled griefs; impervious tombs.

Orpheus and Eurydice

Though there are wild dogs
        Infesting the roads
We have recitals, catalogues
        Of protected birds;

And the rare pale sun
        To water our days.
Men turn to savagery now or turn
        To the laws'

Immutable black and red.
        To be judged for his song,
Traversing the still-moist dead,
        The newly-stung,

Love goes, carrying compassion
        To the rawly-difficult;
His countenance, his hands' motion,
        Serene even to a fault.

In Piam Memoriam

I

Created purely from glass the saint stands,
Exposing his gifted quite empty hands
Like a conjurer about to begin,
A righteous man begging of righteous men.

2

In the sun lily-and-gold-coloured,
Filtering the cruder light, he has endured,
A feature for our regard; and will keep;
Of worldly purity the stained archetype.

3

The scummed pond twitches. The great holly-tree,
Emptied and shut, blows clear of wasting snow,
The common, puddled substance: beneath,
Like a revealed mineral, a new earth.

To the (Supposed) Patron

Prodigal of loves and barbecues,
Expert in the strangest faunas, at home
He considers the lilies, the rewards.
There is no substitute for a rich man.
At his first entering a new province
With new coin, music, the barest glancing
Of steel or gold suffices. There are many
Tremulous dreams secured under that head.
For his delight and his capacity
To absorb, freshly, the inside-succulence
Of untoughened sacrifice, his bronze agents
Speculate among convertible stones
And drink desert sand. That no mirage
Irritate his mild gaze, the lewd noonday
Is housed in cool places, and fountains
Salt the sparse haze. His flesh is made clean.
For the unfallen— the firstborn, or wise
Councillor— prepared vistas extend
As far as harvest; and idyllic death
Where fish at dawn ignite the powdery lake.

King Log

From morall vertue, let us passe on to matter of power and
commandement . . .

The Advancement of Learning

Ovid in the Third Reich

non peccat, quaecumque potest peccasse negare,
solaque famosam culpa professa facit.

Amores III, xiv

I love my work and my children. God
Is distant, difficult. Things happen.
Too near the ancient troughs of blood
Innocence is no earthly weapon.

I have learned one thing: not to look down
So much upon the damned. They, in their sphere,
Harmonize strangely with the divine
Love. I, in mine, celebrate the love-choir.

Annunciations

1

The Word has been abroad, is back, with a tanned look
From its subsistence in the stiffening-mire.
Cleansing has become killing, the reward
Touchable, overt, clean to the touch.
Now at a distance from the steam of beasts,
The loathly neckings and fat shook spawn
(Each specimen-jar fed with delicate spawn)
The searchers with the curers sit at meat
And are satisfied. Such precious things put down
And the flesh eased through turbulence the soul
Purples itself; each eye squats full and mild
While all who attend to fiddle or to harp
For betterment, flavour their decent mouths
With gobbets of the sweetest sacrifice.

2

O Love, subject of the mere diurnal grind,
Forever being pledged to be redeemed,
Expose yourself for charity; be assured
The body is but husk and excrement.
Enter these deaths according to the law,
O visited women, possessed sons. Foreign lusts
Infringe our restraints; the changeable
Soldiery have their goings-out and comings-in
Dying in abundance. Choicest beasts
Suffuse the gutters with their colourful blood.
Our God scatters corruption. Priests, martyrs,
Parade to this imperious theme: 'O Love,
You know what pains succeed; be vigilant; strive
To recognize the damned among your friends.'

Locust Songs

To Allan Seager

The Emblem

So with sweet oaths converting the salt earth
To yield, our fathers verged on Paradise:
Each to his own portion of Paradise,
Stung by the innocent venoms of the earth.

Good Husbandry

Out of the foliage of sensual pride
Those teeming apples. Summer burned well
The dramatic flesh; made work for pride
Forking into the tender mouths of Hell

Heaped windfalls, pulp for the Gadarene
Squealers. This must be our reward:
To smell God writhing over the rich scene.
Gluttons for wrath, we stomach our reward.

Amherst

Redemption spurns parody. The first fruits
Are spoken for beyond the call of shame.
The elect dip their fingers in cruets
Of reason; burnt feathers revive the psalm.

A Daguerreotype

The faultless central parting; stolid jaw;
Frank as a rebel sharpshooter's her eyes
Yet chaste to our promiscuous surprise
Haunt no man's land between vision and law.

Shiloh Church, 1862:
Twenty-three Thousand

O stamping-ground of the shod Word! So hard
On the heels of the damned red-man we came,
Geneva's tribe, outlandish and abhorred—
Bland vistas milky with Jehovah's calm—

Who fell to feasting Nature, the glare
Of buzzards circling; cried to the grim sun
'Jehovah punish us!'; who went too far;
In deserts dropped the odd white turds of bone;

Whose passion was to find out God in this
His natural filth, voyeur of sacrifice, a slow
Bloody unearthing of the God-in-us.
But with what blood, and to what end, Shiloh?

I Had Hope When Violence Was Ceas't

Dawnlight freezes against the east-wire.
The guards cough 'raus! 'raus! We flinch and grin,
Our flesh oozing towards its last outrage.
That which is taken from me is not mine.

September Song

born 19.6.32—deported 24.9.42

Undesirable you may have been, untouchable
you were not. Not forgotten
or passed over at the proper time.

As estimated, you died. Things marched,
sufficient, to that end.
Just so much Zyklon and leather, patented
terror, so many routine cries.

(I have made
an elegy for myself it
is true)

September fattens on vines. Roses
flake from the wall. The smoke
of harmless fires drifts to my eyes.

This is plenty. This is more than enough.

An Order of Service

He was the surveyor of his own ice-world,
Meticulous at the chosen extreme,
Though what he surveyed may have been nothing.

Let a man sacrifice himself, concede
His mortality and have done with it;
There is no end to that sublime appeal.

In such a light dismiss the unappealing
Blank of his gaze, hopelessly vigilant,
Dazzled by renunciation's glare.

The Humanist

The *Venice* portrait: he
Broods, the achieved guest
Tired and word-perfect
At the Muses' table.

Virtue is virtù. These
Lips debate and praise
Some rich aphorism,
A delicate white meat.

The commonplace hands once
Thick with Plato's blood
(Tasteless! tasteless!) are laid
Dryly against the robes.

Funeral Music

William de la Pole, Duke of Suffolk: beheaded 1450
John Tiptoft, Earl of Worcester: beheaded 1470
Anthony Woodville, Earl Rivers: beheaded 1483

Look up these names

↳ Men beheaded in the War of the Roses

I

↗ Commendable, warning, illustration

Processionals in the exemplary cave,

Plato's cave

"Blessing of shadows" could be subjective or objective

Benediction of shadows. Pomfret. London.

↘ Two seats of power

The voice fragrant with mannered humility,

→ someone actually trying to curry favor with the world in their last moments.

With an equable contempt for this world,

Three blows in honor of the Trinity

'In honorem Trinitatis'. Crash. The head
Struck down into a meaty conduit of blood.

A blow to the head.

So these dispose themselves to receive each
Pentecostal blow from axe or seraph,
Spattering block-straw with mortal residue.

very vivid, physical description

Psalteries whine through the empyrean. Fire
Flares in the pit, ghosting upon stone

↑ Heavens

Singing from the psalms

Creatures of such rampant state, vacuous
Ceremony of possession, restless
Habitation, no man's dwelling-place.

⇒ Life is brutal and meaningless, and no one can find rest.

They'd boil the head to preserve it.

"Fire flares in the pit"

↳ Pentecostal reference

↳ The cave image, "ghosting upon stone" those in the pit are still merely shadows.

2

For whom do we scrape our tribute of pain—
For none but the ritual king? We meditate
A rueful mystery; we are dying
To satisfy fat Caritas, those
Wiped jaws of stone. (Suppose all reconciled
By silent music; imagine the future
Flashed back at us, like steel against sun,
Ultimate recompense.) Recall the cold
Of Towton on Palm Sunday before dawn,
Wakefield, Tewkesbury: fastidious trumpets
Shrilling into the ruck; some trampled
Acres, parched, sodden or blanched by sleet,
Stuck with strange-postured dead. Recall the wind's
Flurrying, darkness over the human mire.

[Handwritten annotations:]

Both Henry VI and Edward IV declared for the crown.

A soldier dies

The gargoyles

This poem is from the perspective of a Lancadrian soldier

Longing to, and actually dying.

The soldier wants to be remembered. That is what he

It's a game and war at the same time

3 They thought it was the end of the world

They bespoke doomsday and they meant it by
God, their curved metal rimming the low ridge.

God brings about the end and "by God" is an exclamation

This kind of event only occurs very rarely

But few appearances are like this. Once
Every five hundred years a comet's
Over-riding stillness might reveal men
In such array, livid and featureless,
With England crouched beastwise beneath it all.

Contrast with the grand hope of the Soldier in (2)

— 'Oh, that old northern business . . .' A field
After battle utters its own sound
Which is like nothing on earth, but is earth.

Things after the battle just go back to normal.

Blindly the questing snail, vulnerable
Mole emerge, blindly we lie down, blindly

These are the soldiers, maybe dead or alive.

Among carnage the most delicate souls
Tup in their marriage-blood, gasping 'Jesus'.

Ram and ewe copulating

The reunification of England is like the unification of man and wife.

4

Let <u>mind</u> be more precious than <u>soul</u>; it will not
Endure. Soul grasps its price, begs its own peace,
Settles with tears and sweat, is possibly
Indestructible. That I can believe.
Though I would scorn the mere <u>instinct of faith</u>,
<u>Expediency of assent</u>, if I dared,
What I dare not is a waste history
Or void rule. Averroes, old heathen,
If only you had been right, if Intellect
Itself were absolute law, sufficient grace,
Our lives could be a myth of captivity
Which we might enter: an unpeopled region
Of ever new-fallen snow, a palace blazing
With perpetual silence as with torches.

[handwritten annotations:]

The mind deteriorates temporarily, and perhaps doesn't continue on.

It's easy to assent

Soul tries to make up for its wrongdoings

He has problems with losing his mind in God

we would have no self and our existence would be bland and without change.

Soul vs. Intellect
↳ What goes into God?

Continuing from last section 5

As with torches we go, at <u>wild Christmas,</u>
When we revel in our atonement
Through thirty feasts of unction and slaughter,
What is that but the <u>soul's winter sleep?</u> — *The outward body takes over*
So many things <u>rest</u> under <u>consummate</u> — *Perfected*
Justice as though trumpets purified law,
Spikenard were the real essence of remorse.
The sky gathers up darkness. When we chant
'Ora, ora pro nobis' it is not
Seraphs who descend to pity but ourselves.
Those righteously-accused those vengeful
Racked on articulate looms indulge us
With lingering shows of pain, a flagrant
Tenderness of the damned for their own flesh:

6

My little son, when you could command marvels
Without mercy, outstare the wearisome
Dragon of sleep, I rejoiced above all—
A stranger well-received in your kingdom.
On those pristine fields I saw humankind
As it was named by the Father; fabulous
Beasts rearing in stillness to be blessed.
The world's real cries reached there, turbulence
From remote storms, rumour of solitudes,
A composed mystery. And so it ends.
Some parch for what they were; others are made
Blind to all but one vision, their necessity
To be reconciled. I believe in my
Abandonment, since it is what I have.

7

'Prowess, vanity, mutual regard,
It seemed I stared at them, they at me.
That was the gorgon's true and mortal gaze:
Averted conscience turned against itself.'
A hawk and a hawk-shadow. 'At noon,
As the armies met, each mirrored the other;
Neither was outshone. So they flashed and vanished
And all that survived them was the stark ground
Of this pain. I made no sound, but once
I stiffened as though a remote cry
Had heralded my name. It was nothing . . .'
Reddish ice tinged the reeds; dislodged, a few
Feathers drifted across; carrion birds
Strutted upon the armour of the dead.

8

Not as we are but as we must appear,
Contractual ghosts of pity; not as we
Desire life but as they would have us live,
Set apart in timeless colloquy.
So it is required; so we bear witness,
Despite ourselves, to what is beyond us,
Each distant sphere of harmony forever
Poised, unanswerable. If it is without
Consequence when we vaunt and suffer, or
If it is not, all echoes are the same
In such eternity. Then tell me, love,
How that should comfort us— or anyone
Dragged half-unnerved out of this worldly place,
Crying to the end 'I have not finished'.

Four Poems Regarding the Endurance of Poets

Men Are a Mockery of Angels

i.m. Tommaso Campanella, priest and poet

Some days a shadow through
The high window shares my
Prison. I watch a slug
Scale the glinting pit-side
Of its own slime. The cries
As they come are mine; then
God's: my justice, wounds, love,
Derisive light, bread, filth.

To lie here in my strange
Flesh while glutted Torment
Sleeps, stained with its prompt food,
Is a joy past all care
Of the world, for a time.
But we are commanded
To rise, when, in silence,
I would compose my voice.

A Prayer to the Sun

i.m. Miguel Hernandez

i

Darkness
above all things
the Sun
makes
rise

ii

Vultures
salute their meat
at noon
(Hell is
silent)

iii

Blind Sun
our ravager
bless us
so that
we sleep

'Domaine Public'

i.m. Robert Desnos, died Terezin Camp, 1945

For reading I can recommend
the Fathers. How they
cultivate the corrupting flesh:

toothsome contemplation: cleanly
maggots churning spleen
to milk. For exercise, prolonged

suppression of much improper
speech from proper tombs.
If the ground opens, should men's mouths

open also? 'I am nothing
if not saved now!' or
'Christ, what a pantomime!' The days

of the week are seven pits. Look,
Seigneur, again we
resurrect and the judges come.

Tristia: 1891–1938

A Valediction to Osip Mandelstam

Difficult friend, I would have preferred
You to them. The dead keep their sealed lives
And again I am too late. Too late
The salutes, dust-clouds and brazen cries.

Images rear from desolation
Like ruins upon a plain.
A few men glare at their hands; others
Grovel for food in the roadside field.

Tragedy takes all under regard.
It will not touch us but it is there—
Flawless, insatiate— hard summer sky
Feasting on this, reaching its own end.

The Imaginative Life

Evasive souls, of whom the wise lose track,
Die in each night, who, with their day-tongues, sift
The waking-taste of manna or of blood:

The raw magi, part-barbarians,
Entranced by demons and desert frost,
By the irregular visions of a god,

Suffragans of the true seraphs. Lust
Writhes, is dumb savage and in their way
As a virulence natural to the earth.

Renewed glories batten on the poor bones;
Gargantuan mercies whetted by a scent
Of mortal sweat: as though the sleeping flesh

Adored by Furies, stirred, yawned, were driven
In mid-terror to purging and delight.
As though the dead had *Finis* on their brows.

The Assisi Fragments

To G. Wilson Knight

1

Lion and lioness, the mild
Inflammable beasts,
At their precise peril kept
Distance and repose—
And there the serpent
Innocently shone its head.

2

So the hawk had its pursuit. So Death
Opened its childish eyes. So the angels
Overcame Adam: he was defiled
By balm. Creator, and creature made
Of unnatural earth, he howled
To the raven *find me*; to the wolf
Eat, my brother; and to the fire *I am clean.*

History as Poetry

Poetry as salutation; taste
Of Pentecost's ashen feast. Blue wounds.
The tongue's atrocities. Poetry
Unearths from among the speechless dead

Lazarus mystified, common man
Of death. The lily rears its gouged face
From the provided loam. Fortunate
Auguries; whirrings; tarred golden dung:

'A resurgence' as they say. The old
Laurels wagging with the new: Selah!
Thus laudable the trodden bone thus
Unanswerable the knack of tongues.

Soliloquies

The Stone Man

To Charles Causley

Recall, now, the omens of childhood:
The nettle-clump and rank elder-tree;
The stones waiting in the mason's yard;

Half-recognized kingdom of the dead,
A deeper landscape lit by distant
Flashings from their journey. At nightfall

My father scuffed clay into the house.
He set his boots on the bleak iron
Of the hearth; ate, drank, unbuckled, slept.

I leaned to the lamp; the pallid moths
Clipped its glass, made an autumnal sound.
Words clawed my mind as though they had smelt

Revelation's flesh . . . So, with an ease
That is dreadful, I summon all back.
The sun bellows over its parched swarms.

Old Poet with Distant Admirers

What I lost was not a part of this.
The dark-blistered foxgloves, wet berries
Glinting from shadow, small ferns and stones,

Seem fragments, in the observing mind,
Of its ritual power. Old age
Singles them out as though by first-light,

As though a still-life, preserving some
Portion of the soul's feast, went with me
Everywhere, to be hung in strange rooms,

Loneliness being what it is. If
I knew the exact coin for tribute,
Defeat might be bought, processional

Silence gesture its tokens of earth
At my mouth: as in the great death-songs
Of Propertius (although he died young).

Cowan Bridge

AT THE SITE OF 'LOWOOD SCHOOL'

A lost storm in this temperate place;
The silent direction;
Some ash-trees and foam-patched
Alders at the beck.

All the seasons absorbed
As by a child, safe from rain,
Crouched in the dank
Stench of an elder-bush.

So much that was not justice,
So much that is;
The vulnerable pieties
Not willingly let die;
By chance unmolested
The modesty of her rage.

Fantasia on 'Horbury'

John Bacchus Dykes, 1859

Dry walls, and nettles battered by the dust,
Odours from gathered water, muddled storm-clouds
Disastrous over the manufactured West Riding.

Mind— a fritter of excrement; step
Aside, step aside, sir! Ah, but a priest
In his prime watches where he goes. He goes

To tender his confession. Forgiveness
Journeys towards him like a brisk traveller
On the same road. Is this Horbury?

Yes: and he will perpetuate this refuge.
Yes: and he will weaken, scribbling, at the end,
Of unspeakable desolation. Really? Good Lord!

Consider him thus animated,
That outworn piety and those plush tunes
Restored for the sake of a paradox

And the too-fashionable North. Or, again,
Consider him catspawed by an indolent poem,
This place not of his choosing, this menace

From concave stormlight a freak suggestion . . .
These heads of nettles lopped into the dust . . .

Three Baroque Meditations

I

Do words make up the majesty
Of man, and his justice
Between the stones and the void?

How they watch us, the demons
Plugging their dumb wounds! When
Exorcized they shrivel yet thrive.

An owl plunges to its tryst
With a field-mouse in the sharp night.
My fire squeals and lies still.

Minerva, receive this hard
Praise: I speak well of Death;
I confess to the priest in me;

I am shadowed by the wise bird
Of necessity, the lithe
Paradigm Sleep-and-Kill.

2

Pain unsated by the replete scream.
Flesh of abnegation: the poem
Moves grudgingly to its extreme form,

Vulnerable, to the lamp's fierce head
Of well-trimmed light. In darkness outside,
Foxes and rain-sleeked stones and the dead—

Aliens of such a theme— endure
Until I could cry 'Death! Death!' as though
To exacerbate that suave power;

But refrain. For I am circumspect,
Lifting the spicy lid of my tact
To sniff at the myrrh. It is perfect

In its impalpable bitterness,
Scent of a further country where worse
Furies promenade and bask their claws.

3 The Dead Bride

So white I was, he would have me cry
'Unclean!' murderously
To heal me with far-fetched blood.

I writhed to conceive of him.
I clawed to becalm him.
Some nights, I witnessed his face in sleep

And dreamed of my father's
House. (By day he professed languages,
Disciplines of languages.)

By day I cleansed my thin tongue
From its nightly prowl, its vixen-skill,
His sacramental mouth

That justified my flesh
And moved well among women
In nuances and imperatives.

This was the poet of a people's
Love. I hated him. He weeps,
Solemnizing his loss.

The Songbook of Sebastian Arrurruz

Sebastian Arrurruz: 1868–1922

I

Ten years without you. For so it happens.
Days make their steady progress, a routine
That is merciful and attracts nobody.

Already, like a disciplined scholar,
I piece fragments together, past conjecture
Establishing true sequences of pain;

For so it is proper to find value
In a bleak skill, as in the thing restored:
The long-lost words of choice and valediction.

Coplas

i

'One cannot lose what one has not possessed.'
So much for that abrasive gem.
I can lose what I want. I want you.

i

Oh my dear one, I shall grieve for you
For the rest of my life with slightly
Varying cadence, oh my dear one.

iii

Half-mocking the half-truth, I note
'The wild brevity of sensual love'.
I am shaken, even by that.

iv

It is to him I write, it is to her
I speak in contained silence. Will they be touched
By the unfamiliar passion between them?

3

What other men do with other women
Is for me neither orgy nor sacrament
Nor a language of foreign candour

But is mere occasion or chance distance
Out of which you might move and speak my name
As I speak yours, bargaining with sleep's

Miscellaneous gods for as much
As I can have: an alien landscape,
The dream where you are always to be found.

4

A workable fancy. Old petulant
Sorrow comes back to us, metamorphosed
And semi-precious. Fortuitous amber.
As though this recompensed our deprivation.
See how each fragment kindles as we turn it,
At the end, into the light of appraisal.

5

Love, oh my love, it will come
Sure enough. A storm
Broods over the dry earth all day.
At night the shutters throb in its downpour.

The metaphor holds; is a snug house.
You are outside, lost somewhere. I find myself
Devouring verses of stranger passion
And exile. The exact words

Are fed into my blank hunger for you.

Postures

I imagine, as I imagine us
Each time more stylized more lovingly
Detailed, that I am not myself
But someone I might have been: sexless,
Indulgent about art, relishing
Let us say the well-schooled
Postures of *St Anthony* or *St Jerome*,
Those peaceful hermaphrodite dreams
Through which the excess of memory
Pursues its own abstinence.

From the Latin

There would have been things to say, quietness
That could feed on our lust, refreshed
Trivia, the occurrences of the day;
And at night my tongue in your furrow.

Without you I am mocked by courtesies
And chat, where satisfied women push
Dutifully toward some unneeded guest
Desirable features of conversation.

A Letter from Armenia

So, remotely, in your part of the world:
the ripe glandular blooms, and cypresses
shivering with heat (which we have borne
also, in our proper ways) I turn my mind
towards delicate pillage, the provenance
of shards glazed and unglazed, the three
kinds of surviving grain. I hesitate amid
circumstantial disasters. I gaze at the
authentic dead.

A Song from Armenia

Roughly-silvered leaves that are the snow
On Ararat seen through those leaves.
The sun lays down a foliage of shade.

A drinking-fountain pulses its head
Two or three inches from the troughed stone.
An old woman sucks there, gripping the rim.

Why do I have to relive, even now,
Your mouth, and your hand running over me
Deft as a lizard, like a sinew of water?

To His Wife

You ventured occasionally—
As though this were another's house—
Not intimate but an acquaintance
Flaunting her modest claim; like one
Idly commiserated by new-mated
Lovers rampant in proper delight
When all their guests have gone.

II

Scarcely speaking: it becomes as a
Coolness between neighbours. Often
There is this orgy of sleep. I wake
To caress propriety with odd words
And enjoy abstinence in a vocation
Of now-almost-meaningless despair.

Mercian Hymns

The conduct of government rests upon the same foundation and encounters the same difficulties as the conduct of private persons: that is, as to its object and justification, for as to its methods, or technical part, there is all the difference which separates the person from the group, the man acting on behalf of himself from the man acting on behalf of many. The technical part, in government as in private conduct, is now the only one which is publicly or at any rate generally recognised, as if by this evasion the more difficult part of the subject, which relates to ends, could be avoided. Upon 'the law of nature and the law of revelation', Blackstone said, 'depend all human laws.' This quaint language, which would at once be derided if it were introduced now into public discussion, conceals a difficulty which is no less ours than it was our ancestors'.

C. H. SISSON

I

King of the perennial holly-groves, the riven sand-
stone: overlord of the M5: architect of the his-
toric rampart and ditch, the citadel at Tamworth,
the summer hermitage in Holy Cross: guardian of
the Welsh Bridge and the Iron Bridge: contractor
to the desirable new estates: saltmaster: money-
changer: commissioner for oaths: martyrologist:
the friend of Charlemagne.

'I liked that,' said Offa, 'sing it again.'

II

A pet-name, a common name. Best-selling brand, curt
    graffito. A laugh; a cough. A syndicate. A specious
    gift. Scoffed-at horned phonograph.

The starting-cry of a race. A name to conjure with.

III

On the morning of the crowning we chorused our re-
mission from school. It was like Easter: hankies
and gift-mugs approved by his foreign gaze, the
village-lintels curlered with paper flags.

We gaped at the car-park of 'The Stag's Head' where
a bonfire of beer-crates and holly-boughs whistled
above the tar. And the chef stood there, a king in
his new-risen hat, sealing his brisk largesse with
'any mustard?'

IV

I was invested in mother-earth, the crypt of roots
    and endings. Child's-play. I abode there, bided my
    time: where the mole

shouldered the clogged wheel, his gold solidus; where
    dry-dust badgers thronged the Roman flues, the
    long-unlooked-for mansions of our tribe.

V

So much for the elves' wergild, the true governance
of England, the gaunt warrior-gospel armoured in
engraved stone. I wormed my way heavenward for
ages amid barbaric ivy, scrollwork of fern.

Exile or pilgrim set me once more upon that ground:
my rich and desolate childhood. Dreamy, smug-
faced, sick on outings — I who was taken to be a
king of some kind, a prodigy, a maimed one.

VI

The princes of Mercia were badger and raven. Thrall
  to their freedom, I dug and hoarded. Orchards
  fruited above clefts. I drank from honeycombs of
  chill sandstone.

'A boy at odds in the house, lonely among brothers.'
  But I, who had none, fostered a strangeness; gave
  myself to unattainable toys.

Candles of gnarled resin, apple-branches, the tacky
  mistletoe. 'Look' they said and again 'look.' But
  I ran slowly; the landscape flowed away, back to
  its source.

In the schoolyard, in the cloakrooms, the children
  boasted their scars of dried snot; wrists and
  knees garnished with impetigo.

VII

Gasholders, russet among fields. Milldams, marlpools
    that lay unstirring. Eel-swarms. Coagulations of
    frogs; once, with branches and half-bricks, he
    battered a ditchful; then sidled away from the
    stillness and silence.

Ceolred was his friend and remained so, even after
    the day of the lost fighter: a biplane, already
    obsolete and irreplaceable, two inches of heavy
    snub silver. Ceolred let it spin through a hole
    in the classroom-floorboards, softly, into the
    rat-droppings and coins.

After school he lured Ceolred, who was sniggering
    with fright, down to the old quarries, and flayed
    him. Then, leaving Ceolred, he journeyed for hours,
    calm and alone, in his private derelict sandlorry
    named *Albion*.

VIII

The mad are predators. Too often lately they harbour
    against us. A novel heresy exculpates all maimed
    souls. Abjure it! I am the King of Mercia, and
    I know.

Threatened by phone-calls at midnight, venomous let-
    ters, forewarned I have thwarted their imminent
    devices.

Today I name them; tomorrow I shall express the new
    law. I dedicate my awakening to this matter.

IX

The strange church smelled a bit 'high', of censers
and polish. The strange curate was just as ap-
propriate: he took off into the marriage-service.
No-one cared to challenge that gambit.

Then he dismissed you, and the rest of us followed,
sheepish next-of-kin, to the place without the
walls: spoil-heaps of chrysanths dead in their
plastic macs, eldorado of washstand-marble.

Embarrassed, we dismissed ourselves: the three mute
great-aunts borne away down St Chad's Garth in
a stiff-backed Edwardian Rolls.

I unburden the saga of your burial, my dear. You had
lived long enough to see things 'nicely settled'.

X

He adored the desk, its brown-oak inlaid with ebony,
     assorted prize pens, the seals of gold and base
     metal into which he had sunk his name.

It was there that he drew upon grievances from the
     people; attended to signatures and retributions;
     forgave the death-howls of his rival. And there
     he exchanged gifts with the Muse of History.

What should a man make of remorse, that it might
     profit his soul? Tell me. Tell everything to
     Mother, darling, and God bless.

He swayed in sunlight, in mild dreams. He tested the
     little pears. He smeared catmint on his palm for
     his cat Smut to lick. He wept, attempting to mas-
     ter *ancilla* and *servus*.

XI

Coins handsome as Nero's; of good substance and
weight. *Offa Rex* resonant in silver, and the
names of his moneyers. They struck with account-
able tact. They could alter the king's face.

Exactness of design was to deter imitation; muti-
lation if that failed. Exemplary metal, ripe for
commerce. Value from a sparse people, scrapers
of salt-pans and byres.

Swathed bodies in the long ditch; one eye upstaring.
It is safe to presume, here, the king's anger. He
reigned forty years. Seasons touched and retouched
the soil.

Heathland, new-made watermeadow. Charlock, marsh-
marigold. Crepitant oak forest where the boar
furrowed black mould, his snout intimate with
worms and leaves.

XII

Their spades grafted through the variably-resistant
    soil. They clove to the hoard. They ransacked
    epiphanies, vertebrae of the chimera, armour of
    wild bees' larvae. They struck the fire-dragon's
    faceted skin.

The men were paid to caulk water-pipes. They brewed
    and pissed amid splendour; their latrine seethed
    its estuary through nettles. They are scattered
    to your collations, moldywarp.

It is autumn. Chestnut-boughs clash their inflamed
    leaves. The garden festers for attention: telluric
    cultures enriched with shards, corms, nodules, the
    sunk solids of gravity. I have raked up a golden
    and stinking blaze.

XIII

Trim the lamp; polish the lens; draw, one by one, rare
    coins to the light. Ringed by its own lustre, the
    masterful head emerges, kempt and jutting, out
    of England's well. Far from his underkingdom of crin-
    oid and crayfish, the rune-stone's province, *Rex
    Totius Anglorum Patriae*, coiffured and ageless,
    portrays the self-possession of his possession,
    cushioned on a legend.

XIV

Dismissing reports and men, he put pressure on the wax, blistered it to a crest. He threatened malefactors with ash from his noon cigar.

When the sky cleared above Malvern, he lingered in his orchard; by the quiet hammer-pond. Trout-fry simmered there, translucent, as though forming the water's underskin. He had a care for natural minutiae. What his gaze touched was his tenderness. Woodlice sat pellet-like in the cracked bark and a snail sugared its new stone.

At dinner, he relished the mockery of drinking his family's health. He did this whenever it suited him, which was not often.

XV

Tutting, he wrenched at a snarled root of dead crab-
apple. It rose against him. In brief cavort he was
Cernunnos, the branched god, lightly concussed.

He divided his realm. It lay there like a dream. An
ancient land, full of strategy. Ramparts of com-
post pioneered by red-helmeted worms. Hemlock in
ambush, night-soil, tetanus. A wasps' nest en-
sconced in the hedge-bank, a reliquary or wrapped
head, the corpse of Cernunnos pitching dayward
its feral horns.

XVI

Clash of salutation. As keels thrust into shingle.
　　Ambassadors, pilgrims. What is carried over? The
　　Frankish gift, two-edged, regaled with slaughter.

The sword is in the king's hands; the crux a crafts-
　　man's triumph. Metal effusing its own fragrance,
　　a variety of balm. And other miracles, other
　　exchanges.

Shafts from the winter sun homing upon earth's rim.
　　Christ's mass: in the thick of a snowy forest the
　　flickering evergreen fissured with light.

Attributes assumed, retribution entertained. What is
　　borne amongst them? Too much or too little. In-
　　dulgences of bartered acclaim; an expenditure, a
　　hissing. Wine, urine and ashes.

XVII

He drove at evening through the hushed Vosges. The
car radio, glimmering, received broken utterance
from the horizon of storms . . .

'God's honour — our bikes touched; he skidded and
came off.' 'Liar.' A timid father's protective bellow.
Disfigurement of a village-king. 'Just look at
the bugger . . .'

His maroon GT chanted then overtook. He lavished on
the high valleys its *haleine*.

XVIII

At Pavia, a visitation of some sorrow. Boethius'
   dungeon. He shut his eyes, gave rise to a tower
   out of the earth. He willed the instruments of
   violence to break upon meditation. Iron buckles
   gagged; flesh leaked rennet over them; the men
   stooped, disentangled the body.

He wiped his lips and hands. He strolled back to the
   car, with discreet souvenirs for consolation and
   philosophy. He set in motion the furtherance of
   his journey. To watch the Tiber foaming out
   much blood.

XIX

Behind the thorn-trees thin smoke, scutch-grass or
    wattle smouldering. At this distance it is hard
    to tell. Far cries impinge like the faint tink-
    ing of iron.

We have a kitchen-garden riddled with toy-shards,
    with splinters of habitation. The children shriek
    and scavenge, play havoc. They incinerate boxes,
    rags and old tyres. They haul a sodden log, hung
    with soft shields of fungus, and launch it upon
    the flames.

XX

Primeval heathland spattered with the bones of mice
and birds; where adders basked and bees made pro-
vision, mantling the inner walls of their burh:

Coiled entrenched England: brickwork and paintwork
stalwart above hacked marl. The clashing primary
colours — 'Ethandune', 'Catraeth', 'Maldon', 'Pen-
gwern'. Steel against yew and privet. Fresh
dynasties of smiths.

XXI

Cohorts of charabancs fanfared Offa's province and
    his concern, negotiating the by-ways from Teme
    to Trent. Their windshields dripped butterflies.
    Stranded on hilltops they signalled with plumes
    of steam. Twilight menaced the land. The young
    women wept and surrendered.

Still, everyone was cheerful, heedless in such days:
    at summer weekends dipping into valleys beyond
    Mercia's dyke. Tea was enjoyed, by lakesides
    where all might fancy carillons of real Camelot vi-
    brating through the silent water.

Gradually, during the years, deciduous velvet peeled
    from evergreen albums and during the years more
    treasures were mislaid: the harp-shaped brooches,
    the nuggets of fool's gold.

XXII

We ran across the meadow scabbed with cow-dung, past
the crab-apple trees and camouflaged nissen hut.
It was curfew-time for our war-band.

At home the curtains were drawn. The wireless boomed
its commands. I loved the battle-anthems and the
gregarious news.

Then, in the earthy shelter, warmed by a blue-glassed
storm-lantern, I huddled with stories of dragon-
tailed airships and warriors who took wing im-
mortal as phantoms.

XXIII

In tapestries, in dreams, they gathered, as it was en-
acted, the return, the re-entry of transcendence
into this sublunary world. *Opus Anglicanum*, their
stringent mystery riddled by needles: the silver
veining, the gold leaf, voluted grape-vine, master-
works of treacherous thread.

They trudged out of the dark, scraping their boots
free from lime-splodges and phlegm. They munched
cold bacon. The lamps grew plump with oily re-
liable light.

XXIV

Itinerant through numerous domains, of his lord's
  retinue, to Compostela. Then home for a lifetime
  amid West Mercia this master-mason as I envisage
  him, intent to pester upon tympanum and chancel-
  arch his moody testament, confusing warrior with
  lion, dragon-coils, tendrils of the stony vine.

Where best to stand? Easter sunrays catch the ob-
  lique face of Adam scrumping through leaves; pale
  spree of evangelists and, there, a cross Christ
  mumming child Adam out of Hell

('Et exspecto resurrectionem mortuorum' dust in the
  eyes, on clawing wings, and lips).

XXV

Brooding on the eightieth letter of *Fors Clavigera*,
I speak this in memory of my grandmother, whose
childhood and prime womanhood were spent in the
nailer's darg.

The nailshop stood back of the cottage, by the fold.
It reeked stale mineral sweat. Sparks had furred its
low roof. In dawn-light the troughed water
floated a damson-bloom of dust

not to be shaken by posthumous clamour. It is one
thing to celebrate the 'quick forge', another to
cradle a face hare-lipped by the searing wire.

Brooding on the eightieth letter of *Fors Clavigera*,
I speak this in memory of my grandmother, whose
childhood and prime womanhood were spent in the
nailer's darg.

XXVI

Fortified in their front parlours, at Yuletide men
    are the more murderous. Drunk, they defy battle-
    axes, bellow of whale-bone and dung.

Troll-wives, groaners in sweetness, tooth-bewitchers,
    you too must purge for the surfeit of England —
    who have scattered peppermint and confetti, your
    hundreds-and-thousands.

XXVII

'Now when King Offa was alive and dead', they were
all there, the funereal gleemen: papal legate and
rural dean; Merovingian car-dealers, Welsh mercen-
aries; a shuffle of house-carls.

He was defunct. They were perfunctory. The ceremony
stood acclaimed. The mob received memorial vouch-
ers and signs.

After that shadowy, thrashing midsummer hail-storm,
Earth lay for a while, the ghost-bride of livid
Thor, butcher of strawberries, and the shire-tree
dripped red in the arena of its uprooting.

XXVIII

Processes of generation; deeds of settlement. The
urge to marry well; wit to invest in the proper-
ties of healing-springs. Our children and our
children's children, o my masters.

Tracks of ancient occupation. Frail ironworks rust-
ing in the thorn-thicket. Hearthstones; charred
lullabies. A solitary axe-blow that is the echo
of a lost sound.

Tumult recedes as though into the long rain. Groves
of legendary holly; silverdark the ridged gleam.

XXIX

'Not strangeness, but strange likeness. Obstinate,
  outclassed forefathers, I too concede, I am your
  staggeringly-gifted child.'

So, murmurous, he withdrew from them. Gran lit the
  gas, his dice whirred in the ludo-cup, he entered
  into the last dream of Offa the King.

XXX

And it seemed, while we waited, he began to walk to-
wards us   he vanished

he left behind coins, for his lodging, and traces of
red mud.

Tenebrae

This is a very ancient land indeed;
Aiaia formerly or Cythera
Or Celidon the hollow forest called;
This is the country Ulysses and Hermod
Entered afraid; by ageing poets sought . . .

SIDNEY KEYES

The Pentecost Castle

It is terrible to desire and not possess, and terrible to possess and not desire.

W. B. YEATS

What we love in other human beings is the hoped-for satisfaction of our desire. We do not love their desire. If what we loved in them was their desire, then we should love them as ourself.

SIMONE WEIL

1

They slew by night
upon the road
Medina's pride
Olmedo's flower

shadows warned him
not to go
not to go
along that road

weep for your lord
Medina's pride
Olmedo's flower
there in the road

2

Down in the orchard
I met my death
under the briar rose
I lie slain

I was going
to gather flowers
my love waited
among the trees

down in the orchard
I met my death
under the briar rose
I lie slain

3

You watchers on the wall
grown old with care
I too looked from the wall
I shall look no more

tell us what you saw
the lord I sought to serve
caught in the thorn grove
his blood on his brow

you keepers of the wall
what friend or enemy
sets free the cry
of the bell

4

At dawn the Mass
burgeons from stone
a Jesse tree
of resurrection

budding with candle
flames the gold
and the white wafers
of the feast

and ghosts for love
void a few tears
of wax upon
forlorn altars

5

Goldfinch and hawk
and the grey aspen tree
I have run to the river
mother call me home

the leaves glint in the wind
turning their quiet song
the wings flash and are still
I sleep in the shade

when I cried out you
made no reply
tonight I shall pass by
without a sound

6

Slowly my heron flies
pierced by the blade
mounting in slow pain
strikes the air with its cries

goes seeking the high rocks
where no man can climb
where the wild balsam stirs
by the little stream

the rocks the high rocks
are brimming with flowers
there love grows and there love
rests and is saved

7

I went out early
to the far field
ermine and lily
and yet a child

Love stood before me
in that place
prayers could not lure me
to Christ's house

Christ the deceiver
took all I had
his darkness ever
my fair reward

8

And you my spent heart's treasure
my yet unspent desire
measurer past all measure
cold paradox of fire

as seeker so forsaken
consentingly denied
your solitude a token
the sentries at your side

fulfilment to my sorrow
indulgence of your prey
the sparrowhawk the sparrow
the nothing that you say

9

This love will see me dead
he has the place in mind
where I am free to die
be true at last true love

my love meet me half-way
I bear no sword of fear
where you dwell I
dwell also says my lord

dealing his five wounds
so cunning and so true
of love to rouse this death
I die to sleep in love

10

St James and St John
bless the road she has gone
St John and St James
a rosary of names

child-beads of fingered bread
never-depleted heart's food
the nominal the real
subsistence past recall

bread we shall never break
love-runes we cannot speak
scrolled effigy of a cry
our passion its display

11

If the night is dark
and the way short
if the way you take
is to my heart

say that I never
see you again
touch me I shall shiver
at the unseen

the night is so dark
the way so short
yet you do not wake
against my heart

12

Married and not for love
you of all women
you of all women
my soul's darling my love

faithful to my desire
lost in the dream's grasp where
shall I find you everywhere
unmatched in my desire

each of us dispossessed
so richly in my sleep
I rise out of my sleep
crying like one possessed

13

Splendidly-shining darkness
proud citadel of meekness
likening us our unlikeness
majesty of our distress

emptiness ever thronging
untenable belonging
how long until this longing
end in unending song

and soul for soul discover
no strangeness to dissever
and lover keep with lover
a moment and for ever

14

As he is wounded
I am hurt
he bleeds from pride
I from my heart

as he is dying
I shall live
in grief desiring
still to grieve

as he is living
I shall die
sick of forgiving
such honesty

15

I shall go down
to the lovers' well
and wash this wound
that will not heal

beloved soul
what shall you see
nothing at all
yet eye to eye

depths of non-being
perhaps too clear
my desire dying
as I desire

Lachrimae

OR

SEVEN TEARS FIGURED IN SEVEN PASSIONATE PAVANS

Passions I allow, and loves I approve, onely I would wishe that men would alter their object and better their intent.

ST ROBERT SOUTHWELL, *Marie Magdalens Funeral Teares*, 1591

1 Lachrimae Verae

Crucified Lord, you swim upon your cross
and never move. Sometimes in dreams of hell
the body moves but moves to no avail
and is at one with that eternal loss.

You are the castaway of drowned remorse,
you are the world's atonement on the hill.
This is your body twisted by our skill
into a patience proper for redress.

I cannot turn aside from what I do;
you cannot turn away from what I am.
You do not dwell in me nor I in you

however much I pander to your name
or answer to your lords of revenue,
surrendering the joys that they condemn.

2 The Masque of Blackness

Splendour of life so splendidly contained,
brilliance made bearable. It is the east
light's embodiment, fit to be caressed,
the god Amor with his eyes of diamond,

celestial worldliness on which has dawned
intelligence of angels, Midas' feast,
the stony hunger of the dispossessed
locked into Eden by their own demand.

Self-love, the slavish master of this trade,
conquistador of fashion and remark,
models new heavens in his masquerade,

its images intense with starry work,
until he tires and all that he has made
vanishes in the chaos of the dark.

3 Martyrium

The Jesus-faced man walking crowned with flies
who swats the roadside grass or glances up
at the streaked gibbet with its birds that swoop,
who scans his breviary while the sweat dries,

fades, now, among the fading tapestries,
brooches of crimson tears where no eyes weep,
a mouth unstitched into a rimless cup,
torn clouds the cauldrons of the martyrs' cries.

Clamorous love, its faint and baffled shout,
its grief that would betray him to our fear,
he suffers for our sake, or does not hear

above the hiss of shadows on the wheat.
Viaticum transfigures earth's desire
in rising vernicles of summer air.

4 Lachrimae Coactae

Crucified Lord, however much I burn
to be enamoured of your paradise,
knowing what ceases and what will not cease,
frightened of hell, not knowing where to turn,

I fall between harsh grace and hurtful scorn.
You are the crucified who crucifies,
self-withdrawn even from your own device,
your trim-plugged body, wreath of rakish thorn.

What grips me then, or what does my soul grasp?
If I grasp nothing what is there to break?
You are beyond me, innermost true light,

uttermost exile for no exile's sake,
king of our earth not caring to unclasp
its void embrace, the semblance of your quiet.

5 Pavana Dolorosa

Loves I allow and passions I approve:
Ash-Wednesday feasts, ascetic opulence,
the wincing lute, so real in its pretence,
itself a passion amorous of love.

Self-wounding martyrdom, what joys you have,
true-torn among this fictive consonance,
music's creation of the moveless dance,
the decreation to which all must move.

Self-seeking hunter of forms, there is no end
to such pursuits. None can revoke your cry.
Your silence is an ecstasy of sound

and your nocturnals blaze upon the day.
I founder in desire for things unfound.
I stay amid the things that will not stay.

6 Lachrimae Antiquae Novae

Crucified Lord, so naked to the world,
you live unseen within that nakedness,
consigned by proxy to the judas-kiss
of our devotion, bowed beneath the gold,

with re-enactments, penances foretold:
scentings of love across a wilderness
of retrospection, wild and objectless
longings incarnate in the carnal child.

Beautiful for themselves the icons fade;
the lions and the hermits disappear.
Triumphalism feasts on empty dread,

fulfilling triumphs of the festal year.
We find you wounded by the token spear.
Dominion is swallowed with your blood.

7 Lachrimae Amantis

What is there in my heart that you should sue
so fiercely for its love? What kind of care
brings you as though a stranger to my door
through the long night and in the icy dew

seeking the heart that will not harbour you,
that keeps itself religiously secure?
At this dark solstice filled with frost and fire
your passion's ancient wounds must bleed anew.

So many nights the angel of my house
has fed such urgent comfort through a dream,
whispered 'your lord is coming, he is close'

that I have drowsed half-faithful for a time
bathed in pure tones of promise and remorse:
'tomorrow I shall wake to welcome him.'

An Apology for the Revival of Christian Architecture in England

the spiritual, Platonic old England ... S. T. COLERIDGE, *Anima Poetae*

In the valley at our feet, still half hidden in mist, lay farms, cottages, villas, the railway, the colliery and the densely teeming streets of the men who worked there . . . [Sir George] turned and spoke in the wistful, nostalgic tones of a castaway, yet of a castaway who was reconciled to his solitude. 'You see', he said, 'there is *no one* between us and the Locker-Lampsons'.

EVELYN WAUGH in Osbert Sitwell, *Laughter in the Next Room*

1 Quaint Mazes

And, after all, it is to them we return.
Their triumph is to rise and be our hosts:
lords of unquiet or of quiet sojourn,
those muddy-hued and midge-tormented ghosts.

On blustery lilac-bush and terrace-urn
bedaubed with bloom Linnaean pentecosts
put their pronged light; the chilly fountains burn.
Religion of the heart, with trysts and quests

and pangs of consolation, its hawk's hood
twitched off for sweet carnality, again
rejoices in old hymns of servitude,

haunting the sacred well, the hidden shrine.
It is the ravage of the heron wood;
it is the rood blazing upon the green.

2 Damon's Lament for His Clorinda, Yorkshire 1654

November rips gold foil from the oak ridges.
Dour folk huddle in High Hoyland, Penistone.
The tributaries of the Sheaf and Don
bulge their dull spate, cramming the poor bridges.

The North Sea batters our shepherds' cottages
from sixty miles. No sooner has the sun
swung clear above earth's rim than it is gone.
We live like gleaners of its vestiges

knowing we flourish, though each year a child
with the set face of a tomb-weeper is put down
for ever and ever. Why does the air grow cold

in the region of mirrors? And who is this clown
doffing his mask at the masked threshold
to selfless raptures that are all his own?

3 Who Are These Coming to the Sacrifice?

High voices in domestic chapels; praise;
praise-worthy feuds; new-burgeoned spires that sprung
crisp-leaved as though from dropping-wells. The young
ferns root among our vitrified tears.

What an elopement that was: the hired chaise
tore through the fir-grove, scattered kinsmen flung
buckshot and bridles, and the tocsin swung
from the tarred bellcote dappled with dove-smears.

Wires tarnish in gilt corridors, in each room
stiff with the bric-a-brac of loss and gain.
Love fled, truly outwitted, through a swirl

of long-laid dust. Today you sip and smile
though still not quite yourself. Guarding its pane
the spider looms against another storm.

4 A Short History of British India (I)

Make miniatures of the once-monstrous theme:
the red-coat devotees, mêlées of wheels,
Jagannath's lovers. With indifferent aim
unleash the rutting cannon at the walls

of forts and palaces; pollute the wells.
Impound the memoirs for their bankrupt shame,
fantasies of true destiny that kills
'under the sanction of the English name'.

Be moved by faith, obedience without fault,
the flawless hubris of heroic guilt,
the grace of visitation; and be stirred

by all her god-quests, her idolatries,
in conclave of abiding injuries,
sated upon the stillness of the bride.

5 A Short History of British India (II)

Suppose they sweltered here three thousand years
patient for our destruction. There is a greeting
beyond the act. Destiny is the great thing,
true lord of annexation and arrears.

Our law-books overrule the emperors.
The mango is the bride-bed of light. Spring
jostles the flame-tree. But new mandates bring
new images of faith, good subahdars!

The flittering candles of the wayside shrines
melt into dawn. The sun surmounts the dust.
Krishna from Radha lovingly untwines.

Lugging the earth, the oxen bow their heads.
The alien conscience of our days is lost
among the ruins and on endless roads.

6 A Short History of British India (III)

Malcolm and Frere, Colebrooke and Elphinstone,
the life of empire like the life of the mind
'simple, sensuous, passionate', attuned
to the clear theme of justice and order, gone.

Gone the prized ascetic pastimes, Persian
scholarship, the wild boar run to ground,
the watercolours of the sun and wind.
Names rise like outcrops from a rich terrain,

like carapaces of the Mughal tombs
lop-sided among rice-fields, boarded-up
near railway-crossings and small aerodromes.

'India's a peacock-shrine next to a shop
selling mangola, sitars, lucky charms,
heavenly Buddhas smiling in their sleep.'

7 Loss and Gain

Pitched high above the shallows of the sea
lone bells in gritty belfries do not ring
but coil a far and inward echoing
out of the air that thrums. Enduringly,

fuchsia-hedges fend between cliff and sky;
brown stumps of headstones tamp into the ling
the ruined and the ruinously strong.
Platonic England grasps its tenantry

where wild-eyed poppies raddle tawny farms
and wild swans root in lily-clouded lakes.
Vulnerable to each other the twin forms

of sleep and waking touch the man who wakes
to sudden light, who thinks that this becalms
even the phantoms of untold mistakes.

8 Vocations

While friends defected, you stayed and were sure,
fervent in reason, watchful of each name:
a signet-seal's unostentatious gem
gleams against walnut on the escritoire,

focus of reckoning and judicious prayer.
This is the durable covenant, a room
quietly furnished with stuff of martyrdom,
lit by the flowers and moths from your own shire,

by silvery vistas frothed with convolvulus,
radiance of dreams hardly to be denied.
The twittering pipistrelle, so strange and close,

plucks its curt flight through the moist eventide;
the children thread among old avenues
of snowberries, clear-calling as they fade.

9 The Laurel Axe

Autumn resumes the land, ruffles the woods
with smoky wings, entangles them. Trees shine
out from their leaves, rocks mildew to moss-green;
the avenues are spread with brittle floods.

Platonic England, house of solitudes,
rests in its laurels and its injured stone,
replete with complex fortunes that are gone,
beset by dynasties of moods and clouds.

It stands, as though at ease with its own world,
the mannerly extortions, languid praise,
all that devotion long since bought and sold,

the rooms of cedar and soft-thudding baize,
tremulous boudoirs where the crystals kissed
in cabinets of amethyst and frost.

10 Fidelities

Remember how, at seven years, the decrees
were brought home: child-soul must register
for Christ's dole, be allotted its first Easter,
blanch-white and empty, chilled by the lilies,

betrothed among the well-wishers and spies.
Reverend Mother, breakfastless, could feast her
constraint on terracotta and alabaster
and brimstone and the sweets of paradise.

Theology makes good bedside reading. Some
who are lost covet scholastic proof,
subsistence of probation, modest balm.

The wooden wings of justice borne aloof,
we close our eyes to Anselm and lie calm.
All night the cisterns whisper in the roof.

11 Idylls of the King

The pigeon purrs in the wood; the wood has gone;
dark leaves that flick to silver in the gust,
and the marsh-orchids and the heron's nest,
goldgrimy shafts and pillars of the sun.

Weightless magnificence upholds the past.
Cement recesses smell of fur and bone
and berries wrinkle in the badger-run
and wiry heath-fern scatters its fresh rust.

'O clap your hands' so that the dove takes flight,
bursts through the leaves with an untidy sound,
plunges its wings into the green twilight

above this long-sought and forsaken ground,
the half-built ruins of the new estate,
warheads of mushrooms round the filter-pond.

12 The Eve of St Mark

Stroke the small silk with your whispering hands,
godmother; nod and nod from the half-gloom;
broochlight intermittent between the fronds,
the owl immortal in its crystal dome.

Along the mantelpiece veined lustres trill,
the clock discounts us with a telling chime.
Familiar ministrants, clerks-of-appeal,
burnish upon the threshold of the dream:

churchwardens in wing-collars bearing scrolls
of copyhold well-tinctured and well-tied.
Your photo-albums loved by the boy-king

preserve in sepia waterglass the souls
of distant cousins, virgin till they died,
and the lost delicate suitors who could sing.

13 The Herefordshire Carol

So to celebrate that kingdom: it grows
greener in winter, essence of the year;
the apple-branches musty with green fur.
In the viridian darkness of its yews

it is an enclave of perpetual vows
broken in time. Its truth shows disrepair,
disfigured shrines, their stones of gossamer,
Old Moore's astrology, all hallows,

the squire's effigy bewigged with frost,
and hobnails cracking puddles before dawn.
In grange and cottage girls rise from their beds

by candlelight and mend their ruined braids.
Touched by the cry of the iconoclast,
how the rose-window blossoms with the sun!

Two Chorale-Preludes

ON MELODIES BY PAUL CELAN

1 Ave Regina Coelorum

Es ist ein Land Verloren . . .

There is a land called Lost
at peace inside our heads.
The moon, full on the frost,
vivifies these stone heads.

Moods of the verb 'to stare',
split selfhoods, conjugate
ice-facets from the air,
the light glazing the light.

Look at us, Queen of Heaven.
Our solitudes drift by
your solitudes, the seven
dead stars in your sky.

2 Te Lucis Ante Terminum

Wir gehen dir, Heimat, ins Garn . . .

Centaury with your staunch bloom
you there alder beech you fern,
midsummer closeness my far home,
fresh traces of lost origin.

Silvery the black cherries hang,
the plum-tree oozes through each cleft
and horse-flies siphon the green dung,
glued to the sweetness of their graft:

immortal transience, a 'kind
of otherness', self-understood,
BE FAITHFUL grows upon the mind
as lichen glimmers on the wood.

A Pre-Raphaelite Notebook

Primroses; salutations; the miry skull
of a half-eaten ram; viscous wounds in earth
opening. What seraphs are afoot.

Gold seraph to gold worm in the pierced slime:
greetings. Advent of power-in-grace. The power
of flies distracts the working of our souls.

Earth's abundance. The God-ejected Word
resorts to flesh, procures carrion, satisfies
its white hunger. Salvation's travesty

a deathless metaphor: the stale head
sauced in original blood; the little feast
foaming with cries of rapture and despair.

Terribilis Est Locus Iste

GAUGUIN AND THE PONT-AVEN SCHOOL

Briefly they are amazed. The marigold-fields
mell and shudder and the travellers,
in sudden exile burdened with remote
hieratic gestures, journey to no end

beyond the vivid severance of each day,
strangeness at doors, a different solitude
between the mirror and the window, marked
visible absences, colours of the mind,

marginal angels lightning-sketched in red
chalk on the month's accounts or marigolds
in paint runnily embossed, or the disowned
self-portrait with a seraph and a storm.

Veni Coronaberis

A Garland for Helen Waddell

The crocus armies from the dead
rise up; the realm of love renews
the battle it was born to lose,
though for a time the snows have fled

and old stones blossom in the south
with sculpted vine and psaltery
and half-effaced adultery
the bird-dung dribbling from its mouth;

and abstinence crowns all our care
with martyr-laurels for this day.
Towers and steeples rise away
into the towering gulfs of air.

Florentines

Horses, black-lidded mouths peeled back
to white: well-groomed these warriors ride,
their feuds forgotten, remembered, forgotten . . .
a cavalcade passing, night not far-off;
the stricken faces damnable and serene.

'Christmas Trees'

Bonhoeffer in his skylit cell
bleached by the flares' candescent fall,
pacing out his own citadel,

restores the broken themes of praise,
encourages our borrowed days,
by logic of his sacrifice.

Against wild reasons of the state
his words are quiet but not too quiet.
We hear too late or not too late.

Tenebrae

He was so tired that he was scarcely able to hear a note of the songs: he felt imprisoned in a cold region where his brain was numb and his spirit was isolated.

1

Requite this angel whose
flushed and thirsting face
stoops to the sacrifice
out of which it arose.
This is the lord Eros
of grief who pities
no one; it is
Lazarus with his sores.

2

And you, who with your soft but searching voice
drew me out of the sleep where I was lost,
who held me near your heart that I might rest
confiding in the darkness of your choice:
possessed by you I chose to have no choice,
fulfilled in you I sought no further quest.
You keep me, now, in dread that quenches trust,
in desolation where my sins rejoice.
As I am passionate so you with pain
turn my desire; as you seem passionless
so I recoil from all that I would gain,
wounding myself upon forgetfulness,
false ecstasies, which you in truth sustain
as you sustain each item of your cross.

3

Veni Redemptor, but not in our time.
Christus Resurgens, quite out of this world.
'Ave' we cry; the echoes are returned.
Amor Carnalis is our dwelling-place.

4

O light of light, supreme delight;
grace on our lips to our disgrace.
Time roosts on all such golden wrists;
our leanness is our luxury.
Our love is what we love to have;
our faith is in our festivals.

5

Stupefying images of grief-in-dream,
succubae to my natural grief of heart,
cling to me, then; you who will not desert
your love nor lose him in some blank of time.
You come with all the licence of her name
to tell me you are mine. But you are not
and she is not. Can my own breath be hurt
by breathless shadows groaning in their game?
It can. The best societies of hell
acknowledge this, aroused by what they know:
consummate rage recaptured there in full
as faithfulness demands it, blow for blow,
and rectitude that mimics its own fall
reeling with sensual abstinence and woe.

6

This is the ash-pit of the lily-fire,
this is the questioning at the long tables,
this is true marriage of the self-in-self,
this is a raging solitude of desire,
this is the chorus of obscene consent,
this is a single voice of purest praise.

7

He wounds with ecstasy. All
the wounds are his own.
He wears the martyr's crown.
He is the Lord of Misrule.
He is the Master of the Leaping Figures,
the motley factions.
Revelling in auguries
he is the Weeper of the Valedictions.

8

Music survives, composing her own sphere,
Angel of Tones, Medusa, Queen of the Air,
and when we would accost her with real cries
silver on silver thrills itself to ice.

The Mystery of
the Charity of
Charles Péguy

In loving memory of Sarah Ann Hands (1869–1967)

Nous sommes les derniers. Presque les après-derniers. Aussitôt après nous commence un autre âge, un tout autre monde, le monde de ceux qui ne croient plus à rien, qui s'en font gloire et orgueil.

CHARLES PÉGUY

I

Begins race of Péguy to join war.

Crack of a starting-pistol. Jean Jaurès

Wine in café blood looks like wine

dies in a wine-puddle. Who or what stares
through the café-window crêped in powder-smoke? → Raoul Villain
The bill for the new farce reads *Sleepers Awake*.

play

History is a farcical clown who is rehearsing another assassination

History commands the stage wielding a toy gun,
rehearsing another scene. It has raged so before,
countless times; and will do, countless times more,
in the guise of supreme clown, dire tragedian.

In Brutus' name martyr and mountebank — *Charlatan*
ghost Caesar's ghost, his wounds of air and ink
painlessly spouting. Jaurès' blood lies stiff
on menu-card, shirt-front and handkerchief.

He wrote the article saying that Jaurès should go

Did Péguy kill Jaurès? Did he incite
the assassin? Must men stand by what they write
as by their camp-beds or their weaponry
or shell-shocked comrades while they sag and cry?

Would Péguy answer—stubbornly on guard
among the *Cahiers*, with his army cape
and steely pince-nez and his hermit's beard,
brooding on conscience and embattled hope?

Could either teach Truth or truly teach. Relates him and the assassin

Truth's pedagogue, braving an entrenched class
of fools and scoundrels, children of the world,
his eyes caged and hostile behind glass—
still Péguy said that Hope is a little child. — *Hope is unrealistic weak*

Violent contrariety of men and days; calm
juddery bombardment of a silent film
showing such things: its canvas slashed with rain
and St Elmo's fire. Victory of the machine!

The brisk celluloid clatters through the gate;
the cortège of the century dances in the street;
and over and over the jolly cartoon
armies of France go reeling towards Verdun.

2

Rage and regret are tireless to explain
stratagems of the out-manoeuvred man,
the charge and counter-charge. You know the drill,
raw veteran, poet with the head of a bull.

Footslogger of genius, skirmisher with grace
and ill-luck, sentinel of the sacrifice,
without vantage of vanity, though mortal-proud,
defend your first position to the last word.

The sun-tanned earth is your centurion;
you are its tribune. On the hard-won
high places the old soldiers of old France
crowd like good children wrapped in obedience

and sleep, and ready to be taken home.
Whatever that vision, it is not a child's;
it is what a child's vision can become.
Memory, Imagination, harvesters of those fields,

our gifts are spoils, our virtues epitaphs,
our substance is the grass upon the graves.
'Du calme, mon vieux, du calme.' How studiously
one cultivates the sugars of decay,

pâtisserie-tinklings of angels ''sieur-'dame',
the smile of the dead novice in its plush frame,
while greed and disaffection are ingrained
like chalk-dust in the ranklings of the mind.

'Rather the Marne than the *Cahiers*.' True enough,
you took yourself off. Dying, your whole life
fell into place. ''Sieurs-'dames, this is the wall
where he leaned and rested, this is the well

from which he drank.' Péguy, you mock us now.
History takes the measure of your brow
in blank-eyed bronze, brave mediocre work
of *Niclausse, sculpteur*, cornered in the park

among the stout dogs and lame patriots
and all those ghosts, far-gazing in mid-stride,
rising from where they fell, still on parade,
covered in glory and the gleet of beetroots.

3

Vistas of richness and reward. The cedar
uprears its lawns of black cirrus. You have found
hundred-fold return though in the land
of exile. You are Joseph the Provider;

and in the fable this is your proper home;
three sides of a courtyard where the bees thrum
in the crimped hedges and the pigeons flirt
and paddle, and sunlight pierces the heart-

shaped shutter-patterns in the afternoon,
shadows of fleur-de-lys on the stone floors.
Here life is labour and pastime and orison
like something from a simple book of hours;

and immortality, your measured task,
inscribes its antique scars on the new desk
among your relics, bits of ivory quartz
and dented snuffbox won at Austerlitz.

The proofs pile up; the dead are made alive
to their posthumous fame. Here is the archive
of your stewardship; here is your true domaine,
its fields of discourse ripening to the Marne.

Château de Trie is yours, Chartres is yours,
and the carved knight of Gisors with the hound;
Colombey-les-deux-Eglises; St Cyr's
cadres and echelons are yours to command.

Yours is their dream of France, militant-pastoral:
musky red gillyvors, the wicker bark
of clematis braided across old brick
and the slow chain that cranks out of the well

morning and evening. It is Domrémy
restored; the mystic strategy of Foch
and Bergson with its time-scent, dour panache
deserving of martyrdom. It is an army

of poets, converts, vine-dressers, men skilled
in wood or metal, peasants from the Beauce,
terse teachers of Latin and those unschooled
in all but the hard rudiments of grace.

Such dreams portend, the dreamer prophesies,
is this not true? Truly, if you are wise,
deny such wisdom; bid the grim bonne-femme
defend your door: 'M'sieur is not at home.'

4

This world is different, belongs to them—
the lords of limit and of contumely.
It matters little whether you go tamely
or with rage and defiance to your doom.

This is your enemies' country which they took
in the small hours an age before you woke,
went to the window, saw the mist-hewn
statues of the lean kine emerge at dawn.

Outflanked again, too bad! You still have pride,
haggard obliquities: those that take remorse
and the contempt of others for a muse,
bound to the alexandrine as to the *Code*

Napoléon. Thus the bereaved soul returns
upon itself, grows resolute at chess,
in war-games hurling dice of immense loss
into the breach; thus punitively mourns.

This is no old Beauce manoir that you keep
but the rue de la Sorbonne, the cramped shop,
its unsold *Cahiers* built like barricades,
its fierce disciples, disciplines and feuds,

the camelot-cry of 'sticks!' As Tharaud says,
'all through your life the sound of broken glass.'
So much for Jaurès murdered in cold pique
by some vexed shadow of the belle époque,

some guignol strutting at the window-frame.
But what of you, Péguy, who came to 'exult',
to be called 'wolfish' by your friends? The guilt
belongs to time; and you must leave on time.

Jaurès was killed blindly, yet with reason:
'let us have drums to beat down his great voice.'
So you spoke to the blood. So, you have risen
above all that and fallen flat on your face

5

among the beetroots, where we are constrained
to leave you sleeping and to step aside
from the fleshed bayonets, the fusillade
of red-rimmed smoke like stubble being burned;

to turn away and contemplate the working
of the radical soul—instinct, intelligence,
memory, call it what you will—waking
into the foreboding of its inheritance,

its landscape and inner domain; images
of earth and grace. Across Artois the rois-mages
march on Bethlehem; sun-showers fall
slantwise over the kalefield, the canal.

Hedgers and ditchers, quarrymen, thick-shod
curés de campagne, each with his load,
shake off those cares and burdens; they become,
in a bleak visionary instant, seraphim

looking towards Chartres, the spired sheaves,
stone-thronged annunciations, winged ogives
uplifted and uplifting from the winter-gleaned
furrows of that criss-cross-trodden ground.

Or say it is Pentecost: the hawthorn-tree,
set with coagulate magnified flowers of may,
blooms in a haze of light; old chalk-pits brim
with seminal verdure from the roots of time.

Landscape is like revelation; it is both
singular crystal and the remotest things.
Cloud-shadows of seasons revisit the earth,
odourless myrrh borne by the wandering kings.

Happy are they who, under the gaze of God,
die for the 'terre charnelle', marry her blood
to theirs, and, in strange Christian hope, go down
into the darkness of resurrection,

into sap, ragwort, melancholy thistle,
almondy meadowsweet, the freshet-brook
rising and running through small wilds of oak,
past the elder-tump that is the child's castle.

Inevitable high summer, richly scarred
with furze and grief; winds drumming the fame
of the tin legions lost in haystack and stream.
Here the lost are blest, the scarred most sacred:

odd village workshops grimed and peppercorned
in a dust of dead spiders, paper-crowned
sunflowers with the bleached heads of rag dolls,
brushes in aspic, clay pots, twisted nails;

the clinking anvil and clear sheepbell-sound,
at noon and evening, of the angelus;
coifed girls like geese, labourers cap in hand,
and walled gardens espaliered with angels;

solitary bookish ecstasies, proud tears,
proud tears, for the forlorn hope, the guerdon
of Sedan ('oh les braves gens!'), martyred Gordon
stepping down sedately into the spears.

Patience hardens to a pittance, courage
unflinchingly declines into sour rage,
the cobweb-banners, the shrill bugle-bands
and the bronze warriors resting on their wounds.

These fatal decencies, they make us lords
over ourselves: familial debts and dreads,
keepers of old scores, the kindly ones
telling their beady sous, the child-eyed crones

who guard the votive candles and the faint
invalid's night-light of the sacrament,
a host of lilies and the table laid
for early mass from which you stood aside

to find salvation, your novena cleaving
brusquely against the grain of its own myth,
its truth and justice, to a kind of truth,
a justice hard to justify. 'Having

spoken his mind he'd a mind to be silent.'
But who would credit that, that one talent
dug from the claggy Beauce and returned to it
with love, honour, suchlike bitter fruit?

6

To dispense, with justice; or, to dispense
with justice. Thus the catholic god of France,
with honours all even, honours all, even
the damned in the brazen Invalides of Heaven.

Here there should be a section without words
for military band alone: 'Sambre et Meuse',
the 'Sidi Brahim' or 'Le Roi s'Amuse';
white gloves and monocles and polished swords

and Dreyfus with his buttons off, chalk-faced
but standing to attention, the school prig
caught in some act and properly disgraced.
A puffy satrap prances on one leg

to snap the traitor's sword, his ordered rage
bursting with 'cran et gloire' and gouts of rouge.
The chargers click and shiver. There is no stir
in the drawn ranks, among the hosts of the air,

all draped and gathered by the weird storm-light
cheap wood-engravings cast on those who fought
at Mars-la-Tour, Sedan; or on the men
in the world-famous stories of Jules Verne

or nailed at Golgotha. Drumrap and fife
hit the right note: 'A mort le Juif! Le Juif
à la lanterne!' Serenely the mob howls,
its silent mouthings hammered into scrolls

torn from *Apocalypse*. No wonder why
we fall to violence out of apathy,
redeemed by falling and restored to grace
beyond the dreams of mystic avarice.

But who are 'we', since history is law,
clad in our skins of silver, steel and hide,
or in our rags, with rotten teeth askew,
heroes or knaves as Clio shall decide?

'We' are crucified Pilate, Caiaphas
in his thin soutane and Judas with the face
of a man who has drunk wormwood. We come
back empty-handed from Jerusalem

counting our blessings, honestly admire
the wrath of the peacemakers, for example
Christ driving the money-changers from the temple,
applaud the Roman steadiness under fire.

We are the occasional just men who sit
in gaunt self-judgement on their self-defeat,
the élite hermits, secret orators
of an old faith devoted to new wars.

We are 'embusqués', having no wounds to show
save from the thorns, ecstatic at such pain.
Once more the truth advances; and again
the metaphors of blood begin to flow.

7

Salute us all, Christus with your iron
garlands of poppies and ripe carrion.
No, sleep where you stand; let some boy-officer
take up your vigil with your dungfork spear.

What vigil is this, then, among the polled
willows, cart-shafts uptilted against skies,
translucent rain at jutting calvaries;
on paths that are rutted and broken-walled?

What is this relic fumbled with such care
by mittened fingers in dugout or bomb-
tattered, jangling estaminet's upper room?
The incense from a treasured tabatière,

you watchmen at the Passion. Péguy said
'why do I write of war? Simply because
I have not been there. In time I shall cease
to invoke it.' We still dutifully read

'heureux ceux qui sont morts.' Drawn on the past
these presences endure; they have not ceased
to act, suffer, crouching into the hail
like labourers of their own memorial

or those who worship at its marble rote,
their many names one name, the common 'dur'
built into duration, the endurance of war;
blind Vigil herself, helpless and obdurate.

And yet what sights: Saul groping in the dust
for his broken glasses, or the men far-gone
on the road to Emmaus who saw the ghost.
Commit all this to memory. The line

falters, reforms, vanishes into the smoke
of its own unknowing; mother, dad,
gone in that shell-burst, with the other dead,
'pour la patrie', according to the book.

8

Dear lords of life, stump-toothed, with ragged breath,
throng after throng cast out upon the earth,
flesh into dust, who slowly come to use
dreams of oblivion in lieu of paradise,

push on, push on!—through struggle, exhaustion,
indignities of all kinds, the impious Christian
oratory, 'vos morituri', through berserk fear,
laughing, howling, 'servitude et grandeur'

in other words, in nameless gobbets thrown
up by the blast, names issuing from mouths
of the dying, with their dying breaths.
But rest assured, bristly-brave gentlemen

of Normandie and Loire. Death does you proud,
every heroic commonplace, 'Amor',
'Fidelitas', polished like old armour,
stamped forever into the featureless mud.

Poilus and sous-officiers who plod
to your lives' end, name your own recompense,
expecting nothing but the grace of France,
drawn to her arms, her august plenitude.

The blaze of death goes out, the mind leaps
for its salvation, is at once extinct;
its last thoughts tetter the furrows, distinct
in dawn twilight, caught on the barbed loops.

Whatever strikes and maims us it is not
fate, to our knowledge. En avant, Péguy!
The irony of advancement. Say 'we
possess nothing; try to hold on to that.'

9

There is an ancient landscape of green branches—
true tempérament de droite, you have your wish—
crosshatching twigs and light, goldfinches
among the peppery lilac, the small fish

pencilled into the stream. Ah, such a land
the Ile de France once was. Virelai and horn
wind through the meadows, the dawn-masses sound
fresh triumphs for our Saviour crowned with scorn.

Good governors and captains, by your leave,
you also were sore-wounded but those wars
are ended. Iron men who bell the hours,
marshals of porte-cochère and carriage-drive,

this is indeed perfection, this is the heart
of the mystère. Yet one would not suppose
Péguy's 'defeat', 'affliction', your lost cause.
Old Bourbons view-hallooing for regret

among the cobwebs and the ghostly wine,
you dream of warrior-poets and the Meuse
flowing so sweetly; the androgynous Muse
your priest-confessor, sister-châtelaine.

How the mood swells to greet the gathering storm!
The chestnut trees begin to thresh and cast
huge canisters of blossom at each gust.
Coup de tonnerre! Bismarck is in the room!

Bad memories, seigneurs? Such wraiths appear
on summer evenings when the gnat-swarm spins
a dying moment on the tremulous air.
The curtains billow and the rain begins

its night-long vigil. Sombre heartwoods gleam,
the clocks replenish the small hours' advance
and not a soul has faltered from its trance.
'*Je* est un autre', that fatal telegram,

floats past you in the darkness, unreceived.
Connoisseurs of obligation, history
stands, a blank instant, awaiting your reply:
'If we but move a finger France is saved!'

10

Down in the river-garden a grey-gold
dawnlight begins to silhouette the ash.
A rooster wails remotely over the marsh
like Mr Punch mimicking a lost child.

At Villeroy the copybook lines of men
rise up and are erased. Péguy's cropped skull
dribbles its ichor, its poor thimbleful,
a simple lesion of the complex brain.

Woefully battered but not too bloody,
smeared by fraternal root-crops and at one
with the fritillary and the veined stone,
having composed his great work, his small body,

for the last rites of truth, whatever they are,
or the Last Judgement which is much the same,
or Mercy, even, with her tears and fire,
he commends us to nothing, leaves a name

for the burial-detail to gather up
with rank and number, personal effects,
the next-of-kin and a few other facts;
his arm over his face as though in sleep

or to ward off the sun: the body's prayer,
the tribute of his true passion, for Chartres
steadfastly cleaving to the Beauce, for her,
the Virgin of innumerable charities.

'Encore plus douloureux et doux.' Note how
sweetness devours sorrow, renders it again,
turns to affliction each more carnal pain.
Whatever is fulfilled is now the law

where law is grace, that grace won by inches,
inched years. The men of sorrows do their stint,
whose golgothas are the moon's trenches,
the sun's blear flare over the salient.

J'accuse! j'accuse!—making the silver prance
and curvet, and the dust-motes jig to war
across the shaky vistas of old France,
the gilt-edged maps of Strasbourg and the Saar.

Low tragedy, high farce, fight for command,
march, counter-march, and come to the salute
at every hole-and-corner burial-rite
bellowed with hoarse dignity into the wind.

Take that for your example! But still mourn,
being so moved: éloge and elegy
so moving on the scene as if to cry
'in memory of those things these words were born.'

Hymns to
Our Lady of Chartres

1982–2012

In piam memoriam René Gallet (1944–2012)

the Argument:

that the doctrine of the Immaculate Conception of the Blessed Virgin in the womb of Anna, unlike the doctrine of the Immaculate Conception of Christ in the womb of Mary, is a sentimental late intrusion that infantilizes faith:

that, as Henry Adams observed at Chartres, the twin powers of the modern world are inertia and velocity:

and that, as Péguy said, all begins in *mystique* and ends in *politique*.

I

Retainers out: that *florid grim music*
broken by grunts and shrieks. No motion else.
Amorous bonding putty, mosaic
that breaks up features and wears colours false,

discovered, how? I am pensionable
and you have no news. When last we laid bare
our manifest othernesses cable
television had not been installed here.

For what other reason are there notebooks,
intemperate archives? Bring me to dance,
who cannot dance, your features of botox
and I shall reconsider temperance.

You are my fancy; nor do I accost
her royal highness directly: Virgin
to the eccentric spires where I went lost
tracking down Péguy and faith resurgent.

How febrile, how distrait, this has become:
it was meant as greeting, to reconcile
inconstant memory with constant shame,
(*broken by grunts and shrieks*), impassive style.

2

Velocity and inertia Adams
plumbed at Chartres; fixing grief's effigy
caped in a spout-downpour; nature's bad sums
righted by grace not time's coprophagy:

Dante, politicized wizard, braved wings
of lead and caustic, de-icers that foul
trailing-edges with slush and glaxy strings.
Believed angel in earthen apparel.

Petrarch's *Secretum* cracked I gave away
ignorant that any code forbade it;
distressed wisdom rivulets of white clay.
Shit, even, can be further degraded.

Faith for old-timers gets more difficult,
shorted of breath. How distantly it seems
those phrases, first sprung up within the fault,
became the properties of what becomes.

Ought I submit to some means-test of gifts?
It is no Virgin that I here apprise.
Deeply flawed vow, sophisticate of crafts,
confirms as alien such majesties.

3

Making the innocent subject confess
to his first interview is indecent
politics. Let me give you this address
that you may attach my wits, complacent

Ministers of Oaths and for High Culture.
From the vile slough, black as tar-macadam,
lug the Black Virgin: gross her sepulture.
May I cite you indirectly, Madame,

as someone I knew briefly; who could speak,
through intermediaries if called upon,
attesting to my virtues as a freak?
Truth lies in its case, an untried weapon,

and I have no great practice. Innate skill
fails my speech when I most need you. Bearing
upon the matter voices soft and shrill,
attrition by remorse like sand scouring.

When do I come to trial, even? No
messages before noon. Glasses of hock
and soda water settled Lord Byron
before crass assonance felled him with shock.

4

Portrait of a centurion, haggard, shot
to glory: Third Republic uniform;
mort au champ d'honneur. Well, good for him.
Képi, white gloves, pantalon rouge, the lot.

But there are certainly others: the child
who restores justice, the officer
standing over the heart; and some who bear
the weight of sorrow to the driven fold.

How many centurions áre there in the New
Testament? Have I miscounted? One
spoke with authority of discipline
brought to salvation. Yet another slew

Christ with a thrust straight out of army school.
One guarded the Sepulchre: he's portrayed
all of a heap, slack-jawed plebeian dread.
One made himself responsible to St. Paul.

One I think was blinded and then saved
through blindness by a superflux of faith;
soured wine of Cana sweet upon the breath,
Christ's mourners risen as the unbereaved.

5

Prayers are imprecations for a start;
piety may be possible with time;
plodding through metric and four-square of rhyme;
a soul's conviction, ill-conditioned heart.

Tinctured by death as blood sinks into sand,
befouled by our fecundity the earth
construes itself embrangled in Cain's wrath,
the serpent of the tree long gone to ground;

you new-arising through a cosmic web
of truth and fable to a signal reign;
grand misconceivings we ourselves assign;
interminably thus, the Goat, the Crab—

cursing I say: never so much betrayed,
Regina Coeli; onerous desire
something implanted in the viscera,
a sensual migraine shafting eye through head;

cries of assent from those displaced in mind.
Childhood, Annunciation, the Dormition:
rich in theology our poor contrition;
late snow ravelling off along the wind.

6

Handbells might do it, jews' harps, risible
tuckets of salutation. Otherwise
gnashing and gnawing sound out your praise.
Salve regina. Visible, invisible,

powers, presences, in and beyond the blue
glass, radiantly-occluded Sion, pour
festal light at the feet of the new poor,
scavengers upon grace, if grace is true;

if not, then, as they say, all is allowed.
Where chronic devoirs clatter to adore
la Dame du Pilier and her wooden stare,
the priests come nodding by, dainty and shrewd,

like virgins with trim lamps devoutly oiled,
to do the honours of your mysteries.
Through what straits might I come to worship this,
and kneel before you, and be reconciled,

among the flowering lances, the heathen
gold phalanxes of flame; at the high seats
where Mercy is redeemed from its own threats;
with dumb-struck martyrs trumpeted to heaven?

7

Trumpets again, as this is Sion's twin city
or city-in-law. Across France the great west
windows are full of the sun's holocaust,
the dying blazons of eternity

secured in mazy lead and bevelled stone.
Outside the glass, pigeons rancid as gulls
roost in their stucco-dung on the tiered sills.
The candles blur the air before your throne.

Love is at odds. Your beauty has gone out
too many times, too vividly has flared
through the mild dreams of Herod undeterred.
His eyes are like the eyes of the devout.

O dulcis Virgo, you are the stained world's
ransom, bear its image, live through your
perpetual exile in its courts of prayer.
'This is the carnal rose that re-enfolds

heaven into earth.' They say you are disposed
to acts of grace: tumblers and holy fools.
Child-saints rejoice you, small immaculate souls,
and mundane sorrows mystically espoused.

8

Redemptrice of all vows and fealties, Dame
de Sous-Terre, pray for us, pitched beneath
your mantle of limestone and sifted earth.
Assoil your present and lost children; some

mettled by virtue, briskly taking Christ,
and some as captives; those to whom the kiss
of peace is torment in the midst of mass,
those who salute you with a raised fist.

Spes nostra, salve! Your strange countenance
is our remaking. Turn, then, its remote
familial smile upon this Christian rote.
Sly innocence of the blood seized in a trance

by violent knowledge—what it is to know
our strength. Pray for those neophytes who found
in you, the source of life, their secret wound.
The seraphim with stark pinions aglow

look blankly at us: we who may be spared,
as well as other ecstasies, the hues
of burning and the damned at their old cries,
your varied mercies, variously adored.

9

A match crack-scuffs, a flame spurts in the fosse,
faces bow to cupped hands, a thing archaic,
a gesture proletarian and stoic;
Homeric, even; look at Odysseus,

who was of course a prince in his own country,
champing on Gauloises; Hector of the taut
monocle, dragged helplessly by a foot.
Other manners, another century.

Herod was dire but he was not the Shoah.
What do you say, Vierge, to this Jewish child
fixed at your breast, in the great glass annealed,
Himself the threefold shattering of Chaos?

Another language, such as your Dai Greatcoat
unerringly presented: *misadventure*
for the machine gun's cunningly-loosed ceinture
binding in blood all those who late set out—

Jehovah's time not ours. We might have given
the temple scroll for Péguy to repair,
indomitable, as an unsold *Cahier*,
mystique and *politique* there intershriven.

10

Return, if in mauvais esprit, to Chartres;
there's my old pension; the rue St-Jacques;
there Notre-Dame stone-turbining to Pâques
slices the gloom with radiance of martyrs.

On the cleft hill that odd man jousting blame,
Péguy, to whom Olivier Messiaen
part-offered *Et exspecto*, something brazen;
Jean Moulin whom they also thrust at fame,

his agony finessed to silver wire,
received by Malraux at the Panthéon
with words of platitudinous haut ton,
that France might clamour, swoon, and rise entire.

Entre lutte et louange, deep-tolled sonorities,
the makers work and sleep and have their sex.
Travestied Judas reddish as a fox
swings on his pendulum and never dies.

Malraux negotiates the elevation:
the organ barking mad, the iron vats
terraced with candles wallowing in their fats.
This passage of great things your conflagration.

11

Further to extradition, that could seem
extravagant enough. Whose is the mark
put to such question? Why question, why talk?
Let be to oversee mere epigram

where the begged word is mere. I should not think
in relation to deficit, but hold
occultation and the myrrhian gold
the means to purge authority of rank.

She, prejudged to common wantonness
in a land racked for tribute, takes pity
on us by virtue of the Nativity
which was not without shock, although faultless;

and not devoid, some say, of blood and pain.
I place no call to sleeping heresies.
The three adventurers whom we deem wise—
pedigree of imperious Iran—

or Botticelli's angels on the thatch
did not deplore the tearlessness of things;
lawlessness, yes. Anarchy is what brings
the pinions of her grace to fullest stretch.

12

Grands-blessés crêped, proto-surrealists,
their deaths disband. Bitty ends of Gothic
Assumption, scribblings of hyperlithic,
serrate the vista, crudsoot-furcate crests.

Fancy her mutilée—how light deceives—
there's an odd thing—Parnassian pattern-block
cleft by joint strokes of gravitas and schlock,
dissonance contrabanded through sweet sieves.

Mastery of avowal, wrath's weak eyes.
Stilted and splinted, set about with gripes,
gross thirst mismatched to Lucozade and grapes,
stuck with prosthetic twizzlers and squirt ties,

Invention stalks its wards, distended dreams,
nude cellophanes. Enjambments wrestle still
a truculence of spirit minus will;
sick verses mate with gymnopteric mimes.

All metaphysics here negotiable—
requital's price, blessing's defoliant,
shrewd thrust mistimed. Mystery's assailant!—
cleave to hierarchy and the raw stable.

13

Mildewy twigs make pale light; a green sheen
rubs off at a touch and holds but barely
a radiance of domain. Unsurely
words appear to meet me on what I mean;

fumble eternity. To rescind is
no object. But animation: well then,
reflect. Imagination dwells again
with complex patterns of humankindness;

makes much of little if you could name it,
but does fall otherwise. Slur me your gifts:
Eden upstarting from its unsealed clefts,
Joy's resurrection tolled old-Adamite.

Péguy spun radicals in his trim script.
Later went beyond touch or reach. Orchards
hover against death; and seraphs touch swords.
Resistances of things crown the inept.

I do not see that this could be bettered,
given the time. Surrender a marvel.
The sun comes up and that is survival;
the wound birth opens mundanely sutured.

14

Impossible to think of you as France.
You could be in Yunnan, probably are;
I sent you out of my mind for a dare
centuries past and have heard nothing since.

What a deciduous nonsense there is
when the climate changes, my evergreen!
It is not you I address, great Chartreine,
nor the abundance of your known mercies;

though I confuse many by writing so
much on the cusp of devotion, so set
in the metrics. And I misinterpret
myself many times as inviting you.

This is a primitive animation.
I am bemused that it works; but work it
does, with sparks breaking out of the circuit—
old tramwires, old dodgems' besplat motion.

In a school lab I severed a live flex,
the shock like a bursting bag, my heart's
pace snagged among the bunsens and retorts:
sparkler-haired scarecrow, idiot-crucifix.

15

Will not now say hów I contract prayers
through agencies. Caritas, dismood me
consequence and redress. Let Talmud lie
impenetrable, its adhered layers,

even when things cry out for direction
in common time; appropriate justice
working apace with bluebags and thrust ice;
sensuous half-rhymes delay reaction.

Dig out a testamentary reproach
to lightness of tongue. All such responses
made as a gel to set. Distilled pensées.
Maybe that truth for which I barely vouch.

Simplicitas does not secure vain gibe
from the strait order of things. So conjure
righteous block of Sodom, last non-juror;
transfiguration like a blast of strobe.

Péguy's children were oblates to his grave.
No-one will credit this. Queen and Virgin,
claim your eccentrics from the waste margin.
Concentric the grand singing of the hive.

16

Harrowing is hallowing in some guides
that I would be loath to trust. Admit me
where I may do least harm to the timid
but meet my match in temerity's brides.

Older than Falstaff or Lear I have crap
perfuming my right hand. Spurn confession
unless to strut with Osric-like fashion.
Crazy Saint-Newton who skippered a slave-trip

shanghaied Cowper crazier than himself
to the great benefit of poetry.
Posthumous fame weeps at the lottery.
Dust down the Chartres Virgin from the shelf.

Unless or until Peer Gynt skitters sled-
drunk through my door, scattering the six cats
from their dishes of liver and cold cuts,
She shall be the confidante of my need.

Things are desperate here as I believe
you know, Lady. The poor in heart possess
three fewer skins; subsist on swallowed glass;
Commedia constrained to no reprieve.

17

Overprized charms, one a moulin mystique
from Vézelay: a pilgrims' plaster cast
which on occasion rouses interest,
the cogs of the grinder going clack-click

though you have to catch that on faith's ratchet.
Nothing has moved in thirty years. Mary,
Mother of us, this is no diary
of things spiritual. Accept the racket.

I would submit a prayer for your scald
Aleksander Wat, whose incessant pain
forced a kind of ontological grin
into his features; for the work that roiled.

I think he thought you had forsaken him—
things are, forgive me, too easily said
within the testing limits of this trade.
Dragonfly-blue the azure of your hem

when we are lucky. He went without hope
from a grey region into one greyer.
These limping metrics receive as prayer;
absolve their being uttered true to type.

18

Must you acquit me of this fresh desire
before conceiving my witness? Truly
there are the seeds of puissance in the air.
The consequences of the thing foully

engender. It should not be so. Effect
drives from no cause the cause of its being.
The toad is yet a prince before the fact.
A knavish rigmarole confirms him king.

Where is the sense in this? I have letters
still to write you in my old-fashioned hand
that brings to articulation fetters
of aery trial, being themselves bound.

Can you smell *Sonnets* in this? I confess
myself his adulator unrivalled,
supposing him to have breathed. What distress
sublimes thus to far oceans caravelled?

Too many questions. In a fashion steer
dangerous currents towards non-debate:
the untried, condescending to appear
familiar with language, cannot write.

19

That, and indulgent rhythms in my stride,
will deny me. How can you suffer such
application of flimsies to abrade?
Who would touch brimstone for a sense of touch?

Tacky fingers, remoulades of treacle:
as one considers lyric poetry
fit relaxation, like a song-cycle
after fiscal, *robust*, oratory.

You are incautious: have her thus accost
your sixty years of accreted banter;
so be accredited to fortune lost,
narration spent, an urge to disinter—

anything—spark recognition, aflame
in eyes of gauze. Syntax so confusing
encodes its own message before your name
is put to it, discovered carousing

and set up. I cannot find that motion
regarding normal abhorrence. The books
balance between lust and admonition,
between arrival and time's after-shocks.

20

And no-one cares even for heraldry
as if they cared. Two lions per ten pence
is brute *lèse majesté*. This a cold try
at making meaning without making sense

though to the observant let it comprise
nodded-in complicity. Whose spirit
goes up and out in filmed trajectories
of tragic sentiment, of mean merit?

Mostly it is like playing slow *I spy*
in a sparsely furnished guardroom. Repeat
after me the alphabet of the day.
I shall write of the Hesperides yet

in a stranger key than you would commend
as I imagine such favours. Return
me somehow to that hinterland your mind
where the dumb ox squares up to the unicorn

to keep heraldry thriving though off-track
(to mark the tug of sanity), ardour
of immolation and late passion's mock
vespers near-pagan in their sweet sordor.

21

Orchard and *Paradise* (from the Persian)
I would claim for my paradigm the two
most beautiful words we have. Persuasion
has different roots. I use what I know,

voiding the authority of the scholar.
Lady of International Acclaim,
I am not alone in such bi-polar
addiction to the figment of true stem.

Grafting constrains me to the mistletoe
of chill celebration: *mystery's end*
in these imperfect spheres that seem to glow
even in broad daylight across the land;

and yet a leper too might show such skin
in medieval mimicries of Wrath.
Complex necessity, simple the stain;
spirit so inconsiderately earth.

Judge this a lyrical intermission
to acts yet unwritten; not a coda
unaccepting of the late occasion,
the toll of disenchanted Xanadu.

Canaan

In memory of Jack Hallas

So ye children of Israél did wickedly in the sight of the Lord, & forgate the Lord their God, & serued Baalím, and Asheróth . . . Yea, they offred their sonnes, and their daughters vnto diuels, And shed innocent blood, euen the blood of their sonnes, and of their daughters, whome they offred vnto the idols of Canáan, and the lande was defiled with blood. Thus were they steined with their owne workes, and went a whoring with their owne inuentions . . . ô Canáan, the land of the Philistims, I wil euen destroy thee without an inhabitant.

Judges 3:7; Psalm 106:37–9; Zephaniah 2:5
(from the 'Geneva' Bible of 1560)

To the High Court of Parliament

November 1994

Where's probity in this—
            the slither-frisk
to lordship of a kind
as rats to a bird-table?

England—now of genius
            the eidolon—
unsubstantial yet voiding
substance like quicklime:

privatize to the dead
her memory:
            let her wounds weep
into the lens of oblivion.

That Man as a Rational Animal Desires
the Knowledge Which Is His Perfection

Abiding provenance I would have said
the question stands
                              even in adoration
clause upon clause
                              with or without assent
reason and desire on the same loop—
I imagine singing I imagine

getting it right—the knowledge
of sensuous intelligence
                        entering into the work—
spontaneous happiness as it was once
given our sleeping nature to awake by
                                        and know
innocence of first inscription

Sobieski's Shield

1

The blackberry, white
field-rose, all others
of that family:

steadfast is the word

and the star-gazing planet out of which
lamentation is spun.

2

Brusque as the year
      purple garish-brown
aster chrysanthemum
      signally restored
to a subsistence of slant light
as one might assert
          Justice Equity
or Sobieski's Shield even
         the names
and what they have about them dark to dark.

Of Coming into Being and Passing Away

To Aileen Ireland

Rosa sericea: its red
spurs
      blooded with amber
each lit and holy grain
the sun
       makes much of
as of all our shadows—

prodigal ever returning
darkness that in such circuits
reflects diuturnity
          to itself
and to our selves
          yields nothing
finally—

      but by occasion
visions of truth or dreams
as they arise—
        to terms of grace
where grace has surprised us—
the unsustaining
          wondrously sustained

De Anima

Salutation: it is as though
effortlessly—to reprise—
        the unsung spirit
gestures of no account
become accountable
           such matters arising
whatever it is that is sought

           through metaphysics
research into angelic song
ending as praise itself
the absolute yet again
atoned with the contingent—
             typology
incarnate—Bethlehem the open field—

still to conceive no otherwise: an
aphasia of staring wisdom
the soul's images glassily exposed
           fading to silverpoint
still to be at the last
ourselves and masters of all
           humility—

Whether the Virtues are Emotions

Overnight—overnight—
                              the inmost
self made outcast: here
plighting annihilations
                              unfinished
business of eros
                    the common numen

of waking
          reverie where you had dreamt
to be absolved:
                    and with the day
forsakenness
              the new bride brought forth:
carnal desuetude

her mystic equity
her nature's ripped hardihood
the radiant
              windrows where a storm
emptied its creels
thrusting ailanthus that is called
                    the Tree of Heaven

Whether Moral Virtue Comes by Habituation

It is said that sometimes even fear
drops away—
    exhausted—I would not
deny that: self
expression—you could argue—the first to go—
immolated
   selfhood the last:

deprivation therefore
      dereliction even
become the things we rise to:
ethereal conjecture
    taking on
humankind's heaviness of purchase
the moral nebulae

    common as lichen
the entire corpus of ruinous sagesse
moved by some rite
     and pace of being
as by earth in her slow
      approaches to withdrawal
the processionals of seared array

Ritornelli

For Hugh Wood on his 60th Birthday

i

Angel of Tones
                    flame of accord
exacting mercies
                    answerable
to rage as solace

I will have you sing

ii

For so the judgement
passes
            it is not
otherwise
            hereafter
you will see them resolved
in tears
            they shall bear
your crowns of redress

iii

Lost to no thought
of triumph he returns
upon himself goes down
among water and ash
and wailing sounds confused
with sounds of joy

To William Cobbett: In Absentia

I say it is not faithless
to stand without faith, keeping open
vigil at the site.
Who shall endure? What force throws off
the verdict of each day's
idle and taunting honours,
the lottery, the trade in grief,
the outrageous quittance, the shiftless
orders of fools?
I say let stand the entire
deposed authority
of vision just as it fell;
your righteous unjust and cordial anger,
your singular pitch where labour is spoken of,
your labour that brought to pass
reborn Commodity with uplifted hands
awed by its own predation.

Canaan

I

They march at God's
pleasure through Flanders
with machine-pistols,
chorales, cannon
of obese bronze,
with groaning pushcarts,
to topple Baal. At
crossroads they hoist
corpses and soiled
banners of the Lamb.
The sun takes assize.
Aloof the blades
of oblation
rise, fall, as though they
were not obstructed
by blades of bone.

II

Fourier's children
their steeds, kazoos,
the splashed fetlocks—
deliquescent manna
that most resembles
a sudden urban sleet—
shedding innocent blood
their ragged fusillade
a bit of a laugh
indifferent hatred
stained with their own works:
détentes of corpse-gas
                              reactive
furnaces of the spirit
immemorial
                 sightings in Canaan:
fig trees and planted vines
and the groves
                    unguarded
messuage for jackals.

III

Iniquity passes
and rectitude.
They do not spare
the sucking child nor are they
sparing with trumpets.
Now it is
Moloch his ovens
and the dropped babes naked
swung by an arm
or a leg like flails.

Dark-Land

Aspiring Grantham
rises above itself.
Tall churches wade the fen
on their stilts of glass.

Crowned Ely stands beset
by winds of straw-burning,
by the crouched run of flame.
Cambridge lies dark, and dead

predestined Elstow
where Bunyan struck his fear—
flint creed, tinder of wrath—
to flagrant mercies.

Mysticism and Democracy

Open me the gates of righteousness: That I may go into them . . .

You see the terrain he has won back from but not won;
the ravaged moon is a mere cranium, a mandarin crown,
                              compared to these craters.
He is indeed a survivor and of the intolerable elect.
Enforce for jollity's sake a solemn retaking
of the earth that has been his, many times over, by deed.
Project through lanterns of hot oil the festive advance—
                              it is at once a retreat
to that furthest point where lines of vanishing converge.
The obscurities through which you have armed his way,
night marches, down-draughts of coal smoke,
                   many-chambered fog lit from within,
become to hurled applause: the Veil of the Nations, the Final
Transformation-Scene-and-Curtain, Apocalypse-Hippodrome!

Scenes with Harlequins

In memoriam Aleksandr Blok

Joyfully I accept this strange book, joyfully and with fear—in it there is so much beauty, poetry, death. I await the accomplishment of your task.

VOLOKHOVA TO BLOK, 1907

All the sounds have gone silent. Can't you hear that there aren't any sounds any more?

BLOK, 1920

I

Distance is on edge;
the level tide
stands rimmed with mercury.
Again the estranged spirit

is possessed of light.
The common things
glitter uncommonly.
City besieged by the sun

amid sibylline
galas, a dust
pluming the chariots
of tyrants and invalids,

peppered with mica,
granite-faced seer
scathed by invisible
planets as men dream of war

like a fresh sea-wind
like the lilac
at your petrified heart
as something anciently known . . .

II

The day preens, the birds
gust from the square.
Ferrous sulphate
vapours in the dens

of dead photographers.
With white seraphic
hair against the sun
who are these strangers—

or who are these
charred spirits glaring
their vitreous eyes
towards apocalypse?

They are not of our flesh
to do them justice.
Still they outshine us
among the prophets.

III

Beautiful Lady,
with reverence
in sorrow in masquerade,
how else should we have lived?

Tempestuous fantasies,
blood-tinted opaline
essential clouds,
I am not myself

I think in this last act
without end. Lordly
and faithful servant of Life—
what can one say?

By humour of lament,
spontaneous word of stone,
inspired débâcle
many times rehearsed,

look to abide
tyrannous egality
and freedom led forth
blinded by prophecies.

Now it is gleeting Venus
who so decrees and now
it is parched Mars,
Beautiful Lady.

IV

The risen Christ! Once more
faith is upon us,
a jubilant brief keening
without respite:

Obedience, bitter joy,
the elements, clouds,
winds, louvres where the bell
makes its wild mouths:

Holy Rus—into the rain's
horizons, peacock-dyed
tail-feathers of storm,
so it goes on.

V

Even now one is amazed
by transience: how it
outlasts us all.
Motley of shadow

dabbles the earth,
the malachite-pocked
nymphs and sea gods, the pear tree's
motionless wooden leaves.

In this light, constrained spirit,
be a lord of your age.
Rejoice; let the strange
legends begin.

VI

Of Rumor, of Clamor,
I shall be silent;
I will not deal
in the vatic exchanges

between committees,
mysticism by the book.
History is adorned
with bookish fires.

Begone you grave jewellers
and you spartan hoplites
in masks of foil.
Orthodox arcane

interpreters of repute,
this is understood.
Why should I hear
further what you propose?

Exegetes may come
to speak to the silence
that has arisen. It is
not unheard of.

VII

Decembrist blood! We are taxed
for their visions. The earth
turns, returns, through cycles
of declamation;

with feuilletons and iron
fantasies of the state.
Rhadamanthine the grim
torches of naphtha,

the unspeakable dull woe
of which I may have had
foreknowledge—I forget—
in 'Retribution'.

Postlude

Rose–douched ammoniac
arch goddess
of intimate apparel,
brutal and bijou,

regarding the sensual
imperative despair,
see: there are worse times,
this blank platz,

the bronze humps
of Gaea and Kronos;
spates of fat snow-melt
swallow their parturitions.

Algabal

Stefan George, 1868–1933

Rhine-rentier,
contemptuous bankrupt,
you placed sacraments
in the hands of receivers.

Contempt is in order: one
        would give much
to see those Frankish
rites nobly concluded.

Almost, for Childe Stauffenberg,
it fell so;
but this was tragedy
botched, unimagined,

within that circle.
Medallion-profile
           of hauteur,
Caesarian abstinence!

Your desk is a pure altar;
        it is not
for the coarse earthen things
to bleed their spirit;

but for a vital
scintillant atrophy,
a trophy
of the ageless champion.

Mysticism and Democracy

i

Do not stand witness; observe only
natures and polities aligned with rectitude
                    yet not of it;
commonweal their lodestar, inordinate
and thrusting dominion their enterprise;
purposed ambition not to be confined
                    by reason of defect.

ii

To some, self-found, defected, secret resources,
tacit amnesties beyond denial,
like botanists' or scholars' chance marginalia,
certain debts of trust
                    in commendation.
There being now such riotous shows of justice,
yet, of righteousness, the fading nimbus
remains to us, as a perceived glory.

iii

Is it then by default that we do not
stoop to their honours? It is not wholly true
that what the world commands is a lesser thing.
Who shall restore the way, reclaim lost footage,
achieve too late prescient telegraphy,
take to themselves otherness of common woe,
devotion bought from abeyance,
                    fortitude to be held
at the mercy of door-chimes?

Dark-Land

Wherein Wesley stood
up from his father's grave,
summoned familiar dust
for strange salvation:

whereto England rous'd,
ignorant, her inane
Midas-like hunger: smoke
engrossed, cloud-cumbered,

a spectral people
raking among the ash;
its freedom a lost haul
of entailed riches.

To the Nieuport Scout

How swiftly they cease to be
incredible
            how incredible
the sudden immortals—

a tilt   a flare
as though of mirrors—

dared by their luck
they outdare it
                and spin
from the fumy towers
taking England with them—
flame-tattered
                pirouettes
quenched in a cloud.

Parentalia

The here-and-now finds vigil transfiguring
whatever is
               yet ignorant of your beauty.
Any one of us, given a certain light,
             shall make and be immortal:
streets of Jerusalem, seraphs the passers-by,
and other extras, artisans per diem,
imperative in hindsight
                a brief blessing.
I cannot tell how we might be otherwise
drawn to the things occluded, manifold,
the measureless that stands
                  even so depleted
in the faint rasp of dry autumnal flowers.

Respublica

The strident high
civic trumpeting
of misrule. It is
what we stand for.

Wild insolence,
aggregates without
distinction. Courage
of common men:

spent in the ruck
their remnant witness
after centuries
is granted them

like a pardon.
And other fealties
other fortitudes
broken as named—

Respublica
brokenly recalled,
its archaic laws
and hymnody;

and destroyed hope
that so many times
is brought with triumph
back from the dead.

De Jure Belli ac Pacis

i.m. Hans-Bernd von Haeften, 1905–1944

I

The people moves as one spirit unfettered
claim our assessors of stone.
                       When the nations
fall dispossessed such conjurings possess them,
elaborate barren fountains, projected
aqueducts
            where water is no longer found.
Where would one find Grotius for that matter,
the secular justice clamant among psalms,
huge-fisted visionary Comenius . . . ?
Could none predict these haughty degradations
as now your high-strung
                   martyred resistance serves
to consecrate the liberties of Maastricht?

II

. . . sah er den Erzengel Michael im Kampf gegen den Drachen, Michael,
den Engel der deutschen Geschichte . . .

The iron-beamed engine-shed has chapel windows.
Glare-eyed, you spun. The hooks are still in the beam;
a sun-patch drains to nothing; here the chocked
blade sluiced into place, here the abused blood
                  set its own wreaths.
Time passes, strengthening and fading. Europa
hetaera displays her parts, her triumph
to tax even Dürer's resplendent economy
in rictus and graven sorrow.
                      On some envisioned
rathaus clock, geared like a mill, the dragon
strikes,
      the Archangel, unseeing, unbowed,
chimes with each stroke.

III

You foretold us, hazarding the proscribed tongue
of piety and shame; plain righteousness
committed with much else to Kreisau's bees
for their particular keeping. We might have kept
your Christian inhibitions—faithful, non-jurant,
in the singing-court of dread
                              at the grid of extortion—
but chose pity. This pity is shameless
unlike memory, though both can draw
sugar from iron.
                              Pity, alone with its rage,
settles on multitudes
                              as the phoenix sought
from a hundred cities tribute of requiting flame.

IV

In Plötzensee where you were hanged
                              they now hang
tokens of reparation and in good faith
compound with Cicero's maxims, Schiller's chant,
your silenced verities.
                        To the high-minded
base-metal forgers of this common Europe,
community of parody, you stand ec-
centric as a prophet. There is no better
vision that I can summon: you were upheld
on the strong wings of the Psalms before you died.
Evil is not good's absence but gravity's
everlasting bedrock and its fatal chains
inert, violent, the suffrage of our days.

V

Not harmonies—harmonics, astral whisperings
light-years above the stave; groans, murmurs, cries,
tappings from cell to cell. It is a night-watch,
indeterminate and of vast concentration,
of those redeeming their pledged fear, who strike
faith from the hard rock of God's fallenness;
their pain draws recompense beyond our grasp
of recapitulation.
              Slurred clangour,
cavernous and chained haltings, echo from time's
inchoate music, the theme standing proclaimed
only in the final measures—
                      Vexilla regis
uplifted by Rüdiger Schleicher's violin.

VI

der Tod . . . nahm über uns Gewalt,
Hielt uns in seinem Reich gefangen.
Hallelujah!

Those three eternal days Christus did not lie
shackled in death:
                but found out your stark reich,
deep-buried hypocausts dense for the harrowing,
held there—since time so holds within itself—
slow precise Fellgiebel, chivalrous Hofacker,
clamped in their silence:
                keeps also Goerdeler's
doubled, many-times-consummated, agony:
in whatever fortress, on whatever foundation,
then, now, in eternum, the spirit bears witness
                through its broken flesh:
to grace more enduring even than mortal corruption,
ineradicable, and rightly so.

VII

Smart whip-tap at boot-top, absolute
                   licence of the demons
to wreak their correction; elsewhere they are fixed
self-torches in sulphur; as there is a God,
                   elsewhere, of jealous mercy
this is not news: the book of Daniel's strength
unwritten, Zion's resurgent lamentation
in Kreisau's witnessing here undenizened
to the sand, to the old waste.
                   So let the rights
be speculation, fantastic pickings, late
                   gold of Europa
in her brief modish rags—
                   Schindler! Schindler!

VIII

Hinrichtungsstätte war ein Schuppen im Gefängnis . . .

But if—but if; and if nowhere
                    but here
archives for catacombs; letters, codes, prayers,
film-scraps, dossiers, shale of crunched shellac,
new depths of invention, children's
                    songs to mask torture . . .
Christus, it is not your stable: it will serve
as well as any other den or shippen
the arraigned truth, the chorus with its gifts
of humiliation, incense and fumitory,
                    Lucerna,
the soul-flame, as it has stood through such ages,
ebbing, and again, lambent, replenished,
                    in its stoup of clay.

Cycle

William Arrowsmith, 1924–1992

1

Natural strange beatitudes
                        the leafless tints
of spring touch red through brimstone
what do you mean   praise and lament
it is the willow
              first then
larch or alder

2

The heart feels for its own
                   patience
reflects upon itself
light is everywhere
              the spiders'
galaxies
        droppings of the
star wormwood

3

So there   there it is   past
reason and measure
                sustaining
the constancy of mischance
its occlusion
        a spasm
a psalm

4

Are we not moved by
            'savage
indignation' or whatever
strange
     natürlich
dance with antlers
paces over and
          over the same
ground

5

Larch or alder
     first
then willow
      leafless tints
of spring touch red through brimstone

praise and lament
praise and lament

what do you mean
         praise
lament
    praise and lament
what do you mean
        do you mean
beatitudes

Sorrel

Very common and widely distributed . . . It is called Sorrow . . . in some
parts of Worcestershire.

Memory worsening—let it go as rain
streams on half-visible clatter of the wind
                    lapsing and rising,
that clouds the pond's green mistletoe of spawn,
seeps among nettlebeds and threadbare sorrel,
perpetual ivy burrowed by weak light,
makes carved shapes crumble: the ill-weathering stone
salvation's troth-plight, plumed, of the elect.

Parentalia

Daniel 12:3–4, 9

Go your ways, as if in thanksgiving:
Daniel finally instructed of the Lord.
The book is closed for your time; it will not
                              open again to the slow
round of the psalms, the prophets of righteousness.
But go, as instrumental, of the Lord,
                     life-bound to his foreknowledge
and in his absence making your return
to the generations, the rosaceae,
the things of earth snagging the things of grace,
darkened hawthorn, its late flare, that stands
illustrious, and the darkening season—
Harvest Festival to Armistice Day
                        the other harvest.

Mysticism and Democracy

I am of Dark-land, for there I was born, and there my Father and Mother
are still.

To the Evangelicals: a moving image
of multitudes turned aside—
                 into the fields—
with staves and bundles, through the patched sloughs,
broken-down hedges, among brickstacks:
unerring the voice, the direction, though the truth
             is difficult to follow,
a track of peculiar virtue—English—which so often
              deceives us by the way.
Exhaustion is of the essence, though in the meantime
what song has befallen those who were laggard
pilgrims, or none. It is as you see. I would not
trouble greatly to proclaim this.
              But shelve it under Mercies.

Churchill's Funeral

I

... one dark day in the Guildhall: looking at the memorials of the city's great past & knowing well the history of its unending charity, I seemed to hear far away in the dim roof a theme, an echo of some noble melody ...

Endless London
mourns for that knowledge
under the dim roofs
of smoke-stained glass,

the men hefting
their accoutrements
of webbed tin, many
in bandages,

with cigarettes,
with scuffed hands aflare,
as though exhaustion
drew them to life;

as if by some
miraculous draft
of enforced journeys
their peace were made

strange homecoming
into sleep, blighties,
and untouched people
among the maimed:

nobilmente it
rises from silence,
the grand tune, and goes
something like this.

II

Suppose the subject of inquiry, instead of being House-law (*Oikonomia*), had been star-law (*Astronomia*), and that, ignoring distinction between stars fixed and wandering, as here between wealth radiant and wealth reflective, the writer had begun thus:

> Innocent soul
> ghosting for its lost
> twin, the afflicted one,
> born law-giver;
>
> uncanny wraith
> kindled afar-off
> like the evening star,
> res publica
>
> seen by itself
> with its whole shining
> history discerned
> through shining air,
>
> both origin
> and consequence, its
> hierarchies of sorts,
> fierce tea-making
>
> in time of war,
> courage and kindness
> as the marvel is
> the common weal
>
> that will always,
> simply as of right,
> keep faith, ignorant
> of right or fear:
>
> who is to judge
> who can judge of this?
> Maestros of the world
> not you not them.

III

Los listens to the Cry of the Poor Man; his Cloud
Over London in volume terrific low bended in anger.

The copper clouds
are not of this light;
Lambeth is no more
the house of the lamb.

The meek shall die rich
would you believe:
with such poverty
lavished upon them,

with their obsequies
the Heinkels' lourd drone
and Fame darkening
her theatres

to sirens, laughter,
the frizzed angels
of visitation
powdered by the blast,

the catafalques
like gin-palaces
where she entertains
the comedians.

IV

St Mary Abchurch, St Mary Aldermanbury, St Mary-le-Bow . . .

       Stone Pietà
       for which the city
       offers up incense
       and ashes, blitzed

       firecrews, martyrs
       crying to the Lord,
       their mangled voices
       within the flame;

       to which we bring
       litanies of scant
       survival and all
       random mercies,

       with the ragwort
       and the willow-herb
       as edifiers
       of ruined things.

V

. . . every minute particular, the jewels of Albion, running down
The kennels of the streets & lanes as if they were abhorr'd.

The brazed city
reorders its own
destruction, admits
the strutting lords

to the temple,
vandals of sprayed blood—
obliterations
to make their mark.

The spouting head
spiked as prophetic
is ancient news.
Once more the keeper

of the dung-gate
tells his own story;
so too the harlot
of many tears.

Speak now regardless
judges of the hour:
what verdict, what people?
Hem of whose garment?

Whose Jerusalem—
at usance for its bones'
redemption and last
salvo of poppies?

To the High Court of Parliament

November 1994

Amos 3:8–11

Keep what in repair?
Or place what further
toll on the cyclic
agony of empire?

Judgement and mourning
come round yet again
like a festival
of scratched heroic film.

I cannot say how
much is still owing
to the merchant house
of Saxe-Coburg-Gotha

from your right ranters,
proud tribunes, place-men,
shape-shifting nabobs,
come the millennium,

judged by the ill-fitted,
the narrow oblong-
sutured, jaws of knee-
puppets jerked to riposte,

by final probate
or by exception—
the voice of Amos
past its own enduring.

Pisgah

I am ashamed and grieve, having seen you then,
those many times, as now
                              you turn to speak
with someone standing deeper in the shade;
or fork a row, or pace to the top end
where the steep garden overlooks the house;
around you the cane loggias, tent-poles, trellises,
the flitter of sweet peas caught in their strings,
the scarlet runners, blossom that seems to burn
an incandescent aura towards evening.
This half-puzzled, awkward surprise is yours;
you cannot hear me or quite make me out.
Formalities preserve us:
                              perhaps I too am a shade.

To John Constable: In Absentia

Eheu! quam tenui e filo pendet
Quicquid in vita maxime arridet.

Anxious griefs, grievous anxieties, are not to be
sublimed through chiaroscuro. Knowing this,
                          you framed it clearly.
To mourn is to mourn; the ancient words suffice,
Latin or English, worn channels for the rain,
                          charged and electric.
We suffer commonly, where we are quite alone,
not the real but the actual natures of things;
and there is now, assuredly, no telling
how spirit readied the hand to engineer
a perceptible radiance—arched and spectral—
the abrupt rainbow's errant visitation.

Dark-Land

Are these last things reduced
to the imagining
of shadow-eternals?
Suddenly in the day's flame

very late he saw it
at Dedham: the English
church as it must be
charred in its own standing,

small, distinct, monochrome,
blazed at from rayed clouds,
rallying to that place,
Sheol if not Shiloh.

Mysticism and Democracy

i

Ill-conceived, ill-ordained, heart's rhetoric:
hour into hour the iron nib hardly
                             pausing at the well—
inscribed silver, facets of Stourbridge glass,
polished desk surface; the darkling mirrors
                             to an occult terrain:
mystical democracy, ill-gotten, ill-bestowed,
as if, long since, we had cheated them,
                             our rightful, righteous
masters, as though they would pay us back
                                        terrific freedoms—
Severn at the flood, streaked pools that are called
                                            flashes
wind-beaten to a louring shine.

ii

Let this not fall imputed to our native
                             obdurate credulities.
Contrariwise within its own doctrine it spins,
remote saturnian orb: oblivious
the imperial granites, braided, bunched and wreathed;
                             the gilded ornature
ennobling lowly errors—exacted, from exalted—
                             tortuous in their simplicity;
the last unblemished records of service
                                        left hanging
in air yellowed with a late half-light
as votive depositions
                             not to be taken down.

Ezekiel's Wheel

i.m. Christopher Okigbo, 1932–1967

I

Consider now the valley
of Hinnom—the trucks
from the abattoir — *slaughter house*
skidding their loads,
the shameless body parts.
Ezekiel's wheel
shall encompass all:
each flame-warped spirit — *Children offered as burnt sacrifices in the valley.*
dancing unshriven,
the righteous no less
than the jettisoned
gobbets in limbo.
Here too the shrieking
of witness, zealots
high on propane
                    cracked
faces in the smoke.

II

Praise-song for oil drums,
a psalm of spillage:
these things these men
named and unnamed
sold and selfsold
to the generations.
Ezekiel's wheel
shall eternize all
but to no end—
posthumous sodalities
of the traduced
feasting traduction.
Cannot? Why—what
cannot you not think?
Is it that you are cast,
wan ghosts of the ditch,
as in all things equal
unequally gifted
to the wild dog?

III

Summon again the epoch
serving photographers
envoys and rhapsodists
importunate to the sight.
Have them memorize
a blast-furrowed
nameless carrefour
half-way to Jericho
strewn with your rags.
That from old prophecy,
this to lament.
Let the brittle
devourers, the locusts
of pity, enrobe you;
let the veteran
maimed fig tree stand
stark out of the waste.

IV

The scroll is final:
last breath of the ruah — Holy spirit
self-quenched in wrath.
Ezekiel's wheel
engenders all
living and dying
even in Christ
and Mary who raised
Christ and is risen with him.
Her migrant accursed
Moabite blood
obscurely pardoned,
at the far limit
for our atonement
still she follows Ruth
gleaning to the last
corner of the worst field
the bane of Judah.

Psalms of Assize

I

Hinc vagantur in tenebris misere, quia non credunt veritati ipsi . . .
Querunt lumen confisi ipsis et non inveniunt.

> Why should I strike you with my name
> why trade impress of proud wounds
> come now belated
>   patrons of wrath
> anxieties are not rectitudes
> holiness itself falls
> to unholy rejoicing
> to resurrect the dead
> myth
>   of our salvation
> blasphemies no less
> mercies
>   let us pray
> Gabriel descend
> as a mood almost
>   a monody
> of chloroform
> or florist's roses
> consensual angel spinning his words'
>   thread
> he descends
>   and light
> sensitive darkness
>   follows him down

II

Non potest quisquam utrisque servire, simulque ascendere et descendere;
aut ascendas aut descendas oportet . . .

Ascend through declension
the mass the matter
the gross refinement
        gravitas
everlasting obsession
vanity by grace
the starred
                misattributed
works of survival
attributes even now
hallowing consequence
chants of the trace elements
the Elohim
                unearthly music
given to the world
message what message
                doubtless
the Lord knows
when he will find us
                if ever
we shall see him
with the elect
                justified
to his right hand

III

Prima actio cultus [dei], ex quo consuetudo colendi et [mos] religiosus . . .

Sentences garbled
anger
      indignities
foisted as sorrow
silently acclaimed
in the magisterium
of the lily
      unbroken
the tried and retried
spirit
      the steady
reading of such default
disinheritance also
is inherited
like plenitude
awesome in its way
look provost
for constancy
        the stars
lucent as ardent
as by deeds assigned
to the ephemera
        to our
unending distress

IV

Hac sola ratione semper eris liber: si volueris quaequumque fiunt ita fieri,
et omnia in bonam partem verte.

Seeing how they stand
with what odds
                    by what rule
of accidence resolved
the irresolute
                    the feats
of hapless jubilo
                    the gifts
set down to derision
rejoice in them
as things that are mourned
loving kindness
                    and mercy
righteousness
patient abiding
and whatever good
is held
              untenable
the entire complex dance
of simple atonement
as in a far fetched
                        comedy
making of sleep and time
timeless healers

V

Collige autoritates et presentia et preterita cerne.

Urbs Sion Mystica
                    how comely
the ambient lamps
                    impendent
and instruments of brass
                    and calloused
labourers at the word
a fine miracle
swung by its ways
                    too soon
too soon the fanfare
of visions
            the godly
and noble design
blown to ungoverned
laws of rancour
as freedom dictates
the feast is finished
our cryptic lord of the talents
has left us
            asperged
with lumpen spittle
                    amen
say amen as in mammon

VI

Homini autem nulla umbra sapientie magis in promptu est quam sua ignorans natura.

And yet
             the instinctive
salutation
             that now must seem
willed and awkward
we cannot know God
                          we cannot
deny his sequestered
power
             in a marred nature
if eloquent at all
                          it is
with the inuring of scars
and speechlessness
it does not improve Sion
it has no place
                          among psalms
to the chief musician
it goes without lament
                          it is not
the almond branch prophetic
                          wakefulness
nor is it any kind of blessing
                          given this people

VII

Victo carne et sanguine restant demones; numquam vitabimus. Huc illuc
semper adest.

> The great O of advent
>   cum sibylla
> O that nothing may touch
> this unapproachable
> levity of the creator
> conscience and guilt
> the formal alchemy
> not held to trial
> for what is beyond
> such mercurial reckoning
> its ultimate
>   cadence
> its fall impeccable
> the condign
>   salvation
> pure carnival in the spirit
>   even so
> God of miracles the crying
>   even so
> this is how it ends
> how it goes at the last day
>   spargens sonum
> the day of bitten tongues
> say what you like

A Song of Degrees

It is said Adonai your hidden word
declares itself
             even from obscurity
through energies dispersed
             fallen upon stasis
brought by strangers to interpretation,
aspirant to the common plight.

Destined, as natural heirs of the spirit,
your prodigal unholy fools
             raised stones
in deserts; in the temples cast them down;
things past and things to come unshaken
empire of chagrin,
             of the chronically betrayed.

Plight into plight; there you commit your law
to chance
             inescapable witness:
a centurion's cry, the women
bearing their oil or blood; here you release
Bartimeus for ever
             to his blind faith.

Of Constancy and Measure

i.m. Ivor Gurney

One sees again how it goes:
rubble ploughed in and salted
                    the blood's
haphazard fatalities
our scattering selves allowed
their glimpse of restitution—
                  the orchards
of Sarras or Severn bare
plenitude first and last—
as if constancy were in time
given its own for keeping
                  as such gifts belong
to the unfailing burden of the planet
with so much else believed to be fire and air

To William Law: In Absentia

To fall asleep in the flesh
is nothing. Resurrection
challenges torment. There is always
the deists' Eden, a measured exile
at home among our mourning cedars.
Looking back, it is you I see stand
quiet, exact, under the tree of conviction—
image to mirage, mirage withdrawing
                                    to skeined light,
light to the unmoved miraculous
                          pool of Siloam.

Concerning Inheritance

It is with civic matters as with some questions
of conventional faith: as with professors of strict
canon who vehemently follow nature,
enthusiasts of sublime emptiness
mountaineering into old age, worshippers
of the unassailable ice-flower:
                      as to prize apologists
for plebeian nobleness, who would have found it hard
telling one servitor from another, who spun
half-crowns to enlightenment—*I take this penny*—
grant inequity from afar to be in equity's covenant,
its paradigm drawn on the fiducial stars,
its aegis anciently a divine shield
                           over the city.

Mysticism and Democracy

Great gifts foreclosed on; loss and waste offset
by thrifty oddities of survival—
dittander and black saltwort that are found
                    flourishing on the midland brine.
Flesh has its own spirit, confused with torpor,
deeper than most rooted faiths, deeper than Passchendaele.
Piety is less enduring though it endures much
and with its own stiff diligence keeps the ground
                    set for humiliation.
There was a time any Methodist could have told you
Ebenezer means stone of help.
                    As for the rest,
ruunt in servitium, crammed vacancy's rabble—
this also is admitted: *introit turba*.

To the High Court of Parliament

November 1994

—who could outbalance poised
                        Marvell; balk the strength
of Gillray's unrelenting, unreconciling mind;
grandees risen from scavenge; to whom Milton
                        addressed his ideal censure:
once more, singular, ill-attended,
staid and bitter Commedia—as she is called—
delivers to your mirth her veiled presence.

None the less amazing: Barry's and Pugin's grand
dark-lantern above the incumbent Thames.
You: as by custom unillumined
                        masters of servile counsel.
Who can now speak for despoiled merit,
                        the fouled catchments of Demos,
as 'thy' high lamp presides with sovereign
equity, over against us, across this
densely reflective, long-drawn, procession of waters?

The Triumph of Love

For Alice and for Luc

Tempus aedificandi tempus destruendi

I

Sun-blazed, over Romsley, a livid rain-scarp.

II

Guilts were incurred in that place, now I am convinced:
self-molestation of the child-soul, would that be it?

III

Petronius Arbiter, take us in charge;
carry us with you to the house of correction.
Angelus Silesius, guard us while we are there.

IV

Ever more protracted foreplay,
never ending—*o Ewigkeit*—no act
the act of oblivion, the blown
aorta pelting out blood.

V

Obstinate old man—*senex*
sapiens it is not. What is he saying;
why is he still so angry? He says, I cannot
forgive myself. We are immortal.
Where was I? Prick him.

VI

Between bay window and hedge the impenetrable holly
strikes up again taut wintry vibrations.
The hellebore is there still,
half-buried; the crocuses are surviving.
From the front room I might be able to see
the coal fire's image planted in a circle
of cut-back rose bushes. Nothing is changed
by the strength of this reflection.

VII

Romsley, of all places!—Spraddled ridge-
village sacred to the boy-martyr,
Kenelm, his mouth full of blood and toffee.

A stocky water tower built like the stump
of a super-dreadnought's foremast. It could have set
Coventry ablaze with pretend
broadsides, some years before that armoured
city suddenly went down, guns
firing, beneath the horizon; huge silent whumphs
of flame-shadow bronzing the nocturnal
cloud-base of her now legendary dust.

VIII

But how could there not be a difficult
confronting of systematics—the scale
of articulation notched up one grade at a time?
They have conceded me—I think, beyond question—
power of determination but without
force of edict.
If I were to grasp once, in emulation,
work of the absolute, origin-creating mind,
its *opus est*, its conclusive
otherness, the veil
of certitude discovered as itself
that which is to be revealed,
I should hold for my own, my self-giving,
my retort upon Emerson's 'alienated majesty',
the *De Causa Dei* of Thomas Bradwardine.

IX

On chance occasions—
and others have observed this—you can see the wind,
as it moves, barely a separate thing,
the inner wall, the cell, of an hourglass, humming
vortices, bright particles in dissolution,
a roiling plug of sand picked up
as a small dancing funnel. It is how
the purest apprehension might appear
to take corporeal shape.

X

Last things first; the slow haul to forgive them:
Chamberlain's compliant vanity, his pawn ticket saved
from the antepenultimate ultimatum; their strict
pudency, but not to national honour; callous
discretion; their inwardness with things of the world;

their hearing as a profound music
the hollow lion-roar of the slammed vaults;
the decent burials at the eleventh hour:
their Authorized Version—it had seen better days—
'nation shall not lift up sword against nation'
or 'nation shall rise up against nation' (a later
much-revised draft of the treaty). In either case
a telling figure out of rhetoric,
epanalepsis, the same word first and last.

XI

Above Dunkirk, the sheared anvil-
head of the oil-smoke column, the wind
beginning to turn, turning on itself, spiralling,
shaped on its potter's wheel. But no fire-storm:
such phenomena were as yet unvisited
upon Judeo-Christian-Senecan Europe.
It is to *Daniel*, as to our own
tragic satire, that one returns
for mastery of the business; well-timed,
intermitted terror. How else recall
Mierendorff's ancient, instant, final cry—
madness—in Leipzig, out of the sevenfold
fiery furnace?

XII

Even the things that stood,
stood in unlikeness. The Hauptbahnhofsplatz,
only, had been bulldozed clear. There were some
particulars to be recalled; the wind
bore an unmistakable sour tang
of paper-rubble, close-packed ream on ream
scorched into flaking slab, slowly damped down,
fire- and water-ruin. He could not reconcile,
he said, either Pity or Terror with the justice
of their dereliction:
bacterial supernovae, half-life contaminants,
multi-cellular mischance, myriad-
tongued anomie, are as shadows, vapours to it;
creative nihilism, Götterdämmerung's toy
theatre (and here he cited Benn, Ernst Jünger).
Even with that Parisian oblation
of worked, reworked, burin-and-acid griming,
Rouault's then unknown, desolate

masterwork, the *Miserere*, even
there, he concluded, it seems we must be brought
hard up against the unlovely
body of Aesthetics.

XIII

Whose lives are hidden in God? Whose?
Who can now tell what was taken, or where,
or how, or whether it was received:
how ditched, divested, clamped, sifted, over-
laid, raked over, grassed over, spread around,
rotted down with leafmould, accepted
as civic concrete, reinforceable
base cinderblocks:
tipped into Danube, Rhine, Vistula, dredged up
with the Baltic and the Pontic sludge:
committed *in absentia* to solemn elevation,
Trauermusik, musique funèbre, funeral
music, for male and female
voices ringingly *a cappella*,
made for double string choirs, congregated brass,
choice performers on baroque trumpets hefting,
like glassblowers, inventions
of supreme order?

XIV

As to bad faith, Malebranche might argue
it rests with inattention. Stupidity
is not admissible. However, the status
of apprehension remains at issue.
Some qualities are best
left unrecognized. Needless to say,
unrecognized is not
unacknowledged. Unnamed is not nameless.

XV

Britannia's own narrow
miracle of survival
was gifted to us by cryptanalysts,
unpredictable Polish
virtuosi, it is now revealed,
grudgingly. One might have guessed.
Why, then, did Poland require

that last sacrifice of her cavalry
while she possessed such
instruments of cryptic-helio-
tropic strength, like the sunflower
that is both flamen
and lumen of her noble fields?
Flamen I draw darkly out of flame.
Lumen is a measure of light.
Lumens are not luminaries. A great
Polish luminary of our time is the obscure
Aleksander Wat.

XVI

Turing played well in defence.
Turing did not
play well in defence. Attack both
positions. Admit defeat.

XVII

If the gospel is heard, all else follows:
the scattering, the diaspora,
the shtetlach, ash pits, pits of indigo dye.
Penitence can be spoken of, it is said,
but is itself beyond words;
even broken speech presumes. Those Christian Jews
of the first Church, huddled sabbath-survivors,
keepers of the word; silent inside twenty years,
doubly outcast: even so I would remember—
the scattering, the diaspora.
We do not know the saints.
His mercy is greater even than his wisdom.
If the gospel is heard, all else follows.
We shall rise again, clutching our wounds.

XVIII

                                   It is not
whether we have the Psalms in Latin or Hebrew
nor by what authority such things are committed,
dismissed among the aeonic dense snowflurries:
it is not in the mortgaged conversions—the synagogues,
the cathedrals—to Caesar and the great Pharaoh.
Distinctions are as nothing, but identity
is pulled apart. Try definition—is this a dead
march or a death march? It is a dead march.

XIX

If you so wish to construe this, I shall say
only: the Jew is not beholden
to forgiveness, of pity. You will have to
go forward block by block, for pity's sake,
irresolute as granite. Now
move to the next section.

XX

From the *Book of Daniel*, am I correct?
Quite correct, sir. Permit me:
refocus that Jew—yes there,
that one. You see him burning,
dropping feet first, in a composed manner,
still in suspension,
from the housetop.
It will take him for ever
caught at this instant
of world-exposure.
In close-up he maintains appearance—
Semitic ur-Engel—
terminal agony none the less
interminable, the young
martyrs ageing in the fire—
thank you, Hauptmann Schauspieler.
Run it through again and for ever
he stretches his wings of flame
upon instruction.

XXI

What did I miss?—as the man said,
silence twanging over the sprung
trap. Soothsayers of Suetonius and the *Annals*,
touting fatal omniscience, what
actors they were! Steady
professionals, escapologists,
illuminati of smoke and stench,
to their blackened fingers' ends.
Should I leave it like this? Or should I add
that, for the life of me, I cannot
see my own future in prediction?

XXII

What *flagitia* ought to have meant
in good time to our senators, the Hebrews
pronounced upon daily in their estranged tongue.
They also, it is true, maintained
market-place charlatans and gross sibyls,
guilds of inclusive debasement.
But the solitary great ones—Isaiah, Amos,
Ezekiel—if only these could have been
translated into our statutes, if deified
Caesar alone were their agent of resurrection.

XXIII

What remains? You may well ask. Construction
or deconstruction? There is some poor
mimicry of choice, whether you build or destroy.
But the Psalms—they remain; and certain exultant
canzoni of repentance, secular oppugnancy. *Laus
et vituperatio*, the worst
remembered, least understood, of the modes.
Add political satire. Add the irrefutable
grammar of Abdiel's defiance.
And if not wisdom, then something
that approaches it nearly. And if not faith,
then something through which it is made possible
to give credence—if only to Isaiah's prophetically
suffering servant; if only by evidence
of the faithful women, Ruth and Naomi,
as they were, and as Rembrandt sees them,
the widowed generations, the irrevocable
covenant with Abraham which you
scarcely recall.

XXIV

Summon the leaders, the leaping captions,
numbers rolled from a drum: Cardanus
on the significance of eclipses,
Rathenau, 'industrialist and philosopher',
famous unnamed assassins' open tourers,
a road slicked in its dressing of lime pollen.
After some early clouds burn off
as predicted by the harbour master

we will have a clear day—
lake water chopping under paddle-boxes,
the scroll-wave motion of a carrousel,
jelly-green celluloid eye-shields; children
overexcited by rampageous clowns,
fire-breathers, artists of inept escape.

XXV

The hierarchies are here to be questioned. Lead on
Angelus Novus; show onetime experts presenting
aniline dyes as the intensest expressions
of coal-tar; let others develop 'man's
determinate action', for so Peirce dubbed it
in the wake of Chickamauga. Failing these,
bring others well-tried in the practical
worlds of illusion, builders of fabled masks,
their dancing clients
vanishing into the work
made up as lords and spiky blackamoors.
Unveil the dust-wrapped, post-war architects'
immediate prize-designs in balsa wood,
excelling fantasies, sparsely inhabited
by spaced-out, pinhead model citizens;
Florentine piazzas for Antarctica.
The augurs, finally: strangely possessed by doubt
whether to address the saturnine magistrates
concerning the asteroid, or the asteroid
on the nature of destiny and calculation.

XXVI

Grief—now, after sixty years—exacerbated
through its very absurdity; anger stalled again
for nations twice betrayed by our appeasements'
false equities of common ash; the moral
imagination an eccentric failure.
Laus et vituperatio, public, forensic,
yet with a vehement
private ambition for the people's
greater good—*Joannis
Miltoni, Angli, pro Populo Angli-
cano Defensio*: this and other tracts,
day-laboured-at, under great imposition:
as powers, far-radiant, inspiring
a broadly conceded European fame.

Laus et vituperatio, lost, rediscovered,
renewed on few occasions this century:
Guernica perhaps; or Prague itself,
the Charles Bridge with Hradčany, keeping watch,
in Kokoschka's sixty-year-old triple portrait,
beside Komensky and Tomáš Masaryk.

XXVII

One could hardly foresee the vintage hearse
exploding on impact. God—what a mess!
Instantaneous peristalsis: his eight
Brownings plus the gun-camera—all over
the evening editions—I'm not surprised:
Councillors of State exposed, 'their privy members
like unto those of horses'; nakedness
'unavoidable for duration'. Those
poor, ruined umbrellas.
This: '*ad Socium*'? A hefty
packet for All Souls, I shouldn't wonder.
Fresh intercepts too—the Bletchley magi—
to the Master of St John's, 'for his advisement';
for the Provost of King's Coll:, less than nothing.
As to my Lord Protector: nothing
but name and number.

XXVIII

As I have at times imagined: Melancholy,
the more inert we are, thrusts us
into the way of things violently
uprooted. And there, for her own
increase, grants us a little possession,
that we may then lose all. *Boerenverdriet*—
peasant sorrow? peasant affliction?—you cannot
cease feeling their uncouth terror, whose flesh
is our own. The slaughterers relish this work
of sport: *landsknechts* as Callot depicts them,
hideously-festive-death's foragers;
so he draws them among us,
slouch-feathered, shin-booted, jangle
of sloven-worn iron: *ruyter*, *ritterkind*,
rutterkin, over the low shrub hill—hoyda!
hoyda!—heel-kicking their nags.

XXIX

What is this strange tree that bears so well
such heavy fruit commingled with new blossom;
and who are these
hanging amid the branches,
in bonds of remonstrance,
like traitors like martyrs?
This is our Upas tree; it is a tree of sleep
that never breaks; it is our politic
transcendent shade.
It is England's
iron-bound storm-tree turbulently at rest.

XXX

Bring out Behemoth—so; a sullen beast—
unentreated of the people. It has come
close to your name, with nominal disclaimer,
for your single glory, should that be spoken of,
your ignominy by nameless attribution.

XXXI

Scab-picking old scab: why should we be salted
with the scurf of his sores?

XXXII

Well-set imperial fixture—Victory's
equestrian bronze cancan topping out
Constitution Arch. The city snarls,
the noon guns' heavy ripple shakes the dead.
What guns? Which dead? Haig, whom they justified
in his self-image to the tune of thousands?
The luckless stop-press vacancies? The regiments
rehiring by the week,
hoisting the dead-beat with galvanic
blatter of trumpets?

XXXIII

Trumpets? Come off it—that was cavalry!
Wavering bugles took the Chums and Pals.

XXXIV

Boom-boom! Obnoxious chthonic old fart,
boom-boom, boom-boom! No thanks to that stiff
Korzeniowski. Obsolete, shallow-draught,
fifteen-inch gun, ex-imperial
monitor, perched
rudderless on a mudbank in mid-river,
exposing himself to Borrioboola-Gha.

XXXV

Even now, I tell myself, there is a language
to which I might speak and which
would rightly hear me;
responding with eloquence; in its turn,
negotiating sense without insult
given or injury taken.
Familiar to those who already know it
elsewhere as justice,
it is met also in the form of silence.

XXXVI

You can say you are deaf in several languages—
lass es in Ruhe, mon vieux, hic scriptum est.

XXXVII

Shameless old man, bent on committing
more public nuisance. Incontinent
fury wetting the air. Impotently
bereft satire. Charged with erudition,
put up by the defence to be
his own accuser.

XXXVIII

Widely established yet with particular
local intensities, the snow
half-thawed now hardens over again,
glassen-ridged, or pashed
like fish-ice: refracted light
red against copper. The hedged sun
draws into itself for its self-quenching.

If one is so minded, these modalities
stoop to re-enter the subterrane of faith—
faith, that is, in real Being;
the real being God or, more comprehensively, Christ—
as a sanctuary lamp treadles its low flame
or as the long-exiled *Salve Regina* was sung
in the crypt at Lastingham on the threshold
of a millennium.

XXXIX

Rancorous, narcissistic old sod—what
makes him go on? We thought, hoped rather,
he might be dead. Too bad. So how
much more does he have of injury time?

XL

For wordly, read worldly; for in equity, inequity;
for religious read religiose; for distinction
detestation. Take accessible to mean
acceptable, accommodating, openly servile.
Is that right, Missis, or is that right? I don't
care what I say, do I?

XLI

For iconic priesthood, read worldly pique and ambition.
Change insightfully caring to pruriently intrusive.
Delete chastened and humbled. Insert humiliated.
Interpret slain in the spirit as browbeaten to exhaustion.
For hardness of heart read costly dislike of cant.

XLII

Excuse me—excuse me—I did not
say the pain is lifting. I said the pain is in
the lifting. No—please—forget it.

XLIII

This is quite dreadful—he's become obsessed.
There you go, there you go—narrow it down to obsession!

XLIV

Cry pax. Not that anything is forgiven;
not that there seems anything new to forgive
in this assemblance. Not that the assemblance
might be tempted into the fertile
wilderness of unspirituality. Not that I
know the way out, or in. So be it;
let us continue to abuse one another
with the kiss of peace.

XLV

It is believed—argued—they offered him
some kind of painkiller, which
is plausible. In any event
he would not touch it.
Morus, humble and witty at the end,
glad of a clean death;
Southwell, addressing the cordial
cordially: 'it does my heart good'.
Fifty years without limbs, or in an iron
lung, is that possible? I lose
courage but courage is not lost.

XLVI

Not always. Not even. Hand me that *Latin
Through Pictures*. A thing
given is not always, or even, a gift,
Deodatus; sing *dona nobis*.
A gift is a donation. Donors are permitted
to give of themselves, with saints and martyrs,
kneeling at the altarpiece's edge,
catechumens of final judgement.
Unversed in our data, the secular
conjuring of insurances,
amid droughts, floods, plagues,
how delicate in self-exaction
they appear; with what severity
of graciousness in these and in like matters
they keep their places.
How carnally nonetheless
such things of the spirit are wrought by attrition;
what misplaced, mistimed,

hammering perfects them: the ephemeral
attacking the absolute
with ruining and/or ruined force.

XLVII

Movie-vocals cracked, her patter still
bright as the basement gents' brass taps at the Town Hall.
Benevolent, like a Young Fabians' Club
vision of labour; invariable routine
produced the same hot water, brought to the boil
her honest yodelling. So she fetched home the lads
from France, as once she had marched the lasses back
to a silent mill. She, and her armed
aspidistra, last off the beaches.

XLVIII

Sir, your 'Arts/Life' column claims that Gracie
Fields sang at Dunkirk. Is this
a misprint? For sang read sank? [Phew,
what a 'prang'!—ED]

XLIX

A clear half-face of the moon
at mid-day, above the cupola's intricately
graceful wind-vane's confected silver.
Everything sharp, bright. Memory in its recesses
pierced directly—*Lucifer*
ante portas. Why that?

L

Trimalchio, bouncing up from a brief seventh
bout of financial ruin, pledges us
his high-spent poverty with distasteful feast.
He is himself already, so he claims,
in his seventh element.
He merits, I would say, a loaded rumour
among the legends that now circulate
about Canary Wharf, the Isle of Dogs,
new comets whiffling in and out of orbit.
Time's satire, for its part, allows his status
not worse than that clay-footed emperor—
barely saluted at his last ascension—flung

arse-over-tip to belching Tartarus,
with coarsest imputations, by the gods:
roof-crashing his own dull funeral-orgy,
the never-finished ritual deification,
making a clown-shaped hole in the sacred floor.
Trimalchio readjusts his mask of laughter.

LI

Whatever may be meant by *moral landscape*,
it is for me increasingly a terrain
seen in cross-section: igneous, sedimentary,
conglomerate, metamorphic rock-
strata, in which particular grace,
individual love, decency, endurance,
are traceable across the faults.

LII

Admittedly at times this moral landscape
to my exasperated ear emits
archaic burrings like a small, high-fenced
electricity sub-station of uncertain age
in a field corner where the flies
gather and old horses shake their sides.

LIII

But leave it now, leave it; as you left
a washed-out day at Stourport or the Lickey,
improvised rainhats mulch for papier-mâché,
and the chips floating.
Leave it now, leave it; give it over
to that all-gathering general English light,
in which each separate bead
of drizzle at its own thorn-tip stands
as revelation.

LIV

Entertainment overkill: that amplifier
acts as the brain of the putsch. The old
elixir-salesmen had no such entourage
though their product was superior; as was
their cunning oratory.
For the essentials of the cadre, Wordsworth's
'savage torpor' can hardly be bettered

or his prescience refuted.
What it is they possess—and, at some mean
level, Europe lies naked to their abuse—
is not immediately
in the grasp of their hand. They are vassal-
lord-puppet-strutters, not great scourges of God.
A simple text would strike them
dumb, and is awaited. Meanwhile
they are undeniable powers of this world,
closely attended in their performance
of sacral baseness, like kings at stool.

LV

Vergine bella—it is here that I require
a canzone of some substance. There are sound
precedents for this, of a plain eloquence
which might be telling. One cannot purchase
the goodwill of your arduously simple faith
as one would acquire a tobacconist's-cum-paper shop
or a small convenience-store
established by aloof, hardworking Muslims.
Nor is language, now, what it once was
even in—wait a tick—nineteen hundred and forty-
five of the common era, when your blast-scarred face
appeared staring, seemingly in disbelief,
shocked beyond recollection, unable to recognize
the mighty and the tender salutations
that slowly, with innumerable false starts, the ages
had put together for your glory
in words and in the harmonies of stone.
But you have long known and endured all things
since you first suffered the Incarnation:
endless the extortions, endless the dragging
in of your name. *Vergine bella*, as you
are well aware, I here follow
Petrarch, who was your follower,
a sinner devoted to your service.
I ask that you acknowledge the work
as being contributive to your high praise,
even if no-one else shall be reconciled
to a final understanding of it in that light.

LVI

Less cryptic but still with a touch
of the enigmatic? Very well: how did
the ladies ride? What were they not wearing?
Who put their scent-mark on him
like a cat spraying? For what amour
did he wear a woman's wig? Who tried
to set fire to it?
Relate the *mystique* of Catchems End,
Worcestershire, to the *politique*
of incomprehensible verse-sequences.
Is he or is he not posing *dévoué*
outside the Boutique des Cahiers
in the rue de la Sorbonne?—
his face is turned from the militant display
towards some other vision.
How would you define his body-language?
Stoic consensuality? Sceptic paranoia?
What was meant by 'the greatness
of the flame'? Who cried from the midst of it
'if this is *kenosis*, I want out'?

LVII

My dear and awkward love, we may not need
to burn the furniture; though, like you,
I understand by this time all too well
despair at the kiln-door—the first moment's
ultimate ruin of the final prize.

LVIII

Portrait of mourning's autodidact: proud,
not willing to drop the increasingly
evident burden of shamed
gratitude: to his own dead,
and to those not his own—Pandora
Barraclough, for instance;
his desire to keep alive
recollection of what they were put to, though
not for his sake, not for this future, and not
'rooted', God help us; they were as he
now is; dispossessed
even in the scant subsistence

of disturbed folk-memory. Each time,
the salving of the waste
less and less expected;
yet time and again salvific—
like the barely recognized
beauty of the potato vine in its places
of lowly flowering.

LIX

By *unearned grandiloquence* is to be understood:
congées not given, *pourboires*, backhanders,
neither passed nor winked at in passing.
But—yes—wounded pride is clownish, deadly.
I have a mind to recast this
as mere entertainment-interludes: crowned
Ignorance time-honoured; and Justice running
widdershins with a dagger of lath.

LX

Return of *Angelus Novus*. How that
must have shaken you—the anima
touched like a snare-drum
or the middle ear.
New conjugations, fine as hair-springs,
the seconds-hand twitching it-
self into shock.
Try it again—again you leap
aside and are riven.

LXI

A se stesso.
Not unworded. Enworded.
But in the extremity
of coherence. You will be taken up.
A se stesso.

LXII

A happy investment, Lord Trimalchio:
forasmuch as Blake laboured
in Hercules Buildings, and as 'up Dryden's
alley' is where he was set upon
to the unstinting plaudits of the trade;

as 'mob' and 'fun' came in at the same time:
forasmuch as the world stands,
in a small part, exposed for what it is—
tyrant-entertainment, master of the crowds.

LXIII

Those obscenities which—as you say—you fancy
perverting the consecration; you hear them all right
even if they are unspoken, as most are. It is
difficult always to catch the tacit
echoes of self-resonance. Is prayer
residual in imprecation? Only
as we equivocate. When I examine
my soul's heart's blood I find it the blood
of bulls and goats.
Things unspoken as spoken give us away.
What else can I now sell myself, filched
from Lenten *Hebrews*?

LXIV

Delete: sell myself; filched from. Inert:
tell myself; fetched from. For inert read insect.

LXV

Who posed as Britannia—one of royalty's
rare vestals, was it? Across the years so much
has been taken, too much given away—
more like evidence let
slip than as alms bestowed or restitution
arrived at. What we arrived at without fail,
national débâcle, was sometimes called victory.
India did for us finally, hideous
sub-continental death-rites, the widowed Queen-
Empress felled like Lenin, melted down; new
sacred monsters bellowing at the pyre.

LXVI

Christ has risen yet again to their
ritual supplication. It seems weird
that the comedy never self-destructs.
Actually it is strengthened—if
attenuation is strength. (Donne

said as much of gold. Come back,
Donne, I forgive you; and lovely Herbert.)
But what strange guild is this
that practises daily
synchronized genuflection and takes pride
in hazing my Jewish wife? If Christ
be not risen, Christians are petty
temple-schismatics, justly
cast out of the law. Worse things
have befallen Israel. But since he is
risen, he is risen even for these
high-handed underlings of self-
worship: who, as by obedience,
proclaim him risen indeed.

LXVII

Instruct me further in your travail,
blind interpreter. Suppose I cannot
unearth what it was they buried: research
is not anamnesis. Nor is this a primer
of innocence exactly. Did the centurion
see nothing irregular before the abnormal
light seared his eyeballs? Why do I
take as my gift a wounded and wounding
introspection? The rule is clear enough: last
alleluias *forte*, followed by indifferent
coffee and fellowship.

LXVIII

Remove my heart of stone. Replace
my heart of stone. Inspire
cardio-vascular prophylaxis. Stir
psychotic iconoclasts—Jan
van Leyden's crew—to a fresh blood-feast.
Shall I cease to abide by the tables
of Mosaic law, the intractable
midrashim of the rabbi who died
slowly by torture? Must I make my peace
with Clausewitz; or with Hobbes's law, the timid
aggressor, the stoner of providence?

LXIX

What choice do you have? These are false questions.
Fear is your absolute, yet in each feature
infinitely variable, Manichean beyond dispute,
for you alone, the skeletal maple, a loose wire
tapping the wind.

LXX

Active virtue: that which shall contain
its own passion in the public weal—
do you follow?—or can you at least
take the drift of the thing? The struggle
for a noble vernacular: this
did not end with Petrarch. But where is it?
Where has it got us? Does it stop, in our case,
with Dryden, or, perhaps,
Milton's political sonnets?—the cherished stock
hacked into ransom and ruin; the voices
of distinction, far back, indistinct.
Still, I'm convinced that shaping,
voicing, are types of civic action. Or, slightly
to refashion this, that Wordsworth's two
Prefaces stand with his great tract
on the Convention of Cintra, witnessing
to the praesidium in the sacred name
of things betrayed. *Intrinsic value*
I am somewhat less sure of. It seems
implicate with active virtue but I cannot
say how, precisely. Partaking of both
fact and recognition, it must be, therefore,
in effect, at once agent and predicate:
imponderables brought home
to the brute mass and detail of the world;
there, by some, to be pondered.

LXXI

If slab faces can be wolfish this appears
in the tall glare of sodium light on snow.
Fairground-mirror distortion kneads us all
stocking-masks. I have not forgotten
crowd-demonry, the pulley-grins of the Flemish
tormentors. Should I subpoena Callot's

and Goya's witness to that which is in
(read: of) the natural archetype? It is the sheer
descent, the acceleration, that for us
now is terrible: unselfbeing—each held
distracted in the doomed body-cockpit
by a velocity which is also inertia,
round-the-clock idle talk-down to impact.

LXXII

Ethics at the far edge: give the old
bugger a shove / gentleman a shout.

LXXIII

I may be gone some time. *Hallelujah!*
Confession and recantation in fridge.

LXXIV

For Cinna the Poet, see under *errata*.

LXXV

Corner to corner, the careful
fabric of our lives ripped through
by the steel claws of contingency. We are made
to make ourselves instruments
of violence and cunning. There seems no
hook on which we are not caught
except, by lot, those of the thorns and nails.
Vergine bella, now I am half-way
and lost—need I say—in this maze of my own
devising. I would go back and start
again; or not start at all, which might
be wiser. No. Delete the last four words.
Talking to oneself is in fact
a colloquy with occasion—*eppur*
si muove—or so I tell myself.
Extraordinary how *N.* and *N.* contrive
to run their depilators off the great turbine—
the raw voltage could flay them. Such
intimate buzzing and smooth toiletry,
mingled with a few squeals, may yet
draw blood from bloodless Stockholm. *Mea culpa*,
I am too much moved by hate—

pardon, ma'am?—add greed, self-pity, sick
scrupulosity, frequent fetal regression, *and*
a twisted libido? Oh yes—much
better out than in. *Morosa*
delectatio was his expression, that Irish
professor of rhetoric—forget his name.
Forget my own name next *in hac*
lacrimarum valle. But, to continue—

LXXVI

At seven, even, I knew the much-vaunted
Battle was a dud. First it was a dud,
then a gallant write-off. Honour the young men
whose eager fate was to steer that droopy *coque*
against the Meuse bridgeheads. The Fairey
Swordfish had an ungainly frail strength,
cranking in at sea level, wheels whacked
by Channel spindrift. Ingratitude
still gets to me, the unfairness
and waste of survival; a nation
with so many memorials but no memory.

LXXVII

By what law did Keyes, or my cousin's
Lancaster, or the trapped below-decks watch
of Peter's clangorous old destroyer-escort,
serve to enfranchise these strange children
pitiless in their ignorance and contempt?
I know places where grief has stood mute-
howling for half a century, self
grafted to unself till it is something like
these now-familiar alien hatreds,
coarse efflorescence over the dead
proprieties; strong words of Christian hope,
sub rosa, the unmentionable graffiti.

LXXVIII

You say how you are struck by the unnatural
brightness of marigolds; and is this manic,
or what. Are clowns depressives? The open
secret is to act well. Can the now silent
witnesses be questioned? What hope remains
to get him out alive? I'm sorry, her.

Tomorrow he died, became war-dead, picked
off the sky's face. Fifty years back, the dead
will hear and be broken. Get off the line.
Who are you to say I sound funny?

LXXIX

Time for a quick one, Petronius. Charged
with a violation of overnight
sumptuary laws, Custodian
of the Eyes, do not tempt further
the wrath of Priapus. Lie back. Enjoy.
Enjoy. Open another vein.

LXXX

Hopelessly-lost storyteller found.
Self-styled czar of ultimate
disaster movies says
everything must go. *Daniel*
a closed book.

LXXXI

Everyone on heat; *N.* and *N.* stinking,
unsated. Exposure to be at your ripest
discretion, Petronius Arbiter.

LXXXII

Go back to Romsley, pick up the pieces, becomes
a somewhat unhappy figure. I speak
deliberately like an old man who last saw it—
Romsley—through a spinning bike-wheel, as indeed
Kenelm may have done. That hook of ridge,
Waseley to Walton, was enemy country. Now
I overrun it in fiction. But Fairfield repels
my imperium, and always did. Its complex
anarchy of laws would have defeated Athelstan,
let alone Ine. High swine-pasture it was,
long before Domesday; and will be again,
albeit briefly, at the flash of Judgement.

LXXXIII

To have lost dignity is not the same
as to be humble. Is it so unjust
to say to the State Church you lack pride
and are not ashamed? But I have checked
pride with *Cruden*: fifty citations, three
in the new covenant, and not once
does it stand for a good will. I should call
Daniel proud but not high-minded, worthy
of all admiration. And Ruth, of her
lineage. Is Abdiel proud? Or the unknown
singer of Deborah? What am I to do
with these shards of downright majesty, this
ever-doubtful certitude, our curse,
our blessing, impacted as Hebrew?

LXXXIV

When you lift up your eyes and behold
afar off—look at it this way, not much
is expected of most AND (to have one's own
expectations) something of what they are | leaps
to be recognized—when you lift up
your eyes and behold afar off: how
amazing it still is, the awaited name
hailed through our streets, under the pale leafage,
springing from the hierarchies of splendour
and salutation, prodigious messengers
with their own heralds and outriders—
yes, look! the Kenyan runners, look, there they go,
stippled with silver, shaking off the light
garlands of sweat—

LXXXV

A centrally-placed small round window, closed
under a pediment, caught and stared back my fear
centuries before I opened *The Franchise
Affair*. I am not unusually
sensitive to atmosphere, but one or two
fiery dreams of houses held
mid-day séance through my seventh year.
Photo-negatives I now accept
as the originals of this peculiar dread:

black façades, gap-windowed with solid-
glare flame, and with stark
figures caught in some unhuman
intimate torment I could not grasp
until I came to stills of the burning ghetto.

LXXXVI

Well over half-way now; still no response
from Angelus Silesius. These are harsh times
with hag Faith going the rounds. It is good
to be tempted and not fall. I remember
the Telgte synod: Grass in the chair,
vehemently imperturbable. Angelus
stayed for my paper. Was that Grass's suggestion?
Our theme was timely: '*Kinesis* to *Kenosis*:
Guilt and Redemption in the *Trauerspiel*'.

LXXXVII

Forgive me, *Vergine bella*, if I return
to splenetics; they are not seemly,
a threat to both health
and salvation. A girl I once
courted competitively has died
aged sixty-three. Salve my uncouth pretence
at love, her small strained courtesies. Forgive
lapses in grace, common yet of one's self,
although it is too late. Bless,
of your charity, for your orator's sake,
prize *N.* and *N.* made Swedish millionaires.

LXXXVIII

Let him alone, let him
have his way, let him be touched
by his own angel, it will come to nothing:
born again, but stillborn.

LXXXIX

Stunned words of victory less memorable
than those urged from defeat; not that the vanquished
are more to be believed. In effect
it cries out for silence: whose
silence, would you say? I say endure

by way of enduring: the secular
masques, *laus et vituperatio*. What
is ƎƆИA⅃UᗺMA you may ask; has it come
down to us from the dead language of Canaan?

XC

Ur? Yes? Pardon? Miss a throe. Go to gaol.

XCI

Celebrate yet again the mind's eye's
dreadful kink or reach of resurrection—
the British walking-wounded—these are like
bunched final stragglers in a three-legged
marathon—last-gasp survivors, loud roll-calls
of the mute orphans, child-victims
in mill and mine. Here's your Lost Empire
Medal for a life spent giving blood. Not
celebrate. Calibrate. Seniors
to synchronize watches. Last rum and fireworks.

XCII

No way, Jane Grey, uncrowned bright
humanist: Boethius, Tully; Seneca, 'the old
moral man'; no way. The common
elm—*ulmus procera*—also gone
under, with the shires; though deer
are cared for, and the rare white cattle; as
is memory in this tranche of frozen sunlight.

XCIII

One thing then another, eh, dour
old Gower? Even in Latin your satire
well understands itself not well-disposed.
But in contempt—*Geffe juvat*, star-shards
rattling the coulter—and without leave,
under protest, with formal complaint, by
chance right of reply, the people—

XCIV

Suddenly they are upon us, the long
columns, the immense details
of betrayal: as always predicted
yet wholly unforeseen.
Incidents at the frontier—it is not
courage that is now in question.

XCV

This is not Duino. I have found no sign
that you are visited by any angel
of suffering creation. Violent
sensitivity is not vision, nor is vision
itself order. You may be possessed
of neurasthenic intelligence as others
have been tormented by helpless self-
knowledge, though I doubt it. In any event
I would not parade comparisons. Naked
experience as you preen it is a mild
indecency, like old-style London revue.
Indecent in turn, let me here interpose
the body of a parenthesis (do we indeed
not know ourselves?). You can always
say *I call you*, forcing my superior
hand at rhetoric. My question is
rhetorical, in that I expect
no answer. Would it be fairer to say
that I do not invite one? Let me allow
this to be no defence, merely a registration
of shock; and that, of course, I am putting
words in your mouth. Even so, I propose to
stay with this, perhaps to carry some meaning
of our imperfection.

XCVI

Ignorant, assured, there comes to us a voice—
unchallengeable—of the foundations,
distinct authority devoted
to indistinction. With what proximity
to justice stands the record of mischance,
heroic hit-or-miss, the air
so full of flak and tracer, legend says,

you pray to live unnoticed. Mr Ives
took Emersonian self-reliance the whole
way on that. Melville, half-immolated,
rebuilt the pyre. Holst, some time later,
stumbled on dharma. What can I say?—
At worst and best a blind ennoblement,
flood-water, hunched, shouldering at the weir,
the hatred that is in the nature of love.

XCVII

Devouring our names they possess and destroy
by numbers: the numbered, the numberless
as graphs of totality pose annihilation.
Each sensate corpse, in its fatal
mass-solitariness, excites
multiples of infliction. A particular
dull yard on a dull, smoky day. This, and this,
the unique face, indistinguishable, this, these,
choked in a cess-pit of leaking Sheol.

XCVIII

You will have seen how a big humming-top
walks its ferrule on a few inches of floor,
as if rehearsing the Torah. You see also
how this man's creepy, though not creeping, wit—
he fancies himself a token Jew by marriage,
a Jew by token marriage—has buzzed, droned,
round a half-dozen topics travestying
The Testament of Beauty. Denial
seems the *mot juste*. What did he say? He said,
I think, 'for Ashkenazic read Sephardic'.

XCIX

So be that jaw- and rib-stove
gabardine hump of pain
sopping the cobble-slime with its rag beard.
Don't even pray. Don't give them any more
to work on—I can understand that. If
witness meant witness, all could be martyrs.

C

Blitzkrieg crazes the map-face. Europa wakes
abruptly multi-fissured, the demiurge
rewriting things in her dust. *Mit welchem Recht?*—
Freud's outburst, strange as it seems, though he
meant being lied to. Courage is exposed
to the crack of nerves and pétards. *I
don't wish to know that!* I don't wish to crow.
Here's a better suggestion: have
black-out for sixty years and find her again
irreparably repaired.

CI

Though already too late we must
set out early, taking the cinder
path by the old scythe-works. There will be
no quarrel between us—all this time—
a light rain unceasing, the moist woods
full of wild garlic.

CII

You are right, of course; I neither stand
my ground nor run. In whatever direction
kinesis takes me, it is no distance.
In part like Blake's carnalists—*they
became what they beheld*—I am seen
to work my daysman's stint in the foul mill.
One could say that Hobbes (of Malmesbury), whom I
would call the last great
projector of Europe prior to Hudson
(Hudson the Railway King) is radical
as we are *déracinés*; granted that *Leviathan*
towers on basics rather than from roots;
and that *roots* itself, unhappily, is now
a gnostic sign among the Corinthians.

CIII

Parades of strength are not, in the long view,
Aristotle's magnitudes. Langgasse,
in Danzig, sparked a short fuse. The massed
hakenkreuz-banners appeared as machine-fresh

robust street-hangings, crests of the phalanx,
terror's new standards. I do not recall which
death-camp it was that sheltered Goethe's oak
inside the perimeter. I cannot
tell you who told me or in what footnote
it sat hidden. This and other *disjecta*
membra, the abused here drawn
together with pain for their further dis-
memberment, I offer to the presiding
judge of our art, self-pleasured *Ironia*.

CIV

Self-pleasured, as retching on a voided
stomach pleasures self. Savage indignations
plighted with self-disgust become one flesh.
Pasternak, for example: *shestdesyat*
shestoy, they shout—give us the sixty-
sixth (sonnet, of Shakespeare). You could say
that to yourself in the darkness before sleep
and perhaps be reconciled. Nothing true
is easy—is that true? Or, how true is it?
It must be worth something, some sacrifice. I
write for the dead; *N., N.*, for the living
dead. No joke, though, self-defenestration.

CV

Mea culpa, mea culpa, Geffe juvat.
Take out supposition. Insert suppository.
For definitely the right era, read: deaf in the right ear.

CVI

You: with your regular morning and evening
glossolalia timed like the angelus;
your high mass choreographed by smoke-
sacristy ephebes—*choreograph* is the word
revealed to them; who are you to protest?
You: with the mantra sewn into your alb,
your rigidity and your abandonment,
your proud ignorance of doctrine, contempt
for the protracted, indeterminate,
passion-through-history of the English Church,
the Church of Wesley, Newman, and George Bell.

CVII

Flos campi time again among the small
ruins, vestiges, memorials, of the uprooted
midlands railways. How suggestive the odour
of hawthorn, building from the rubble
of craft and graft. What was it that growing
girls could get from *Virol*? Were boys forbidden it
for their green-sickness? Could it have fed
our mutually immature desires? How
English, how vivid, how inapposite
to the disnatured century: a slow, Lydian-mode
wayfaring theme for unaccompanied viola.

CVIII

—Well as I hear I hear you but as I
hear you you are in dumb-show—

CIX

Oculos tuos ad nos converte: convert
your eyes, *Vergine bella*: you gave us
a bit of a turn there. Not unnaturally—
but not naturally, either—they conceived
light to be the prime agent,
or mover, of generation. And as that
light embraced you, so you embraced
this conception; became—secured
by the eternal—its mortal source
and tenure: though many, perhaps most,
would argue against the relevance
of the Scholastics. What do you mean,
what have they to do with it, and have I
studied *The Sceptical Chymist*? Salt, sulphur,
mercury: more potent by far
than metaphysics whose demoted angels
have been caught dancing
with impropriety. Who's Impropriety? *Mea
culpa*, ma'am. Wit-spasm.
Since when has our ultimate reprobation
turned (*oculos tuos ad nos con-
verte*) on the conversion or
reconversion of brain chemicals—
the taking up of serotonin? I

must confess to receiving the latest
elements, *Vergine bella*, as a signal
mystery, mercy, of these latter days.
No matter that the grace is so belated;
no matter who staked out and reaps
the patent-commodity; no matter how
grace is confused, repeatedly, with chill
euphoria. *Ad te suspiramus,*
gementes, flentes: which, being interpreted,
commits and commends us to loving
desperately, yet not with despair, not
even in desperation.

CX

This glowering carnival, kermesse of wrath
and resentment, how early—? Very. Very deep
among elementary mayhem: *Seventy Years*
a Showman, A Book of Golden Deeds, The Worst
Journey in the World: Finders. Keepers:
Dandy, Beano, Film Fun, Radio Fun, mis-
teachers of survival: Laurel and Hardy
cutting, pacing, repacing, their
flawless shambles. In Scripture class,
under the desk lid, perilous comic strips
of dentures blown from trumpets. Swift
economy of outline evidenced
by aircraft recognition cards: six days
a week—Saturdays off—the sustained,
inattentive, absorbing of King James' English.

CXI

But is such anger genuine or factitious,
Mr Editor? Inquires a sincere
correspondent of the *Pink 'Un*. To which
that proper rag makes answer rhadamanthine: Patriot Blood
is a great horse, so is Eurovista,
Kristallnacht is at stud. The odds
are against High Prophecy. Heap
ashes on your head and split your sides.
Since you have asked, however, we can say
the donkey Nehemiah has been lamed
but not withdrawn. Seán O'Shem
said—trenchantly—that the man's epigraphs
are his audience. He needs to be heard.

A draft typescript: caulk on caulk
of liquid eraser, illegible, overwrought,
more like psoriasis or scabies than
genuine inspiration.

CXII

The glowering carnival, kermesse of wrath,
caravans of the hermaphrodite
children of Plato, their genius
'strangely neglected': a man in an iron cage
lifted from Bunyan; the magic
lantern found among Empson's effects—
'works like a dream, lacking some slides of Hell'—
rare *tableaux morts-vivants*, the gift
of Ruysch-Leopardi; a mindless
cogitation and final
exhaustion of the automata;
the once-unequalled broken to advance
the unequal captains; general apocalyptic
uninventiveness on all sides: rumour
of Jewish alchemy, Rathenau
cold in his furs.

CXIII

Boerenverdriet? You eat it—it's Dutch liverwurst.

CXIV

From the Angels of Irrational
Decision and of Reversed Order
to the Angel of Improvisation:
from the Angel of Improvisation
to the Angels of Tannic
Acid, Salicyl, and Plain Water:
from the Angel of Advantage—where is
the Angel of Recorded Delivery?—
from the Angels of Advantage
Lost, of Sacrifice, of Surrender,
to the Angels of Merciful
Intervention and Final Custody.

CXV

Overburdened with levity, the spirit found
in carnal disarray—so what do you know,
Amarilli, mia bella? Say it is not
true that mockery is self-debasement;
though already I have your answer: We
are to keep faith, even with self-pity,
with faith's ingenuity, self-rectifying cadence,
perfectly imperfected: e.g., the lyric
art of Spanish baroque, seventeenth–
eighteenth-century Italian song,
which so aspires to make adamant *I
am melting*, the erotic, thrilled and chaste.
(End with that reference, in the Ludlow masque,
to *haemony*, plant of exilic virtue.)

CXVI

What a fool! And what folly—I should have pledged
Lucian from the start. Erasmus, More
the fool, how could it fail, that lineage?
As before, the question stands as one
of rhetoric. Wealth—*copia*—was required
to buy moderation: Lucianic
or Erasmian moderation, that is. *Morus*
enacted extreme measures, though not
overmuch—now and then a Lutheran
zealot *in flagrante*. And though the line did
fail, it was not from that cause nor
for any reason. Memory
and attention died, *comme ça*,
which is not reasonable. Polity regroups
and is guarded, where on D-Day men
drowned by the gross, in surf-dreck, still harnessed
to their lethal impedimenta.
Moderation can wring Jonah for comedy—
see Lucian, *supra*, and other analogues—
Despondency will bend iron, and *Much-afraid*
was a strong man's daughter—he said,
setting aside his stalled ode for thirty
vicarious rounds of bare-knuckle.

CXVII

A noble vernacular? We could screw him,
finish him, for all that. Then he ought
to be happy: a reborn ageing child,
privileged to no place of honour, sated
with dissatisfactions; his wardrobe
of curial cast-offs,
student of Livy in his father's house,
his father being the bailiff—three pounds
a week, rent-free. But all that *unheimlich*
work of his: salutes and cenotaphs,
and vessels moving seaward, the ebb tide
purled in their wake. We cannot
have some great instauration occurring
by default, can we?

CXVIII

By default, as it so happens, here we have
good and bad angels caught burning
themselves characteristic antiphons;
and here the true and the false
shepherds discovered
already deep into their hollow debate.
Is that all? No, add spinners of fine
calumny, confectioners of sugared
malice; add those who find sincerity
in heartless weeping. Add the pained,
painful clowns, brinksmen of perdition.
Sidney: best realizer and arguer
of music, that 'divine
striker upon the senses', steady my
music to your Augustinian grace-notes
with your high craft of fret. I am glad
to have learned how it goes
with you and with Italianate-
Hebraic Milton: your voices pitched exactly—
somewhere—between *Laus Deo* and defiance.

CXIX

And yes—bugger you, MacSikker et al.,—I do
mourn and resent your desolation of learning:
Scientia that enabled, if it did not secure,

forms of understanding, far from despicable,
and furthest now, as they are most despised.
By understanding I understand diligence
and attention, appropriately understood
as actuated self-knowledge, a daily acknowledgement
of what is owed the dead.

CXX

As with the Gospels, which it is allowed to resemble,
in *Measure for Measure* moral uplift
is not the issue. Scrupulosity, diffidence,
shrill spirituality, conviction, free expression,
come off as poorly as deceit or lust.
The ethical *motiv* is—so we may hazard—
opportunism, redemptive and redeemed;
case-hardened on case-law, casuistry's
own redemption; the general temper
a caustic equity.

CXXI

So what is faith if it is not
inescapable endurance? Unrevisited, the ferns
are head-high, breast-high, the days
lustrous, with their hinterlands of thunder.
Light is this instant, far-seeing
into itself, its own
signature on things that recognize
salvation. I
am an old man, a child, the horizon
is Traherne's country.

CXXII

Sitting up, I drift
in and out of sleep. It now appears
too much is owed, impossible to repay:
Memoria, the loan-shark.

CXXIII

The secular masque, advanced
by computation, has not otherwise
progressed. Millennial authority
makes necromantic the fire-targeted

century. African new-old
holocaust suffers up against
the all-time Hebrew *shoah*. But shaking
with aeonial palsy the screens
have failed Tomorrow and the victory
altars of the sacrificed engineers.

CXXIV

The glowering carnival, kermesse of wrath—
the pressure's beginning to tell now, you
can hear it, the creaking bounce
of the Miltonics: *But to my task . . . But
to my task*, I ask you! He also cribs
from Dryden and *Vox Clamantis*. Recently
it's got much worse; like a provincial
actor-manager. What's more—when Arno
blundered at Firenze and the bronze
Baptistry doors bulged like tarpaulins, when
the flesh of the frescoes knew corruption—
he wasn't there, as Croker pointed out.

CXXV

I have been working towards this for some time,
Vergine bella. I am not too far from the end
[of the sequence—ED]. It may indeed be my last
occasion for approaching you in modes
of rhetoric to which I have addressed myself
throughout the course of this discourse. Custom
is strange—as I believe, ma'am, you well know—
not least in its familiar
power of estrangement. Estrangement itself
is strange, though less so than the metaphysics
of tautology, which is at once *vain
repetition* and *the logic of the world*
(Wittgenstein). Some of its moves—I mean
tautology's—call to mind chess-moves: moves
that are in being before you—even as
you—make them. An actual play-through
from the Last Quartets could prove superfluous,
except to a deaf auditor. Then there is this
Augustinian-Pascalian thing about seeking
that which is already found. Tautology,
for Wittgenstein, manifests the condition
of unconditional truth. Mysticism is not

affects but grammar. There is nothing
mysterious in grammar; it constitutes
its own mystery, its *practicum*. Though certain
neologisms—Coleridge's 'tautegorical'
for example—clown out along the edge,
τὸ αὐτό enjoys its essential being
in theology as in logic. The intellectual
beauty of Bradwardine's thesis rests
in what it springs from: the Creator's grace
praecedentem tempore et natura ['Strewth!
'already present in time as in nature'?—ED]
and in what it returns to—our arrival
at a necessary salvation. So much
for the good news. The bad is its correlate—
everlasting torments of the non-elect; guaranteed
damnation for dead children unbaptized.
Wyclif and Dame Julian would have raised
few objections or none to those symmetries.
The Church's first martyrs, the Holy Innocents,
unbaptized Jewish infants, surrogates
of the Jewish child we call our Child-King—
small impediments that Policy deals with,
takes care of: *baptized in blood*. But surely
every new-born child is baptized in blood.
Still, there they are: crying shame to the cant,
the unending *negotium*,
the expediencies, enforcements, and rigged evidence.
Vergine bella, forgive us the cunning
and the reactive, over-righteous
indignation, the self-approving
obtuse wisdom after the event,
our aesthetics and our crude arrangements.
I have been working up to this. The Scholastics
mean more to me than the New Science. All
things are eternally present in time and nature.

CXXVI

To the short-sighted Citizen
Angel, the Angel of Assimilation—
'I will not run, dance, kow-tow, to entertain
thugs, perverts, parvenus, perjurers'—
from the stifled Lamentation Angel.
To that dying power from the trim,
well-clad Angel of Death: his insignia
and instruments.

From that, to the violated Angel
of Eternal Audit. And to eternity,
the ashen-fleshed, wrenched-silent,
untouched, unhearing, Angel of Forgiveness.

CXXVII

In loco parentis—devoured
by mad dad. Hideous—hideous—and many like it.

CXXVIII

The rough-edged, increasingly concave,
line of advance
stops dead: machine-guns do the work
of trick photography. The next trick also
requires apparatus: a sector
chitters brave tries at synchronized push-ups;
by magic the order stands—to remain—pitched
slightly forward against unseen resistance.
Cocteau *flânéed* the First War. After the Second
he moved angles, elevations, to revitalize
young gay men mercurial whom he lifted
out of the tribunals, fabled interrogations,
the cellars, of his fantastical *milice*.
Dipping their (rubber-sheathed) hands to the wrist
in vats of quicksilver, they were absorbed
by bedroom-mirrors through which the interchange
of life with death began and ended. It
is hard now to recover how his debellated,
debellished land bore to inaugurate
towers of remembrance, the massive
verticals, to lean on fields of the dead;
the fields of preservation, with ranging
shadows cast by the black bulk
of light, that are formal sorrow, mourning,
in its conjurations of triumphs.

CXXIX

One or two illustrations might help us—
Geffe—to take a fix on your position,
anomalous as it is. Two Kokoschkas
and one Rembrandt: Rembrandt's unfinished
The Concord of the State, OK? The Masaryk
portrait and *What We Are Fighting For*, OK. OK?
ta-Rah ta-Rah ta-rarara Rah

CXXX

Milton—the political pamphlets. Blake
in old age reaffirming the hierarchies.
Péguy *passim*, virtually. Bernanos,
if only for having written *la colère
des imbéciles remplit le monde*. Radnóti
at Bór. The great self-recovery of Wat.
ta-Rah ta-Rah ta-rarara Rah

CXXXI

Mourning registers as celebration. Haydn
at sixty-six, his clowning majesty
of invention never bettered (I mean,
I think, the late 'Erdődy' Quartets).
Bartók dying in New York, unfinished
music among the sickbed detritus:
ta-Rah ta-Rah ta-rarara Rah

CXXXII

I would have liked to know—I may yet know—
whether the hidden part which most engages me
is closer to nub, crux, crank, or orifice.
Crank, probably. The system which converts
rotary to rectilinear motion is called
the eccentric. Whichever it is, it has my tie.
ta-Rah ta-Rah ta-rarara Rah

CXXXIII

The nerve required to keep standing, pedalling,
grinning inanely, strikes me (*splat!*) as more
than temperamental luck. It is a formal
self-distancing, but like choreography.
You could clog to some late Haydn without
injuring either tradition. Please—my *foot*—
ta-*Rah* ta-*Rah* ta-*rarara* *Rah*

CXXXIV

It surprises me not at all that your
private, marginal, uncommitted writing—
this is to be in code—came at the end
to the forum of world acclaim. *Decenza*—
your term—I leave unchallenged; decorum
aloof from conformity; not a mask
of power's harsh suavities. (Internal
evidence identifies the late
Eugenio Montale as the undoubted
subject of this address.) It sets you
high among the virtuous *avvocati*—
the judges with a grasp of such vocation—
even among the place-brokers, purveyors
of counsel, publishers, editors,
and senators-for-life; a civic conscience
attested by comedy: twenty-five years
with the *Nuovo Corriere della Sera*
as leader-writer and critic of first nights;
still your own man; publicities, public life,
the anteroom to the presence-chamber
of self-containment. (Machiavelli described
entering his study, robed as if for Court.)
But one man's privacy is another's
crowded *at home*—we are that circumscribed.
Machado who, to say the least, is your
grand equal, sat out his solitude, habitué
of small, shaky, wicker or zinc tables—
still-life with bottle, glass, scrawled school-*cahiers*—
put his own voice to slow-drawn induration.
I admire you and have trained my ear
to your muted discords. This rage twists
me, for no reason, other than the sight
of anarchy coming to irregular order

with laurels; now with wreaths: Duomo drone-
bell, parade-mask shout, beautifully-caught
scatter of pigeons in brusque upward tumble,
wingbeats held by a blink.

CXXXV

So what about the dark wood, eh?
When do we come to the dark wood?
We have already been sent to the dark
wood, by misdirection: Trônes, Montauban,
High Wood, Delville, Mametz. We have been there,
and are there still, in a manner of speaking.

CXXXVI

But only in a manner of speaking.
I was not there, nor were you. We are children
of the Thirties, the sour dissipation;
England at once too weepy and too cold.

CXXXVII

The glowering carnival: nightly solar-flare
from the Black Country; minatory beacons
of ironstone, sulphur. Then, greying, east-northeast,
Lawrence's wasted pit-villages rising early,
spinning-wheel gear-iron girding above each
iron garth; old stanchions wet with field-dew.

CXXXVIII

Confound you, Croker—you and your righteous
censure! I have admitted, many times,
my absence from the Salient, from the coal-face
in Combs Pit, Thornhill. Yes, to my shame,
I high-tailed it at Pozières (Butterworth
died in my place). At Arras I sacrificed
Edward Thomas (the chief cause of your
hostility—why can't you say so?). I find
your certitudes offensive. My cowardice
is not contested. I am saying (simply)
what is to become of memory? Yes—I know—
I've asked that before.

CXXXIX

Concerning the elective will, *arbitrium*.
Concerning wilfulness and determination:
in so far as the elective is elect
it will not now be chosen. It may choose
non-election, as things stand. The Florentine
academies conjoined
grammar and the Fall, made a case of *casus*.
All things by that argument are bound
to the nature of disordinance,
Judgement's two minds, the broken
span of consequence. How can our
witty sorrows try the frame of such
unsecured security—nothing between
election and reprobation, except vertigo
and a household word-game of tit-for-tat
with family values. Milton writes of those
who 'comming to Curse . . . have stumbled into
a kind of Blessing'; but if you suppose him
to invoke a stirrup-and-ground-type mercy, think
again. It's a Plutarchan twist: even our foes
further us, though against their will
and purpose. Hopkins gave his best
self-coinings of the self—*inscape*,
instress—to inventing Lucifer:
non serviam: sweetness of absolute
hatred, which shall embrace self-hatred,
encompass self-extinction, annihilation's
demonic angelism. Hereditary
depression is something else again. You
can draw up Plutarch against yourself; yourself
the enemy (*do it and be damned*). Hopkins
had things so nearly right, as did Herbert,
though neither would have flown solo (the Angel
of the Agony was in attendance).
As for the rest of us, must we describe
Finnegans Wake as a dead end? (*Over
my dead body*, says Slow.)

CXL

A se stesso: of Self, the lost cause to end all
lost causes; and which you are not (are you?)
so hopeless as to hope to defend. You've

what? Leopardi for the New Age? Mirageous
laterite highway—every few miles
a clump of vultures, the vile spread.
Fama, for *Fame*: celebrity and hunger
gorging on road-kill. *A se stesso.*

CXLI

From the terrible Angel of Procreation
to the Angel-in-hiding of Senility.
To the Autonomous Angel
from the several Angels of Solitude:
cc Angel of Self-Alienation,
Angel of Solitary Confinement.
From the Angel of the Morning Gold-fix
to the Angels of Mandragora and Rip-off.
To the Demotic Angels from the Angels
of Repulsion-Attraction, the loud-
winged Angels of Equal Sacrifice, the sole
Angel standing in for Hope and Despair.

CXLII

To the Angel of the Approved Estimates,
to the Angels of Promise Across the Entire
Spectrum. To the Surplus Angels of Acquisition.
I cannot even hear the new instructions,
let alone obey them. Where,
you will say, does explanation
end and confession begin? To know all
is to forgive all: a maxim more wicked,
even, than it is stupid—forgive me,
would you, ever?—But that, by my reckoning,
is not the sum. I have introduced,
it is true, *Laus et vituperatio*
as a formality; still this formal thing
is less clear *in situ*. That—
possibly—is why I appeal to it. The Angels
of Sacral Equivocation, they now tell me,
are redundant: we have lost the *Bloody Question.*
Though you can count on there being some
bloody question or other, one does more
than barely survive. Less hangs on the outcome,
or by, or around, it. Why do I think—
urgently—of beach-sewage? At one source,
Moltke, the two Bonhoeffers, von Haeften,

suffered the Bloody Question and did
nobly thereby. Late praise costs nothing.
To the Angels of Inconclusive Right
on Both Sides, to the Angel of the Last
Minutes, to the Angel of Our
Estimated Times of Arrival and Departure.

CXLIII

Power and sycophancy, sycophancy in power:
power's own cringing to extrapolation
and false prophecy. Subways of white tile
smeared with obscene brown banners. Foucault
running there for his life. Synaesthesia
of appeasement's brain-stench.

CXLIV

Now, for the Law, the Prophets, must we take
inspired guesswork; for inspired guesswork, inter-
locked ignorance, vanity, fear, hope?
It's a difficult line—I can just hear
Unwisdom grinding like fury, the farthest
breaking of Nations. Even beyond that,
distorted sound-patterns of grace. Is this
Manichean? No—Manichean! What?
Lauda? Lauda? Lauda Sion? LAUDA!

CXLV

Incantation or incontinence—the lyric cry?
Believe me, he's not
told you the half of it. (*All who are able may stand.*)

CXLVI

The whole-keeping of Augustine's City of God
is our witness; vindicated—even to us—
in a widow's portion of the Law's
majesty of surrender. A hundred
words—or fewer—engrafted by Tyndale's
unshowy diligence: it is all there
but we are not all there, read that how you will.
Cursed be he that removeth his neighbour's mark:
Mosaic statute, to which Ruskin was steadfast.
(If Pound had stood so, he would not have foundered.)

Paul's reinscription of the Kenotic Hymn—
*God . . . made himself of no reputation . . . took
the shape of a servant*—is our manumission,
Zion new-centred at the circumference
of the world's concentration. Ruskin's wedded
incapacity, for which he has been scourged
many times with derision, does not
render his vision blind or his suffering
impotent. Fellow-labouring master-
servant of *Fors Clavigera*, to us he appears
some half-fabulous field-ditcher who prised
up, from a stone-wedged hedge-root, the lost
amazing crown.

CXLVII

To go so far with the elaborately-
vested Angel of Naked Truth:
and where are we, finally? Don't
say that—we are nowhere
finally. And nowhere are you—
nowhere are you—any more—more
cryptic than a schoolyard truce. Cry
Kings, Cross, or Crosses, cry Pax,
cry Pax, but to be healed. But to be
healed, and die.

CXLVIII

Obnoxious means, far back within itself,
easily wounded. But vulnerable, proud
anger is, I find, a related self
of covetousness. I came late
to seeing that. Actually, I had to be
shown it. What I saw was rough, and still
pains me. Perhaps it should pain me more.
Pride is our crux: be angry, but not proud
where that means vainglorious. Take Leopardi's
words or—to be accurate—BV's English
cast of them: when he found Tasso's poor
scratch of a memorial barely showing
among the cold slabs of defunct pomp. It
seemed *a sad and angry consolation.*
So—Croker, MacSikker, O'Shem—I ask you:
what are poems for? They are to console us
with their own gift, which is like perfect pitch.

Let us commit that to our dust. What
ought a poem to be? Answer, *a sad
and angry consolation.* What is
the poem? What figures? Say,
a sad and angry consolation. That's
beautiful. Once more? *A sad and angry
consolation.*

CXLIX

Obstinate old man—*senex
sapiens,* it is not. Is he still
writing? What is he writing now? He
has just written: I find it hard
to forgive myself. We are immortal. Where
was I?—

CL

Sun-blazed, over Romsley, the livid rain-scarp.

Speech! Speech!

In memory of David Wright

At tuba terribili sonitu taratantara dixit.

ENNIUS

Vorhang, bevor du den Beifall begreifst.

GÜNTER GRASS

1

Erudition. Pain. Light. Imagine it great
unavoidable work; although: heroic
verse a non-starter, says PEOPLE. Some believe
we over-employ our gifts. Given identical
street parties, confusion, rapid exposure,
practise self-emulation: music for crossed
hands; for two fingers; music
for taxiing to take-off; for cremation.
Archaic means files pillaged and erased
in one generation. Judge the distance.
Innocent bystanders on stand-by. Painful
scenes mar final auto-da-fé.

2

Interpose a fire-curtain; stop the applause
from getting through. But would Herr Grass accept
the dedication—our names
unromantically linked? I owe him; he
owes me nothing. Here's an awkward
question going spare to be asked: do
you, as I do, sit late by the Aga
with clues received from sputtering
agents of Marconi; from Imre Nagy;
from Scott of the Antarctic frozen in time
before the first crossword? Decent old Böll—
why me, why not Günter? Help him, someone.

3

How is it tuned, how can it be untuned,
with lithium, this harp of nerves? Fare well
my daimon, inconstant
measures, mood- and mind-stress, heart's rhythm
suspensive; earth-stalled the wings of suspension.
To persist without sureties take
any accommodation. What if Scattergood
Commodity took all? Very well, you
shall have on demand, by return, *presto*,
my contractual retraction.
Laser it off the barcode or simply
cut here—

4

Reformation woodcuts enscrolled such things
between the lips of magistrates, prophets,
and visionary infants. To me it sounds
like communications breakdown, somebody
promoting his (say her) fanatical
expressionless self-creation on a stuck track.
Our show-host has died many times; the words
of welcome dismiss us.
Anomie is as good a word as any;
so pick any; who on earth will protest?
Whatever is said now I shall believe it
of the unnamed god.

5

Enforcer! What will you have? What can I
freely give you? The usual twist
perfected with some pain. Remind me:
for how long did my guardian spirit
cry out under your interrogation?
What intact part of her was found
to sate your inquiry? *Salaam. Shalom.*
Napoo Finee. Finally, dental records.
Strengthen your signal I AM LOSING YOU. That
always gets to them. Reglue the fetish
pig made of terra cotta. Remind me:
bienvenue—is that arrival or welcome?

6

They invested—were invested—in proprieties,
where cost can outweigh reward. Decency, duty,
fell through the floorboards (*applause*). I cannot
do more now than gape or grin
haplessly. On self-advisement I erased
WE, though I is a shade too painful, even
among these figures tying confession
to parody (*laughter*). But surely that's
not all? Rorke's Drift, the great-furnaced
ships off Jutland? They have their own
grandeur, those formal impromptus played
on instruments of the period (*speech! speech!*).

7

Not all they coúld do they háve done; but bring
atonement beyond dispute. Harps
in Beulah. In Hut Eight the rotors. So few
among many true arbiters: thát much
is already knowledge. Now to admit
heroes of lost chance, profundity's
astronauts missing their stars; their breakages
chargeable to all parties. Still, broken
ingemination, they cannot
charge us again for that. Claimant
Fatality appears and acts
mannerist through and through. Citations please.

8

Be stiffened by rectitude kept
rigid with indecision. Say: coherence
though not at any price. Would I exchange
my best gift, say, for new spools of applause,
roulette set pieces (YOU OWE US MONEY)?
Cameo actors can make killings
their legacies. Even so, dereliction
is seminal, to the zillionth power
indicted (*vide* Augustine). But for that
primal occasion I cannot believe us
absolutely struck off. And—yes—Lilith
we háve met [|] and do I knów you?

9

Going attrition. Give me any advance
on attrition. Eternal progress? To the unseen
man in the corner, now gone. I will not
put up anyhow to attract their tictac.
This being the centennial of some half-
heard plea I AM AND HAVE NOTHING pass
round the one remnant candle of vigilance.
Most things are still in the dark. Í should be,
not glad, but able, to recall these wíth you
at some time, rabbi, sometime this century,
as they are here—immediate—to our powers.
But *welch ein Gruss*, what kind of pitch is that?

10

From the beginning the question how to end
has been part of the act. One cannot have sex
fantasies (any way) as the final
answer to life. Shiftless,
we are working at it, butt-headed
Sothsegger for one, between bouts of sleep
and community arm-wrestling, elbows
in spilt beer. TALK ABOUT LAUGH, TALK ABOUT
ANGRY. But don't count, don't bet,
on who or what ends uppermost, the franchise
of slavishness being free to all comers
without distinction.

11

Is MUST a true imperative of OUGHT? Is it
that which impels? In the small hours a red
biro clown-paints my pyjamas. Mirrors
disclose no exit-wound. Scrupulosity
unnerved so, *Gelassenheit* is a becoming
right order, heart's ease, a gift in faith,
most difficult among freedoms. That's
fair enough, given injustice. Each strafe
throws in some duds, freak chances. The libido
of eunuchs, they say, is terrible. God
how I'd like to, if I could only,
shuffle off alive.

12

I have the instructions. Now they read REMIT
NOTHING AT THÍS TIME BUT REFER YOUR PAIN—
you being me. Excuse us, please. The rules:
they stand for our redemption. Or whatever.
Your heart has to be in it, swiftly
and sharply dealt with, but alive
to its own beating; sometimes likened,
by misconception, to a creative
phase of the moment. How is it you were clad—
Balzac, you said—in the wild ass's skin?
Penitence easy-over. Penance | blood
from the leper's dish.

13

If I am failing you sense this, a blind
date of exclusion; the milieux, each mêlée,
whether in wrath, or hope, or enraged sorrow.
This for Max Perutz, brilliant alien star
of observation. Always our blind Fates.
Inheritance is a power among powers
out of its keeping. To these |
honours, titles, are like wreaths delivered
in the name of the PEOPLE; that is to say
in name only. The acclaimed chorus
overrehearses silence. Listen: I ám—this
also ís—broken. For instance see *passim*.

14

What is it you seek and are caught seeking
in mirrors, for variety? The grammarians'
so-called accusative of recollection: that is,
recollection in the act? VARIETY
seems a misnomer if, when, it sustains
Abraham weeping for Sarah ánd Hagar's
travail. Having through-revised the instruction,
make mourning instrumental. Spare us
a little for what follows: axiomatic
redemption grafted to the condemned stock
of original justice; contestant juries
dealing out faith for faith.

15

About time and about this time, when all
her days are fulfilled: as at Pentecost
or at the Nativity, the Godhead
with her in spirit, like a flint arrow-tip
touched to a vapour, a flame. *Intacta*,
through many roads despoiled. The bride of tongues
intimately perfect, perfect though untimely;
not our day. Believe it [|] Augustine
saved himself for this: the City of God
riding her storm-sewers, towering
at watch and ward, prophetic, exposed
to obscurity, hidden in revelation.

16

First day of the first week: rain
on perennial ground cover, a sheen
like oil of verdure where the rock shows through;
dark ochre patched more dark, with stubborn glaze;
rough soggy drystone clinging to the fell,
broken by hawthorns. What survives
of memory you can call indigenous
if you recall anything. Finally
untranscribable, that which ís wrests back
more than can be revived; inuring us
through deprivation, below and beyond life,
hard-come-by loss of self self's restitution.

17

That's not WORKERS' PLAYTIME. Trust Dad
to find the wrong wavelength. Trust Aunty Beeb
to screech like a tart. Trust the Old Man
to pawn his dentures. Trust Grandma to have to go.
Trust Ted-next-door to swear that his stuffed
parrot still talks. Trust Irish Jim
to call it a grand wake. Trust rich Uncle Tony
to drink from the saucer because we're watching,
and because he's rich. Trust Mad Bess
to queen it in purple. Trust your Mother
to notice who's missing. Trust Sandy
MacPherson to blow us to Kingdom Come.

18

Who now says the divine spirit does grammar
to the power x? I want. You want.
You want I should write. Write what, I ask.
Like, write this down, maybe. BEHOLDEN
I love it. Tell me: when were we ever
not beholden? And yes, righteousness
sticks át it íf unrecognized. Steadfast
witnesses you might have called us, pharisees
not philistines. Rate zero on RECENT PAST
AS DISTRESSED SUBTEXT. Penalties. Plead
fax or e-mail. Cut out the funny speech.
Commit to landfill. Or recycle waste.

19

For stately archaic detail tag Dürer's
LORD MORLEY with POMEGRANATE: self-shielding,
facet-compacted, its glitter-heart scarce-
broken FIDUCIA. Go easy: think GRENADE.
Faithfulness wrong-footed (this, now, in re
Colonel F. Fajuyi, late Nigerian Army)
asks and receives praise-songs in lieu. The sun
scans Cancer to Capricorn: emergent
cohorts mass for mutation. Semiotics
rule semiautomatics: is the surreal
any more our defence? Call the tribunals
to order but not right now.

20

THEY tell you that? Spiritual osmosis
mystique of argot—I like the gestures
that come with it: a kind of dumb thieves' cant.
SPI–RI–TU–AL–I–TY I salute you.
Ich kann nicht anders. It was not so much
cultic pathology I had in mind
as ethical satire; but you wriggle so,
old shape-shifter. Since I am compromised
I shall say more. Assume the earphones. Not
music. Hebrew. Poetry aspires
to the condition of Hebrew. Say that it ís
a wind in the mulberry trees: who will know?

21

SURREAL is natural, so you can discount
ethics and suchlike. Try perpetuity
in vitro, find out how far is HOW FAR.
I'd call that self ⏐ inflicted. Pitch it
to the CHORUS like admonition. Stoics
have answers, but not one I go for.
Think surreal the loss of peripheral
vision vis-à-vis conduct. See if Í care
any less than did Desnos, but he cannot
now be recovered. Sights unseen. Body
language my eye. Regarding the shrimp
as predator: EYE TO EYE IT IS TRUE.

22

Age of mass consent: go global with her.
Challenge satellite failure, the primal
violent day-star moody as Herod.
Forget nothing. Reprieve no-one. Exempt
only her bloodline's *jus natalium*.
Pledge to immoderacy the outraged
hardly forgiven mourning of the PEOPLE,
inexorable, though in compliance,
media-conjured. Inscrutable Í call
her spirit now on this island: memory
subsiding into darkness, nowhere
coming to rest.

23

It has its own voice, certainly, though that
fails to come through. Try Hilversum. The Dutch
are heroes living as they have to. Give
Luxembourg a miss for old times' sake.
Recall the atmospherics. Stoicism
may well serve | fill its own vacancy.
Step forward, you. Speak at the red light.
What else proclaims us? More suggestions please.
Autographed hate-mail preferred. Everything sounds
THE CRY OF THE AFFLICTED. That any cause
to delete other options? Talk me through this,
Gallant Little Belgium | I still hear you.

24

Diminishment the long-withheld secret
of dying. The mind's threatened attention spared
by what it gives up; as by these dark
roses in rain-bleached tubs. Things to be taken
further let me confess. Strategies
are not salvation: far from it. Even so
REDUCE means LEAD BACK (into the right way),
mortal self-recognition. Patience
is hard, reductive. What comes next?
What shall I say: we múst be animal
to some purpose? My God, who else heard UN-
HINGE YOUR JAW, DO IT LIKE A PYTHON and díd she?

25

As I believe I heard, the astounding
percussionist is deaf. David said once
he could draw music up through heel of hand
(not Saul's David; David of DEAFNESS, late,
silenced by throat cancer) though the instrument
in this connection was indeed a harp.
Sympathy is more material than empathy:
só I interpret your response as you
register such *unbeschreiblich* . . . Luck
is against the many; and to be gifted
as she is also with striking
and instrumental beauty cannot be bad.

26

No time at all really, a thousand years.
When are computers peerless, folk
festivals not health hazards? Why and how
in these orations do I twist my text?
APPLY FOR FAST RELIEF. Dystopia
on Internet: profiles of the new age;
great gifts unprized; craven audacity's
shockers; glow-in-the-dark geriatric
wigs from old candy-floss (*cat-calls, cheers*).
Starved fourteenth-century mystics write of LOVE.
When in doubt perform. Stick to the much-used
CHECKMATE condom (*laughter, cries of 'shame'*).

27

Something of London shook itself apart—
vibrant Yiddish Theatre—was swept away
with the street-flares of Whitechapel. It was not
music to all ears. Rosenberg mostly
ignored it as he avoided Hebrew. His LOUSE
HUNTING, nonetheless, remakes, re-masters,
redeems farce. He did not wholly imagine
rats, lice, the sole victors. His last efforts
to survive—like THROUGH THESE PALE COLD DAYS—
appear belated and timely acts
of atonement. Are you serious? Well I'm
not joking exactly.

28

LONG TERM counted as thirty days. Hoarding,
looting, twinned by nature. Haruspicate
over the unmentionable, the occult signs
of bladder and bowel. More mental hygiene
urgently called for to forget oneself.
THOSE WHOM IN IGNORANCE I HAVE KNOWN
AND CHARMED BARREN. Scrupulosity can kill
like inattention. How will this be judged?
How shall I plead as one greatly
gifted with hindsight: those dead and dying
dropped there to maim the irresistible
beauty of the advance?

29

The sanctuary hung with entrails. Blood
on the sackcloth. And still we are not
word-perfect. HARUSPICATE; what does that
say to you? CLEARING YOUR THROAT. Between us
is the Pope to be trusted? Can he divide
night from day? What is his sphere of desire?
What price the menorah's one-octave
chant of candles? No-hope to redeem
all covenants. In visions you can tell
NOTHING has changed. Now as ever the sun
roars, is black-rimmed, the moon burns, fire
quenches water.

30

Symbolic labour spinning straw to gold.
Not the hard labour of procrastination.
However you look at it you might
fancy yourself saved by some careless genie
numerate but illiterate. Courtesy
titles re-auctioned like licence plates.
Rage here as variant hobby. Proclaim
NO SWEAT in the tongues—coarse triumphalist
Australian-Tuscan. Culture shock—in fact
there's nothing to it. I mean make real
your fantasy. What did I tell you—see—
they can't touch us.

31

This WORD, the word you are so strenuously
enacting: could it be CHARADE? Or CHIE?
Nót CHIE? *Merde* then | I pass. Daumier
was his latest Muse: now there's a thought
difficult to let drop. Even at the end
I overreach your stake with the viziers.
Soccer versus Islam. Rip through thís lot:
END OF THE WORLD CUP. GO EASY WI' T' SENNA.
PECCAVI RESCINDED. THE AMUSEMENT
PARK TWISTER AND OTHER STORIES. MORE FAUNA
OF THE AUGEAN. BELT UP. PHAZZ. TAKE
TIME OUT, SIMONE WEIL.

32

Take issue. About time. Why not shout down
darkness above all? Invent the telegraph
you would be wise to. Some go
dancing, some set fire to their beds.
Anyone for a mock-up? It is not
easy to make do or make
reparation. MAKE ANSWER here
submits a bulk recognizance: e.g.,
as to the brain a telling of lost sensation;
as in heart's blood slammers against appeal;
if instress then with unselfknowing temper
confessional to the bone.

33

YES, I know: fantasies see us out
like a general amnesty, with *son
et lumière* and civic freedoms.
Something múst give, make common cause,
in frank exchange with defamation.
So talk telegraphese, say: FORTITUDE
NEVER MY FORTE. BLOOD-IN-URINE SAMPLES
RUIN EURO-CULTURE. Try NO to each
succession of expenses; nominal
acceptance, each makeshift honour botched
as though by royal appointment. And PASS to all
duties, rights, privileges, of despair.

34

That caught-short trot-pace of early film: did minds
adjust automatically then? Could they
watch the stiff gallantry jig-jog, go knees up
into, half-over, the wire ⏐ follow it and know
this was not farce—whatever else in thát line
might get them howling, have them dress ranks
to Chaplin's forwards-backwards fame and luck?
Such formalities! Thís after a rare
projection of WINGS: heroic lip-readers
in action—one last sortie and—bingo!—
ventriloquists on sight, choked mouthings PER
ARDUA, the eloquent belly-blood.

35

Say you dispute the audit—no offence
to her intended (or to her intended)—
pending the hierarchies so soon to be
remade, though not with her demotic splendour.
Fantastic, apocryphal, near fatalistic
love of one's country, bearing with it
always something under- or over-subscribed,
bound to its modicum of the outrageous,
cartoon-animation: jovial, martial,
charwomen, their armour bristles and pails,
dancing—marching—in and out of time—
to Holst's JUPITER ás to JERUSALEM.

36

Huntress? No not that huntress but some
other creature of fable. And then for her
like being hunted. Or inescapably
beholden (this should sound tired but not
emotional to excess). Half forgotten
in one lifetime the funeral sentences
instantly resurrected—hów can they do it?
Whatever of our loves here lies apart,
whatever it is you look for in sleep:
simple bio-degradation, a slather
of half-rotted black willow leaves
at the lake's edge.

37

These I imagine are the humble homes
the egalitarian anti-élitist SUN
condescends to daily. Democracy
is in the voice—Churchill's or some other—
I cannot now hear; and the missing clue
WANHOPE: missing, that is, from the game
celebrity plays us for; not lost, since I
still seem to possess it. You too, Jack!—
know who I mean, eh?—poet and scholar
caught sashaying your shadow self. Say that
at normal walking speed, toes on the line.
Say: SURE SUCCESS OF RAP PAR FOR THE COURSE.

38

Do nothing but assume the PEOPLE'S voice,
its speaking looks of dumb insolence.
Xenophobic still the Brits are heroes
living as they have to—short-cuts, thwartings,
one circus act after another, the Powers
enlightened, vengeful: no darkness more
difficult of encounter. Show the folks
Caravaggio's FLAGELLATION—what's it worth?—
sensational, unfeeling. Award
damages for and against the press.
Why is the wreck still singing? All at once
to speak well of this—A FINE STORY!

39

All right push off $^|$ any second and I
have outlived you. Your pioneer flight
not mistimed, albeit without coverage.
How aboút thát: light-heavy solid husk
the body in perspective striking
absently—almost—on ribs of coal-staithes,
and blistered hardtop. How *nerdlich* to probe
sick personality, each stagnant
puddle a maelstrom? Describe being
in shock $^|$ Í'll sáy. OR what routine
visionary surveillance has failed
to return from patrol.

40

The Poles are heroes living as they have to
(put PAYABLE TO BEARER): the exploded
city they made fly together again,
courtesy of Canaletto and the PEOPLE.
Gouvernement Géneral a drawn furnace
of things unmentionable. So that
would be your lot then would it or is there more
Germanic-Slavic mirth? Like *Galgenfreude*,
hideous place-names long ago tattooed
into our bones. Brush-up mnemonics. Unearth
survival kit. Activate motto (the Poles
et cetera). Change date of expiry.

.

41

And what would not be Lusitanian
sorrow were you to raise it: is this
rhetoric? Write NO or NO COMMENT. Hands up
all those too easily won over—*hoch*
to *Hochzeit*. Dreadful translations. Give out
the IOUs. The Christmas of the truce
even as it was | was passing: fróm and fór them.
Take that man's name and voice, Sarn't, íf you
judge him unfit to match late-night *dévots*,
spoilsports from Devil's Island, Fenian Men
bloody and sententious, the Stahlhelm
trumpeted, the Lambeg pounding its beat.

42

Grace to withdraw—enter—an appeal if
there is leeway? Recidivist Í shall
restore a lost glory to your circuits.
So argue righteousness, fee'd by the drab
ill-fortune of the Rand. Confess, Sir
Edward (alias Marshall) Hall,
I merit my nark's wages. As, at times,
you played to be unmasked. Here we are: caught
with eau-de-Luce, vitriol, defiling *Pearl*.
No, no; not a word. The jury is out, hung
on forensic oratory. Your last defence
laughed us to tears.

43

You must be blind | VERITAS to stare so.
In the required half-minute it sounds good
to cast our intercessions for the grand
chefs of World Order. Still: how to attest
with least defilement? Sieve it? Not that.
Authorize the inauthentic with sincere
fraudulence of empathy. Is there some
precedent for my 'slanders': in the Roman
love elegists, or perhaps three-headed
PUBLIUS, who cannot now be released
from the FEDERALIST PAPERS, a monster
of exact foresight?

44

It now seems probable that I have had
a vision or seizure—some stroke of luck
(see thirty-nine, *supra*). HE'S GOT A NERVE!
Cross-hatch the basilisk behind bars.
Cryptic third-degree: is the dandelion
alone parthenogenic, strange virgin tribe
of scorched earth? STOP WRITING. HANDS ON HEADS.
Meanwhile, without our knowledge, the conjectured
difficult child begins to understand
history. Do not refuse him his loss:
wanting things to change and to stay; briefly
comforted by snowfall.

45

Shocks, alignments, brake-fluids, slackened
memory, checked and adjusted. No, not
MORTIFIED. That was last season's key.
How strange it sounds, a fable of common
life: like Thanksgiving—neither
at one with the world nor with ourselves. GO HOME |
ŒCONOMY. A word pertaining to households,
inoperative, at the heart. And you,
a shade importunate. Least said; this said;
to be said at least: If I can see my own
way to forgiveness | I am MERCY your
blind daughter.

46

Champ d'honneur versus *Schlachtfeld*: from this
affray Prussia emerges the clear victor.
Is VECTOR now more widely used—if so,
how exactly? *Die Zuckerzange, bitte!*
Please pass the forceps—you might have said.
Tea with the Hohenzollerns. All the best.
Had fallen by thís time, my own ticket
long overdue. Somewhere in No Man's Land
I took SAKI for SAPPER. *Tray no bong.*
That piece of his, lambasting England's
luxury underclass, was right on target—
SAKI 'as is', Lance-Sergeant BEF.

47

The moon in its stained ice-clouds; ice-clouds
themselves memorable. How sharply they recall
the years of my late driving, the hoping
not to arrive. IS THIS CANONICAL?
COULD IT BE EPOCH-MAKING? Slow down here;
turn at the volta. Unstoppable work
schedules can only be envied. I need
blanks for the world-surfing quote research
unquote of your average junk-maestro.
BLANK BLANK BLANK BLANK. BEÉN THERE
DÓNE THAT. My own titles could well prove
épuisés by instantly wiped applause.

48

As pellitory, among other common
signatories of the wall, stands to old faith—
step back a step, even if expected—
the fieldstone, intricately veined and seamed;
moss, lichen, dobbed with white crut of birds;
Credo (car radio) even as I muse
through tactics, passive aggressions, wound-up
laughter from the claques. HAS BEEN | EDITED.
NOT CLEARED FOR PUBLICATION. Don't bleep shop.
Accept contingencies. Honour
the *duende*. Revoke a late
vocation to silence. THÁT'S ALL RIGHT THEN.

49

Not to forget Colonel Fajuyi, dead
before I arrived (having lost out to Customs).
That means I was robbed; a sweat-pulped cache
of small ten-shilling notes (Nigerian). He
had worse things to contend with. I don't doubt
his courage, his slow dying—smell my fear!—
protracted hide and seek to the bushed kill. Faithful's
death was as foul but he | went like Elijah.
Remaindered UN helmets, weapons, fatigues,
show up here, neo-tribal. Where did you
ditch the platoon? What have they done with Major
Nzeogwu's eyes?

50

Old men to their own battles. It may be
troublesome to restart these. On advisement
I make ACTION THIS DAY. And about time.
Carry this through in some order, armatured
at the salute. Even if it kills me.
Empty your pockets for the cage. Re-jig
HM's ageing right profile on sterling
zinc of the realm. Can I say that and not
seem attracted by censure? *Vieillard,*
go to the door. The threshold-angels
will soon come calling. Those with the gifts
have long since been and gone. You were asleep.

51

INORDINATE wording of Common Prayer
find here dilated. Outrage is ripped loose
from the vast scope and body of SORROW,
our hulks moving in convoy. Destroyers—
one has heard of—self-destroyed—boomerangs
from tin fish. Enemas *de rigueur*: no
mud in the proctologist's third eye; no glycol
jellying hís windshield. Now he expatiates.
POSTERITY how daring! Waste of effort?
You may conclude so. I do not
so understand it. You may
write this off, but it shall not be read so.

52

Strange working of the body; how it knows
its own time. Thát after all ⏐ and more—
seventy years near enough—the resin-knurled
damson tree, crookt at black gable-end,
stands in the sight of him departing. LORD ⏐
THOU HAST BEEN OUR DWELLING PLACE—FROM ONE
GENERATION ⏐ TO ANOTHER (*lento*). So barely
out of step ⏐ bow and return. Charles Ives's
Ninetieth Psalm, found late, as grief's thanksgiving;
as full tide with ebb tide, the one in the other,
slow-settling bell arpeggios. Time, here renewed
ás tíme, hów it páces and salútes ús ⏐ in its wáys.

53

Fine figure of a man, say it. Try
this for size. Say it, why are we waiting?
Get stuck in. Hurdy-gurdy the starter
handle to make backfire. Call monthlies
double strength stale *fleurs du mal*. Too close
for comfort, say it, *Herr Präsident*, weep
lubricant and brimstone, wipe yo' smile.
COMPETITIVE DEVALUATION—a great find
wasted on pleasantries of intermission.
Say it: licence to silence; say it: me
Tarzan, you | diva of multiple choice,
rode proud on our arousal-cárrousel.

54

Take it, the plenary immanence, to be
eternal: this passing hence of summer:
and you as being wholly the obscure
origin, the clairvoyance, the giving. *Mein
Ariel, hast du, der Luft nur ist . . . ?* And by
these words the gifted and recovered
cycles of the unstable, sins not counted.
Contemplation as love's estate, wild aster,
with goldenrod, with the still untorn
awnings of sumac. Consider how this sways
argument across the line | if
it ís argument. OH I BELIEVE YOU.

55

As many as the days that were ⏐ of SODOM.
If this is to be exorcism. Is it?
You turn me on. Hoick out another clue.
THE LENGTH OF THE THING. Let them imagine
some signal blessing sent but not received,
saying: I am in the pink. Wish you were here.
In Abraham's tent and bosom. DID YOU EVER . . . ?
I said I believe you AND here I háve you.
Among the ellipses trail-marks cut in salt.
Tristis lupus, I cannot now construe
other than as impeachment. Watch my lips.
This is more end-stopped than usual. WHY?

56

Flanders poppy no trial variant. Does
my bad breath offend you? Pick a name
of the unknown YPRES MASTER as alias.
Abandoned MARK IV tanks, rostered by sex,
Marlbrough s'en va-t-en . . . frozen mud wrestlers
entertaining: dead Jocks. Arrest yourself
for grief of no known cause, excuse me.
A superflux among bit players, which
happens to be the best part: unnatural
wear and tear but finished by Christmas.
Beef of Old England's off. You can eat cake.
YEOMANRY HORSEPLAY FAILS AS LIGHT RELIEF.

57

Show you something. Shakespeare's elliptical
late syntax renders clear the occlusions,
calls us to account. For what is abundance
understand redemption. Who—where—are our
clowns WET 'N' DRY: will the photographs
reveal all? Só hate to be caught in mid-
gesture, you knów thát, noble CARITAS,
proud AMOR—pledge your uncommon thoughts.
See all as miracle, a natural graft,
as mistletoe ravelling the winter boughs
with nests that shine. And some recensions
better than thát I should hope.

58

Better than that I should hópe, assign me
to bond with some other fatedness
coveted as free will. I can read
dry-eyed—C. Brontë cleared it with a word—
Olney's own castaway *en famille*. Manic
depressive, wrote about hares. PERFORCE
hís word. Better than thát I should hope: my
word is my bond, my surety, my entail.
Twelve press-ups at a time; such heaviness
increased like due allowance. *Entre-nous*
the mad are predators. Forgive me. Cry CHILD
OVERBOARD—the self-righting hull shears on.

59

Everyone a self-trafficker. I asked
for stone and so received a toad. Alongside,
low-slung jets blizzard the surface-water,
jockey from gate to air-gate: next the sea-gate
tilts out its lights. Blackness is to be
distinguished from blankness. The Laureates
process blank-faced for you to name them.
Did I sáy another trip ruined by bursts
of atrocious static, England My Country?
Mine, I say, *mine*: damn Skinflint's last onion.
And nów whose England áre you ⏐ but then which
England wére you? Were you ever! NOW THEN!

60

I think now I sháll get through. Even
a bit of a breather. Nothing heavy.
No heavy come-on. On thy way, Friend.
Up the Hill Difficulty. How do I find thee?
That's a good name—APOLLYON. Too many
stuck for a treatise maybe but so what,
Sister Perversity, ANON on his knees,
sinuses choked with shit. Is there anyone
not a promoter of simple gifts? Keep
with it, PILGRIM ⏐ nó more nine days' wonder,
Cambridge, full of thy learning. Flash:
Bucer signs for England—*De Regno Christi*.

61

Open to every season, the known bountiful
or as bare for our good. The frosted mantle
over the shot-tower—spectacular—
vivifies cold; once and for all
resumes its corolla, crowns the instant:
I mean the sun's befogged radiance,
our violent infirmities, our dead.
It is not Ceres' living child I see
broken asprawl inside the wind-tunnel,
from limo to limbo in a soundbite,
fuck-up as obligation. ENGLAND AWAKE.
You fell for Aladdin's Uncle—one of those.

62

Witness the untutored, unchastened heart
labouring with its bereavements—thát's
occupied—of time, service; of reward.
Look at the face! But daughters do forgive
fathers—PORTRAIT OF DINORA—unrivalled
even as shadows. The woman. The man.
Grace before arbitration. Is it
the artist only who gets burnt, unalloyed
unallured TETRAGRAMMATON? You
see, I have this blurred vision of Bomberg,
old, dying, *peon* on donkey, lop-
sided, terrible.

63

Court of Auditors: applause from far back.
Would I have spoken so freely if not
under constraint? EITHER WAY THEY GET YOU.
Providence cited as creditor, who
would credit providence without payment?
Once or twice cheap entr'acte music moves
towards the sublime. Ageing, I am happy.
What price now forgiveness and likelihood?
Togetherness after sixteen years? You're on.
There is a final tableau of discovery
and rehabilitation. Not everything
is as we want it.

64

In for the long haul. Course correction. Go
automatic until relief strikes you: spitted
up to—and into—the caecum. No sign there
of most-favoured malignancy. Meanwhile
the sitar's humming-bird finger-blur—
free in-house video, dizzying
play and replay: life's adjacent realm
with full and frank exchange of love-bites—
how coarse we are, I had forgotten. *Puir
auld sod*. Lift-off but no window. Leibniz's
monad is one thing. One thing or another—
we are altogether something else again.

65

Fragments of short score: inspirational I
find them. Visionary insights also
as they are called. Clouds of dark discernment
part wrath, part thankfulness, the full spectrum
rekindling; the rainbow still to be
fully wrought. Don't say you have forgotten.
I HAVE FORGOTTEN MORE THAN YOU KNOW.
It is not nature but nurture brings
redemption to mind. *Mein Ariel,*
hast du, der Luft nur ist . . . ? So name your own
sentence. Any sentence. You can have
life if you want it ǀ appeal to music.

66

I feel myself the secret keeper of your
engorged smile—this is still my delusion—
Dolores—the sign-language, *bouts-rimés,*
each turn immaculate, drawn, held, on a tight breath,
nothing spoken, the crouch and spatter, each
deferring to the mirror. Never a hair
fetishist I am almost ashamed
to confess; have always envied Füssli's
auto-erotic pencil, self-mastery of abasement.
Nothing between lust and friendship, one gibed,
though not of Füssli. RE-ENACT THE URINE
CEREMONY: OBSCENITY'S ETIQUETTE.

67

Can't do dialogue even when the dramaturge
purposes confrontation. Snatched asides
pass for exchanges. I have composed
clinching *mots de l'escalier* in mid-flight.
The public claims these besieged privities
like, when to act entitled by a laugh;
like, kick yourself for courage, doubling up
as your dead stand-in; like, to go under
only to be insensately revived.
Dolores—LILITH, I should have said—
nothing we did was real. I ask
your pardon. Check my prosthetic tears.

68

Justice: not in order. Valetudinarian
ex-captives to chew dirt. See them sequestered
in alien unforgetting, a lost tribe
whose rites are grief and indignation,
whose speech is primitive, uncomprehending;
incomprehensible, though with a few
loan-words scavenged from Burmese dialects.
The dead can be struck eloquent. These
dying, cannot—shabbily unsorrowed—
unless you call this eloquence. GO ON:
Justice, transparent bale-fire of vanities:
massive, shimmering through incoherence.

69

Collegiality: their grand rule
of unreason, service-formalities
in common disservice. What was I thinking—
Bergmanesque tragic farce? I have come
so far, anarchy must be in it:
flames ransacking the last scene, as by right
of origin and survival; sheer possession,
threatening the silver and private bride.
No final retribution—háve I said that,
and if so, why? Some innocent couple
sleeps through it. Say this was my idea. THIS
WAS MY IDEA.

70

As the train curved into Groton I woke
and looked out for you—whoever you are
or may be—sadly, without desire (poor
mawkish adverb; either milk it or clip it.
Is that machine turned on?) The State is held
to the character of its citizens. Surrogate
is what Í am. They can have my views
on all such matters: the fabrication
of natural light, the poison-runnels
greening with slick. If not hierarchy
then general dynamics. As the train
curved into Groton I looked oút for you.

71

I trust that she's now done with the body
search, close interrogation, the finger-
printing, the restless limbo of the *Quais*,
the depilatory and ritual bath,
the ultimate in cosmetics;
that, for the last time, she has wakened
to cameras, lust, vindictive protocol,
the snarl-ups in the lobby of false friends,
the go-betweens and other betrayers
to public knowledge. I cannot think how
else to commit, commend, her: a botched business,
out of our hands, reduced to the Sublime.

72

Parrot Prophet X—ad lib PRETTY
BLOODY PRETTY BLOODY. Those bloody Scots
basted in contumacy: new Bannockburn,
old dereliction. Sullen Welsh pride,
the carp half-glimpsed, a glow and shadow
deep amid water-smoke, potent, unheld....
Our Irish trespass, not to be thought of.
What phoenix, Coventry—out of whose fire,
heartless Brummagem, Worcester, grace-abandoned,
self-estranged Althorp, grief's interest,
Handelian measures, freedom hardly won,
forsaken in the act? MAKE RESERVATIONS.

73

A set of courtly clogging dances I
fancy him up and doing: kick and shuffle
for solemn cod mugshots, self-artificious
plebeian things of hard edges, effortless
and practised dumb-show. His gifts given us
almost in passing—this is not a problem—
as the dance-master floor-chalks original
steps of memory. It is BEHEMOTH
which, among all his works, most flexes
violence under restraint: this being
created neither tó music, nor
fróm music, nór, altogether, fór silence.

74

Bucer's England—*De regno Christi*—even then
it was not on, not really. The more
you require it, the more it slips from focus,
skews in the frame, the true
commonweal out of true. Bucer knew this,
no-one exempted; nothing of fraudulent
greatness, even so. And Í say: accept
no substitute; but the body's natural
immunity to reason you máy suffer;
at best by proxy. End of scholastic
disputation. Now the theatricals:
enter SCATOLOGY, *dancing, with* DESIRE.

75

From your vantage, with your parallel latitude,
it may be possible to gaze across—
there's a taped commentary. Call the place
ETRURIA and watch me signal you,
rehearsed, miming in character, as one
taught to bear up ǀ but nó goód at it.
The bearings must be out, though. Look, we've slipped
two generations, perhaps three; a scene,
noble, sorrowful, in recognition:
stable- or smithy-yard, rough-surfaced
with dirt and clinker-rammel, stomped
by snurring drayhorses.

76

O CLEVER Memory, to take my name
for acts indifferent and true to type.
How formally this begins. There are accidents
you can see coming, whose actual
speed of occurrence is in slow motion.
This is not one. *Ben trovato*, jaws clamp
shut on floating perception and hang there:
now gaffed and despatched. PISCATOR
the ever watchful, curd-faced LADY LUCK.
Just so I worked the celebrated
elaborate Italian locks, the self-barbed
open-to-shut *concetti* of blind eyes.

77

Revive the antimasque of baroque
methane: time and death—that rot, a fake
Shakespearean girning, a mouth's pained O,
the soul exhaled as a perfect smoke-ring,
clownish efforts made to bind the corpse-jaw,
skeletal geezers like kids again with bad
joke-book toothache, Dr Donne's top-knot shroud,
coroneted bag-pudding (*show-off!*). Face
the all but final degradation—FAMED
PILLAR OF THE CHURCH A STIFF—reorder
the Jacobean Sermon, re-set Burton's
Anatomy, endorse the Resurrection.

78

That's great they say nów I have come thís far.
But still, my brothers and sisters, baroque
ís beautiful. You also have beauty.
Why could I not have foreseen this: we
were meant for each other. Consensual
the gifts of sex, of oratory, in both
unequalled. Ogled by reborn commerce,
nó, I will nót speak straightly but abide
my chainhood on the block. As I can show you:
the bronze equestrian Union trumpeter,
coated with a green patina of swamps,
up from the Wilderness: léss strange now than wé are.

79

Sleep as and when you can. Write this.
We are almost there. *Mein Ariel, hast du,
der Luft nur ist . . .?* Captive, regain
immortality's incarnate lease. Endure
vigil's identity with entrapment.
There are worse obsessions. YOU HAVE MY LEAVE,
GO NOW, free spirit shaped by captivity,
forsaken in the telling, so to speak,
the end of contemplation: overnight
the first frail ice edging across the pond,
self-making otherness by recognition
even as I describe it.

80

Ice—*augenblick*—four chordal horns—baritone
invocation of mute powers. The grammar
of the centurion, formed to obedience,
pitched in disorder, unfocused zealotry. THIS
MAY BE INSUBSTANTIAL. RESUBMIT.
The nadir of your triumph to do duty
in place of outright failure, erosions,
worn synapses. Even today the light
is beautiful, you can hardly avoid
seeing that: shadows, reflections, on reeds
and grasses, deepening visibility;
the mind's invisible cold conflagration.

81

Again: the saltmarsh in winter. By dawn
drain-mouths grow yellow beards. Old man's duty,
vigilance so engrained, shabby observance,
dirty habit, wavelets chinning the shore-line.
Rich in decrepit analogues, he sees:
archipelagos, collops of sewage,
wormed ribs jutting through rime. Sun-glanced,
it is striking, vacant, a far consequence,
immaterial reflection beautifully
primed, the decommissioned lighthouse
no longer geared to darkness with clock-shifts
of steady alignment.

82

Plutarchan parallels to special order.
End of a calendar year. The double
lives of lost veterans haunt me. How much
further does this take them? I should guess
nowhere by you, openers of the new age,
winners all ways, fawning with sharp elbows,
teeth, to make *lebensraum*, pledging dead loves
to the brokers of Pity, pitiless
resurrection men. O bad luck, Anna,
Boris; bad luck, Dmitri, Laika: you missed us.
Next year same time, same place. Let's all retrench,
get together for shared únrecognition.

83

Of an age to lapse or revert, bring back
Künstlerschuld, regrettable souvenirs.
Long undetected or overlooked, false
claims of veteran status finally
hauled to account. Even so, childish
anger at the injustice of it. *Jedermann*,
call me *Jedermann*, for the seductive
pleasure of strange mouthings. Say *den Haag*:
heavy old-gold Rembrandts, Dutch-Jewish,
by chance of bestowal: bankrupts, timely
survivors. Making, breaking, things familiar.
At twenty, ignorance was my best judgement.

84

Had none or made none. This may as well
tick over, keeping itself vacant
asking for it, conviction. Not transferrable.
Sit as beggars in justice—pardon
the officialdom. And there you háve me.
WELCOME TO THE PEACE PALACE, banging
carillons en suite. As I observed—
twenty-three, *supra*—the Dutch are heroes
living as they have to. Easier said.
I can't say better. Speak as you find.
Whát do Í find? A good question. OVER
TO YOU, BRER FIRE, SENATOR, MISS WORLD.

85

Ruin smell of cat's urine with a small gin.
Develop the anagram—care to go psychic?
Psych a new age, the same old dizzy spell.
Force-field of breakdown near the edge. Now
to work | backwards not like breaking down.
Seek modem-demo, memos to dawn-broker,
duty-savant. CODEBREAKERS our salvation.
Logos of futures, world-scam, meniscus
brinking, about to break, unbroken. Science
not beyond reason. Ultimate hope. Take,
e.g., Democracy—or try to take it—
as cryptic but convenient acronym.

86

He voids each twelve-line block | a head
solemnly breaking water. Not at this time
Poseidon, but convulsively mortal,
spouting, eyes bulging, green man. Say again,
care to be psychic and by how much.
Is there ever a good time? What's on offer?
NIGHT AND FOG named as the losing answer
out of thousands submitted: albeit unjust
to slapdash courage. Not all is ruin
if you can hold a final salvo. Rouse
Hipper, advise floundering Jellicoe, make
signal of requiem, cast wreaths of iron.

87

If I could once focus—Rimbaud's career,
Nigerian careerists—on a single factor,
self-centre of anomie, I might present
to the examiners in whose shadow I am,
a plainly disordered thesis which they
must receive to reject: indifferent
drummers-up for all markets. BIAFRA RULES.
That long-dead young Igbo master who transferred—
so abruptly—his panache and command-flag
from Latin eclogue, from Ovid's *Amores*,
to POLITICS, ESPIONAGE, AND TRAVEL died
with or without judgement. Style undisputed.

88

Night and fog it is then, comrades, *Nacht
und Nebel*: goes always for the throat—
pharynx, jugular. Once for all costs
of live demonstration waived. A few
dead women late admitted heroes
on generous terms. Sign here with broken
hands patched up for the occasion. Thank you
Odette, Violette, no further questions
commensurate with your knowledge. Stand at ease
against the wall. Unflattering photographs,
almost without exception, cracked and stained.
Darkest at finest hour. Add salt to taste.

89

Write out a cause: crazed sanity, untreated
logomachic sarcoma. Unveiled stuff
of grand malpractice. Parts of the interlocked
post-doctrinal foul-up. Cheers!—Augustine's
fellow who could fart, with most sweet savour,
angels' song: tones passing as angels' song.
Cross-reference ODOUR OF SANCTITY and run.
I give you ten yards cross-examination,
thwart man without allies (with friends, yes).
Don't overstretch it, asshole. Don't say TIME
WIPES ALL THINGS CLEAN. Don't let them hear CUR
DEUS HOMO—thát kind of filthy talk.

90

Mediation means business, the apostles' jets
muster in strength, their afterburners
glowing post-prandial cigars. Mere duty
so empowered it is like furlough
with millionaires' playthings, a galaxy
of voices, leaping ⏐ static. Animus
is what I home on, even as to pitch.
You can say thát again. Or not at all.
Split second's chance allowed, no second chance.
My God, he can pack it in—suddenly
come to his temple, its standing ⏐ here destroyed.
(Rum place for a cigar, *Herr Präsident* . . .)

91

Thís lays it ón ⎟ a shade: in the arms
of his claustral love. A pun, then, *arms*? He's that
sort of a mind. Another one on *lays*:
lays it ⎟ on a sháde—are you still with me
yet wandering, blocked words hung round neck
on a noose of twine: his own name included.
Not the usual idyll, dazed ingenuities
filling the vacant days. A well-trained child
yawning at the recital. *Mein Ariel,*
hast du, der Luft nur ist . . .? Teach patience,
SISTER PERVERSITY; how I desired your
variant dolours. FRIGID BITCH DOLORES!

92

Either the thing moves, RAPMASTER, or it
does not. I disclaim spontaneity,
the appearance of which is power. I will
match you fake pindaric for trite
violence, evil twin. Here I address
fresh auditors: suppose you have gone the full
distance. Take up—on line—the true nature
of this achievement. Prove that you have fixed
the manifold. Dismiss the non-appearance
of peculiar mercies. Presume to examine
the brain in its electric cauldron
regarding the Brazen Head.

93

Pardon is incumbent, RAPMASTER, or it
is not. On balance I think not. So
get in line, SNUFF-MAN—with PRINCE OF FEATHERS—
PRATFALL his oppo—mourning Persephone
lost in September tribute, England's daughter.
Hack violence to yourself, brief miracle
confessions overridden. None of these
gifts us self-knowledge: she is beyond it
and you are nowhere, spielers of abuse.
Slow burn, slow double-take. The Northampton
MADONNA AND CHILD. She there? Can it be
the grief matronal? I shall return to that.

94

Hopefully, RAPMASTER, I can take stock
how best to out-rap you. Like Herod
raging in the street-pageants, work the crowd.
Bit short of puff these days. Swig any one
elixir to revive the *membrum*. Squeeze
both tubes for instant bonding. IT'S HIS CALL.
In the Algarve, places like that, the Brits
are heroes living as they have to.
Where áre we? Lourdes? Some sodden mystery tour.
What do you mean | a break? Don't give me that.
Great singer, Elton John; though, Christ
Almighty, even the buses are kneeling!

95

Politics, RAPMASTER, must be a part
of our conformable mystery, this
twinship of loathing and true commonweal.
As yoú haunt Tudor polity so I
re-gaze the gaze of Holbein, my drawn face
a breath, a dust, of chalk-bloom; pettish
client between porch and easel. Skelton Laureate
was a right rapper: outdance yoú with your shades
any day. And is gone. Moriscos, hatchet-men,
yoú would have been and are. *De*
Regno Christi: breeding up good and ill,
breaker of Eurostallions.

96

Tune up an old saw: the name-broker
is carnifex. Forms of enhanced
interrogation by the book. Footnotes
to explain BIRKENAU, BUCHENWALD, BURNHAM
BEECHES, DUMBARTON OAKS, HOLLYWOOD.
Masters of arts toiling as they are bent
to Saturn's justice in praetorian bunkers,
pourrying tortured figures from foundry sand
with suspect blood and their own fecal matter.
As many days as are the days of Sodom:
count all one hundred and twenty, then shriek
I'M COMING.

97

In re: radical powerlessnesss of God
to be reconceived. Not for millennial
doom-mood, nihilism's palindrome,
but for what it is and we are: no use
against backed-up inertia, ignorance,
proclivity. What was it like before
Adam made incest with the red earth
his matrix? Their ruination, litter,
our sacred sites for depravity, cells
of Moloch, Baal's palaces: the díscharge
of violence filling the screen—projectile
vomiting en masse.

98

TAKE TWO: the Northampton MADONNA AND CHILD:
an offering up of deep surfaces; chalk
sleepers from the underground risen to this.
(Moore also became a figure.) Her bulk
and posture, load-bearing right hip-bone,
inward, understood, projected, wrought.
The child's face, though [|] prim, sweetened, incurious.
Absent here even the unfocused selving
close to vacuity, Stanley Spencer's fixation,
crazed-neighbourly, which ís a truth of England
alongside manifest others,
an energy altogether of our kind.

99

How many more times? Customs not customs!
Fajuyi was dead by then, though Major Nzeogwu
still had his eyes. Can't you read English? What
do I mean by praise-songs? I could weep.
This is a praise-song. These are songs of praise.
Shall I hyphenate-fór-you? Syntax
is a dead language, your incoherence
the volatility of a dead age—
vintage Brook Farm, adulterate founders' bin;
and you the *faex Romuli* the dregs.
AUTHENTIC SELF a stinker; pass it on,
nasum in ano, the contagious circles.

100

Onto these near-Stygian sets the PEOPLE
enters and is discovered: courtesy
Balzac, courtesy Honoré Daumier. Additional
acknowledgements to Balzac, apologies
to Daumier. Could keep this up all night
rigid with *joie de vivre.* The mountebank
is a poor honest fellow with a drum
and a kitchen chair, a coral-boned
tumbler for a child. The guignol
carries more weight and is, I suspect,
the better artist, fixing on these faces
torpor, avidity: master of light and shade.

101

Virtue is all in timing; it cán be put
down to instinctive balance: the group leans
into the camera, the unstable darkness.
Let us interpret their eyes, their uncondoned
self-recognition. Look, to be lost's as good
as being tethered: Oates míght have been found
dead on all fours behind the tent. But they
sat measuring posthumous averages
of bitter legend. The Great War did not
occur to them. In time Shackleton came
close to missing it and was frozen out:
far off the glacier floated ⏐ a white feather.

102

A pale full sun, draining its winter light,
illuminates the bracken and the bracken-coloured
leaves of stubborn oak. Intermittently
the wind spoors over salt inlets
and the whiteish grass between the zones,
apprehension's covenant. Could this
perhaps end here: a *Paradiso*
not accounted for, unaccountable,
eternally in prospect, memory's blank
heliograph picketing the lost estate?
AND ís this vision enough, unnamed, unknown
bird of immediate flight, of estuaries?

103

BY AND LARGE: after the renowned, retired,
circus troupe of that name. Cross-
dressing in mid-twist, salvation in mid-fall.
No better choice. Go for baroque. Cán you
máke it? Questions, questions. Show me a mark
of interrogation, I'll show yoú my
exclamation points. Fly me! LOST THE PEACE
BY SUPERHUMAN SKIVING: true or false?
Three out of ten: brave cockney rhyming
slang on an epic scale! Across the board
the Brits are heroes: twenty-four-hour
convenience machismo—IN YOUR FACE!

104

V. poór linguist, *nota bene*: loved
Latin, German, for love of the uncanny—
unheimlich. What's weird in Latin? Inuit
not too secure these days. Stubborn
metaphysics calls for German above all,
über alles. Where do I go, *Leiermann*?
Where cán I go? Soul-brother, show a light!
EQUITY, ELIGIBILITY, CULPABILITY,
heard through a cloud—acoustic din—the rage;
that THEATRE OF VOICES, noble íf nót
ridiculous. Forsaken in the telling—
pelagic diasporas [LEAVE UNFINISHED]

105

Absolutely untouched by the contingent,
as he believes he ís, master
academician of rotor-wisdom,
indispensable, self-made, *thaumaturge*,
until dispensed with, disposed of. THAT RIGHT?
What is the present standing of injustice
among those who know? Would we, without Churchill,
have concluded a Vichy peace? That's
hard to say. Daventry and Droitwich
are still transmitting: cries of disbelief,
recognizance, evasions that return
with a comet's faithfulness of assignation.

106

DE MORTUIS—bitterness of those journeys:
the rail-ice thawed by acetylene
and coke-braziers; chipped-free semaphore
arms tilting to right of way. *Arbeit*,
heraús, were nót words Í knew in those
deep years of the dead: the eight-coupled
coal engines, shaken viaducts, compounded
smoke of manufacture and destruction.
If you can still remember, put me down
as terror-stricken, unteachable.
Or hold me to my first promise. *Sadly*
I máy show up in time for your last laugh.

107

Look on the bright side. WHADDYA WHADDYA
call thís—script or prescription? Cite your own
stiff going-price. Dysfunctional [|] THIS
ALSO IS THOU, NEITHER IS THÍS THOÚ.
Act through a few poor mime faces; pose late
reflexion. As not unreflecting try
posterity. Become vindictive in self-
vindication? Fall then victor among
the secondary infections. Claimed as latest
pastmaster of the grand infarctions
caught in mid-stride, savaged beyond speech
(Pray for us sinners) YOU THÉRE [|] LADY?

108

Not love even, airhead; some *tendresse*
of creatures, young at age. Whát do you knów!
It's better inside but don't mind clothes.
Share, not nothing but not much: THE POLISH
RIDER is wonderful. When was he
ever in Poland? Even these late
colloquies are fictions. No more games
I can imagine. Responsible
or not, I will hold you as if for once
I would be held ín you. Who is this?
Come here nearer the light. Are yoú
the Shunammite woman?

109

Oh, yoú again, DOLORES! I hate shows
of past disaffection; hate-comedies
knocking perverse sainthood. Did the socks
not rot on those feet: for ús beggars?
Thorough-bloodied his potsherds. But new
era, new hero. Am I in error here?
Waked Erin, too—that ís, herself the grave
setting of comedy. Stout-hearted filmscript
charms loot from Lotto. *Bodhráns* pitch me wild
with dancing excitement. Confirm that? I
sháll | in closed-circuit confession. AND práy
for John Reidy otherwise Seán Ó Riada.

110

Ám discomfited | not now being able
to take as fact even my own dying—
the apprehension or prospect thereof. My
faux-legalisms plead to be vouched for,
even if unwitnessed, as are many things
I could indicate but not show. What I cán
stand are unfixable fell-gusts ratching
the cranky chimney-cowls; their smokes blown
hárd dówn or tugged ragged; shade and shine
the chapel wind-vane's blistery fake gold.
I imagine yoú see this also: such
is the flare through memory of desire.

III

Mid-stride say I eject from the planet—
if only in spirit—though without notice,
though fully housebroken, drop a dead
weight, shocking, malodorous (draw *pudor*
over it, let it lie) say: I know myself
in some form beholden to grand Orion
long contemplated for yoúr sake, way out
as you can be; to Andromeda in full
rig, exactly as GURNEY last saw her,
Cassiopeia, her constancy; to the small
unnamed constellation I get to name
Constellation Kreisau.

112

Eight-block coda to the CITY OF GOD—
don't tempt me, Tempter, demon overreacher,
or not in my own voice. It was agreed
my topos is SODOM, grandiose
unoriginal. I woúld be myself
stuck in some other *bolgia* yet scarcely
recall what it was I promised, or even
what promise ís, damned liar that I am:
trying on broken accents, reading Dante
as if for the first time. This ís the first
time, better admit it. If back on standard
self-therapy so much the worse.

113

What is a *vitrine*—how does it connect
with the world of ANSELM KIEFER? This
is what we have come to: ash and shivered
glass. Memorialized dead-centres without
focus. Atrocious glamour grime-plastered,
corrosive, corroded; road salts, metals.
Single abrupt frame of violent
disassembly: identical frame pulled
back into being. In the obscure
soteriologies of these things, the lines
created are destructive and vital.
Auction. Autopsy. Scrap-avatar.

114

When all else fails CORINTHIANS will be read
by a man in too-tight shoes. No matter. You
shall not degrade or debauch the word LOVE
beyond redemption. As she redeems it.
Six times this trip I have brought round my wreath
to the vulgar gates. Let Thames take over,
not grandiosely, our plebeian grief.
Evangelical high prelates caught
disarrayed in full raiment. Guardsmen
make heroic bearers: even their wry-necks
crick in alignment. Comedienne to act
SORRY for hostile nation. CURTAINS. CREDITS.

115

Where CODA to the CITY OF GOD? Restore
what decrepit organ? Who has a mind
to improvise? You say it is all
improvisation—*dú, mein Ariel.*
Flit off, there's a love. Under half-dead
wistaria, crudely cut back, the stone
lintel, newly snail-cobbled, glitters
with their mucilage. Not bad as an aubade;
not quite the final gasp. Extrapolate
LAST POST into reveille. Re evil—
relive, revile, revalue | self-
revelation. EASY NOW, SOUL-BROTHER!

116

How could you have lived through him so long?
Don't take it for an accusation, you
write as if sleep-walking. I never
walk in my sleep. I fall off chairs. But,
yes, it's a lengthy haul to the diploma.
Self-correction without tears: see me reverse
tango this juggernaut onto the road.
TEN DEGREES BACKWARD, Isaiah says.
Ezekiel's the better mechanic but less—
you know—beautiful! All eighteen
wheels engaging the hardtop and no
body-damage to speak of. RIDE IT, PREACHER!

117

No nearer Jerusalem. Self-justifying
hatred taken for all its worth. Worth what?
Just as unjust. I know the game,
for and against. Poetics of self-rule.
Why nót twist Luther [|] practised self-parodist?
Justified self-accusation at list price.
CAPITALS, STAGE DIRECTIONS AND OTHER
FORMS OF SUBPOENA. *Italics*, words
with which I—*sometimes*—surprise *myself*.
Unapproachable City of God. *Lost*
estate (WESLEY?) [|] though if the towers stand [|] wróng
way úp [|] it's probably not a mirage.

118

Inconstant even in this the dead
heart of the matter: laughter no joy.
Thin veil of libel up for bids. You áre
wantonly obscure, *man sagt*. ACCESSIBLE
traded as DEMOCRATIC, he answers
as he answers most things these days, easily.
Except in thís one craft he shows himself
open to a fault, shaken by others' weeping;
duty's memorialist for the known-unknown
servants of Empire, for such unburied:
the spirit's gift upheld, impenetrable;
the bone-cage speared by lilies of the veldt.

119

Shambles of peripeteia to discover
history if not to make it. Loud laughter
track poór compensation for the bad show.
This needs working on but then who needs it?
AMICUS, his own worst enemy? Make a good
ending, as they used to say. So give me
your prescription for the good life and I
will tear thróugh it. Dissever sensual
from sensuous, licence from freedom; choose
between real status and real authority.
Clever move that—Catullus's sure-
footed imitation [|] of the Limper.

120

English Limper [|] after the English Sapphic. This
has to be seen. But what a way to go.
Given a free mínd Í would present Daumier's
effigies as supreme honours: gouged,
wrenched, and sagging clay; self-made
corruption ravaged, inexhaustible,
FUROR's own purity. *English*, you clown—
líke at the ALDWYCH. So what cognómen
will become me at last? O TIME-LIFE, do
try to be reasonable; you háve the power.
At least pass me the oxygen. Too late.
AMOR. MAN IN A COMA, MA'AM. NEMO. AMEN.

THE ORCHARDS
OF SYON

To my children and grandchildren

Later, but before I had become a student of theology, that truth of which I have spoken struck me like a radiant light of grace. It seemed that I saw, though at a distance, within the image or form of Truth (this being wholly transparent), God's grace already present in time as in nature, before any good works existed.

THOMAS BRADWARDINE, *De Causa Dei*

Tom Brangwen's mood of inspiration began to pass away. He forgot all about it, and was soon roaring and shouting with the rest . . . Only the bride and bridegroom sat with shining eyes and strange, bright faces, and scarcely sang, or only with just moving lips . . .

The five men went out. The night was flashing with stars. Sirius blazed like a signal at the side of the hill. Orion, stately and magnificent, was sloping along . . .

'It's a fine night,' said Tom.

D. H. LAWRENCE, *The Rainbow*

Everything was at rest, free, and immortal.

THOMAS TRAHERNE, *Centuries of Meditations*

I

Now there is no due season. Do not
mourn unduly. You have sometimes said
that I project a show more
stressful than delightful. Watch my hands
confabulate their shadowed rhetoric,
gestures of benediction; maledictions
by arrangement. For us there is
no deadline, neither for stand nor standoff.
I can prolong the act at times
to rival Augustine, this shutter
play among words, befitting
a pact with light, the contra-Faustian heist
from judgement to mercy.
I shall promote our going and coming,
as shadows, in expressive light; take
my belief, if only through a process
taxing salvation—may I proceed?—
not merely to divert with faith and fiction,
to ease peregrination, what a life!
Has it ever been staged
seriously outside Spain, I mean
La vida es sueño? Tell me, is this the way
to the Orchards of Syon
where I left you thinking I would return?

II

Something escapes committal; in my name
recalls itself to being. Mystic
durables are not the prime good, nor
lust the sole licenser. Shakespeare
clearly heard many voices. No secret:
voicing means hearing, at a price a gift,
affliction chiefly, whereas despair
clamps and is speechless. Donne in his time
also heard voices he preserved on wax
cylinders. Some of these I possess
and am possessed by. Persistence tells,
even when you are past speech, gurneyed
from *Death's Duel*. As for posterity,
whose lips are sealed, I do prefer
Polish to Czech though, not speaking
either language, I am unable to say
why. Starting with these,
I wish I understood myself
more clearly or less well.
Go back to cast off several lives. Find
all have godlike elements
divided among them: such suffering,
you can imagine, driven, murderous,
albeit under notice of grace.

III

La vida es sueño as shadow-play. This
takes me back. Genuflect to the gutted
tabernacle, no-one will wonder in what sense
words are consequential to the cartoon.
How is this life adjudged
derelict, a stress-bearer since Eden?
Think ahead: your name
finally out of alignment, its
dates crammed in; they might be self-inflicted
wounds of morose delectation
borne lightly out of primal throes, a last
remittance from doomed childhood.
Unwise or wise choices do make
gymnasts of anchorites, if that
means what Í mean. You say you have me there
which is all we have here, in the Orchards
of Syon that are like Goldengrove
season beyond season. Neither day nor hour
to determine the tinder
chemistry of exchange. If I were you, would
you believe? Ripe vastage of estate,
the Fall revived with death-songs. Set this down
as anomy's coherence, and the full-
blooded scrub maples torch themselves in the swamp.

IV

We are—what, all of us?—near death. So wave
me your solution. *Cupio dissolvi*,
Saul's vital near-death experience more
sandblasted than lasered. *Beam
us up, Asrael.* High talk, dissolution
expansive, all pervasive; here it coils
back into density: dark angel, fused,
rubberoid, shrunk, foetal, as though raked
from Zeppelin ashes. Immortal
Death, lovely suppliant!
Orphée I saw six times in the one week.
Du calme counsels the Princess, Maria
Casarès, newly *enceinte* with sorrow
not hers alone. Her tragic shadow—pulled
through—down and across—is swept
off the blank end wall. Truth not so hot,
unobliging, even at the last count.
I understand Hell's surreal ruins to be
those of the blitzed Académie de St Cyr,
with wind machines off camera, all elements
miming a solemn music.
Bite on yr death wish. As for faith,
expose it finally, like ignorance.
Coming or going, do the circuits again.

V

Baroque says nothing broken, though to break
off labours the point,
and it judders and all.
Nonetheless I would clinch this
as music's invocation, the tuned
drums *glissando*. You
can elide changes of pressure. I believe
creation ís self-healing, a self-stanched
issue of blood. It is also
furtherance of slow exile, but enjoy—
best to enjoy—riding that *vague*.
Requite self-envying, to eat the heart out
for the heart's satisfaction, is this
wisdom? Well, as the wise man said,
I know it when I see it. So much
of time is rubble. Under the sky's
great clearances, not oúr time only.
How beautiful the world unrecognized
through most of seventy years, the may-tree filling
with visionary silent laughter. *Comme si
l'aubépine*—Frénaud—*était un présage.*
The hawthorn all the more fulfilling its beauty.
Comme si les dieux nous avaient aimés.
As if the gods even now had faith in us.

VI

I know breakthrough as I tell
the dream surpassed. *The Art of Fugue* resembles
water-springs in the Negev. No
longer much to write home about,
endurances give us forty years
post-visionary so far. Weak fulfilment
while the joke empties. This is a joke?
Not when ajar. *Adieu, mon capitaine*,
go spare, go Immelmann, spared flamer,
straight through the climacteric, no avoidance.
In threads of chaos anarchy remains
the cryptic absolute whose clue is reason,
lost achievements, music lost among them,
deeper than we imagined, protracted
jealous exhaustion holding the floor.
Applaud, won't you, if only first time round,
and I alone escaped to tell thee. Don't
abreact to all blind self-exposure
permitted the Resistance. Heavenly music!
As order moves by instinct I say trust
faith so far as it goes, or as far as you
can hold its attention. Cite Emmanuel:
the man of sorrows whose blood burns us.
Le misericordieux qui nous brûle le sang.

VII

Our fealties taken to be your places
of refuge and defence. Author? Author
is all one word, like Faculties. Can you
receive me? Unwise to make wise choices
too early. Incorrigible in any case
the human spirit or its spin-offs,
cogent, unreadable, and at some
personal cost a public nuisance:
not ineradicable but not soon
put down or uprooted. Best early flowering
or in the sere. Music arguably
not implicated in the loss of Eden,
held to its resolution. No
question an affirmation. Tell him he ís
alive—someone—and responsible. He may
respond to that, as to other electrodes,
as Lear to the sour-sweet music of viols,
as some to oils of unction or to Gospel.
Tune him to Gospel: *Over my head*
I hear music, music in the air. That
Gospel? Súre that Gospel! Thát sure
Gospel music in my head. Oh my sole
sister, you, little sister-my-soul,
this mý Gospel, thís sure músic in mý head.

VIII

No mystery I tell you, though in the first
instance it ís a gift, one that you owe me,
the square-stemmed woundwort I have been brought
to consider, precious as peppercorn
once was. No description
merely for beauty's sake, so Flaubert said,
or wounded Maupassant, or someone poisonous.
You owe me, Albion, I should have added
in Gurney's name not mine. Let them be:
tenacity of accent, leaching phosphates,
stringy Welsh poppy, its alien yellow. Is it
anything of significance that I
ceased to attend? Headlands are where ploughs turned
back over English durance. As I recall.
The labours of the months are now memory,
indigent wordplay, stubborn, isolate
language of inner exile.
The curlew's pitch distracts us from her nest.
But: end this for all in some shape other
than vexed bafflement; each triangular
wall-cope cladded with tight moss
springy as a terrier's pelt, buttonhole
emerald polypodae, sprung tremblers
within the burring air of the fell?

IX

The year rounds, takes fragments round with it. Some
tryst this is, image-conscious iconoclast!
The well-worn pattern, familiar abutments,
abraded angles, in the nature of limestone,
unfinished to perfection. Say something, you
have a name for it. Curlews on call,
high and abroad, to be identified
quartering the topmost fields; and other
alarm cries, known but not placed, *chich
chich, chich chich*. Penumbrate, a lily
distinctly shines, talisman
to that which is key-cold ín me, and sealed.
Could be haemony, from some remote
and gracious fable, upholding the rod
or stem of sharp judgement, finally spared.
Are you still with us, spirit of difficult
forgiveness íf I may so term you? The man
is old; it is more than age he girns for.
And Í said: is there anything you think
you should tell me? Was there a mirror
and did it breathe cold speculation?
He is knackered and there are no
schemes to revive him. The year unlocks,
hunkers, swings, its anniversary-round.

X

Sleep to incubate diamond. What a find,
a self-awarded *donnée* if ever
I knew one. If that one was ever you,
wrestle, wrestle with me, my love, my dirty
fighter. I can't say much
plainer than that. *T'souviens-toi*
Tom-mee? Tom Wyatt, his lute and grating,
his torturing, tortured friends.
I place myself in a seven-year pre-
survival bracket, with options. Nod
if you can't speak and let me charge it
to my own account. The Lambeth
Prophecies, The Good Friday Agreement.
Even now I confess
difficulty in pronouncing such words
as absolution. Suggested manual
of handsignals might work the trick.
Strophe after strophe. *Achilles*
from *Ajax*: power-loss imminent, the split
voice-tube welts blood. Dead Tragedy threatening,
death of Comedy is perhaps a worse
dereliction. Strophe after strophe
ever more catastrophic. Did I say
strophe? I meant salvo, sorry.

XI

Begin with golden curtains; sometimes helps
to anticipate THE END. How did they make
insouciant comedy so like innocence?
By way of Ealing, charm in confusion
through to last checkpoints. Impudent,
feckless. Watch them frogmarched off.
The Day of Judgement dire codicil
to human mood and thought; elect
doctrine on show, its common other side
exposed in saturnalia. I salute
your good self—the stout party—bounding
egalitarian cockiness its *forte*,
sensual, unfallen. Dreams have charted
levels of sleep both complex and perplexing
I understand. It's a safe bet we're all
potentially impotent. Again, you coúld
say that I give myself
to well-failed causes. If this failed
to make the last connection I'd be sorry
from my own viewpoint, rarely now entranced
by calf love, light-fingered cockneys. Pimlico
is not Silvertown though,
on the screen, it might appear so. Exit—
through heavy resistant side-doors—in a daze.

XII

Might gain eras of promise, collages
of dashed peace, many-headed the field
rose, dog rose, tossing in bright squalls,
all things self-verifying. A ferrous
atmospheric tang between lightning-bouts
has similar potencies, its presentiments
in the instant abundance, superflux,
familiar chill inspiration, self-
charged shock beyond shock. Show how many
succeed, rising again undiscovered,
turning at a breath: exhalation,
threshold and lintel, the unknown
to be entered, yet to be desired;
on a timekeeper's schedule if need be.
Exhalation ah, not inspiration! the Orchards
of Syon exhaling green into gold,
gold to candescent red. Like ancient
rhetoric, both florid and threadbare,
showing the *stemma*. Light-endowed
among the natural shades and shadows; heavy-
browed barbed rugosa, rain-hackled, a streaming
instant unreconciled, magnificently
thrown off—the coda,
the invoked finality, the setting-out.

XIII

No: blessing not mercy. Not that I care
to chance it. Unless there glints our ransom.
Centuries of failed initiates exclaim
against these equities. Whatever
your name is, leaden Mercurius.
Let me review a sometime common
standing or vantage. Patchy weather, quick
showers gusting the fields like clouds of lime.
You thought us held by favours: see above.
Such are the starts of memory, abrupt
blessing slid from confusion. Await
new-fangled light, the slate roofs briefly
caught in scale-nets of silver, then
sheened with thin oils. These signals
I take as apprehension, new-aligned
poetry with truth, and Syon's Orchards
uncannily of the earth.
Jefferies' *ancient sunlight*, Tarka-man
perhaps turning more profit by the phrase.
But pass me over, angel. I've recast
my furthest revelation; it's as much
as you have witnessed, much as I have told:
a massive, shedding, insubstantial substance
blurred and refocused, blurred afresh by rain.

XIV

The fell, through brimming heat-haze, ashen grey,
in a few hours changes to graphite, coral,
rare Libyan sand colour or banded spectrum.
Distant flocks merge into limestone's half-light.
The full moon, now, rears with unhastening speed,
sketches the black ridge-end, slides thin lustre
downward aslant its gouged and watered scree.
Awe is not peace, not one of the sacred
duties in mediation. Memory
finds substance in itself. Whatever's brought,
one to the other, masking and unmasking,
by each particular shift of clarity
wrought and obscurely broken-in upon,
of serene witness, neither mine nor yours,
I will ask bristling centaury to translate.
Saved by immersion, sleep, forgetfulness,
the tinctured willow and frail-textured ash,
untrodden fern-sheaves, a raw-horned oak,
the wavering argents in the darkened river.
Later again, far higher on the fell,
a solitary lamp, *notturna lampa*,
night's focus focusing, Leopardi saw,
himself a stranger, once, returning late
from some forsaken village festival.

XV

Nothing untimely, since we are all
in time checked at dispersal, possibly
for keeps. *La vida es sueño*? I ought
to read it, before they say I haven't.
Memory proves forgetting. Take gipsylike
klezmer, soul music
not everywhere unheard, not at all times
accusingly silent. O Queen of Heaven,
now no wonder
description is trial being of the person
always on call, always answerable,
a witness that can barely be suppressed:
try loyalty or some such common oath.
But having to wake up and always
in a different place, always to the same
postlude of nightmare. *Crimen* is not
the root, *kómē* is your coiffure of fire,
martyrs who reap the flames. Presentable
tribute to the passing down of kings,
Poiesis a sufficient act; I almost
forgot to say this. Otherwise
the transient ever-repeated dream,
the all-forgetful. *La vida es sueño*
or something other. Other, that is, than death.

XVI

Cassandra at twenty, thanks to Ronsard. Or
reshape a clause from Petrarch's book, his thought
wedged in the solid nature of the world
like a doorstop or indeed a dossier.
Expatiate on this, or say *La vita*
nuova the limit. Or change views entirely.
Deep-rucked topsoil where brick lorries turn; Jim
Brindley's iron and stone; Boulton's coin-press;
Baskerville cutting, setting, his plain
and ornamental types; artificers'
resounding mastery of things hard laboured.
My masterwork this patched-up exhibition
and national treasure, memorial
of a non-event, our absurd love
put here to confront us—you can describe it
or I shall—
pace your half-provoking dismayed mirth.
Others such as we were and are themselves
still of sound mind.
Leave undefeated losers to make good.
Life's fatal dance moves as a simple
covenant with time, the circuits of our choice.
How would yoú stress Pavese's axiom—
lavorare stanca—work till you drop?

XVII

Tri-towers, Christ-silos, rise from, retract
into, the broad Ouse levels. Roadside poppies,
hedged bindweed, still beautiful. The kempt fields
basking; intense the murmur of full summer,
more growl than murmur: coast-traffic snarled,
snarling. Hawks over the dual carriageways.
I've jolted from northward across the moors,
not entirely at peace. Memoranda for horizons
in travail—spirit-levels—steadiness
of outlook all too readily measured.
Broadly, I have the measure of myself,
mechanically at bay. I'd not resurrect
Goldengrove, other than as a grove in Syon:
sustainable anomaly, so I
can tell you, though too easily said.
Tommies' lore, re crucifixes and the like;
Tennyson's wild expenditure of bells;
suffering—Batty's—his queer
politics; Owen transfixed by eros:
my difficulties are not with their
forever-earnest speech. The chorus
lines of road-rage shunt to yet more delay.
Masked somewhere, on one side or the other,
the time-struck Minster doles greed by the clock.

XVIII

Comedic my control: with each new old
scenario, keep moving. In the Orchards
of Syon you can delve Los Angeles
or some other holy place.
Havergal Brian's Five Towns extorted
wealth from poverty, but with choral music
held as a birthright: well-tended ground
ripe for the laying waste, the Great War.
Lawrence's Eastwood, Rosenberg
in Stepney and Whitechapel—I'm
ordered to speak plainly, let what is
speak for itself, not to redeem the time
but to get even with it.
Glastonbury mislodged on its mud lake
with jackpot ignorance and freakish thorn;
York trafficking, gridlocking, organ-congas;
medieval hell-mouths less congested
than this sullen Minster. Anarchy coheres.
Incoherence coheres. Stupor animates.
Chaos ordains. But to what depth? Some demon
chobbles its rap-cassette, spits out
pathetic dreadlocks. I had forgotten
Donne's meta-theology. A road-drill
swallowed through tarred slab re-emerges fighting.

XIX

Potestas clavium: the new
day starts as the last, with wrong numbers,
like a dull kind of caprice. You coúld write
smashed as a maenad, vox clamans
in deserto: these are all
standards of forthrightness if rightly taken.
Hedgerow woundwort, this was the healing touch
I brought upon myself through memory
and lack of thought, absence without leave,
weedy ecstasy, or worse. Could
Goldengrove have been at any time
The Wood of the Suicides?
It cán be murder, or murderous
fantasy: wherever you look the leaves
hanging blood-brown, more real than unreal.
This yard's a wilderness: something vital
displays itself, though not in direct
line of vision. I'd chance morning-glory.
But here's no alibi. Provide further
clearance by code. You have a knack, a way
with broken speech; a singular welcome
for rough concurrence. After a time it's all
resolved, in part, through a high formal keening.
And need to work on that and to go higher.

XX

Two nights' and three days' rain, with the Hodder
well up, over its alder roots; tumblings
of shaly late storm light; the despised
ragwort, luminous, standing out,
stereoscopically, across twenty yards,
on the farther bank. The congregants
of air and water, of swift reflection,
vanish between the brightness and shadow.
Mortal beauty is alienation; or not,
as I see it. The rest passagework,
settled beforehand, variable, to be lived through
as far as one can, with uncertain
tenure. Downstream from this Quaker outcrop
Stonyhurst's ample terraces confer
with the violent, comely
nature of Loyola and English weather;
stone, *pelouse*, untouched by carbon droppings,
now, from the spent mills. Indescribable,
a word accustomed through its halting
promptness, comes to be inscribed. The old
artifice so immediate, the delight
comprehends our measure: knowledge granted
at the final withholding, the image that ís
to die, the creature, the rock of transience.

XXI

Staid forms forgathering: it is smeared
vision that finds Goldengrove some inches
from my face. Late Sargent: a Venetian
gilded interior as it transpires.
In the Orchard palliates my distress
with slender familiarity. So much
for schooling of the eyes. I could show other
unstudied transformations, although rare.
Rare for me, I mean: wreathed encounters
on the threshold of late friendships, things
recovered, even if unrestored, sad
Succoth, the feast of booths. Can you stand—
cleft—but in the spirit, as a tree
by lightning, close to the shored heart?
I believe this has been done. Dante
describes it somewhere—I may be mistaken.
Don't look it up this time; the sub-
conscious does well by us; leave well alone.
Address the picture; it may tell you
who you are, but not where
memory is going. Whatever
finally betrays us, it will be
a gift of description, the life
dramatically foreshortened to begin with.

XXII

Ghost-asters edge the trash. I find a crow
on the firehouse steeple no mean omen.
Dawning arousals: call him Posthumus
Fortunatus which could have meant *born*
gifted, but is not my name. Low-laid
at the dayspring: less self-renewing
censure; more mourning sickness. I was *en*
rêve for Goldengrove, which you had elegized
some generations since, untouched, beyond
the Clock House and the Valley Farm
in a different country. I recall
my thoughts as yours, and sounds, far more than thought,
the saw-mill's flintering squeal. Aeons
deepen their recession. To such ends
no-one's drawn gifted. Misrepresentation's
power play. With what fiction
should we defend our verdicts, retransmit
voices along the waveband?
But to conclude. When last were valedictions
chronically distributed? Mistiming
of brain and heart, lately, I find less
bearable: whatever the garlands
and ceremony, the Orchards of Syon,
the heavy-bearing trees bowed towards Fall.

XXIII

Not all palimpsests are this eroded
to mý mind. A late sun buffs the granite.
Autumn lies lightly earthed, her funerals
the yellowed reddle blown bare, still abundant.
Should I say só much for Elijah's
chariot blessing these banked fires? If that
were even half-true I could give my name
to rehabilitation. *Bien-aimées,*
this calls for matching alchemies to make
gold out of loss in the dead season:
Petrarch revived by Char, though not
in so many words, *la flamme sous l'abri,*
the curfew-flame, uncovered. Frénaud,
bleakly resplendent. *Where are you from?*
I said; and he said, *Montceau—
Montceau-les-Mines.*
Once you ask that you can direct this,
objectify fear, sorrow; the well-placed
lip-readers of failure now succeed.
Last days, last things, loom on: I write
to astonish myself. So much for all
plain speaking. Enter
sign under *signum*, I should be so lucky;
false cadence but an ending. Not there yet.

XXIV

Too many times I wake on the wrong
side of the sudden doors, as cloud-
smoke sets the dawn moon into rough eclipse,
though why in the world this light is not
revealed, even so, the paths plum-coloured,
slippery with bruised leaves; shrouded the clear
ponds below Kenwood; such recollection
no more absent from the sorrow-tread
than I from your phantom showings, Goldengrove.
I dreamed I had wakened before this
and not recognized the place, its forever
arbitrary boundaries re-sited,
re-circuited. In no time at all
there's neither duration nor eternity.
Look!—crowning the little rise, that bush,
copper-gold, trembles like a bee swarm.
Coleridge's *living powers*, and other
sacrednesses, whose asylum this was,
did not ordain the sun; but still it serves,
bringing on strongly now each flame-recognizance,
hermeneutics of autumn, time's
continuities tearing us apart.
Make this do for a lifetime, I tell myself.
Rot we shall have for bearing either way.

XXV

Deformed! I know you as a creature
after my heart. Eat it before it stinks
neo-Shakespearian wordplay. Bloody silly
referring to your bankrupt
wisdoms, failed insurers of reputation,
dealers in things despoiled. Are poisons new
to homeopathy? Spill the salt of the earth.
If you can trust my senses Goldengrove,
upstanding from our common soil, arrays
in fiery colours . . .
One of us talks too much if I'm so like you.
Eternal orders flash balancing
acts in the East Window, random and wholly
articulate light. Risen pilgrim, what's
ex cathedra this day? Daniel
into revelation; a great multitude
crying *Hurt not the earth*. Perverse
to persever: the Orchards of Syon
not just any mirage. Bless poetics
if this is what they are. *La*
vida es sueño—see, I remembered! Whose
name had you thought of giving? Eat whose heart out?
I fear, though, you confuse me with Parnell.
Or vice versa. Even him who cares.

XXVI

Dantean eclogues. Relentless, a toothed
mill-wheel baptizes the mill-race. Invisibly
made evident, the wind shapeshifts, towers
in self-turned glassy sheenings. Lofted
swarms build, dark as locusts. *Where are you fróm?*
I said. He said, *La nostra madre comune.*
Saltmarsh or creek-mire where ochre-
and umber-rendered verdure becomes tinder
in a dry spell. Unforgettable
doctrine, *Matrona*: engage with my contrite
heart of anger. All things are possible.
The spirit materializes; once for all
we know its oratory. So moving
to the one outcome I fancy this light
fantastic carries itself as completion
somewhere that I am not. Ions emote
to make and break aeons; yet still I mourn
you, my sister, as for a dead twin.
Terra madre, Terra incognita,
this is the end I imagine, but who
first said we were finished?
Who said, to think about nothing is not
nihilism but superfluity—
just to break even with you in despair?

XXVII

Not all orchards are for carols of death
and betrayal, the first the final
coupling, virgin fatality. Spanish
drama from the Golden Age,
dentro del vergel, misdirects us there.
Equalize this if you can. Survivors
live out their lives as though by will
and freedom, with or without fulfilment.
Not that it matters now: such frequencies
largely dispersed, the myriad-
faceted black holly of endurance
itself, keeping sombre-bright clusters
exilic. By the way, this
has to show winter in its bounty,
Goldengrove laid bare, becalmed,
lightly sketched in snow; peacock
and peahen treading the white grass.
The Master of the Lost Fecundities
retraces leaf-spoor and hieroglyph,
makes equal atonement.
The hellebore, the Christmas rose, is crowned king.
Yes and we have gifts, at one with the other.
Such tendernesses to our selves I mean,
perennial, like the ilex.

XXVIII

Wintry swamp-thickets, brush-heaps of burnt light.
The sky cast-iron, livid with unshed snow.
I cannot say what it is that best
survives these desolations. Something does,
unlovely; indomitable as the mink.
Raise this with the sometime Overseer
for his stiff *Compliments Book*. Nothing left
to take leave of, if by any chance
you happened to be dying before colour
variety leapt to the blank screen. That
helps me to place my thoughts: intelligence
withdrawn convincingly from the eyes
awaiting close-down. Nothing prepares us
for such fidelity of observation,
I would observe. Nothing to be struck out
of like finalities. *Atemwende*,
Celan almost at last gasp, *atem-
wende*, breath-glitch, say; or Hardy, *The Souls
of the Slain*. According to my
palimpsest, always the first despairing
calculation shows through. Frozen
irresolution, eternal stasis;
wintry swamp-thickets, brush-heaps of burnt light,
the sky cast-iron, livid with unshed snow.

XXIX

A Psalm of Reifying for the Feast
of Distances. Yuletide hazard lights
are still up: in dooryards and domestic
backlots, stark shrubbery, stripped espaliers, dwarfed
by high coiffures of lights, the brittle nets
stuck with captive glass ortolans: these
I greet again, out of mail-catalogues;
fantasies bond prettily. You can hear
nightlong—imagine—filaments trill and snap
in all-levelling cold, in frost-held
vibrating darkness. What is power outage
to secular piety? Outage not
outrage. But spare us, Herod, Herodias,
in these way-outward parts of your City.
Masquing automata, the primal bare
literacy of known constellations:
Orbis Sensualium Pictus, our
elementary colleges of Light.
I tell you, ageing is weirder by far
than dying; and vision loses out
to wandering speculation. Yes, but here
look here! chain-store tawdry profiles and all, *les rois*
mages presented as presenting: Gallico-
Sabean praise-bearers open to exile.

XXX

Blurring sharpens: instance, my cold-tears make
flowerets, faceted clusters, out of clear brights,
headlights, eight, twelve, across, signal gantries
like emporium-glitter. I'm not driving |
fortunately. How slowly it all goes
hurtling to oblivion. Line after line
solidly fractured *without*
effort and without discord—Coleridge; the eye
of Imagination passive and a seer.
Think seer as you would stayer. Even
thinking at all earns points; but if this
is the home-straight, where is my fixed home?
City of God unlikely. Then *in medias*
res, interactive with inertia? Or
something fazed mentors called *the lyric cry*?
You can cross frontiers in suspended
animation, homing onto the inner voice.
Lyric cry lyric cry lyric cry, I'll
give them lyric cry!
Whose is the voice, faint, injured and ghostly,
trapped in this cell phone, if it is not mine?
Some voices ride easily the current. Some
lives get away with murder any road.
How slowly—*without discord*—all hurls to oblivion.

XXXI

Yield violence to violence: no end yet
in pain's finale. Who was it said *Wood*
of the Suicides? I had imagined
that was behind us with *The Death of Virgil*:
the hemlocks' rugged outline, sleet-
welded, wind-harrowed, snow-haggard.
Not even halfway tired, I am fed
voices, *neque Hesperus, neque Lucifer,*
sic admirabilis est: Hesperus,
Lucifer, the strong planet that shines
as it sings, beautifully, in the clear
dome of midwinter. Dante's trope
of Justice: my wounds your injuries,
why do these gird us so or edify
such undistinguished tears? *Atemwende*:
catch-breath, breath-ply. If you survive me,
do something with the incorrigible
nature of judgement. This is the way
a mind sits, congested and vacant,
sweating itself at a year's end:
breath-plight and remission, though I can mouse
no conclusion at thís point, the live
screen blizzarded with interference—did I turn
myself on?—overriding MESSIAH.

XXXII

Black, broken-wattled, hedges appear
thinned through, fields an irregular patchwork,
the snow businesslike. I can record
these elements, this bleak satiety:
accustomed ratios of shine to shadow
reversed; inflected when not reversed.
Closer to nightfall the surface light is low-toned.
This is England; ah, love, you must *see* that;
her nature sensing its continuum
with the Beatific Vision. *Atemwende*,
breath-fetch, the eye no more deceived,
beggars translation. Her decencies
stand bare, not barely stand. In the skeletal
Orchards of Syon are flowers
long vanished; I will consult their names.
Climate, gravity, featherlight aesthetics,
pull us down. The extremities of life
draw together. This last embodiment
indefinitely loaned, not quite
the creator's dying gift regardless.
Clear sky, the snow bare-bright. Loud, peat-sodden,
the swaling Hodder. Of itself
age has no pull. Be easy. With immense
labour he can call it a day.

XXXIII

Might pass myself through, as a backward
courier of vision: your *Table Talk*,
her *Trench Poems*, my *Love Elegies*. As if
no-one's of account, or takes, or gives, account
beyond some timeless exigence, the fall
of determined sparrows, a dead son's
postmortem on the father not declared
here as tyrannical; charted, the fretful
wheeling of outmanoeuvred grand
armies, clef-signs from three miles high.
Losing's finality, impacted by noble
and fateful omens, a tundra of scored
waste, unreal: I fought the campaign-maps;
tea caddy, biscuit barrel holding down
rebellious corners. Cry havoc here on all
dream-hypnotists of escape. Destroy
and reassemble. To be an unrivalled
linguist is the deeper hope—Mason
regarding Massignon—*a spirit
that divines the source*. Newly dyed
opacities of the wintry delta stand
gauzed, a red wash, evenings and mornings.
Briefly at noon low ridges fend this light
that flashes a clear verdict from the scales.

XXXIV

The nether way to salvation, if
I so undertake it: *the nether*
way of the flood claims sainted Catherine
speaking of perdition. Life against life
in her scale of plenitude; the flood's
foulness like smashed Warsaw sewers,
with more long-buried rites. Mere violence
now of denial; trees to windward
snow-ghosted; the light
enters upon its own darkness and falls
mute. It must be some
forward observation post. I said
perdition without thinking. This cannot
be Purgatory, neither is it
The Wood of the Suicides, nor dead
Goldengrove alive with mistletoe;
not swirling Venus, even, where a day
goes slower than the year. Redemption
is self-redemption and entails crawling
to the next angle of vision.
Press the right word, the scenes change. Who can
not be affected: Spring releasing, shire-
wide, the nature of waters, a world
that flows and rises for us just as you see it?

XXXV

To gardens, famously resorts of hazard:
a half-day's melt and granites reappear
as if beached, wearing lichens for life-scars,
which they are not. This is a fanciful
way that I have of lauding endurance
in things familiar though still foreign. Béla
Bartók is dead. Once more music
and memory move, each to its own
incomparable haven. *Where are you from?* I said.
He said, *the Orchards of Syon.*
Simply recording these tricky
counterpoints declares faith. And yes I do
fantasize; it was not so much like him,
even on West Fifty-seventh Street,
the intersection-wind pasting new snow.
This well-clued business not ways beyond us—
business here meaning survival, strange lures
of duress, longevities: for the record,
a full sesquicentennium
after Laud's death, by which time the tortoise
itself was archbishop.
Self-fortifying little shell of a creature,
how I would miss you, having seen you, blessed,
draw back your head.

XXXVI

Downhill to go, then up the long curve of field.
December chastens the stream bed; frosted mist
hangs in autumn's leasowe; the far slope
burns hazy yellow where it is spring. I count
our seasons clockwise, with nadir and zenith,
on the year's face. Between five and six, that's
all I can see to tell you. The life-lines
tug briefly, my coming from way back, a child's
journey between worlds: though this is at best
half the fable. *Atemwende*, turn
of breath. *Spinnrad*, turn of wheel. Many
returns melt barriers and the winged
lion roars his obeisance. Not good
chiasma if you cannot make crossing.
Babylon's candles are lit for children
far older than their time, of whom fondly
no-one despairs. I did the Lady
Julian an injustice
which I will leave for evidence against me,
configured by the final stroke. Of course
Hell is empty; or *The End* will erase it
in its due place and order. *Poets
leap over death*—was that Coleridge? If so,
did anyone see him do it and live?

XXXVII

This is a fashion of great day that even
I can wake up and decidedly warm to,
when disparities get spliced and make
sense to each other. Blancoed halyards,
guy-ropes, fresh cordage, stress-tested wires,
tug to attention; new and ascendant
flags thrapping the wind. Memory
hyperactive—poised on time—that word
gyroscope spinning for my balance: *gnōthi
seauton* sounds like adult fun, a trip
to Olympus, or, it could be, Ithaca,
glittery cold Cornell, Château-Thierry's
Chirico-vista'd mausoleum.
In these not simply hilarious scenes
is *goose* sweeter than *gans* I wonder. Love
you, Frank, come on home! Frank being Frank
O'Hara. Faithless and steadfast
loves in arms together. Well,
here you are. And to a hero's welcome.
Speak for one full minute without
deviation, veteran. *Éternel
retour* is not a high-noon locution
I would ever stress lightly. O mý tachy-
cardia, dó I have news for yoú!

XXXVIII

Kindheitslandschaft: I still think they thought
we invented it. That whole time. *The Landscape
of Childhood*. Of more than memory, dead
Ingeborg. And even so, there only.
Did we shield then, believe it, hope to die,
those all-marvelling, unrehearsed
hours, where goldcrests and the great ferns were,
Osmunda regalis, bowing us in and down,
both royal and nesh? I am conversant with
the book of recollection, self-
desolating child, part-changeling. Ancient
vows are unexempted,
in some way signify the natal language
not forgotten. Intermittent
cloud-shadow across roofs. Our loves discerned
like stars depth-hung in water.
Impassively the sempiternal casts
deep for endurance.
And here—and there too—I
wish greatly to believe: that Bromsgrove
was, and is, Goldengrove; that the Orchards
of Syon stand as I once glimpsed them.
But there we are: the heartland remains
heartless; that's the strange beauty of it.

XXXIX

I must have written this off-stage, if it
shows. Be serious. I repeat: ageing
is weirder far than our dying. *Quod erat
demonstrandum*, the sun in the stair-well
through summer dresses. Sensualist
memory, here Í am in this frayed
cyclorama, caught squinting absurdly;
and there is the joker with two heads. Intense
unwasted life, so nearly at an end,
what can I say now, except *Whose wére you?*
Hand out the book prizes, my acceptance
speech is postponed. *Your Children's
Health Under Labour* by Bruce L. Osis
and T. B. D. Klining. What gives? An old
artery slurried with carbide. Language
destroys ideas but not character,
Mercurius. So what díd the Surreal
say to you that now bears repeating
like the ancient power of *Perforce*? Read
Dante's jokes about sex, though best not
for comfort, or pity. Furiously the earth
turns, but without sensation, the moon
adjusts herself to our perspectives. If joy
ís still in waiting, then let it be called.

XL

Still, gratitude to music for making
us vocal: music to find its place here.
Estimable Saint-Saëns, firework cadenzas,
Fourth or Fourteenth of July. Does music
know or care how it sounds? Go, horns
of plenty, clash promiscuous
cymbals! Meyerbeer labours it out;
Widor's a mere thirty-two-foot giant
of shaking subsistence. Order construes
the incoherent, widely as we need.
Here's late Schnittke now, auditor
pro defunctis and all-present, resuscitating
organum. To summon from drone-tomb
commotions of calm. Slavonic eardrums'
requiem aeternam though hís Zion more
Prussian than Russian. *Penitential*
Psalms on *dot edu*. Listen,
Beryozka, birchling, this is so far
true to my acclaim:
aleatoric light that remains unfinished,
as Schnittke and his music multiform,
struck off in mean unpropitious time.
At the end it ís a question of stamina.
Beautiful though grim if thus our long home.

XLI

This should be called *The Second Book* or *Book
of Stone* maybe, or *Tristia*, or
You, Mandelstam. More alive than ever,
the barren land abruptly blazing through
with common flowers. How they oblige us;
it is no mystery to them, nor privilege.
Winter is not the same but, again, we
knew that. Where the sun
reels out slow laden rivers, the genius
of the birches there builds its shadow.
Beryozka, I know this, this remission,
and shall confront my own witness
like a man with a chain-saw, delicately.
Kamen does mean stone, the word
to be proven: as a moving light
narrowly outruns itself on a railed curve;
as the dimmest among us carries his torch
into and beyond the terminus of remembrance;
as the canniest in turn misplaces tape-
records of innocence and guilt, the tundra's
unnameable lichens—meaning that I
have not found and betrayed them—attestations
bled of all secrets but the first or last
secret of survival.

XLII

Up against ageing and dying I stand bemused
by labours of flight: a low-geared heron
retiring to its pool, the shapes that gulls
beat and tack; a motionless
crow butting a head-wind, like carved beam-end;
the smallest birds also that ricochet
from bush to bush but strike nothing; kestrel,
slammed against window-glass, spread-eagled there;
wrenched updraught; slighted harpies
of witness, finally. Lepidoptera
drugged by light into shell havens
of self-destruction. Should these not tally,
metal-toothed winter oak-leaves rap
on shuttered mansards; a trumpet pitches
its high reflection. Something also of grief
baffled, murmurings of Kaddish
proscribed during the Passover; a raw
coffin discreetly manhandled. Cindered gusts
make their eyes water. I record this
among the scattered thrown-out accusations
proper to such scenes; think further of Abe
Klein's Uncle Melech, coming in low across
land newly called Israel, and held to be
unforgiving, that shadow-path a pledged curse.

XLIII

Say what you will, the interim record
of preservation is awesome. First this,
then this, catches the affrighted eye.
Renegotiate the sleep-veil, admit
that other world this fantasizing world
conspires for and against us; our images
drawn out of cold fires: *Christ*
treading upon the Beasts, St Guthlac's
Psalter at Crowland, planted mid-fen,
dun scrolls, clay-moulded almost, basilisk
and cockatrice, creatures harmless enough
in small malevolence. As species
of reproduction far-fetched. Re-apply
Dies Irae with its scarifying
mnemonics to cleanse prayer. Range
how you will, anger, despair, are inbred
monsters: Nebuchadnezzar's crawlingly
bitter egress to gnaw grass; Cain's brood
busy at Heorot. Such startings-up,
slouchings, of self-hatred; a sullen
belch from the ice-maker in the small hours.
All honour to patience, but patience which
as *natural heart's ivy*—Hopkins—must
surely choke it: *it*, here, being the heart.

XLIV

Orchards of the *bocage*, June through October,
sloughed odours of death from tracked armour
gone multiflame. Decaying glider-fabric,
knicker-silk parachutes, umbelliferae,
littering the hedgerows, the barn-rubble,
and splintered crofts.
Blackened as Rouault's *Miserere*, a body
splays for the camera, the camera
staying put, except it probes further
the human midden. Hand-held or swivel,
at the crossroads of Hauts-Vents, machine-carbine,
a reflex action. Then immediately
peace brings *The Armed Vision*, a work of courage
and quick advantage. Who dares show himself
embusqué in this verdurous new terrain
to be fought through? Did Hyman go to the wars?
Empson didn't, nor did I. *Armed Vision*
is of course Coleridge. Meanwhile, *mes capitaines*,
the veterans are dying. And I cannot say
what they care to remember. Whitman,
not James, is the true focuser. Drum-taps,
trouble no more these Orchards of Syon
glutted with spillage; where the blind-worm
excretes her young.

XLV

Listen, Meister Eckhart is here, ready
and eager to tell us his great news:
that we caught aright the revelatory
scream from the carrousel; that there's a divine
presence in destitution; that yes, we loved
bright Harry Heine and Frank O'Hara
as more than passing attractions when
I pass was the catch-phrase and they unheard of;
that the heavy residues from easy loving
render us breathless. Both you and I
who pray with the *dévots* yet practise
every trick in the book: our nuptials
are of the spirit entirely. The topos
of the whole is gratitude. Duino's
cliff-hanger we witnessed, and its consummation.
Wait, I've not finished. A radical
otherness, as it's called, answers
to its own voices: that there should be
language, rituals, weddings, and wedding-nights,
and tapes which spin fast forward, stop, reverse;
that there is even now hawthorn, this bush
pregnant with the wild scent and taint of sex;
that there áre men and women, destinies
interlocked; and dying, and resurrection.

XLVI

To love, determinedly and well, and to be
unfaithful: there should have arisen
particular broken forms to engage this;
brutish presentments heavy as the sea
that rides from darkness onto a skirr
and pash of shingle. Montale, in *Finisterre*,
focused something, his eros, though I can't
quote him or even recall
clearly what he said of desire and absence
of the desired. Such is Eros, pupil
of the moon, with full corolla
presaging migraine; or, as I see it, self
rectifying vision indefinable.
Is anything out there? To love
determinately, to redispose
death in this strange body? Held by evidence
I say again: passion and inertia
overwhelm us, like a waste
surf compounding with its undertow.
Many waters cannot quench Phosphor.
See how it's done, plunderers
of subtext, caught flotsam, even of your own
eye-catching inane flare, these other words
borne out beyond your salvage, there as here.

XLVII

In Terra Pax packed with low-level shots
of the reduced city, laid-waste battery cells,
unroofed dead wasp-combs, gutted termite towers,
monumental shards, trays coagulant
with half-fused lead. In the Orchards of Syon,
also, there are temples and labyrinths
not for the defeated; but how to make them
answerable to such ends: it is this
that confounds me. Come down from your high
thrones of question, good doctors of wisdom.
Now Í am at ground level and must grope,
whereas the blinded archangel stands clear
on his chance tottering ledge. Say then,
enormity has to be got right:
tracking survival instincts of trapped rats
through to the final Syon in her throes.
You thought I had abandoned the dream-sewers?
Well, so I had; I had been blown apart
by universal pity trumpeting
con sord. to *triple forte*. Krenek
or Kurtag I'll scatter around this,
anything from HUNGAROTON; *In Terra Pax*
dark in itself but sighted, as dead stars
that overlook us with a splittering light.

XLVIII

But what a hope, but to have willed so much
upon you. As if I were my true self,
myself the other. Not that you claim this
but we have to invent dialogue—don't ask—
like patience provoked into being. Then
what should I say these are: the gates
of Emanation? Not if you can help?
Pub car-park puddles, radiant cauls of oil.
When all else fails, the great rainbow, as Bert
Lawrence saw it or summoned it. *Va' via*
but not remotely. The entire display
swings on a fulcrum and is repositioned
as the earth tilts and spins. You need to weigh this
by constant reckoning. I am not the judge;
these are not directions. Never let
my voice mislead you. I may be mistaken;
self-mistaken; wrongly self-possessed;
confusing jealousy with righteousness
as I would have it
whatever wrongs we do, one to another;
our midlands far and wide; Lawrence, his
New Jerusalem *in the mind enthroned*,
time for bestowal, shadow into shadow,
St John the Baptist gloaming on its hill.

XLIX

In due consideration of the world's
bulk and selvage, I envision the Orchards
of Syon in terra cotta and yellow brick;
tracts of juniper; beauty still thriving
on squatters' rights. What was Lawrence's
view of *The Blind Girl* if he ever saw it—
he múst have—the two rainbows, the young
woman, unseeing herself, but taken
out of the body, as we are, blindly,
by self-forgetting? The sun, the sudden
prism, rediscover their own time,
whenever that is; bending to our level
they lift us up. Hopkins, who was self-
belaboured, crushed, cried out being uplifted, and he
was stronger than most. He said that creatures
praise the Creator, but are ignorant
of what they do. Imagine your own way
out of necessity; imagine
no need to do this. Good story, bad
ending, if narrative is the element
that so overreaches. Providence
used to be worked-in, somewhere. I, at best,
conjecture divination. The rainbow's
appearance covenants with reality.

L

Covenants, yes; outcries, yes; systemic
disorders like the names of rock-plants, yes;
right side for creativity, yes; and well
if none of ús fails our provision.
Go to the revivalists for vision,
the charismatic troupers. Planets
of alkali, no; a methylated cold
glow in the northern heavens that spells God
the encoder, no. Who is *long suffering*
to us-ward? Oh man! More sensual,
at times craven, clay our solicited
Maker must make do with. This means love
and fear, soul-sister, bounden by deed of gift,
by imputation and by adoption,
by sighs and groans—*uh-húh*—
to stay and sway us, as never before.
O never before heard preaching like it,
saving your presence, maestro, as it soars
spontaneous, by the book, the plenitude
of the oppressed, oppressive and upgathered.
Not condign here to bespeak reprobation,
to exhaust Egypt, rise from a dead sea.
H'm-h'm! Keep her hummin' Lord! The day
of Jubilo, though new to my programme.

LI

LUMEN OBSCURUM. Latin would be my guess.
Try *atemwende*. Take another walk
down to the river, where the darkening flood
churns beneath burnt-out alders, leaps and yaws
across—between—its millstone rocks, mud-yeasty.
Whatever's cryptic is Polish. Explain that,
if only in sign language, and I'll spell you.
And you replied, *wooden, prettily carved,*
with traces of original pigment;
Mateusz six, twenty-one, repeated.
Why not render
atemwende breath-hazard? Start homeward.
Ostracizm's a small foothill town
in the Carpathians that retires at dusk,
battening rumours, telling its safe houses.
Tenacity itself can drive
only so deep. Wat's posthumous *lumen*
obscurum illumes; at the crib of things
settled, creaturely, its fabulous glim
invisible to most. So how did he
sign *tremor cordis* to be no enigma,
smoke out last words, grudge-heavy honey bees
living off self-remitted spoil of the hive?
Where your treasure is, there is your heart also.

LII

Consider these cauteries life-tokens
to a hapless though not hopeless intelligence.
Cicatrice is no dead insect. The balm-
bearing trees are incised. New skin
sets itself in patterns of the old wounds.
Denn wo euer Schatz ist, da ist auch
euer Hertz. Spirit's a tad elsewhere,
brown on the ceiling, caught among the drains,
stashed in some mezzanine. Where your treasure
lies, there your heart lies also. Is this even
to be thought? Whereas each moment's
epiphany's much like a betrayal
of held breath, I feel the need to swing
things and let go. Hourly, on the hour,
somebody fresh floored by the virus
of inspiration. As for mischance, I know
halogen projects Chinese characters
deep into the closed
circus of my eyelids. I'm not blind,
nor blind the world's designer randomness:
schwarzrot of the dying rose, the thick
greenwarped Spanish glass; clashed consanguinity,
rioja against rioja; diverse
affinities; unassuaged; rejoicing.

LIII

Was Orphée's *Princesse* Camus' lover; might
you yet be my lover if we here
believe ourselves projected by a master?
Scavengers find things to love in junkyards
but not junkies. Broken society
be damned. Be damned to *robust* language.
My need: seven lines to be patched with loans;
and of course you. Syntax turns against me,
pledges its joker, wisdom's oversight.
Ingeborg Bachmann you must remember
even as I speak,
surrogate in the lion's mouth, *nella
bocca di Leone*. If we could
reconvene here, what would I have in mind
but to convey you, as with defiance,
ad ulteriorem ripam, Liverpool–
Halifax (Nova Scotia); this despite
Dis's spasmodic hold, with evidence
we were enrolled after the tide had turned,
that I was mishandled by death's angel
on course; or even that this *Cantilena*
is not a long-range reconnaissance
flying-boat overseeing survivors,
winking a vital message to the dead?

LIV

Memory is its own vision, a gift of sight,
from which thought step aside, and frequently,
into the present, where we have possession
more and more denied us. I shall not
deny yoú without recollection.
Query: how far ascribe this to a failed,
no, failing, motor control. I am not less
careful or curious of our durance, *the eye's
elaboration of tears*, Mrs Beeton's
beautiful phrase. She failed at twenty-eight
and went unwept by me. Now you also,
sine nomine, if that is what you are,
earthy-etherial; I desire you
to fathom what I mean. What dó I mean?
I think you are a muse or something,
though too early rejected. The dank
Triassic marl, sandstone like mouldered plaster,
can't all-inhold you. From Burcot to Worms Ash
the rock sweats and trickles, even in winter,
the sun digs silver out of the evergreen.
Orchards of Syon, tenebrous thresholds
of illumination, a Latin love
elegist would comprehend your being
a feature of his everlasting dark.

LV

I desire so not to deny desire's
intransigence. To you I stand
answerable. Correction: must once have stood.
What's this thing, like a clown's eyebrow-brush?
O my lady, it is the fool's confession,
weeping greasepaint, all paint and rhetoric.
Empower the muse; I'm tired. Shakespeare, who scarcely
brooded on perfection, perfect so many times.
Memory! memory! *The eye*
elaborates its tears, but misremembered,
misremembering no less key-clustered
mistletoe, the orchard's châtelaine.
I may well carry my three engraved thoughts
out beyond Shrawley whose broad verges once
throve like spare garden plots with pear and apple
or with wild damson, thinner on the ground.
O my lady, this is a fool's profession
and you may be dead, or with Alzheimer's,
or happily still adoring a different
Duke of Illyria. I have set you up,
I confess thát, so as not to stint
your voice of justice. Love grows in some
way closer to withdrawn theology.
The Deists' orb drops below Ankerdine.

LVI

Suicide-comedy, the panic-laughter
traversing, then cut off; and still a need
to be on the right side of this, survive
myself, garland myself with tribute.
How deeply wedded wére you? A strange
bisexuality of language
in private monodrama ís allowed
although disturbing. Did I disturb
in Klagenfurt or Rome, dead Ingeborg,
when ruins hooked and shelved the broken
cloud-breaking moon? Prophets as fantasists
fulfilled—that's not the issue. *Scotus shows*
necessity reconciled with free will—Hopkins,
himself soul-strung, haggard, though not like you.
You leave me with a ghosted speech to finish
saying we never met. False evidence,
and I'm a stalker—incapacitated—
of my own gifts and yours. Such prurient
language of flowers Parnassian, a blight:
gothic monk's hood, black horehound, but no longer
luxuriantly or *in rare abundance*. Still
inconsolable, sex-haunted, we'll reverse-
charge our challenge to the bridal suite.
Some voice will pick it up before refusing.

LVII

Reading Dante in a mood of angry dislike
for my fellow sufferers and for myself
that I dislike them. Dante is exact
in these conferrals. The words of justice
move on his abacus or make a sudden
psst psst like farrier's hot iron on horn.
The small blue flame of the glass votive lamp
that jibs in the funnelled air at the right
hand of Mary Mediatrix is his also.
From this distance the many barbed divisions
between Purgatory and Hell appear blurred.
You could step across or shake hands. Logic
is fierce, though at the last less feral
than mock-logic that destroys many.
Sensuous is not sensual, but such knowledge
increases with sensuality—*psst psst*—
hissing and crying out, the final throes.
Messaline—Frénaud—*la vulve
insomnieuse*—ever-working valve-part
unsightly, blood-gravid. Look, Virgin
of Czestochowa, shelterer
from the black rain, look, ser Brunetto
whom Dante loved, look, Farinata: the sun
moves a notch forward on the great wheel.

LVIII

La vida es sueño, and about time;
about hanging in there, about my self,
my mind as it is, to be remembered,
regarding timegraphs: these I understand
as the nongrammatical speech of angels.
I mean, they're beyond grammar that reminds
us of our fall, and of hanging out there.
My mind, as I know it, I still discover
in this one-off temerity, arachnidous,
abseiling into a pit, the pit a void,
a black hole, a galaxy in denial.
Life ís a dream. I pitch
and check, balanced against hazard,
self-sustained, credulous; well on the way
to hit by accident a coup de grâce.
Intolerable stress on will and shall,
recovery of sprung rhythms, if not rhythm;
test of creation almost to destruction—
that's a smart line; it can survive me.
In denial not my words. I'm moving
blindly, all feelers out. Cosmic flare-wind
tilts the earth's axis, then returns us,
with our ears singing, our eyes rolled back,
mute, Atlantean.

LIX

Never quite warmed to fiery Wiclif. His
heavenly country meant the Kingdom of Heaven.
Chosen by and for the elect. A man need not
conform to his own words though he enacts
or enables them. Orators marginalized
by their own oratory a recurrent theme,
commonplace the cartographics of dissent.
All along, I'm labouring to try out
a numen that endures, exactly placed:
some upper valley in the high fell country
where millstone grit juts against limestone; shippens
built of random masonry; the home-
croft with its gapped wall and its well,
and black nettles where the privy stood. Ivy
and other evergreens in profusion,
most notably when it's winter. Yet Hardy's
redoubtable friend asked: Our people,
where áre they?—cranky old Barnes—*But óh,*
our peóple, whére are théy? And I could
not answer, but left him there in silence.
Curlew and kestrel trek the fell-sides,
the Hodder burls, a pheasant
steps from the thorny hedgebank beside us,
the stooped pear-tree honours us with its shade.

LX

Stuck on then plucked off: self-surmounting rôles,
each one a self-presumption. Not any more
a wrought Jesuit or young
refusnik with an old heart. These
congested subway cars! We can
always say no, every last one of us.
So much is surely consonant with even
a fool's kind of street-wisdom. The heart
itself made to pull gears. Not now Péguy's
disciples or the helotries of Maurras.
Vanished the threatening and so threatened Jew.
Not for this time a student of war
Clausewitzian, despoiler of Goldengrove
and Syon's Orchards as I have heard
myself say with some reason. Neither a slave
nor the slave's master-mistress. Not her
in such bravery, not him who answers
with proud erectile tissue. Casuistries
for which our tongues' tongue is choric
wherewithal and uninsured third party.
The heart is not beautiful. Exposed
it leaps fattily, apes a sexual motion
as if copulating with itself, *la vulve
insomnieuse*, to re-transplant Frénaud.

LXI

Myth, politics, landscape; with language
seeding and binding them; marram grass or
Milton's broadcast parable *springing up*
armed men. All wisdoms thrown, as clay is thrown
and thrown again by the novice-master.
Our patience proven in the rage of others:
Commonweal their lodestar, inordinate
dominion their enterprise.
Love justice in a word, the knot-garden
of equity. Melech-Melchizedek, great
king among smallholders. *Righteousness*,
word of a decent splendour. Fortuna
our wire-dancer, or gyroscope—better
not look down. Existence ís
advanced mechanics, intuitively structured.
Kierkegaard springs to mind and is gone
as swiftly into the prodigal rainbow.
I can see only so far; I can say
only so much; I trust I shall greet you,
with or without your recognition,
instantly, and at my own expense. To, from,
the body of self-being *kommt Freud und Leid*:
joy, sorrow, as equals. All of this speaks well
for the affinities between us meeting as strangers.

LXII

Not the root of discrimination. That
coúld have been said more clearly: *crimen*. I'm
myself close to the inarticulate. Commonplace
muddledom I grant, extraordinary
common goodness being its twin. I think
of others on such evenings, long forgotten,
placing new flowers in the cemetery;
a sycamore's disproportionate
summer heaviness, engorged with shadow;
yew-bark, its waning glow, fulvous as sandstone;
empurpled bronzings: highlighted,
the beech's massive casque. Such grace
dispeopled, do not ask too much of it,
heart's fulness troubled by its own repose.
But is this asking too much, of nature
and of relationship, of kind? Yes,
to be blunt: eloquence moving
bad conscience forward, backward, across,
like a metal detector. Owen's bled
Pity was effectively burdened. These
new drafts on old devotion: who knows what
bolt has them targeted, what final tour
of sick Compassion: Shock-Horror's century
so unbelievable it must be true.

LXIII

Not quite heat- or rain-scrim, this heavy
blankness, thinning now, presides with a mauve-
tinted wipe-around grey. Noon, yet no distance
to any horizon. The Malverns gone in haze.
I would not, formerly,
have so described bereavement. *Land
of Unlikeness* a similitude, certitude
moves to dissolution. Still, an answer:
misprised, misplaced love,
our routine, is not tragedy;
misadventure at worst. And my self-styled
lament must cover for us both.
Something here to know time by, in all
conscience. In all conscience we
shall lie down together. Dear one, be told
you chose impenetrable absence; I became
commonplace fantasy's
life-sentenced ghost. Allow
our one tolerable *scena* its two minds.
Abruptly the sun's out, striking a new
cleave; skidding the ridge-grass, down steep hangers;
buddleia in dark bloom; a wayward covey
of cabbage-whites this instant balanced
and prinking; the light itself aromatic.

LXIV

Belated grief-dervish: moribund and only
now into the surge and swing of the elements.
And not my words alone, as I commit them
to you also, yoú being my last but one
love. This could as well be lichened rock
or shadows of stained glass, Rossetti-like,
glowing and fading; ebbing, you might say.
Thát tell you what love is, how it stands, how
it opens itself, mirrors itself blind;
how it is self-requiting, not disarmed;
who makes it, who falls hard by the way
like carnal Christians or lost picaros;
poorly attended, guarded, self-exposed,
self-perpetuating, selfless, barren;
poison ivy or shingles for hair-shirt?
Imagination under stress in due
time becomes carbon, which I will not waste.
Who needs retractions? I can torment myself
with simple gratitude, municipal
salvias in the restyled garden of rest
staring my thoughts back. Beleaguered, roughly
unhostile people, many voices raised;
Messiah and *Elijah* filling the slate-
roofed tabernacles of millstone grit.

LXV

Heavy, post-cloudburst, slow drops, earthing, make
dibble-holes under the crouched evergreens.
So far I'm with you, conglomerate roots
of words. I wish I could say more. Even
this much praise is hard going. *Physical
psyche*, Lawrence, also hard going.
Nonetheless it's here: sodden, glaucous
evanescence; ridged *impasto*. I sense
revelation strike obliquely in,
thwartways, to our need.
Pigeon-mobbed, on the play-patch, my own
public madman hurls at the laden air
his archive of bagged injustice. Let us
not follow him into the *Theatre
of Kings and Magistrates*. My polity—
polity!—acts convalescent
with time and matter, each particular seam
of common being; close-set
quotidian marvels, fresh-felled trunks of beech
split thin-clean like slate. I claim elective
affinities as of the root, even.
Even if unenduring. Treat with care
these angry follies of the old monster.
Dig the—mostly uncouth—language of grace.

LXVI

Right, one more time! *Pomerium* will not
pass muster as *orchard*. That place of last
reckoning, at the Berlin Wall,
more resembled it; or say Carthage
chemically defoliate, salt understood
here as a chemical. Or the French con-
nection, *cordon sanitaire*. Contingent
natures of all things save God. Uncompromising
self-sufficiency work for the cockroach.
Difficult to end joyful starting from here,
but I'll surprise us. Inurements
I allow, endurances I approve;
nothing of ours is irreducible
though passion of failed loves remains
in its own selving. So let us
presume to assume the hierarchies,
Goldengrove, even as these senses fall
and die in your yellow grass, your landscape
of deep disquiet, calm in its forms: the Orchards
of Syon, sway-backed with pear and apple,
the plum, in spring and autumn resplendent.
Syon! Syon! that which sustains us and is
not the politics of envy, nor *solidarność*,
a hard-won knowledge of what wears us down.

LXVII

But now and in memory never so
wholly awaited, the breadth of this
autumnal land. In Goldengrove the full
trees trumpet their colours: earth-casualties
majestic; unreal as in life they build
riches of cadence, not yet decadence,
ruin's festival. This much is allowed
us, forever tangling with England
in her quiet ways of betrayal. Natural
mother, good but not enough. Again, bring
recollection forward, weeping with rage.
Debit the lot to our chequered country,
crediting even so her haunted music.
Loyal incoherence not official
but now and then inspired: when circling
Heathrow on hold we are entertained
by Windsor's scaled-down perfect replicas;
or as Sussex, dormant, rippling with shadows
of airflow, tilts, straightens under, and they
switch off the flight-chart.
So much for my conclusion, a small
remembrance, *nos fidelités sont
des citadelles*—Péguy. Our fealties taken
to be your places of refuge and defence.

LXVIII

Never an off season. Call for the voicer
of fair omen. The voice persists
in rising monotone. Talk obsession
to ecstasy. Delete *My Word*. Lie
down in the space provided.
Pollen and basalt—Dame Rainbow, ancient
lover of water, immortal
for want of a better term; self-remnant
in each element of the same desire.
Not as she once was, metaphysical
and, like, wild. Weigh the importunate
nature of being [|] with a light
husk, the grasshopper's, tall
storyteller of the Hesperides
with hymns to divine Aphasia
(*for it is she*). Even so Goldengrove
might have been Silvertown, could be Golders Green;
you can't rule on that. *Finis* was the last
word to escape me. Period. Stop
trying to amuse with such gleeful sorrow.
Here are the Orchards of Syon, neither wisdom
nor illusion of wisdom, not
compensation, not recompense: the Orchards
of Syon whatever harvests we bring them.

Scenes From Comus

For Hugh Wood on his 70th birthday

Who knows not *Circe*
The daughter of the Sun?

JOHN MILTON

The good walk in step. Without knowing anything of them, the others dance around them, dancing the dances of the age.

FRANZ KAFKA

1 The Argument of the Masque

1

Of the personality as a mask;
of character as self-founded, self-founding;
and of *the sacredness of the person*.

Of licence and exorbitance, of scheme
and fidelity; of custom and want of custom;
of dissimulation; of envy

and detraction. Of *bare preservation*,
of *obligation to mutual love*;
and of our covenants with language

contra tyrannos.

2

That we are inordinate creatures
not so ordained of God; that we are
at once rational, irrational, possessed by reason.

That this is no reason for us to despair.
The tragedy of things is not conclusive;
rather, one way by which the spirit moves.

That it moves in circles need not detain us.
Marvel at our contrary orbits. Mine
salutes yours, whenever we pass or cross,

which may be now, might very well be now.

3

Titagrams violate my late aggro.
Mute apathy not now in order, try
provoking our old selves mono-duet.

Say, thirty years until H. M. commands
a small obstruction for the mantelpiece
and senna's called on more than single malt.

Inspiration breathes hard. Still your music
would arouse Milton for me, if he required
such service of us. He doesn't, does he?

Let's go to ground around the grinning cake.

4

Language of occasion has here fallen
into occurrence of outcry, reactive
outcry, like a treatable depression

that happens not to respond. If fate,
then fated like autism. There is some notion,
here, of the sea guffawing off reefs,

to which we compose our daft music
of comprehension. Rain-front on rain-front,
then a sun-gash, clouds moody; the sea's mood

turns from slate-black, to yellow ochre, to green.

5

Add that we're unaccountably held to account;
that we cannot make our short days add up
to the sum demanded. Add, that accountancy

is a chartered profession, like surveying;
that rectitude is a grand directive;
that righteousness has no known charter

and is not, generally speaking, in demand.
That there are immoderate measures in plenty;
that plenty is a term of moderation;

that moderation is by some used to excess.

6

That, in these latter days, language
is the energy of decaying sense;
that sense in this sense means *sensus communis*.

That common sense bids me add: not
all language. If power's fuelled by decay,
so be it—decay being a natural force.

Moral corruption is another matter;
I cannot get beyond pronouncing it
inertia of malevolence, or *pondus*.

This *pondus* has itself nothing to add.

7

That stale enlightenment exacerbates
the incoherence—ask me to explain—
profuse expediency that leaves us speechless,

wordless, even. Their words attack my throat
wordlessly. If it were silence to silence!
Silence is dealt defending a loved child

against incorrigible fact. Mute
suffering's a factor of countless decibels.
I see the pristine hammer hammer alarm.

I see it but I can hear nothing.

8

That the imagination is a type
of reactor. Mine works well with bursts
of winter-sun chill-out in Reykjavik,

orgiastic shuteye. A critical mass:
impression into expression. Where's the many
times caught and expelled, all-sufficient child,

transfigured memory, now that the sun's gone in?
The Monad begetteth the Monad, and doth
reflect upon itself its own fervour.

The man who said this died of alchemy.

9

Draw together the surviving powers,
the *dark Aleph* and the *Father of Lights*.
I imagine them majestic in winter,

though not as they used to be still dangerous.
I say imagine them I mean create them—
another remnant of alchemical twaddle

that ceases to be twaddle in some cases,
and in some degrees, of allayed loathing.
Any fire to transmute these fraudulent base years.

I say create them I mean imagine them.

10

That the receptor and reactor are a unit
making themselves many units of energy;
that the voice of prophecy clings to its logged spar;

that the deep waters toss me about—I shout
from the crests and the troughs, these words that turn
to a spooled marker-dye the colour of vomit;

even so cannot cease from invoking the sea's
unchallengeable voltage, its transforming waste.
The need for good reactors I also accept—

the alchemy the primal infiltration.

11

Sexual love—instinctively alchemical:
early sexual love. Or is the dying
recreation of it the real mystery?

I say that each is true: words troth-plight
to both of us, equal with her, truer
now, than I was or ever could be,

but knowing myself in her. I said
ask me to explain—they won't remember,
forty-six lines back and already buried

with the short day.

12

That *marriage is a hieroglyphic*, stands
in its own garment. Not a possession.
Not always dispossessed. Or to speak

otherwise: it brings ruin and the numen
together; and indeed it can
be a lovely thing when others make it so.

That numen, too, is a hieroglyph—
a shadow brought to bear, a signal.
And that reason is articulate in the will

if you don't think about it.

13

That I mean what I say, saying it obscurely.
I would lie to anyone in all frankness.
Rhetoric is weaponry, should not be allowed

to fiddle the equation. We are a hand's span
from the end of time. Milton thought so
and rejoiced in so thinking. Perhaps

he was right, perhaps it has been and gone,
sudden death trumpets, Armageddon, the taking
up of the elect, their inurement, the totalled

compact reality of all evil fictions.

14

Not in these noises—Milton. *A troubled sea
of noises and hoarse disputes* is also him.
Even short arctic days have a long twilight

as I have time to observe. Gloam lies pulsing
at the sea-skyline, where the *Hood* blew up
surging at full speed, a kind of wake

over the sudden mass grave foul with cordite,
gradually settling. Milton meant civil war
and civil detractions, and the sway of power,

the pull of power, its *pondus*, its gravity.

15

Somewhere I have lost *Milton on Music*
and *The English Masque*. Sometime in the last days.
I thought they were in the bag. Three gross men

and three skeletal women mouth me
the world's disasters. Milton would have laughed.
Save these for the antimasque. The antimasque

will not be saved, not from the winter sea,
the *stormy Hebrides*. My spirit salutes yours
unclaimed. To reduce is to lead back,

to rectify; also, to diminish.

16

That the antimasque is what saves us
challenge by challenge. Still I anticipate.
I did not anticipate the marriage

that I destroyed. It was not then the fashion.
The Ludlow Masque was far from fashionable
though fashioned well. To up the bid, superbly.

Milton's *superbia* is a joy to have:
triumphal reticence, verse to be delivered
badly and to survive; and this by virtue

of Comus' gifts—not meant to be so taken.

17

That actors think too highly of themselves.
Relax this *pondus* of splenetic pride.
Sleet's always driven sideways in my experience;

hard at it now, rustles like harsh tissue
or creaks against the glass. As Milton said,
no more chiding. He had some years to go.

Someone had to forgive him. No, not himself.
His daughters, maybe, though that story's garbled.
He was a cheerful soul and loved your music,

Hugh, as he must have told you many times.

18

I'm wresting myself into simplicity—
exhaustion's bonanza—also I wish to leave
something in trust, something by definition

not by default. Head-on the big crows
halt the wind, the gulls plane in wide curves,
vanishing among the flurries; fields are blue-brown

with a top-dressing of snow. In whose name
such conflagrations of undeeded gifts?
If not Milton then Hardy; if not

Hardy, Lawrence—*Look! We Have Come Through!*

19

That from this noise, this mêlée, there issues
a grand and crabby music. And that I
want my piece of it. Even when not mine.

That vows so made are like lights on snow-ploughs,
purpose and power at once. Look what gets
tossed aside. Massive effects are junked.

And they talk about Heavy Metal. They don't know,
these kids, what weight of the word is,
that in the half dark of commodity most

offers are impositions.

20

That weight of the world, weight of the word, is.
Not wholly irreconcilable. Almost.
Almost we cannot pull free; almost we escape

the leadenness of things. Almost I have walked
the first step upon water. Nothing beyond.
The inconceivable is a basic service;

Not to be too Parnassian about it;
And not to put to strain their erudition
(I mean the learned readers of J. Milton);

And weight of the word, weight of the world, is.

2 Courtly Masquing Dances

nello stile antico

I

Weight of the world, weight of the word, is.
Take it slowly, like walking
through convalescence, the load
bearing not yet adjusted, progress
made with a slight forward and sideways tilt,
or otherways angled, one hip
acting up, strung on a wire.
How heartening it is when it goes right—
the moment of equipollence, a signal.

2

Indebtedness is resolved by paying debts,
strangely enough; justice, not metaphysics;
custom, restitution, setting to rights and rest.
Law-breaking too is in the hierarchy,
and riding westward, post-haste. This
brings us to Michaelmas, its rule and riot,
its light a fading nimbus over Wales.

3

The river the forest, the river is the forest,
the forest the river, swamps of loosestrife
choking fecundity. Sabrina, she also, chaste
genius of teeming and dying,
I fancy her
trailing labiles, placentas, uncomely swags.
My own lines double here as her lianas.

4

The time of our sleeping, all-forthcoming time
in the author's progress. Are you convinced by sleep?
At some level I am, though still forgetful.
You appear largely in possession, Sabrina;
your waters never sleep—now kept in spate
by Cambrian readjustments far up-stream;
your stretch of the interminable
journey to closure
that gathers beauty, bearing as it goes.

5

Inducted by Marvell I have brought along
my *wanton troopers*—squaddies, as we know them.
I watch them urging through, at some low ford,
their rowels nicking. Fawns? There are fawns,
even now, in the still haunted purlieus
between Bewdley and Ludlow; and stags rutting.
Of the sexual lives of children I speak elsewhere.
And of white wood-sorrel long called *alleluia*.
And of the rut of begetting.

6

Masques are booked to be simple, sensuous,
comely, shaped to a fair design;
not over-passionate;
free from dark places and equivocation;
present a tidy challenge, less to the maker
than to the persons in the entertainment,
young noble clones broadly beset by clowns.

7

This our egregious masking: what it entails.
Our sex-masques plague-threatened. Our murrain'd
rustic to-and-fro-ing, lording it here, and there,
craven in vanity. I mean, lawful
lordship, powers that must be, I do not grudge.
Nor do I challenge the power of the Lord
President in Cymru. *Diolch—diolch yn fawr.*

8

I doubt Marvell bought out Milton's fouled life.
But bring on music, sonorous, releasing.
What we have becomes their reticence
within the radius of a storm's hollow
like honey in a tree. Bayed Milton reticent?
Or that wit-bibber from Hull? I say self-being
goes the last word with both, that it goes proud
in its own passion—mystical couvade
with sensual dying, sensuous rebirth.

9

Suppose, ingenious, we tell our loves
haemony's in the script, melts like a pearl,
chemical self-renewal not to be paid for,
retroactively inheres, working forgiveness
within the act, enriches all performance
in the great masquing- or presence-chamber
of reason and desire:
you with your daemon or genius, I with one
who for the fiction's sake must feel betrayed.

10

Suppose I tell it otherwise: haemony
is of the blood (therefore the lovely name);
the elect possess it subject to possession;
it cannot be bought, bartered, part exchanged.
The sun is drawn away, darkness advances
bleeding our scene, mysterious dry ice
tinctured with earth-smoke, Orphic harbinger.

11

Its prickliness closely reckoned, revered—
few others contesting—dim prodigy
uncultivated
and of glummest fruition.
Proffer it then to that transparent virgin
of pregnant chastity;
let her go far afflicted with her friends.

12

Haemony may mean technē ⎮ now he tells me.
Haemony means whatever Milton meant by it.
Wisdom of the blood was not intended.
He was his own man, like Lawrence. Not
proto anything that I can think of.
Nor was Lawrence blood ⎮ wisdom in isolation.
Look at our tangled history. Neptune's
forest submerging, compounding its coal measures,
smoke-enriched England ⎮ her children ashen.

13

Yes, Comus, about time; about time
and justification. That's beginning
to match a laggard forwardness. In touch,
my other self—so held—once it's too late;
my other pulse, beating to Plato's rhythm
heard through circadian circuits of distress.
Loud hissing in the ears may or may not
mean blood pressure soaring, or sex on heat,
or siren voices, or your lisping snakes.

14

I've not pieced out the story. Milton's script
was briefly censored, bits of sex expunged
for the girl's sake. Chastity makes its bed
with sensuality, could not otherwise
use such authoritative vehemence
devoid of knowingness.
It's an attractive doctrine to me now.

15

Hereditary thresholds, I recognize
how often you're mysterious disenchanters,
enablers of some journeys but not this
where England ends half way across a field,
the valley of the Honddu at the cleft
church of Cwm Yoy, its displaced gravity;
and I not moving and yet moving on.

16

The red sandstone forest, fern-shouldering streams;
the Severn also, cliff-cutting, wide-wading,
the commonness of the prodigious journey—
no memory of those lost princes who wait
to be dug up by Grimm—the words of un-
expected and expected salutation;
the young commoner, Lawes's find, not found
at the scene of his making, who might now
be thought well worthy an earl's daughter.

17

Oh, and yes, Comus, back to our vanity;
now I have brought you out, a shared advantage,
to walk and take the air around the moat,
though this smells bad tonight. So be my guest
emissary, or janissary, to the swans
who ride the higher air, when they've a mind,
mysterious radii, not given to tread
with any flesh of spirit, or be trodden
by any but the airiest incubi.

18

This is a fabled England, vivid
in winter bareness; bleakly comforting
the faded orchard's hover of grey-green.
We have come home, say, all is well between us.
Sharp-shining berries bleb a thorn, as blood
beads on a finger or a dove's breast pierced
by an invisible arrow to the heart.

19

Too many of us. I have laid you
waste with such love.
But such waste as becomes fecundity
in the eyes of others: the sun strikes
through these dimensions, cumulus
burns tortoiseshell-umber, lanterned
from inside the mass.

20

To show immediately how it all works:
Platonic theology's flight simulators;
no call to leave the ground of our estate.
There are designs that light the empyrean.
I have more in mind Great Tew's
model symposium that's set in motion
by slow airs fluted on the inlaid grass,
aubades to angels from the sons of earth.
The eternal round's a fixture on their screens.

21

He means the poets, and he has these moments.
Also he has his lines, the dying
swan that chants, enchanted to the stream,
palmed off on you know who. They say the red
kite is back, inland from Aber,
in soaring numbers, some in the Thames Valley,
round Cuddesdon's small, declivitous plateau
where even the snails are different. And the birds.
Near where they set him up with Mary Powell.

22

Sharpened, sharpening, the swifts' wings
track and loop back clear skeins
through vanished arches.
See in what ways the river
lies padded—no, dashed—with light.
Show whether the imaged clouds
are litanies or escorts.

23

Tacitus described the Phoenix once,
mentioning myrrh and semen, which must mean fire.
Steady now, old heart, longevity
is not at all the Heraclitean thing.
See, hear, how sparks
fly from the burning-plumed rôtisserie—
painful the fable ardently re-wound.

24

Alongside these travesties stands my own
vision of right order. Some forms, orders,
travesty themselves. That is today's
communiqué. Tomorrow's order book
will read the same.
World-webbed collusions, clouded diplomacies,
are lightning when they strike and strike us down.
Of marriages I speak, as of right order
among the travesties.

25

It's not impossible to be the child
of Bacchus and Circe, all imagination,
a demon made against his deepest will
a choric figure awed by what he hears.
There ís a dogged beauty in the world,
unembarrassing goodness, honesty unfazed.
There's also the corrupter, the abuser,
the abused corrupted in accepted ways,
the ways of death, the deadliness of life.

26

The corrupter, the abuser, the liverish
ravager of domestic peace. The soi-disant
harmless eccentric. Nobody's harmless.
Neither is comedy. Maybe the polka
injured thousands. In this depleted time
revive me, take me to a blue
movie, hold my hand in the dark.

27

His storm is in our air; light-burdened leaves
electrify his keepings. Love appears
as though by being [|] named an equal self.
Retrieve impulse, enjoy,
without collusion, your own
doubtful self-celebration; say no more.
Conclude, most things offload without a glance.

28

Hard to imagine them so cramped: thirty
feet by sixty?—I can't believe it.
Were the first builders pinched for cash, or what?
Then this thing—sudden—in the midst of them:
Comus, as we must call it, unconfined,
disembarrassing itself of common vesture,
the hyphenated speech of titled actors,
the torches set like wild men on the walls
tossing swart-blooded fire.

29

Can't have been torches in that space; put
candelabra. Candles, torches and all, burn down
to their ugly sockets; and the castle:
a site of gaping sconces, puddled floors,
and sodden tidy grass with gleam of rime.
Need to think about this; if possible, not
wax portentous but not quip it away.
By it he means you, Britannia, his 'deep
and passionate love', high-stepping into ruin.

30

Say that I am gifted—and I'll touch you
for ordinary uncommon happiness. What
a weirdo, you think. Well, yes, I was wired weird.
Back to the forest, then, where still so much
is the matter of legend. I see us getting down
to something long since hallowed and nuptial,
nuptial or nothing, angrily desired.

31

These short ones are the sock-fillers. No,
do my life justice now if anywhere,
register shock-survival, childhood
anaesthesia: like being sucked
down by the *Bismarck*, pressure, multi-
dimensional pain, dead sulphonamides
creaming the mastoid bone.

32

Knowledge does what to sex or, as it comes,
consensual, word of conjure? Certainly
flesh has its own spirit but may not know that.
Would you call an experience with Donne's
Elegies providential? Where are tapers
tapers burning in the immortal vaults of love?
Who is this now approaching
love at first sight? And is excoriate
nót to cry from the heart?

33

Quiet! I'm still trying. Pity,
terror, you might care to empower them
as choruses, though they're as nothing
without judgement
of what instruments can do
to the human voice.
Imagine synthesizers
transforming the desert of our earth-drawn
metaphysical cries.

34

Die Fühlungsmühl: the hollow mill that turns
always full of itself. As master—briefly—
of my own skill, I call this to account
under a dated lintel, the gristing-chamber,
where for a lifetime it has ground me
an unnutritious powder, a black grain
against the grain of the stone.

35

Held by this half-literate grieving excitement,
honey-infused candles, this vigil: patriotism
is not unChristian; it's not Christian either,
I beg to plead. Transcendent indistinction
trashes the thought. Spirit bleeds everywhere
emoting body-pathos, not unlike
ectoplasm, or grease-paint from Hallowe'en.

36

It ejaculates its pain and is not
answered; nor acknowledged wisely.
Give you these, by way of verbiage:
obvious things, patience that has for emblem
seeds oblivious, the flax-plant in its way;
chicory also, its sober chance provision;
the service tree, wild, scarce, with healing willow;
the torchwort or mullein, as it is known,
and comfrey the waste-healer.

37

Harrowed three days, now Lazarus
breaking his fast. Dead Sickert's look-alike.
Post-flu invalid's diet and inappropriate
light-squinnied isolation. Abstemious wolfing,
loose-tied, flop hung, baggy, nappy-cravat,
big dish of mussels, stewed prunes, gleaming black stones,
spoon like a tongue-depresser gobbed straight in.
Poverty parodied—rich sensual man of parts—
death-grip on his revived inheritance.

38

And if by some such hazard something
incomparably finished, something beyond change
as by design, yes, the great memory-surge
of raw beginning: snow-contoured strange Wildmoor
and our stiff ugly tasks; a single storm lamp
not thawing-out the frozen pipes; each pane
of the kitchen window quilted with white ferns.

39

Rewriting his own deepest reading. Thát
fair comment on the wiped out fifty years
from genesis to this? Give me a break
in concentration, so I can concentrate,
as I once did—a Comus child—on pignuts,
on how the tree gum, malleable, came to hand
as damson-amber; which I tried to burn.

40

Go through it all again: Is this
the genius that approached you? Does it
have a name? Said, wish I could draw you,
draw you so that you seem
not to be hiding, wish I could draw you in?
Concede some kind of epic statement.
Sleep alone, fertile and barren friend.
Insulted witness of proven chastity.
Name of hotel?

41

All Saints All Souls, the shades stay with the year;
and prayer has ratted on me; and the leaves
have ratted on the boughs. November First,
variegate, attenuate, Japanese; high
spiritous colours, or wan, or putrid brown.
And I say: watch—watch this phenomenon,
this other selving; it is yours to keep,
whose shadow reaches out, grows, is unhinged,
flung on the shattered pavement, breaks apart.

42

Read *me* throughout, the *du* is self reflexive
though not without exception. There are times
when I consort with music so to speak.
Speaking of which there's your reluctant gift
of sorrow so prolific and my own
fortune spent in mishearings; our voices pitched,
our minds of penury poised upon excess.

43

Their time not ours. They show it; are naked.
Name three still living awarded the Mons Star.
Love will not spare us the past. Old
men of seventy have nuisance value.
I snorkel into contrived sleep, I wake,
I address the mirror: *spare me my own
rancour and ugliness.* It too is naked.

44

I'm tired now the whole time and yet I wish to
take up my bed and walk:
to Compostela, for example,
bush-hat hung round with scallops on return:
or ride the Gulf Stream through to Akureyri
and find a hot spring equal to my bulk
sheltered by palm trees, bowered by frangipani
or bougainvillia, wallowing in *Icelandic
Christian Poetry* till the fish come home.

45

Sprung from stacked cages racing-pigeons
with startling whurrawhurra
crowd to the air,
turning, co-radicate, radiate,
from this focus, the body
of their homing flight.
Where's the sun up to? I can see them
not now a wheel exactly, nor a fan,
more a silver bowl, the silver tarnishing.

46

The light, generous, discovers its ascent,
gives all it can bring us:
a haze, and at odd hours the moon also is there
appearing sea-worn.
But what a hope, the mild attrition
of a dove's call, the body
gradually winding down, becoming vacant.

47

The small oaks crest the ridge, the sun appears
cresting this instant. Their topmost ranks
take fire and vaporize
or find some other form wherewith to be
not of this world. How can I tell you?—
dawn after dawn, immeasurable taking up
of dross and dying.

48

Slouching at senescence. Whereas Ursa Minor
is the real McCoy, the true Cynosure:
whereas, what I believe I give you here
I take as the counterpoint to your own
caustic attrition and noble rest-
oration of music's power to console.
Whereas, thus, in proclaiming, in oration.
Seventeenth-century torch-songs did things well.
No slouches, then, whoever wrote them.

49

The stiff-eyed man in the colonial hat
directs his dotted eyebeams angled sharply
into the ground. Instantly they re-
bound (from mirror or burnished metal)
these rays elliptical, soaring, crown
with high art a solitary stunt pine.
Faith stands confirmed in trigonometry
keeping at nadir and at zenith, both,
its delphic zeal.

50

If this sleep mask is a time machine
a world attends us under a strange star,
our gifts are what we owe, each to the other,
and which we give: now there's no going back,
no *Wedding at the Marsh*, the true fiction
set in the one frame; or the book set down
marked at that page, not closed and not returned to.

51

The ashen-purple soil looks ripe for winter,
as does the succubine ground ivy
snag-wrinkling over it. The wind veers
closer to silence than most things I know
outside your third quartet, music I
strain to catch:
clamours of diminution, abrupt rest.

52

Sei solo, a polished soundfocus, blunt splay fingers
unhasty, the bow attentive, now to be glimpsed
pistoning *tempo di bourrée*, and heard
clawing out four-string polyphony, a form
of high baritone *tessitura*,
groan, almost, and sighing—such depth—the instrument's
power from upthrust, the return
equally measured: an athlete's kind of measure
with and against earth's torque and tricky camber.

53

Heady September heat with shadows thrown
across white walls. Sun fetching us this instant!
Where are we sans our lovers; you name the place?
The place itself is common; I have been here
many times and enough.
Love's grief is full, always popular,
like ghosted memoirs or the old
fashioned chara-tours,
like some Welsh hill smothered in rhododendrons.

54

Absolutely all in all, all in the picture
exhibited to the jury. Aged overnight.
Overnight seduction by a minor art
carries life, and the voyeur, with it
without any major recompense. The charge
is *anadiplosis* and the sentence
the sentence here handed down.

55

A fish-shaped embryo aureoled in flame
glows from the time-scarred retina's
scratch kaleidoscope. A thing even of beauty
I should fancy; less strange than goldfish
on black and white TV. Now Piscis breaks
out into floated plaques and warps of colour.
I'll join you, wobbly swimmers of the eye.

56

Restart from cold: crystallized
microchips on the plane window.
November Thirtieth; the pumice
and verdigris textured coastline of Iceland
steps up slowly as slowly we step down.
Can't tell you how unoften I accost
these graphic isolations. The swept-strewn
groundscape of Keflavik accommodates us,
I cán tell you.

57

Greetings *sul ponte*, fratello mio. If
careen means turning vessels on their side
to claw off barnacles; and if *fulsome*'s
the right word for befouling praise;
if the self servers now in full career—
against whom you stood
and stand no chance, none, stop
scratching and sighing—and if *col
legno* means whacking it with back of bow—

58

Feed the seven cats, pray to the household gods.
Try on the new Timon of Athens face.
Sickert's late 'Lazarus' self-portraits kill me.
To be reborn into love is to live
a posthumous life. Can you, can anyone,
better the telling?
Shakespeare's Timon not born again into love.

59

Something towers and stoops to its own mind
exactly; it is good merely to sense this.
I am, by my kept word,
a disenfranchised stranger. Strange that my fathers
thought they were not. There goes a fox
like a swift perfect image of itself.
Somewhere a frightened skunk squibs rancid musk.

60

Had intended—what had I not intended?
Praise elemental Job's *ur-Weheklag*,
its iron-cleave, lead-scald? Praise all change
this side of chaos, with the immoveable.
Praise hook-wheeled constellations, praise autumn's
dense clearances, its disfiguring splendours,
far-riding glacial rock, the setting
sun like a stoke-hole, the winter woods
gutted by fire.

61

Stations of the cross are not standard school
crossings, unless for non-standard children.
Not stops on any metro. Some police
barracks may resemble them. Show me
what you are thinking—my *forte*
is melodrama—you are free to go.
Data bases serve also: we are all
made to endure. Made, as in *made*
the Heavens and the Earth, as in *made Man*.

62

Now from sun-stalking rainclouds that supreme
engine advances, marshalling
familiar cubist layouts, the half-
harvested fields,
blocking their shift-patterns like dazzle
camouflage
on ships in dry dock during the Great War.

63

The city stands to itself, the late
October sky a sportsdome
of clear Fall blue; Virginia creeper,
with ample cladding, warming the brick walls
to a dark glow, a gross finery.
When I close my eyes the sun
beats in silent clamour against them.

64

Veteran imagination, going down
in wide slow circles, gracefully almost,
like a Fortress over Schweinfurt.
Acquittal here for those no less distinguished,
wound-stripes like velcro scars for him and him.
For her the undead Reichsführer's cryptic doors.
I have made, singularly, a double life
vicarious in parts. Nothing redemptive.
Mouthing aphasias now. Interrogations.

65

Nor is being beside oneself the cue
for revelation, though its arrival stuns:
like the high-piled and brilliantly
toppled bells—their run-of-the-change,
tower-engulfing, average Sunday peal,
a visitation that possesses
foundation and frontage of the shaken air.
Nor is emptiness alone the answer, the tomb
itself open-mouthed.

66

The day, about to be paid off, descends
into its promised adumbrations
which I do not decline: low-
wattaged fuchsia, far-illuminant,
especially at evening when the sun
draws on its constant yet depleted light,
empowers the sum of innate happiness.

67

With splintering noises the ancient tannoy
celebrates more delay like a bequest
or benefaction long overdue.
An ordinary day, one more rehearsal.
Ducking and weaving the last flight goes in,
the voice of reason maddens with its fear;
voices of prophecy assail the dead.

68

Again the wind hauls and my yard-tree
shags itself free of leaves. The house rocks
as if to show that it was built on sand.
Very little now that I do not
take to be hers in lieu of deprivation:
implausible, credible muse whom I
assuage by night. Unbelievable sex-love,
to which I gave such credence, she believes
our slow corruption by the Song of Songs.

69

The cunning is to swing it, be a hinge
of the unhinged time. At very worst
gaping on all, missing what pillage finds;
at best a portal for the hierarchies.
Something done with ⌐ the urge to have begun
in many ways consigned to be regained.
All on the make, and broken, and exact,
says Milton, England's challenge to Petursson.
In Wintry solstice like the shorten'd light.

70

On mounds of winter city-pigeons flame
drab epaulettes. Clouds over cooling towers
lift and sunder. Call me fantasist
lately assigned to reality. Example
is scansion; instance, to suffer so.
Locate exile in a basement of field stone
kept by the soughing furnace.

71

First and last, the Denmark Strait takes all
as if by reversion. The Hallgrimskirkja
rears, preternaturally white,
high and dry on its mount, a tribute
to light's pyromania. Everything's
besprent with rayon prisms. The theatre
of obligation offers us refuge.

72

Win some, lose some. The Younger Brother
said Milton should be topped, his books burnt.
This over royalty and the republic:
close to the bone, the resurrection bone
which never could be found though they raked memory
from end to end. And wrought the sarabande,
Sabrina's theme, ascending through the strings
as though such music rounded out mischance.
Dawn-labouring candles twitched their sallow flames.

73

Four days on floor six of the Radisson
Saga. I am translated: high density,
high intensity spaces
of imagination. Not much else to observe:
one rotary, three intersections, a school,
a pale house trailing the weathered flag
of a Scandinavian kingdom. Sketched susurrus
of tyres through slush. The self-flensing ocean
making haphazard signals, idle, urgent.

74

Think of *Tetrachordon*, or, rather, of Milton's
apologetical sonnet, rhetoric
like the exposed
innards of a jumping jack the slightly
salty gunpowder odour.
High-vaunting Hecla, her sulphurious fire;
as in the obscure, curious madrigal.

75

Anytime, now, the final breath-taker,
of which I shall not judge—
not as gravity judges the vortex
or the stone gravity or the targeting
arrow the bow or the magnet
the pendulum, the pendulum mere
misinformalists of time.

76

Got religion, though, down at the heart
of Reykjavik, its little houses,
the old ones rigged like tin Bethels.
I should have bought in
when Iceland went for sale,
settled myself as a famed incógnito,
folk bed, folk table, with a folk
knocker to my door; the yard
dwarf-flowered, the lava summer-hued.

77

Is nothing if not farce,
your regular antimasque. But I
have run out of farce and out
of patience with this ashkenazic rôle.
Take it, leave it, the serious work's been done.
Listen! that gnawing sound the big jets make
devouring their flight paths. I'll be out of here
before the first blank ice, well before rotten
gutters grow healthy fangs.

78

Bright cutting-edge or not, I intend to give
notice to my own mind. I suppose
sooner or later we encounter evil
and find little to say.
Remembering though to say:
behind incertitude the vaulting
certitudes of flume and flame.

79

No, no. Comus screamed like a peacock
at this conclusion. Moral vanity
is his parole, in the off season,
at any time mere sensuality
seems to lie dormant. I know well
the bristling strut, demonic rectitude,
the rod and glass, the masks of his fixation.

80

While the height-challenged sun fades, clouds become
as black-barren as lava, wholly motionless,
not an ashen wisp out of place, while the sun fades.
While the sun fades its fields glow with dark poppies.
Some plenary hand spreads out, to flaunt an end,
old gold imperial colours. Look back a shade,
Guðríður Þorbjarnardóttir, over your
left shoulder or mine, absolute night comes
high-stalking after us.

3 A Description of the Antimasque

1

Antimasque, the Lady said, not anticlimax.
Then let me give you the Laws of Justinian.
Or Petursson's passion-psalms, even more to the point.

Shall I rejig myself to senile Horner
and get among the women one last time
in a wolf's pelt of harmlessness, holiness even?

Prophecy is too much, the prophets are too many.
The sea is greenish first, then mustard-yellow,
then chevroned, then broken up,

camouflaged in its abundant colours.
Why do I give you this, why, trembling so,
the meniscus of desire?

2

Sought-after pageantries of light
by darkness annulled; as if by chance
something incomparable gets done; the annulment

blazingly carried through. But now
we are on our own, there is no music.
Ask of me what you will, it is not enough.

Thule's irregular reefs, try naming them
natural pindarics. Our duty is to find
consonance in the disparities, like as not,

duty no less than function—how to rise
to ceremonies of speech; when, why, to address
intrusive suffering.

3

Antimasque, stiff buffoon! *Sunburning*,
Moonblasting (Milton my friend) the works.
But judge decorum on a sliding scale

itself a float of courtly masquing dances
John Adson would have envied, not to mention
W. and H. Lawes & Co (strange form of words,

that, *not to mention*—it has a name).
The first Comus, Sabrina, were, are, nameless.
What will you give me for your fifteen minutes

that I would pay myself, or cheat
myself out of, given half a chance,
granted the delicate footwork of a clown?

4

In patches, profusion—rugosa possibly.
Check out Yule beacons, how they flare, die down,
like giant toaster fires. Seasonal folk-skirlers

with *brennivin* and fiddles muster accordingly,
and with many accordions.
I can't see where, how, resolution applies,

but I am not Hallgrimur Petursson.
If fame is erotic I shall go after fame.
Roses, though, at this latitude?

I mean, when the new year is patently launched,
and metamorphosis absorbs the broached resins;
and when night's final combustion caps everything.

5

At dense comedic levels fishes probe,
white, flat, luminous, among volcanic
greaves and fissures; find openings

where they nose past the mystic origins
of leprosy and blindness:
Milton's pearl, the *gutta serena*, Hallgrimur

Petursson, his stricken eloquence
all the more to be hailed. Proportionate
disproportion—or equity—it even turns

on this. On this and that, you say. In fact,
you say nothing, god-given Diodati.
Bare preservation is the speaking power.

6

The pulse of the whole fulfils nominal
metronome keepings. Take this as understood.
The narrative's a kind of figured bass,

stark-sounding in the arias. Of crisis
and denial. Sometimes I wish music
meant less to me. Now it's like standing proxy

in a declaration of unanswered love.
Or something like. Sexual
love—what other kind of love ís there,

even for an amorist
of the abstract eros? Hear me
sight-read these as optional cadenzas.

7

Take this one straight from the floor. Do the vigilant
keep the best vigil? Reversed film is not
magnetic force. A rhetorical

question's essential to the dynamic.
Memory of her body is what carries me. Come!
Even though I have no distance to drive.

Mystery means all that's unobvious
to the inattentive. Axioms
are a dead weight. Or, if you prefer,

they are the tie-rods of argument.
Saved by such rules as these
evoke chaos, chaos that knows its bounds.

8

Image of egg-whites threaded as extruded
through boiling water; Lear's numskull friend
with his tarred whited sockets. *Admit One*

to the theatre, the observatory, to the small
cinema showing new foreign films,
the museum of glances, the Ecclesia

Sancti Pauli in Walton Street.
I had forgotten how the ill-omened road
configures at this point. I catch my breath.

The clue's in the projector, out of focus
for fifty years: a face blurred to declare
itself in some way, some way of saying no.

9

Combative in theory, I hate drawing
my own blood. Blood-line's a different issue,
Severn-side blacksmiths and nailers who must have bled:

I vouch for these, on half-familiar terms.
Ungrateful though they may be for my voice.
Hallgrimur Petursson's closer to them,

although not in Icelandic. I've yet to find
a well-working translation. Petursson found
that he had leprosy. Segregation works.

The English class system works in its own way.
Neither segregation nor assimilation;
pitched as incumbent on declining grace.

10

En route from the belligerent post office
to encounter this: termination's crowd
moving freely about a locked centre,

a thousand, more, in solitary vigil,
residual unpaid weepers; dark eye-spoors;
befouled cerements; chilled waxen flux

draping the plaza's grid of iron birds
stalled upon flight; regular paths dead ends
between sidewalk and office: brought to stand

embarrassed, as for the under-rehearsed
in rote and rite, misspeaking their best lines
anciently taped, spun flailing. Wipe the day.

11

Nightmare arrested, stop-watch still in its
possession, sex undeveloped; stuck film.
Things unattempted yet with sleepmask on.

Try Chaucer's mask: the broad way of the wheel,
the public ruin and the private gain;
no-hope encounters with the witch herself,

Circe or Lilith or Lady Mede;
the living fetish of the murdered love;
the rigid fantasist bowed as if for prayer;

the ultimate fixity of things let slide,
the treaty sealed, the treacheries undisclosed;
disclosed, the voyeur's mirror in the wall.

12

So let there be nothing where it stood,
Ludlow's brief mirage: Comus' spectral
body as its material which might

absently be repaired-to. This in worn
September through Michaelmas. You'd expect
no late miraculous quicksilver in these

quick-falling days. But take the road once more:
the sainted angels bearing themselves aloof,
pre-emptive patrons of trashed Coventry—

curtain-call Michael, out-of-stock artiste,
conjured ineptly; the unriven spire
soars reinspired, alight with a dull rain.

13

Joy is the full sun and the half shadow.
Twelve stands unbalanced, no prize for that—
lurching city fathers. But imbalance

is everywhere. In the tectonic plates
ripping Iceland apart, to cite you basics.
I'm no *Fortuna*-type much as I love

Boethius. And irony has limits. If
this were adjudged Senecan I'd be honoured.
Surrey's bitter proud jousting, his straight-up

elegy for Wyatt, I can find strength in,
ironic or not. Not [|] all other things
being equal. They aren't and never will be.

14

Solemn music and dance, befitting language
drawn with a difficult meeting of the kinds,
History on call, posterity in rehearsal,

may yet carry us through. Voice from the wings
interpellates a chorus. Style for style
Purcell could do me justice, Jonson's words,

or Dryden's, gesture satisfaction. Thus
to counterpoise: so poise it and retire
into the work. Music of false relation,

sufficient harmony's near-mental grist,
bewails a coda: bring it down, I say,
justification's tenor bare of theme.

15

Error-heavy work, to be set right
by final showdown. Say, vision and the Fall
use me to sing. Or, idiot-alibi.

From the outset something of mine failed
the long addition, short détente, between
private and public, purpose, desire, hope.

I was off sick while freedom bells were rung
in three-parts-ruined cities for that age.
Bring back the *Trümmerfrauen*, rubble-women.

I want start-over with a different voice.
Few souls are solitary through force of will.
Here there's no crossing-point from zone to zone.

16

Rilke could read *Bible* in bad light
or shaky script. Most of what I claim
can be so read. This is a summary

as it is a summons. Though not on oath
repeat after me *the interminable
journey to closure*. Here's a beginning

beginning at the end. For a start it was
not interminable: not since we knew ourselves
appropriately immortal. There was joy—

the unbroken immanence to which I speak—
that day upriver, chased by angry swans.
Half-recalled abjurations yet to come.

17

For some cause or other the block stands.
It's like a monument to a mythic poet.
Better, to the commander of a rearguard.

Whether of stone or bronze it is found fractured
if not by vandals by some intrinsic flaw
proper to originality and the medium,

material witness to a state of things
in which our freedom is a type of fate
within the shifting bounds predictable.

A certain way: interpret, sober fear
sprung of a certain knowledge of the odds.
Interpret, crazy shouting on the heath.

18

The reefs of which I spoke: the breakers there
pile with such force you feel their breath expelled
in hearing it. Expelled, never expended,

not off those shores. This is a partial gloss.
I take your challenge. Partiality,
error, relative absolutes,

pitching things into shape. Roman theology
hits us with *culpa*, though that's not a coup
except to unwary punsters. Geophysicists

make much of *fault*: fault, with its proper
natural enormity, a geyser's eye
that bulges like the eyeball of a squid.

19

Nothing is unforgettable but guilt.
Guilt of the moment to be made eternal.
Reading immortal literature's a curse.

Beatrice in *The Changeling* makes me sweat
even more than Faustus' Helen. Recompose
Marlowe's off-stage blasphemous fun with words

or Pound's last words to silence. Well,
let well alone. The gadgetry of nice
determinism makes, breaks, comedians.

All the better if you go mad like Pound
(*grillo*, a cricket; *grido*, a cry from the fields).
The grief of comedy you have to laugh.

20

In Wintry solstice like the shorten'd light
sky closes; and sea parts, ranging itself
from unpredicted sources, radiant

when you'd guess blankness under broad shadow.
Hidden artificers of the visible
withhold what's long been destined to the dark.

In shifting scapes eternity resumes.
I cannot fault its nature, act by act,
gauged by the lost occasions of the sun.

Ephemera's durance, vast particulars
and still momentum measures of the void.
WHAT DID YOU SAY?

Without Title

in omaggio a Eugenio Montale

Here to my mind is the objection to taking love as ultimate. There is no higher form of unity, I can agree. But we do not know love as the complete union of individuals, such that we can predicate of it the entirety of what belongs to them. And if we extend the sense of love and make it higher than what we experience, I do not see myself that we are sure of preserving that amount of self-existence in the individuals which seems necessary for love.

F. H. BRADLEY

The profound nature will have a savage rudeness; the delicate one will be shallow, or the victim of sensibility; the richly accomplished will have some capital absurdity; and so every piece has a crack. 'Tis strange, but this masterpiece is a result of such an extreme delicacy, that the most unobserved flaw in the boy will neutralize the most aspiring genius, and spoil the work.

R. W. EMERSON

Improvisation on
'O Welt ich muss dich lassen'

Traurig as one is between bearers, dancers,
old comrades from the Crem or at the Palais,
that's not the issue. Can't decide among
the cheap comedians. I do panic.
Queer noise going on there like a gander
rehearsing its angry call. I long to stay
immortal and ageless, to stick around
for the Bacchantes' orgy, folk throwing up.
I had a dream in which this is all real,
where we rip off our masks and sing
'O Welt ich muss dich lassen'; medics on cue
for the recite-a-thon. Forget your science.
Dead friends are no remoter than in life.
It's curtains, though, protesting I can tell
limbo-dancers from wizards, chaps who tear
papers to shreds then flap them as by magic
back in one piece, *You're fired* still crisp, pristine.

Without Title

to PMH

Pheromones moribund, but something other
bemuses mourning, more than vows unmade,
shared life aborted. I could write at length
an entailed history, the character
of unfruition, match my fellow townsman,
his grief's pastmaster though long-since cold,
culling the bay bowers to which he
cannot return. His gall his gift,
his sign a bloom-struck cherry bough; ours
flowering currant that close-to stinks of cat.
Ingenuous I recall us, a genius
for misconception making our divorced
selves of love still agelessly at one:
no restitution but with wired laurels.

Chromatic Tunes

to PMH

Each waking I conclude erotic dreams
private mass entertainment. There's
no joy in this, nor do I spend desire
that things should be so. Otherwise I read
of matrimony on your foreign planet
but cannot find the language. Otherwise
featureless idling strews the wintry strands;
woods bare their clutter; sea birds appear
to boister with the waves, to wrench themselves
windborne. The soughing moon-tide's hulkingness,
massive passivity, works its gnarls of light.
Further I cannot judge
whether to go, or stay; or tell how one
might stay, another go, far flung, bereft.

In Ipsley Church Lane 1

More than ever I see through painters' eyes.
The white hedge-parsleys pall, the soot is on them.
Clogged thorn-blossom sticks, like burnt cauliflower,
to the festered hedge-rim. More than I care to think
I am *as one* coarsened by feckless grief.
Storm cloud and sun together bring out the yellow of stone.

But that's lyricism, as Father Guardini
equably names it: autosuggestion, mania,
working off a chagrin close to despair,
ridden by jealousy of all self-healed
in sexual love, each selving each, the gift
of that necessity their elect choice.

Later, as in late autumn, there will be
the mass-produced wax berries, and perhaps
an unearthed wasps' nest like a paper skull,
where fragile cauls of cobweb start to shine.
Where the quick spider mummifies its dead
rage shall move somnolent yet unappeased.

The Jumping Boy

I

Here is the jumping boy, the boy
who jumps as I speak.

He is at home on the king's highway,
in call of the tall house, its blind
gable end, the trees—I know this place.

The road, on broad contourings drawn out of sight,
stops—wherever—but not at Lyonnesse,
though from Lyonnesse I shall bring you,

through grimed orchards, across gorse-hummocked
old common land everywhere given back
to the future of memory.

2

He leaps because he has serious
joy in leaping. The girl's

eyes no way allowed for, or else
she is close in covert and we
are to know that, not knowing how.

I'll bet she worships his plebeian
bullet head, Hermes' winged
plimsolls, the crinkled toy tin hat

held on by elastic. He is winning
a momentous and just war
with gravity.

3

This may be levitation. I
could do that. Give my remembrance
to his new body. These episodes recur.

4

Jump away, jumping boy; the boy I was
shouts go.

On the Reality of the Symbol

I

That he feared death—Karl Rahner—unrevealing.
Fine theologian with or against
the world, in senses that are not the world's,
his symbolism, both
a throwback and way forward, claims its own
cussedness, yet goes with the mystery.
Parturition of psalm like pissing blood
I must say, the formal evidence
so much an issue. Though not painful
pain's in the offing, somewhere signifies
its needled presence. Plus, the prostate's
a nasty beast even at the best of times.
But for translation the old linguaduct
works not too badly. This is a translation.

2

So? Say it again: ephemeralities
ever recurring. There are numerous
things you can't speak or think. Must confess I
sometimes raped her ghost? The olive trees
oblige our buffetings. Scapegoats are not
hunted but driven out. There yet remain
impassioned and strange readings: a remote
cry of the blood sugars.
Try *melos* for desired numbness of breath.
And you a poet in all justice. Too
many signs: call scourings from fouled pipes
purification. There! the white dove plumps
her spectral finery. Building my ark begins
late in the terminal welter of the flood.

3

Pity love could not act us. No scarcity
of drama schools where I live. In some of them
refusal's not much worse than other failings
I won't elaborate. We refused each other:
loss is what we are left with. Re-audition.
They'd take us back, instruct us to be old.
Here's bargain-gelt to move things on a stage.
More than a sexy trial a *Trauerspiel*
needs make-believe to launch the sordid fact.
Does this miscast us as a tragic chorus?
Can't answer that, I'm working on my role.
Shyster's from a Yiddish word for shit.
It's not, you know.
This is late scaffold-humour; turn me off.

4

On vision as a mode of neural tort:
and I could find myself becoming
overseer for rehabilitation,
imprinting with due licence the late-cancelled
stanzas that hymn roulette. Everything mortal
has to give from life. When we're exhausted
by ill-willing, the fictions of our joys,
violin, pleach-toned harp, and grand piano
melodize; the contessa's niece
glitters her gift three lengths of the salon.
Symbol burns off reality: take *The Red Shoes*—
since I'm to show beholden—how for instance
those awkward, svelte, death-struck life enhancers
labour their immortality proclaimed.

5

Gold, silver, to gel-blaze the dark places.
Black has its own gleam. Pascal's
name is a blank to many people; so
also are yours and mine.
There must be unnamed stars but all are numbered
de profundis. Check these on the web
spun by their own light. And does such knowledge
firm up allegiance to the stoic heavens?
And is the question real or rhetorical
when finally the all-or-nothing man
presses his wager? Such extravagance
here to expand on, to elect chaos
where there's a vacancy and peradventure
if chaos is the word.

6

The work of mourning—the *Trauerarbeit*—
bugles dead achievements. Regardless
and in spite of, what a memory
fenced by glittering breakage. Stabs
at the long jump (juniors) from a mired run up,
off a fractured board. Five seconds' freedom
I nominate to be the normal freedom
of the mob-ruled. Subsequent fables,
men of stale will nursing their secret wounds,
the token of the scarecrow as sufferer,
seem done for. Death fancies us but finally
leaves us alone. Metaphysics remain
in common language something of a joke.
Mourning my meaning is what I meant to say.

Insert Here

Fuit d'une fuite éternelle—no, founded
in eternal light. And then what?

. . .

A clash of trodden ashes, if clinker
can be called ashes.

. . .

                The angular
sun on windows or windshields like swans
taking off and alighting.

. . .

Let me be, says the dying man, let me fall
upward towards my roots.

Tu B'Shevat

I

Returning to my own green winter, dense
invocation and slow-growing charge
unlike anywhere: Hebrew alone will serve

this narrative which is a broken thing—
because I cannot well pronounce it
interpreter, mage, teller of righteousness.

Word for the sun found here six-pronged and noble.

The first tree being the almond, the land
Israel, the voice prophetically enlarged,
the end, so far conceived and unprepared for,

absolves witness.

2

Not much to go for there. I can remit you
endurances at worst or transfer funds
on estimates of cost. Subsistence-wrung

and royal Hebrew—*to the chief musician*—
suffering servant, plenitude that mourns,
singer of griefs unsung, the aleph-tav

of others' fruits and vines. Moshe Dayan,
en route to Suez, praised the flourishing
Palestinian date-harvest,

which was not to the purpose. I salute purpose:
festivals where they strip the vital groves,
attune their joy and wish nobody harm.

Children's Games

From laughter to slaughter,
from shul to Sheol,
from Torah to Ahor.
Say Noah-Shoah.
Noah-Shoah! Noah-Shoah!
Tell Bialik.

. . .

The air foil-fêted
and with zinc clatterings,
each new gust slaps
the wire-strung small
neighbourhood flags into wind-
milling windmills.

. . .

For this day and for dread
of Sheol, let the dead remain
under sedation.
These are memory games.
Find Bialik,
he should know.

To Lucien Richard: On Suffering

The undulant road makes the way-out tide
rise and fall. After the merchants' houses
the tarred fishing shacks and places that sell bait;
after the shade trees the gleaned reaches of sand.
Sea-bass are plentiful. Although the smallest
get thrown back—legal—they mostly die,
float for a short while, scales catching the sun.

Granite plugs through sand bluffs. The stub
lighthouses resemble follies or summer homes
for checkerboard painters. Gulls appear
laggard and yet they are sleekly primed.
The fine machinery of instinctual natures
is well adjusted to the environment,
hooks up arrivals to the thermal tower.

I take on Seneca, could have sung like Jonah
at your discretion. So enjoyed it when
the weighted line you cast tore from its rod,
bait and all, and flippered and was gone,
the timing perfect, perfect your chagrin-
charged resignation, mute expressive glare:
no chance to practise custody of the eyes.

So I said to them half-blinded which
of you is the angel? And which angel?
I did not think there were angels. The sea
light was visionary, as it sometimes is
to susceptible people. Dead or alive
we sojourn in the world's refuge and abattoir.
Pity about the tackle. I could have wept.

Wild Clematis in Winter

i.m. William Cookson

Old traveller's joy appears like naked thorn blossom
as we speed citywards through blurry detail:
wild clematis' springing false bloom of seed pods,
the earth lying shotten, the sun shrouded off-white,
wet ferns ripped bare, flat as fishes' backbones,
with the embankment grass frost-hacked and hackled,
wastage, seepage, showing up everywhere
in this blanched apparition.

Offertorium: December 2002

For rain-sprigged yew trees, blockish as they guard
admonitory sparse berries, atrorubent
stone holt of darkness, no, of claustral light:

for late distortions lodged by first mistakes;
for all departing, as our selves, from time;
for random justice held with things half-known,

with restitution if things come to that.

Epiphany at Hurcott

Profoundly silent January shows up
clamant with colour, greening in fine rain,
luminous malachite of twig-thicket and bole
brightest at sundown.

On hedge-banks and small rubbed bluffs the red earth,
dampened to umber, tints the valley sides.
Holly cliffs glitter like cut anthracite.
The lake, reflective, floats, brimfull, its tawny sky.

Epiphany at Saint Mary and All Saints

The wise men, vulnerable in ageing plaster,
are borne as gifts
to be set down among the other treasures
in their familial strangeness, mystery's toys.

Below the church the Stour slovens
through its narrow cut.
On service roads the lights cast amber salt
slatted with a thin rain doubling as snow.

Showings are not unknown: a six-winged seraph
somewhere impends—it is the geste of invention,
not the creative but the creator spirit.
The night air sings a colder spell to come.

Discourse: For Stanley Rosen

I

As to whether there persists—enlighten me—
a dialectic: labour into desire.
Forgive my small vocabulary that tries
and abides your patience. What a wonder's
man the philosopher set on his throne.
What a wonder he is, and how
abysmal. I would not have you say
I speak ungratefully; or that there's self
going spare in our unsparing tribute.
Arbeitsknecht by adoption, I never
hurl down advice, even to shake the building.
Perhaps (but not likely) I may be still
a whizz at ordinary language and you
mishear things.

2

No, put it this way: cancel, expunge, annul,
self-reference. Philosophy keeps up
embarrassment and expense. I'd quit us
of further scars had these now been incurred.
You're magisterial in judgement's gorge
where the rocks are at all angles and the stream
huggers its way through:
let's flip with self-projection's paper boat.
Language not revealing to the elect
only; and wild descenders pierced by good.
So few of us absolved when what we write
sets us to rights on some false scale of justice.
You're magisterial in your own conviction.
And a clown with it, and a judge of clowns.

3

Susurrations of winter: voicing stems mistune
a glass harmonica at my good ear.
The alien's close to home, the changeling's not
too much a prodigy or wastrel; lovers
and children not inimical by rote.
Something here even so. Our well dug-in
language pitches us as it finds—
I tell myself
don't wreck a good phrase simply to boost sense—
granted its dark places, the fabled burden;
its loops and extraordinary progressions;
its mere conundrums forms and rites of discourse;
its bleak littoral swept by bursts of sunlight;
its earthen genius auditing the spheres.

In Ipsley Church Lane 2

Sage-green through olive to oxidized copper,
the rainward stone tower-face. Graveyard
blossom comes off in handfuls; the lilac
turned overnight a rough tobacco brown.
Every few minutes the drizzle shakes
itself like a dog:

substantially the world as is, its heavy body
and its lightnesses emblems, a glitter
held in keel-shaped dock leaves, varieties
of sameness, the pebbles I see sing
polychrome under rainwash,
arrayed in disarray, immortal raiment:

my question, since I am paid a retainer,
is whether the appearances, the astonishments,
stand in their own keepings finally,
or are annulled through the changed measures of light.
Imagination, freakish, dashing every way,
defers annulment.

Improvisations for Jimi Hendrix

Somewhere a Queen is weeping
Somewhere a King has no wife

I

I am the chorus and I urge you
act messenger's idiom from Greek tragedy.
Get to know words like the gods'
inconstant anger.

Stand in for Pasiphaean bull,
exquisite player of neumes!
Enlarge the lionized
apparatus of fucking.
Wacko falsetto of stuck pig.

You can vibe self-defector and know
how to project
Olympian light waves.

The show guitar melts like sealing wax.
It mutes and scalds. Your fingers
burning secrets.

Your legerdemain.

Extraordinary progressions chart
no standard progress.

Call guru noises to task.
There is no good ending admits fade-out.
By rights you shall have
top prize longevity
wiped as a gift.

2

Prime time, whole time, the planet's
run by toupée'd pinkoes: but not ruled.
Not even music rules.

What kind contortions fix hex-mind pyrewise?

Something unexplained—I exempt his music.

No huckster, then, dazed gambler with real grace,
saved possibly; and the hotel rooms
destroyed themselves.

3

Short-changed and on short time let us
walk óh-so óh-so with all new gods.
Showmen kill shaman, dunk parts in late

wag-chat's petty brine. I had a line all
set to go; a lien now. Even the shadow-
death cues further shadows. Take his hand,
Medea, if he can find it. *Lysergic*

also is made up Greek.

4

Sometimes the king of a forbidden country
has his entitlement, his lineage,
adorned by error.

Somehow a king delivers his true bride
in the perilous
marsh of childbirth and all three go safe.

Yes there is weeping and yes some find
the lost miracle and do not know it;

swagger royally, play the pretender
to sinking Atlantis,
drown in their star-dust. Some are reborn.

. . .

Somewhere the slave is master of his desires
and lords it in great music
and the children dance.

To the Teller of Fortunes

I

Spread sand not straw. Salt useless here although
useful elsewhere. Stresses count in a line,
help weld and wield. Take me to task—or worse—
for misappropriation. Pontoon's not
bridge: I understand that by reproof.
Plain speaking still an order I believe.
To which now add: the omens
blood-fuddled and in other ways befouled.
Sounds good.

II

Pointedly they drew daggers in the air.
More to the point he had recast
their programme of intent.
                              More to the point
they stalled the racketing old flail-tank saved
for tyrannicide.
But point taken: to let the children cross.

III

Morbidity thrives. Tiberius' emerald
greening the ulcer-finger.
Observer at the feast of infamy, your
choice abstentions. Stiff place card at table,
carte de visite, the plain memorial card,
redeem a quality of need, the twelve
pearl-handled fruit knives, the figs' entrails,
writs of departure served from the epergne.

IV

Well-taught articulation
                              and the Fates
past all necessity frivolous;
each doll so jointed it moves dis-
jointedly, mime-shocked, smiling.

V

And then they cart us off which is not good,
not good, mea Hostia; so that we lose
sight of our selves before Lethe annuls us.
No more of us without whom there is nothing.

VI

Hail Caesar and the rest. Reviewing language
I am wrought still by how patient it is.
Even in Thule the durability
of light over a century—you
can rely on it, it augurs well.

VII

Chancy but promising. Who's that poet
tarred his horsewhip on aesthetes?
                              If this is just
thirteen syllables I shall survive.

Ex Propertio

Encouraged by a glib-tongued haruspex
to practise divination: what's wrong here?
Soothsayers hold their skills inviolate.
Incited by a renegade conjurer
I bowelled my loyalties to law and love
rhetorical in parts. Love as a necromant
re-infiltrates the dead *whilst* law usurps
upon itself: two elder shades of weight,
authority mere power, power in authority.
The act of love surpassing eloquence,
a shadow there of Amor in his stride.
I shan't recover divination's charm
out of these studs and hooks or Hymen's ring
of decayed iron, or cauterizing brand.

Ars

i.m. Ken Smith

1

Hazardous but press on. Enjambment
drags: hinge of induration
not a patent success.
Comparisons build tautologies yet again.
What is incomparable and are we
making a list?

Don't lay destructive charge if you were booked
for exhibition.
To confess mayhem plead ornate regard.
Ciceronian conclusions, fixed resolve.

Style paradox inertia's mobile face
for the duration. It has been thought
expedient to have us curse and weep
with the same countenance as one inspired.

Delete *delenda est*—exemplary
Carthage her rubbed-in wounds.
Not everything's a joke but we've been had.

2

Nor does vision deny this: the province
of human discourse, error, self-delusion;
the spirit's oblique lifting a leverage
for the entire corpus; distressed paradigms;
and, as some have said, charges to answer.

How risible the solemnized
intentions towards joy.
Unexchangeable password, I have yet
to find the place appointed. It will come.

Over, across, the Pennine scarps and valleys
motorway lights—festal suspension bridge,
high-arching nocturne. I grasp the possible

rightness of certain things
that possess the imagination, however briefly;

the verdict of their patterned randomness.

On the Sophoclean Moment
in English Poetry

A serene draw, the Sophoclean Moment
if only for a moment, issues thence
into the unforestalled or, failing that,
experienced inexperience. *Try again*
may itself be Sophoclean, who's to know.
I think, though, they mean plainer things by far,
but not basics precisely—not clay, schist,
quartz, Hornton greenstone. Words are never stone
except in their appearance. See me out,
long-domiciled epiphanies I trust.
Answer for what I am? No time to answer,
a nerve of ageing touched upon and primed:
as when the jittery leaf snags, is a mouse:
one stop from *Sophocles* to *Sepulchre*.

In the Valley of the Arrow

1

First flowers strike artificial at first sight,
the colours appear concocted, perhaps they are.
Crocus for starters soon looks pretty
much washed out.

Now here's real alchemy—the gorse
on roadside terraces, bristling with static,
spectator of its own prime, inclement challenge

or salutation brusquely in place,
hermetic at full display and rallying,

as best becomes it, spicy orator.

2

Not Bohemia, not Illyria, where dramatic virgins
immortalized, as common grace, rhetoric's
vernacular flowers. Still in your gift, dull stream,

the singing iron footbridges, tense weirs
pebble-dashed with small foam, a shivey blackthorn's
clouded white glass that's darker veined or seamed,

crack willow foliage, pale as a new fern,
silver-plated ivy in the sun's angle—

this for description's sake—
                                        and as the year
ploughs on, gross bramble, more misshapen-
shouldered, hairy, jigging with bees,

beata l'alma.

3

My shadow now resembles my father's: cloth
cap flat-planted with its jutty neb
that prods the leaf-litter. Ineffectually.

What do they think of while they think of nothing?
Thinks: check pulse-rate as last animus
jerks home—spit, spat— *they* of course being *them.*

The finite mind transcends its finitude
with the contrivance of affinities,
on the great wheel that keeps time in suspense.

Dying's no let-up, an atrocious
means of existence: nobody saved;
no sign of ransom if you comprehend me.

Smug bastard.

4

Heart-stab memento giving a side-glimpse
of feared eternity—left at the kiosk—
as on a bright path you might catch the shadow
of your attacker.

Sun off shields in middle distance
and lidded water saurian-scaled.

Standing or going there is always pain;
the machinations of set injuries;
sentiment in collusion with itself.

The wild geese racket and mute swans proceed
in formal agitation round the lake.

Not all his days are this eventful.

5

More than you know it's like dead trees that stay
the same, winter and summer—odds
on how he tells it—sheathed in samurai
mail of black ivy. At it again,

beata l'alma.

Unzipped and found addressing the smeared walls
of an underpass, crying not my
address, no more unnamed accusers,

self-dubbed natural thespian enacts
age, incapacity—judge the witnesses—
brings himself off to video'd provocation.

Pardon my breathing.

Improvisations for Hart Crane

Thou canst read nothing except through appetite.

I

Super-ego crash-meshed idiot-savant.
And what have you.
This has to be the show-stopper. Stay put.
Slumming for rum and rumba, dumb Rimbaud,
he the sortilegist, visionary on parole,
floor-walker watching space, the candy man,
artiste of neon, traffic's orator,
gaunt cantilevers engined by the dawn
of prophecy. A sight to see itself:
he, swinger with the saints in mission belfries,
broken and randy ringing up the toll.
Procrastination's death to be in time,
publish his name, exile's remittancer,
prodigal who reclaimed us brought to book.

2

The Stars-and-Stripes looks best when it's unfurled
stiff as warped board on a declaiming wind
under a cobalt sky; the National
Guard at stand-to, half-tamed weaponry;
the Chief's advisers, unsexed white and black,
good with binoculars and shown to be so;
their photo-faces lit with simple purpose,
their public selves the sanctum, the arcane;
their privacy the secrets of events;
the keys of war bestowed like a small heirloom
of sentimental value to the clan.
Poets are unstable, least to be trusted
with scripts of grand arraignment. All in all
you screwed us, Hart, you and your zany epic.

3

Unwise these thoughts high-spanned. A shade too much
American Primer, liberty
safe on the list, shiny-electric-gated,
sordor its new-old mansions. Heave him in—
'lyric confession slams the bunkum test'—
our self-accusing bard: naked bacardi
and sailors! Straight sex mothered him;
for the witch he performed. I went along
with all that jazz, twizzled the fuzzy dial
to catch Roosevelt. Admit, though, we had plunged
before his first term, faithful old depression
working us all the way. What derelicts
we must have been, ripped off by infancy.
Thou canst grasp nothing except through appetite.

In Ipsley Church Lane 3

One solstice has swung past, the immeasurably
varied, unvarying, profusion of hedge-burgeon
stays richly dulled, immoveable for a while.
Over by Studley the close air is dove-grey,
a hollow without sun
though heat had filled it; shadow-reservoir,

more than a mirage, however you chance to look,
if mirage-like in its reality.
The day does not wear well, the well-kept grounds
of the new offices are uninviting.
There is a kind of sullenness that summer
alone possesses. It passes; will have passed:

not to speak of your heart, that rules and lies
in webs of heavy blood, a clobbering fetish.
Parables come to order; the hurt
is mortal though endurances remain,
as they have to, insufferably so;
hindsight and foresight stationed in their ways.

Offertorium: Suffolk, July 2003

for Annie and Julian

Even in a sparse county there is dense settling
and an unsettling that surfaces here or here
via the low levels, the tide-spiked rivers,
lanesides over-endowed by sovereign fern,
the crowned stalks I call hemlock, with poppies'
      mass vagrancy,
rough forms of mallow, roses' battered shells.
A woodpigeon hauls into late take off,
self-snatched from truck wheels. Abundant hazards,
being and non-being, every fleck through which
      this time affords
unobliterate certainties hidden in light.

Broken Hierarchies

When to depict rain—heavy rain—it stands
in dense verticals diagonally lashed,
chalk-white yet with the chalk translucent;

the roadway sprouts ten thousand flowerets,
storm-paddies instantly reaped, replenished,
and again cut down:

the holding burden of a wistaria
drape amid drape, the sodden
copia of all things flashing and drying:

first here after the storm these butterflies
fixed on each jinking run,
probing, priming, then leaping back,

a babble of silent tongues;
and the flint church also choiring
into dazzle

. . .

like Appalachian music, those
aureate stark sounds
plucked or bowed, a wild patience

replete with loss,
the twankled dulcimer,
scrawny rich fiddle gnawing;

a man's low voice that looms out of the drone:
the humming bird that is not
of these climes; and the great

wanderers like the albatross;
the ocean, ranging-in, laying itself
down on our alien shore.

The Storm

(EUGENIO MONTALE, 'LA BUFERA')

The storm that batters the magnolia's
impermeable leaves, the long-drawn drum roll
of Martian thunder with its hail

(crystal acoustics trembling in your night's lair
disturb you while the gold transfumed
from the mahoganies, the pages' rims
of de luxe books, still burns, a sugar grain
under your eyelid's shell)

lightning that makes stark-white the trees,
the walls, suspending them—
interminable instant—marbled manna
and cataclysm—deep in you sculpted,
borne now as condemnation: this binds you
closer to me, strange sister, than any love.
So, the harsh buskings, bashing of castanets
and tambourines around the spoilers' ditch,
fandango's foot-rap and over all
some gesture still to be defined . . .
                              As when
you turned away and casting with a hand
that cloudy mass of hair from off your forehead

gave me a sign and stepped into the dark.

Luxe, Calme et Volupté

to PMH

Lost is not vanished; nor is it finished;
more like a haunting from the ghosted future
that was not ours and cannot now be called
through into being by too late consent.
Motions towards life are not living
except abstractly I am moved to say.
Both of us here conjoined in epitaph
                   awaiting stone.

Improvisation on
'Warum ist uns das Licht gegeben?'

Scored by folk-genius set to its lathe.
I also am a worker in iron.
Patience be judge, nailers and puddlers,
chained free citizens, battling cortèges,
beyond subsistence, given that you are mine,
hammered to fable as in blood proven.
Against survival something that endures:
win, lose, the paid-up quiet death.

Pindarics

2005–2012

It is not true that, with the passing of years, love becomes less dreadful.

Grief makes one live in a dreamlike world of fantasy where banal, everyday things take on a bewildering, *thrilling* aspect, not always displeasing.

I must find the secret of fusing the fantastic, trenchant vein of *Lavorare stanca* with that of the *pornoteca*: slapstick, realistically declaimed to the people.

CESARE PAVESE, Il mestiere di vivere

I

Could I have known what I had, *Boyhood's End*
and all that? Crowding her so to myself
through strange puberty, Dame Kind her solitudes
a joint possession. Nurture, that charlatan
of genius, how beautifully she would have read
me these ruined photographs, their cracked gloss
smeared by association. If this is abrupt
forgive me; and explain the sequence: she
and I inexplicable, even now, to ourselves.

Pray, kind executor, do not take her
for tutelary goddess. Further reading
may establish her name and age. My scope
grants nothing to dignity, even self-
affronting *dignitas*, matching an art
reactionary as all wars; susceptible,
if things had gone otherwise; the long-
desired solo album many have claimed.
Do not be so abandoned as to care

what I abuse, back from my *rentier*
exile among books. These wits I have
protract through stratagem a formal muse
bemused by how late love retracts its term.
Not you, Ces; pax; I'll talk us sweetly through.

2

The winter cherry already has been and gone
(alexandrines pose a question I cannot answer
within the confessing of England). Elsewhere now
I laboured for Rachel not Leah, but lost her
ere I had numbered pearls in the bride's cache-sexe.
Matings for life aborted by birth, let gannet
shame us—their indifference to all this.
We should trade vows across sea-walls of flinder.
Settlings upon the wind they do superbly.

You shall be that naïf, your mistress-soul
neither here nor there: familiar accounting
given its pregnant blank. How the swans peel
their wings from chaliced rest, half-drag their flight,
I grant you for montage.
The aconite's amazed at our appearance
each time it moves; it never fails us. Guess
what comedy of uncreated kind
draws us to confluence. Stay well apart though;

most explainings are slipshod, sliding in the blood
of mutual offences, ignorance
and post-ignorance, I mean hers and mine.
How one may draw too much to trick and sequel
I am not minded to declare just now.

3

Nomen or numen when you meant nomos.
But at this juncture the strophe stands
incontrovertibly revealed, exact,
with bonum simplex and like civitas,
talismanic in the microchip,
power not to descend to the thing done,
the garbling utile. Chemically discharged
Iambus slurs through spoil-heaps, low and thick
and all-tenacious. Cranking forgotten skills

there must be, somewhere, choices that succeed,
all elements at one within the phase.
People go shuttery, as on a sub
splayed in a crash-dive,
so keep in trim, you and your darling oppo,
is best advice; keep up and take a cause.
While refutation's in the truth-locker,
the body politic that does not die
and is not answerable to any God,

returns a form of grandeur, shame for shame.
Power's not every place that virtue is,
and anarchy by files deploys to order
as if through modes of conduct or of weight:
dactyls advancing against a contrived rest.

4

Rattled emplacements, wind-garbled rookeries
of mistletoe; no traceable shiver
at the world's heart: untouchably not
as we are, not everlasting.
Darkly a primed sun works to expose grand chill;
the nesh yellows of Spring acclimatize
against black soil in lee of the Fleam Dyke.
Bridge me your question from that other country
of speculation which you may enter

without leaving my side. And did I dream you?
Glazed wedges of furrow, tilting shield-angles,
prism a flash hail-squall; light cries *now!*
At any time the strange laurel's transposed.
I will not misquote here for retrieval
such as some reckon with. We did not need this
episodic fabric, this longevity,
a field spread with inexplicable bone-ash
at our return, the gaunt light withdrawing.

Awkward, or still, one comes into self-range
but has never shot or hunted. What appeared an
in-season to the brain? Grotesque as yours
my hid sex thrust like the mounted
head of a fox.

5

After the prize-giving the valedictions;
after the phone call a brief sense
of what happiness would be like; after
the forgiveness a struggle to forgive.
Some discourse is expansive, but some
composed of opposing blocks. Again
the award ceremony as paradigm
for the expected. She gives herself
to the right man. Their exhaled composure.

But, to my purpose, the other, the choice
that is arbitrary, of the free will,
moving the unkeyed sections until they lock.
Not to deflect the wildest things; acceptance
a distinct willing; a reach for truth
like sentences from Tacitus online.
Delirium of order. Not this easy,
but music seems an answer, undisturbed
by other than itself, the keyed answer.

Or crystallography which I
think I misunderstand; it's not Stendhal.
Patterns of lines, mostly, raw in appearance.
I see I've defined a poem; something I'd say
held over, deep in reserve, so that it may strike.

6

Not to unthink the work done: but a dervish
whirlstorm of sepia and sand
occludes it like a twister on the bed
of a shallow sea. Cuttlefish bone survives,
incongruously reft its light-weft grottoes,
in parrots' cages or in books of verse.
Seashells are more elaborate and hiss,
tell childhood fortunes, voyage from Madagascar.
Presence of the intrinsic's here in doubt.

Repetition betrays us, our minds at odds.
How commonplace a stanza's prized array.
Admission charge is the true price of fame;
all else subvention, bonuses, blithe fraud.
What did the Strega pull? It bought no women
(by which I judge such things); no life
even in harm's care; nor did it tip your gift
timely-immortal, dummied-up to death,
for restitution in requital's cave.

Storms at first light our drummers. You
could well outlive the next century,
fatalities allowed for. Can't go further
unless to claim I found such plenitude
one of the dark moon's non-existent seas.

7

Rub two distichs together, wise not to
bet against fire. A view to fail,
repump a washed-up beach ball, palp a god,
cross vows with a convenience metaphor.
All is invention; I am spoiled for choice.
Assign me Pindar's job-lot, born to sing
modernities traduced or what you will;
homeo-pharmacopeia's adagia
spilled upon none that reads. Your votes Ile dig—

I tell a lie—Pindar should live so long
engrossed by fame and fall and techne's pride,
thriving as mafia in fatal throe.
Projecting horoscopes from new-set mouth
who was this this self-maker shall succeed,
contractual-expansive? Steady hand
named boss of spin. The tongues of angels
heal metal fatigue; oracular blessings
licked into being with your aesthete's spittle.

Happily you can best preach woe, abide
assiduous beauty its gross acts of phage.
Consensual this art we so uphold,
the *necessary murder* claimed in passing,
judged out of order, rendered disacclaimed.

8

Act jealous stepmother to our miming gifts
and receive a free mirror. Flamed thing is mute,
lights no face but its own. What do you say
to text virile—*You're fired? Fuck the Pope?*
Elsewhere than here the vatic can win bets.
I take the odd perception to myself:
primed buddleia cone with its thin spiral wire,
electric-copper-green, seems artificial;
big crab-shell flints dug in East Anglia

roundly emblematize, come squat to hand.
That is how you bless things, hymn the random,
the pristine, the primeval, the inert;
as when rhymed legend hoicks excalibur
cack-handed out of stock commodity:
The world as there and I here judging it
Yeats wrote, as if disdaining emulation.
Philosophical Irishry sat well with him,
Swift, Berkeley, Burke: therewith to moon the Crowd

and to subsist with, high upon renown.
That greatness be beholden to our time
snap acronyms, phase hyphenated words
of one syllable, scrabble *par-li-a-ment,*
applying tack-wit to your fingers' ends.

9

It was not so intended. Set this right
as by dictation or from memory,
with nothing to look up. *That can't be true.*
Well-noted passim I am my bent wits'
straight man: terrific lyric repartée,
terse *reportage*. But cowardice in the line
too heavily made light of by one's peers.
Has there been a single *rite de passage*
half-decently accomplished in my name?

The answer must be *no*. Remains unbroached
the box of *virtù* levered from blitzed Belmont,
unlovely relic to have so survived.
Crab into yourself, using a claw–
hammer if that is inventoried.
They would cheat us of imperfections. Did
Shakespeare not write those stock-barren things,
Timon, *All's Well*, that were the making of him?
My sweat I am stuck with; my references

stuck to the plastic. Ah, those cumbrous trees
of autumn gorgeous in their trash! Best try
exultant decreation or a *clang*
of being as some Shaker shaked. Prevails,
the timely setting forth the timeless rout.

10

To Dante *the green cloth*, the attribute—
unsurprised astonishment—his lines confer,
plain to themselves. I would assess this
as one completes a course of penicillin
somewhat like prayers at bedtime. Period.
Not that I'm loosely read or reprobate
as checking reason wholly by the moon's
horoscope for poets. Let there be
a feature that can drive this driverless cab

to high invention. One must broadly read,
ambivalent of riposte. Ambivalence!
To say *fulfils* here means *annihilates
necessary sub-ethics*. Oily and grand
a trombone solo; I would leave you rich
in such effects remembering my voice;
exorcised late redactions of your love.
I scan you for ideas; can attend
that bonny mind more than I find to say.

At whim these are cats' cradles; at will
schools of dolphins applaud us teasingly.
You do not owe me in truth some vacant years
to my last recollection. At the seams
tried lines regraft themselves as best they may.

I I

La bufera. The storm. Yes, but in whose
memory am I to raise this beggared storm,
establish tides of scattery impaction?
E altro and so on. Some say the autumn comet
presages disasters: these portents of our art
more than ever a dead man's. If he demands
authorization I shall track him through
sodden trajectories of blind sycamore.
Ces, and I hold this in as good a faith,

could read presages, lately grew uncanny
as a wild goat grows cunning on the cliffs;
his friends among the stolid Piedmontese
kind enough not to notice. It is scarce
a matter of possession but of station,
of good form even. By what depth, what ire,
should I type-code my storms? It feels good
raising a question that can sound at once
heroic and perplexed. Last steadying beam

begs symmetry of chaos. There's an ape
of innocence with which to guy the end
that thrives by various names including guilt,
spitted on entertainment: outside film
the busiest stuntmen are the torturers.

12

Late April already; the scraggy apple
comes across all bridal—transient coral—
a woodpecker removes rivets, the tree
breaks open and is shown to be dying,
intensely so, *lavorare stanca*,
reams of survival, time-reamed, barren
at the heart only. They say our sap-time
embalms itself as a tree and so is crowned
without effort by our effortful years,

not inebriate *odi*. Begging grandeur
of what is at best a scrawn confluence
I take as justified—the branch mass-corsaged,
well-settled into pigment an inch thick.
The hand not now its own daemon comports
the riven spirit, takes absolved measure.
Whatever we have reckoned with—or not—
discards us lightly. Sky empurpled,
all things change; it is the changeable month

according to prediction. It shall bear
athwart us prime's most fecund judgement
when death blossoms no more: like Revelation.
Now it is enough, the symbol's moment,
beauty's conundrum, rapt and reft-attired.

13

How reconciled, then, Ovid, by such time
as in Vorónezh he was no man's fool?
I'm speaking brutally; the answer holds
in the way that vines hold, or a sloth
holds to the branch if this has been provided;
or like some skill at talk or my invention
misfocused here. In the good neighbour's yard
tyres creak, slurp, on gravel; the yard door splits
an observation, whangs against my greeting.

What Ces describes—*duration of real pain*—
spikes with its radicals the roots of thought.
Hebrew mates word and thing, the acting word,
the basic punning language though not all
punsters are poets nor would wish to be.
The absolute's absolution is itself.
Presence of the intrinsic saved for death
politic power was one uncivil term.
How strange you have to be to stay faithful.

Vorónezh: Ovid thrusts abruptly wide
the ice-locked shutters, discommodes his lyre
to Caesar's harbingers. Interrogation;
whatever is most feared. Truth's fatal vogue,
sad carnifex, self-styled of blood and wax.

14

Say Coriolanus fought from dark to dark,
a thing of blood; such as he told his mind
he could turn cities ashen, being empowered
by slow brain-worm to swift self-travesty;
bespoke *a lonely dragon in his fen*—
that sentimental—something more than huff—
and hitting wild accord, a douce of rage,
blood-tears by contract, servitor of guilt.
Shakespeare's gold-trading; mortgages; a name.

Stress here that Ces was exiled to twelve months
of dire self-catering at Brancaleone.
Musso's block-strutters pinned him in their charts
marked as tame dragon; this at worst was true;
decently wounded, asthma and cockroaches
and self-reproach. Alas they tortured Ginzburg
and Ginzburg died. That was another time.
I have some feeling for his widow's brusqueness.
Implicate wit to air-freshen the fact.

For Coriolanus there is no escape
in the sublime, in God, or melancholy,
no music for his state, no martyrdom,
no reconciling with the truth of things;
but, crazy-passive, a last mêlée of spite.

15

Ces blamed Ruskin for the fascist state.
Intrinsic value's at the root of this;
it can broach either way. So sling your hook.
Ulisse, Ulisse, son io. Pound
was Ruskinian; make that plausible
which is our métier. The presence
of the intrinsic is not here in doubt.
The modus snarls; the modus is what kills
Coriolan's challenge to Malatesta—

neither man the fascist Aufidius was.
You'll find I cannot delegate to reason.
Some things are merely raw; my argument
snuffles among them for the better scraps.
Labour is allowed beauty, an enhanced
beauty labouring our kind. Ventriloquists
earn enviable sums; may attempt satire.
Democracy's not a bad word, though disliked
by some old rhetors; new men steered to rule.

I'm spent, signori; think I would rather
crash out than glide on through. Pound glided
through his own idiocy; in old age
fell upon clarities of incoherence,
muteness's epigrams, things crying off.

16

Moves to embarrass us with wilting stock
but I prevaricate. Applied eugenics
essentially a bearing lost; re-wrought
for the conglomerate that sprung a nation.
Thinking it through I would revive the myth.
Anyone can be chorus; it is not
a thing of station but of rapt possession
(anyone can run, thus, on half a brain).
Think of the poets as of those who swing

by highest office. Stake the estranged its chance
as censors of some neophyte republic:
citations please, say, *Purgatorio*
where they give you time-stamped cards at check-in.
Politic power
was the good Tudor term and stood for something.
When you pitched Nihilist I was disturbed,
trusted you to strike failure; at your triumph
affirmed that trust with grand old-fashioned verbs.

Call in Walt Whitman's love-child and be wise.
Terrible things are done, we none the wiser.
Were you serious *re* eugenics? Why,
what did I say you deemed unlyrical?
Too few the questions proven to affirm.

17

Grade yourself as fidelity avails
even in the trash yard near Gethsemane.
Eternity irradiates couple
jigs a fair recreation of sound bite.
Let nothing slide to waste, or very little.
These are peasant virtues, Ces. Claudel
was of our company; your pardon, *my*.
This fretful strophe I have had replayed
in place of ancient howling. Much too soon.

What assigns *double, treble, reality*
to a single word? Make that *in context*,
I'm yours, free spirit, dead cobber. All in all
Simone outwitted us: *L'enracinement*:
working on multiple planes. Let us suppose
I would entice her with this threnody
like Wordsworth's *Ode to Duty* read too late.
Go make a pile. Vote me treacherous friend:
I take it my pitch catches your emphasis

and that we have entente—forgive the French—
since proof stays out of court. I wish you joy
in your post-pill amazement, brother Ces;
despite the surreptitious afterthought
of your prescription branded with my shame.

18

Whether what we grow is organic soothsaying
time will betray. Until next century
the deluge goes nowhere, the aquifers
slow to revive. But by such time as claims
recur, forgotten riftings will have burgeoned
straitly with cupric and hard-yielding song,
lavorare stanca; the last irruptive
fix on the myth dissolving in flense-water,
mâchés of bylines, ropy-jellied tictac.

Stuck on the weir's lip my last allegory:
how you cried, *I will race you under the bridge,*
die to revive lost skinship. Estranged senses,
near-death experience, gift us our children.
Yet, to convene late classics, show familiar
with things aloof, insupportably nuptial.
Let us bear away this gummed epilogue
though not in so many lines. Within the laws
of hazard we have form. Good form shall keep us,

my fellow suppliants, out of the temple.
I would write of myself, *learns lessons well*
but never in time. Labour transfigures
a mere grotesque zeal of corrumpery
to mort intemperance, souls humped in drag.

19

So much I've read you in the new language
we could do it together: *lavorare stanca*,
which is not what you think. Association
thrives without content; and proximity
fumbles its challenge. I would wrest
corporateness out of your diffidence;
my virtues still modestly exorbitant
for one so gifted. The almond tree
conceives in pure code, zealous, prophetic.

Rapid eye-movements, hint of paralysis,
will not undo us in the court of question.
I put it to you: symbols are well in train,
as Joseph worthy of his singular coat,
mobile out of the pit, his membership
chain of incumbent prophets, sweet revenge
for love; and sacred reinvestiture.
For us, the brickmakers, Pharaonian time,
the sphinx's part-decipherable face.

I put it to you: what is psoriasis
in the eternal economy? Right to silence.
Nothing here amounts to what I scanned
one blue day on the Red Line: *Undefeated.*
Throws in the towel (that promiscuous throng).

20

Someone there has made a chalk drawing
of the common man. In history-time
he came and went so patient he was blind,
blinded, even, a tommy on Somme duckboards;
and his patience was brought against him
as an indictment and with no appeal.
If what I grope for lies above the mud-lid
we shall at some point grasp his calvary.
Other than the story, this tells nothing.

No improvement on a child's stick figure.
As stark as that. Almost too well
you read me, the hard labour to explain
even so demanded. *Enter self-discharged*
I would erase as written. Be abrupt.
In basic English cry for Goethe's light,
two words allowed. Pause for collection
and a chorale-like music; grief inclusive.
Other than the story this tells, nothing.

No courage can do more. There is a gap.
Let us pass through it; the many voices
of peasants and soldiers are reinstated.
The pageants move, stooping, to hallow them.
Nothing tells this story of thee or another.

21

Narrative's easy—up we go and down—
I do not like the structure of that face,
as if the spirit pines in locked regard.
Treason against the self is something I
can go along with in snagged kinds of ways.
This is a tack too late, while opportune
sombre litigation with the body of language
is something else. What did that vow surmise
of sixty years, then seventy? All told

nothing confessed. Add nothing from the heart.
Such fury's best occulted, non è vero?
Sure—if you ask around of those who sleep,
fast-forward indices to crib remorse
for *things ill-done and done to others' harm*;
unrivalled fear of intimate disclosure
straight from the can. Some claim the end of things
the sun cooling toward our brands, our
synaesthesias from gruff solar storms,

as though an epode now should take the stand
devoid of counterturn. Who needs this? Pitch
here exceeds the very worst of tone: *if*
you had not already pledged each other
with morning-after vomit on the step.

22

Ces was bad vibes, a weakling in his loves,
though there only. To render *Moby-Dick*
speaks courage in grand style. (Myself dispatched,
a play toward, trim raincoat over arm
like a sommelier's napkin, tickets prick-eared
blazer breast pocket—a college *Hamlet*
starring her tyger love unheard-of since.)
The sequence is: struck-through you do not squeal.
I plead Aristotle on metaphor.

But did I then rip out the dedication
from a half-righted poem lust-inscribed
though with a sacred title? It seems not.
The busy hammers closing rivets up
is heady, sinewed work, by odds enthralled,
bathetic flesh, tang of coke-seasoned iron.
Boys have gone mystic for less, displeasingly
celibate, though from chained whim not
poetry's blessing (which is down to earth).

Gyring Ann Lee: her people sense-impelled
to profligate abstinence;
gifted their brute stock selves annihilate;
force that evolves its own essential form
would be true bonding sprung aloof by grace.

23

Had they dreamt wings rigid they could have flown.
At what stage are you? With such pindarics
I would be slow to bet on your survival.
Graced by a small legacy of terrors
does not read well; but try Italian.
The kestrel's now a common bird; so touch
it sparely: glinting in a turn of verse
let it fall as if shot. Goodbye, Miss Dowling,
I meant to say; untowardly famous

as you were; and of exalted kind
known briefly. The most generous would see
a small hawk riding the wind well into time,
inerrantly: so death exceeds its powers.
In the garden the fresh-planted medlar
is thriving. I would not count on its fruit.
Works and Days missold us as drought-proof,
no question. I was taught to look skyward
for enemies; and we are of an age.

Rephrase for written-out: are dogs
irritated by their own tails; or does each
chase it for fun? What a gift I bring you,
patron of small claims. Ambiguously ridden
the leaper Memory comports its will.

24

Convenes and prospers, being espoused
neither to bag-lady, nor yet to enraged
flamenco-dancer; untargeted by fishwife;
no crosslegged succubus, no semi-retired
scrapping-bitch his barren mate.
Yet lust's the ground of wedlock, even sublimed
like alcohol in a stew. And mutual comfort
rides on the pelvic bone. As Ces says,
you can deny him nothing. Nothing,

when in the counterturn all is absurd:
I'm running a slight fever—anniversaries
unman me—meeting not with substance,
finishing against the clock in swive
and swive about, begotten of spoilt skin
late chancred by exile;
plea-bargainer for annulment self-repealed.
You my lost soul of grace, provider
of differentials, calculated stress,

stand here: the passing wonder's not of age.
I watch us in this ersatz Globe, made famous
by our effrontery, less tragic thus
than we were as children. First symmetries
ex chaos as of now fine in their place.

25

Pitched *labouring ships* so well that I took off
but botched the dating. Must I yet go back,
the process over (he said), over the process?
Procession so ill-grounded; thoughts rethought
without conviction, processing the pace,
sad ingenuity, its thrice-nicked blessing.
Ah, words, that made her stammer to respond,
which here are unsealed urns of scantling ash,
stock trunk, with our raw-cicatriced initials,

long-since felled; and the sedged heron-pool
drained for a bypass. I said, *there is a light
between us, cara, and that light is you.*
How could she not concur? Beech: I reclaim it,
smoothed elephant-hide bark. The English sun,
Ces, chills so rapidly. And I make knock
repetitive with imagined fellow feeling,
Du, nachbar Gott, and all (you might translate
this). I cannot think how else to come about.

Obscurity is what it is. Leave well
untried the Herculean gate. Concede
those labouring ships their laboured progeny
among which we are borne. Contrary tides
clamour to beauty as flared light scuds through.

26

Sometime a nation of sentiment, rotted now
with sentimentality. Is that a defence?
I love the detritus of my own body
such as earwax; maintain an itching head
condemned as heretical. That look—
priceless!—and yet it costs them nothing
in self-esteem or status. Fart moral.
I have (say) fallen foul through eighty years
to be an observer of wits, baroque divas,

god-haunched castrati clapped in periwigs,
indecent song. *But the real, tremendous,*
truth is this: suffering serves no purpose
whatsoever. Scrapbox of body parts,
dried schoolroom mucus. Achieving climax
never that easy; they missold us there.
Can't use elastoplast on the wise wound
the lady said. I effectively remember
that stumbling engine-note desynchronized;
we staring upward; they, up there, gaze down.

Contrivance whereby Circe might bestow
her dripping câche on an unvirile lover—
they say this is obscene—eludes me still.
Sometimes, in a lost *Pathology*, I
dedicate, to, and, with, you, our, little, death.

27

Conjubilant the hawthorn crusts and crests
with blossom, part-submerges its own growth,
patched opulence; metallic spreads of rape
take on familiar fields, adapt the contours
to alien brilliance, reflecting signals.
So much of us is coded. Spindly lime
is now also in leaf. A faintish ringing,
metal plied with soft hammers far abroad,
I do not find to name: the rape perhaps

reverting to its near-galactic chime.
I draw again something held undeclared
among the fulness; water shadows it
from time to time; reflections spin desire
to liquefaction, odd regular pebbles
appear as algorithmic: these to be sensed
without sensing the foil; and to be gathered
because I did not gather her to myself
when our first May rode its weird homely flare.

To that close-proximate scene I am a man
with half his head gone, gnawn by foxes
and other creatures, obdurate in decay;
and all for folly that is even now
remonstrance of the wound. Rewind the spring.

28

The remonstrance is mine, farther than you
could make to cast it. I cannot describe
my animus to your containment; and it moves
in ways unadmirable, even while one keeps
attention at the salute. *Could I forbear this?*
attracts no answer. Making is exhaustive;
I will renew my vows on its detritus.
Give me the time of day, formal agreement
to my existence in the common need;

though this will scarce absolve the weathering earth
its inspiration. Systole, diastole,
incur things of the mind, even at no
remove. Invent from nothing each new scene,
an oblique shaft of sunlight, odd squat tower,
diversities of lichen, ripe spawn of hope,
wistaria's spindly rambling before it takes
fast hold; novelty brickwork an embarrassment.
Blocked out, the runny ink, *No Blacks or Irish.*

Manipulate necessity to end
even as salutation. Set us down
into our loop; and we repeat ourselves
only as mute desire. We do not open
the fatal book nor match up sighs that steal.

29

Whether *Fleem* or *Flame*, with the recumbent
sun flooding us, a quibble. In the old Fen
fastness vast reed-masses so flared up
in deep-mawed conflagration by chance grace
of our quirked northern light's refractions.
I have dismayed you, forgive me; you
follow too closely for your wisest good.
These strophes are protracted and it tells.
What is noble in England is a question.

Our friendships hold by a thread, spiders' webs
are stronger and finer. Look, these filaments
suggest perspectives of accuracy
borne out by imagination. Stand
to stare through: is it *instress*? Fineness
appears waxed in this strange evening glow.
All things glide by, everything remains
untainted by finesse of hope or
by invention; as by invention of hope.

Without marriage in heaven it becomes harder
to take bearings. Yet loved, at any time
my soul was oddly vacant, as if stillborn,
even into old age; let us not lose
this last astonishment untaxed by grief.

30

Agèd time is revived in these undulations of light,
on stream banks fulfilment's music is offered up . . .
the clarity of water brings me back to myself—
to a maternal cherishing—the blue sky hazy . . .
great boughs of sweet chestnut my guardians, the hawthorn also
makes faithful resort; but why this silence,
even now, amid the plumage of birds?
Ah, Frénaud! Were you Welsh this would be *hiraeth.*
What luck to encounter you so; to ride

the staid Elbe to its source, to find Bourgogne
regrafting soul to her eternal vines,
their roots in misery, one scarcely doubts,
poor poilu. Sentries—you bribed them? But with what?
Shots of naïf happiness most likely.
I cannot think what to say. You were—
delirious sane man—keyed hostage
by grammars of fortune; maestro-victim
set to *record*. You built with love

Messalina's bed, and took counsel there.
I hoard that epigram, shield it from the guards,
this undermanned night staff. Ovid's metamorphs,
again we are reborn and no-one warned us.
I'll bury these rags in sand under the pines.

3I

Sullen rewriting but by whose desire
is the open secret a wound? Decline
to be written off against currency
disclosures in some posthumous reckoning
somewhere out of mind, as by oversight.
Of equal justice [|] equity its type
hove-to, fix-traded for votive gestures,
how simply things respond to certain vantage,
remaindered legend burnished by occasion.

Symbol's wild garlic overstrung of late
shrives in extremis; lyric élan
pages its time inspiriting the nul.
Cities relapse, are sanctuaries, chance havens;
things unnameable cleansing the unclean
slicked parterres. (Cast Hebrew Bible for foxes.)
Truth may deploy ruth that redeems nothing,
delusion let invoke love's palindrome.
Deafness on call s(urr)eals the inner ear.

Lived experience finally is death's
chef de mission. Dance, merciless coda,
old in your ways. I play you sealed witness.
Pity the circumstance; retire with lame
felicity, quick-fixed misstep of rhyme.

32

Origen, *Stars*; *Aquinas on Angels*;
it seems to go on for ever. Spirits
are serious business though we care
too little about them. Stars have no soul,
he was way out there; and hierarchies
of angels rarely keep beneficent order
in these relative times; but can appear
in surprising places: that surprise us,
not of course them. This is as close to votive

as I can get and yet engage reason.
Registration of mind, even one so cramped
into its barrel, to propose a world
even by that squint light! *Calmatevi*, Ces:
despairingly cynical out of love
is not cynical though it is despairing.
We cannot mourn like this; there is too much,
even *andata*; we need *e ritorno*.
From where? Obviously from the wrong Solesmes

where she quoted Villon on hunger and wolves.
Stars cannot, angels will not, indemnify
against derived madness; participants,
even co-conspirators. Dissipative
yet congealing: the heavens are filled with their hail.

33

Well-versed public acts: with long inurement
I've brought myself athwart them. Be inured,
the spikier the better, you waaa'z blood.
Begloried, sheer of state, armed by the sea,
all-thumping eloquence stuck in its shoals
for curiosity, bones of Leviathan,
with a wrenched hook or two, compose this plaint.
Bravo for constitution of report
and barren empire barking on its tides.

How could one swim so well and yet despair?
Let them lament at will who never saw you.
Close-kept release of life, the body-lagged
spirit, draws up engrafted induration.
Women become contagious abstinence,
afflictions of the skin. What has been heard
of my impediment's productive charm?
Impediment's not the right word; hold
Contagious. Meanwhile my writing fingers weep.

Ovid would have our number. Definitely.
Look at yourself; it makes no difference
the mirror is upside down. Judicial
stay on writ won at eleventh hour
changes nothing. Small hotels are to die in.

34

Spin this like a thimble on a needle's end
for meditation; quiddities discharged.
He was a shade before his time, Propertius;
conceived its power—sexual polity—
as Ovid did not, save by experience
or its equivalent. The élite
is a smaller crowd. You must accept this
as I must. Myths for venting? The best
song studies the gyre and is steadied thereby.

If things strike home that follow the earth's curve
those 'skeined' wild geese direct exilic order;
the rigours of such flight an imitation
as though they intone verse; where stress takes up
directionless lament, makes something of it.
Elsewhere their myth; the vatic can lie idle;
it is the beat that counts. Do other things
to maintain credit; surfing, say, or kite-
flying in storms, with and without the key;

or call collect and have cracked codes put through.
Who is addressed here—surely I would have said?
Such were your lineaments and I missed you—
dare I say?—*lord of life*; dissertations
lining the epoch where we stand proclaimed.

A Treatise of Civil Power

To Ken Haynes

Justyce now is dede;
Trowth with a drowsy hede,
As hevy as the lede,
Is layd down to slepe,
And takith no kepe;
And Ryght is over the fallows
Gone to seke hallows,
With Reason together,
No man can tell whether.
No man wyll undertake
The first twayne to wake;
And the twayne last
Be withholde so fast
With mony, as men sayne,
They can not come agayne.

JOHN SKELTON

The Minor Prophets

Joel in particular; between the Porch
and the Altar—something about dancing
or not dancing. No, *weeping*; but in the Bible
there's so much about dance; often of ill omen;
the threats of scorched earth and someone who resembles
the Scorpion King. They should film Joel:
A fire devoureth before them; and behind
them a flame burneth.

Citations I

This not quite knowing what the earth requires:
earthiness, earthliness, or things ethereal;
whether spiritus mundi notices bad faith
or if it cares; defraudings at the source,
the bare usury of the species. In the end
one is as broken as the vows and tatters,
petitions with blood on them, the charred prayers
spiralling godwards on intense thermals.

No decent modicum, agreed. I'd claim
the actual is at once cruder and finer,
without fuss carrying its own weight. Still
I think of poetry as it was said
of Alanbrooke's war diary: a work done
to gain, or regain, *possession of himself,*
as a means of survival and, in that sense,
a mode of moral life.

Citations II

Whether power rides on arias or recitatives
is not entirely an idle question.
Recitatives mainly I'd say although
people keep asking why your lyric mojo
atrophied at around ninety. I'd
swear myself blind atrophy's not the word
but that invention reinvents itself
every so often in the line of death.

Or if not why not: call writing nothing
but self-indemnity for what is denied it?
Yes, to be blunt, the pitiless wrench between
truth and metre, though you can scarcely hear this.
For yes read possibly. The train's just stopped
at the Jewellery Quarter. Perhaps if I alighted
I too would stroll a city of emerald
or at least zircon.

On Reading *Milton and the English Revolution*

I

The craft of vision is what I make of this.
They did so labour salvation, the dispossessed
their triumphal example. England
can do without most of us. For us
also language is a part-broken league.
Fix your own tail to the Jerusalem donkey.

II

Radiant urim; also the discreet
seraphic viscera. I say again it
can seem too much. The seeds of virtue
implanted by some mystical generation:
He that hath obtained to know this
goes without answer.

III

Wiped the old slur between liberty and licence.
Wisdom is back. How did it go, Wisdom?
The soul knows there no difference of sex.
Sympathy flows, utterance is end-stopped.
As if that stopped collusion. Perhaps it does.
Memory too returns, her key still in the lock.

IV

God himself is our Zion *where all creatures*
are fellow citizens: the ox with the butterfly,
the butchers in meaty aprons, Aaron's jewels,
a Commonwealth shilling from an oddments box;
great contrariety of mind; old reprobates
stuck with new-risen saints. Now cry *Amen.*

V

The mind closes or the imagination
turns itself down: if for no other cause
than play-catharsis. That being said,
choice or necessity to play Cromwell
with laryngitis? A simulacrum
of living speech strikes the aggrieved ear.

VI

Debridement that means reaming out the mock
virginity of the wound. Idiolect
that could be idiot dialect but isn't,
wrinching and spraining the text for clown-comedy
amid the pain, *the inward and irremediable
disposition of man*—this I can live with.

VII

The remnant is the redeemed. Forge the true key;
we shall insert as ordered, not *wrinching
and spraining* since I have strained myself.
How certainly words are at one with *all
corruptible things*. Bow down, bow down,
at the great stone altar sacred to billiards.

VIII

Getting into the act I ordain a *dishonoured
and discredited nation.*
Milton or Clarendon might well approve.
Can't say who else would. It smacks rather
of moral presumption. Things are not that bad.
Mirren is super.

IX

Everything is holy and we will reign
in our young bodies and make good our age.
O earth, earth, earth, Fairfield and Wribbenhall
shall resurrect like Cookham; Bagshot Heath
grow vines: for us—how else should I prophesy,
misguided, misconceiving, mis-inspired?

X

Joy is freewilling but—more—freeloading.
In the Book of Enoch, how the angels cover
all—is it all?—all the daughters of men.
I brood on this and am repelled by it
less than by my own gaffes of citation.
They have cut down our choice cedars. Curse for blessing.

XI

If God were not light—how does it go on?
Or at whose say so? Trouble the hypothesis
to be an immortal fact. It is enough
even mortalists concede the nub. *Save God's
being light, spirit could not have been.*
The marvellous webs are rimed with eternity.

XII

But to go out with all that surrogate
history turmoiling in your wake,
a load of screw-wrath.
Regret cannot now get closer to target.
Sibylline interdict spells blunder—*resign!*—
though resignation itself proclaims the finder.

Holbein

I

The other Cromwell, that strange muse of Wyatt
and master of last things: it makes a fine
edge—wisdom so near miswielding power.
I think of the headsman balancing that
extraordinary axe for a long instant
without breaking the skin; then the engine
cuts its ascending outline on the air,
wharrs its velocity, dreadful, perhaps
merciful. And that moment of spreading
wide the arms as a signal. In fact it's all
signals. Pray, sirs, remember Cromwell's trim
wit on the scaffold, that saved Wyatt's neck;
the one blubbing—talk of the *quiet mind*!—
the other a scoundrel, yet this redeems him.

II

Imagine Hercules mated with the Hydra,
this king of bloody trunks their monster child.
More would have so rated him the arch
cleaver of women and old holy men.
Cerebral incest, his sperm a witch broth.
And Surrey, with his hierarchy of verse.
Meticulous the apportioning of time
in its reserve, Virgilian rectitude,
as though a full pavane of the elect
were the ten syllables to which they trod
as to the noblest music in the land,
lovely fecundity of barren heath,
Hillarby Bay, the Alde's thin-ribboned course;
sudden clouds harrowing the Anglian sky.

Parallel Lives

I

The Quyete of Mynde was a tough home assignment,
but you know that. The style seems to be made
with those like us, stranded and crying out
as brittle things in Virgil and Dante
that when you snag them flock the air with blood
making a mess of anger and lament:
the violent spendthrifts of their own hearts
to whom no quarter is given, no
quality of grace shown. The harpies have them.

II

The leathern wings belabour and I get
carried away. Plutarch writes of being
overdrawn by the affections. Quiet mind,
in Wyatt's English, is far from slumber
or waking lassitude. It is parsed here
because, since Wyatt wrote, that *continent
temper* which could play equivocation,
land it and slit it, find there the gold ring
of truth safe in its gut, is history.

Masques

Jonson also was excellent on work
within his mansions of erected wit.
For him it was defiance of the mob,
his adversaries mouthing at his call;
it was the shape of things held by the world
in various columns with the Latin scrolls
conspicuous like the Ralegh frontispiece.
I see Inigo Jones' great arches
in my mind's eye, his water-inky clouds,
the paraphernalia of a royal masque;
dung and detritus in the crazy streets,
the big coaches bellying in their skirts
pothole to pothole, and the men of fire,
the link-boys slouching and the rainy wind.

Harmonia Sacra

Harmonia sacra, a few sacred crumbs,
and we're a scared people. Not even now
sapped or snapped, the willing of the form
of nationhood, royalist, republican,
the seventeenth-century vision of harmony
that all gave voice to and that most betrayed.
This sounds like Herrick though without his grace.
I sing of times trans-shifting were his words.

On Reading *Blake:*
Prophet Against Empire

I

Everything swings with the times. Cynicism
becomes innocence—such is my gash of thought.
Before you can say *Quid* or *Obtuse Angle*
or *Mrs Nannicantipot*, the milk tooth
hangs from the door-knob by its cotton thread.
Terror is opportune as is relief from terror.

II

This is where the cryptic opens. Blake
was afraid, shaken by the Law's dice-rattle;
but could have been an opportunist also
if luck had offered, or held, or just begun.
Coarser radicates nobler, by a kind
of sublime compromise with accident.

III

As to the sublime, don't take
my gloss on it. *The Spiritual Form
of Nelson Guiding Leviathan*: you behold
only the hero, the corpses, and the coils
of his victories, grandly weighed and spread.
For a long age you do not see the monster,

IV

the visual syntax so conducive to awe.
Which is why, in *Jerusalem*, he could
contradict and contain multitudes (I've
cribbed Whitman, you stickler—short of a phrase).
One poet is very like another and rejoices
in the final artifice. I mean great poets.

V

If *counting gold* is not *abundant living*
nothing else counts. That there are over-
flowing granaries of Imagination
stands neither here nor there. Money is fertile
and genius falls by the way. It doesn't—
but stays in its own room, growing confused

VI

as I suppose Will: Blake did, overwhelmed
by the spoiled harvest of *The Four Zoas*.

VII

At this end there is the mere amazement
for one's own dumbness and that of res publica
which do not correlate or even collide
except for public utilities, tyrants
of unaccountable error,
whose names are *Quid*, *Skofield*, and *Inflammable Gass*.

VIII

One dies dutifully, of fearful exhaustion,
or of *one's wrathful self*, self's baffle-plates
contrived with the dexterity of a lifetime.
Nobody listens or contradicts the screen;
though, homeward-bound, some find combustious
sights to be stepped aside from—an old body

IX

its mouth working.

To the Lord Protector Cromwell

I

1

Cut our loss. Make *Prognosticks* a back-list.

2

For labour of petty conundrums use

3

any commonplace book as model: strings

4

of synonyms, cramped maxims, anecdotes

5

nine-tenths botched in conveyance. *Turtle* is first

6

found in the Protectorate, meaning of course

7

the *sea-tortoise*; something having to do

8

with English sailors. England went maritime

9

and imperial; stared the world down;

10

rousing her own ire. Keep to this strong voice

11

like Milton's sonnet with its signal purpose;

12

your known affect for Jewry and for music;

13

far-sighted blindness as the reach of vision;

14

like Burford's Levellers raked into their mounds.

2

1

Testudo is Butler. I note your strength enshelled

2

in that coarse-featured death mask, even so

3

better than a boiled skull, the mock of Tyburn.

4

How that exposed them, their French lisping,

5

their twenty-four fiddlers, the new theatre,

6

lascivious strolling and the royal whores.

7

But why history? Nothing appeals to it

8

except for murdered reporters: that's

9

not history, a folk-huddle more like,

10

with marathons and talk shows, brief Diana.

11

They made a film about you, that tough actor.

12

Guinness outplayed him as he finally

13

outplayed himself. Then there's the other thing,

14

Veronica Guerin's guilt-subliming wake.

3

1

Clue here is *Ireland*, not a conclusive one.

2

Below Times standard (old style). Dublin drug-heads

3

and Drogheda won't fit down or across.

4

Or if they will, then in a different warp.

5

Wanted: the well-judged end. You judged; were lost.

6

Luck of the common man at fifty-something.

7

Oblivion, self-oblivion, attend our needs.

8

It all goes on for ever. In that style

9

best known to himself, Milton pledged you immortal.

10

You made yourself with mortal stratagem:

11

the bowels of Christ, baubles, encumbrances,

12

with Ireton and the swaying major-generals,

13

the power-inducted saints and speculators.

14

You were above that, somewhere below God.

4

1

If the word be not with us, what is our

2

present legal position? I could answer

3

though possibly incorrectly. Say I would beg

4

out of this hire-house of ceaseless allusion.

5

I want out from this mire, say, of bluish flame.

6

Look up aphasia and aporia their origins.

7

The mystery of our being rests on such knowledge

8

if we're in neither of the sad sloughs.

9

I had a calling for England: that silver piece

10

I would pierce and hang at my neck, anyday.

11

There's an unfinished psalm doing the rounds

12

in the vicinity of my skull. My tongue

13

informs me this is not Hebrew but English

14

or Brobdingnagian if I may so construe it.

On Reading *Crowds and Power*

Cloven, we are incorporate, our wounds
simple but mysterious. We have
some wherewithal to bide our time on earth.
Endurance is fantastic; ambulances
battling at intersections, the city
intolerably en fête. My reflexes
are words themselves rather than standard
flexures of civil power. In all of this
Cassiopeia's a blessing
as is steady Orion beloved of poets.
Quotidian natures ours for the time being
I do not know
how we should be absolved or what is fate.

A Cloud in Aquila

1

Get him out of there—Turing, out of
the *Turing Machine*. Some hope, if the rules
of immortality can be bent. I
should hope so.

2

The world of his prediction is not ours
as he conceived it. If there is innocence
it was as here: phase, segment; region
of Aquila

3

that validates and haunts first love, verifies
disappointment itself, *meaningless
in the absence of spirit*, whatever
the mechanism

4

of the thing, desire, the singing calculus;
impossible pseudo-science, Eddington,
McTaggart: their measure of the mind
nubilate, precise,

5

roving existence at call. Any way
the idea of love is what joins us thus far
though not past all question in the same
tissue of body;

6

and Morcom is well dead and Turing with him;
the Clock House demolished. At the sharp turn
where it was always dark the road steepens
to Housman's Pisgah.

In Framlingham Church

Surrey's ornate, unsatisfactory tomb,
not to the life at any rate, stiff
inaccurate pietas some seventy years delayed.
No point posting the card sonnet to Clere.
Nothing atones ever, but for a moment,
Holbein's unfinished sketch perhaps, as if
the sitter could not wait for the rich detail
that so delighted his proud port or span
when what proclaimed him was the wake of Troy.

De Necessitate

But that was Holbein's way not Surrey's whim
impetuous and impatient though he was:
the features finally rounded, trappings roughed
for later ornament, a word or two
to indicate style, colour—Henry's new men—
perjury, extortion—cut off at the neck,
a martyr here, or feckless victim; some
who would die safe in bed, some born to pass
into the shadow of the ragged stone.

After Reading *Children of Albion* (1969)

1

Time-expired accusation, a tendresse
of news-hounds, a cave of judges, a judgement
confounded, a covenant of fuddled sleep.
Children of Albion now old men and women
compromised by the deeds they signed in Eden
forsaking dearth.

2

Kemp's Jig was hard labour—London to Norwich.
I saw a man enact it for an hour,
his stage about the space of a kitchenette.
Theatrical darkness, sound only, a hish,
a hisp, tissue of little bells. Then—bingo!—
lights! and a gold Albion uprearing,
electric with a static declamation,
a stance-prancer to his motionless fingers' ends.

3

The dancers, faces oblivious & grave,—
testing testing
the dancers face oblivion and the grave.

Integer Vitae

1

Did you then say
circumscribed betrayal; did you say, the years,
the years alone have done this, circumambient,
did you so propose?

2

The years will not
answer for what they have done, that much is
certain. There is no shaking them, we
might have foreseen this

3

but refused.
No, refusal's too much said for such freedom.
What fails here is fail-safe, our modus
conjured by slide-rule.

4

Ha! we can choose,
vivify what we catch from others' voices.
Thence to imperatives if you stall in
any manner of theme.

5

Non-concurrent
the freedom and constraint outside of this
transient lock that is itself both
end and motive

6

juggling music
for piccolo and snare-drum, for any other
ad hoc hocketing of joy, always provided
there remains silence.

On Looking Through *50 Jahre im Bild:*
Bundesrepublik Deutschland

It is not a matter of justice. Justice is in another world.
Or of injustice even; that is beside the point, or almost.
Nor even of the continuity of hirelings, the resourceful;
those who are obese—the excellent heads of hair—
the beautiful or plain wives, secretaries and translators.
The riots and demonstrations that now appear
like interludes, masques, or pageants, or students' rags;
the police water-cannon: you look for the film's director
but cannot find him. There is the captioned Wall;
there the Reichstag, the Brandenburger Tor
variously refurbished, with and without wire;
there's Willy Brandt kneeling at the Ghetto Memorial
on his visit to Warsaw, December of Nineteen Seventy:
I did what people do when words fail them.

A Précis or Memorandum of Civil Power

I

Could so have managed not to be flinging
down this challenge.
True way is homeless but the better gods
go with the house. *Cogito a bare*
threshold, as G. Marcel sagely declares,
of what's valid.
Come round to the idea, even so
belated, and knock. Echo the answer
in spare strophes that yield almost nothing
to the knowledge
outside them raw with late wisdom.
Quatuor pour la Fin du Temps not Gide's
doctrine of the moment which passes
as verity
in veritable suffusion. Grace
appears hardly spontaneous in that sense;
and in no sense whatever of the bloc-
veto or grab
of reality to our self-desires
as in a telling run of worldly luck
eminently worthy of these maimed lives.
I would forgo
this chant and others if I were not
more than a shade distressed. The sacrament
in its little hutch, the geyser's patio
of scalded earth,
beauty and disfigurement, all interest
set on the bias, accrued poverty
breaking every bank. The light exhaled
by spirits of *great*
purity is also in the finest painters
transfigured common light, *the crown*
of their achievements. Sage Marcel
withholds this gift
from artists of the word no doubt exactly
according to his lights which are quite something.
Knowledge, self-mastery, the self-embedded
body not ours
by deed of possession though suffering
possesses it and makes it ours in time.

I trust the arbiter—that's difficult.
My marginal
ontological reader, let her recoup
a line or two delivered without pathos.

II

I cannot work much closer to the slub
or perhaps it's
diffused like rumour, meaning diffused power.
How awkward this must sound. I'm reading Cornford
from a split paperback almost my age.
John Cornford dead
in Spain at twenty-one. Ninety this year.
Plaudits for Lenin and for Bela Kun.
Time turns sincerity to false witness
abetted by
our clear-headed stupidities; on occasion
a kind of brutishness conferred as love.
Heart of the heartless world he took from Marx
for a poem
part-way to timeless. Fine by either book.
The power-and-beauty mob has my bequest.

III

Not to skip detail, such as finches brisking
on stripped haw-bush;
the watered gold that February drains
out of the overcast; nomadic aconites
that in their trek recover beautifully
our sense of place,
the snowdrop fettled on its hinge, waxwings
becoming *sportif* in the grimy air.

IV

I accept, now, we make history; it's not some
abysmal power,
though making it kills us as we die to loss.
What lives is the arcane; by our decision
a lifetime's misdirection and a trophy
of some renown
or else nothing; the menagerie
of tinnitus crowding a deaf man's skull
has more to say. Woman's if you so rule.

It's gibberish
we bend to or are balked by on the spot,
treatise untreatised and the staring eyes.
The windflower has more stamina to fail,
the Lent lily,
the autumn crocus with its saffron fuse,
all that we fancy and make music of,
like Shakespeare's metaphors for governance,
nature itself
brought in to conserve polity; hives of gold
proclaim a gift few of us can afford.

V

Say everything works well but that it works
just like mischance.
Something of value is derived regardless
of our botched loves, uncalled-for, unconnived-at.
Civil power now smuggles more retractions
than hitherto;
public apology ad libs its charter,
well-misjudged villainy gets compensated.
I still can't tell you what that power is.
The statute books
suffer us here and there to lift a voice,
judge calls prosecutor to brief account,
juries may be stubborn to work good
like a brave child
standing its ground knowing it's in the right.
Letters to the editor can show wisdom.

VI

Well, there's a fortune in it if you sail
once round the world
faster than Jules Verne in his fantasy.
Fantasy makes a power of money too.
Money's not civil power in itself;
more the enforcer.
Types of physical prowess are a gift,
also computer-skills at a high pitch.
I lack the staying power of the grand
minimalist:
gnarl and burr, whoops of recycled basso,
the off-key sweetness of a single bell,
the world-wide reputation, decent life.

Let's all shore up
half-decent lives this Lent, *happy and holy*.
Two or three people I would call saints
without lust for sincerity which
Marcel describes,
*an exaltation in one's negative
powers*. I aim to cite correctly
but admit licence when the words won't match
with my own brief
to set this tricky artefact on line
for the realm of primal justice and accord.

VII

Why *Quatuor pour la Fin du Temps*, this has
nothing to do
surely with civil power? But it strikes chords
direct and angular: the terrible
unreadiness of France to hold her own:
nineteen forty
and what Marc Bloch entitled *Strange Defeat*;
prisoners, of whom Messiaen was one,
the unconventional quartet for which
the *Quatuor*
was fashioned as a thing beyond the time,
beyond the sick decorum of betrayal,
Pétain, Laval, the shabby prim hotels,
senility
fortified with spa waters. (When I said
grand minimalist I'd someone else in mind—
just to avoid confusion on that score.)
Strike up, augment,
irregular beauties contra the New Order.
Make do with cogent if austere finale.

G. F. Handel, Opus 6

Monumentality and *bidding*: words
neither yours nor mine, but like his music.
Stalwart and tender by turns, the fugues
and larghettos, staid, *bürgerlich*,
up to the wide gaunt leaps of invention.
Repetition of theme a reaffirming,
like figures in harmony with their right consorts,
with the world also, broadly understood;
each of itself a treatise of civil power,
every phrase instinct with deliberation
both upon power and towards civility.
At the rehearsing always I think of you
and fancy: with what concordance I
would thus steadily regret and regard her,
though to speak truth you are ever in my mind;
such is eros, such philia, their composure
these arias, predetermined, of our choice.

An Emblem

Among the slag remonstrances of this land
memory reinterprets us, as with
a Heraclitean emblem. On a sudden,
sunslanting rain intensifies, the roses
twitch more rapidly, flights
of invisible wing-roots lift
from the lighter branches; a purple sky
ushering a rainbow. Now it is gone.

The Peacock at Alderton

Nothing to tell why I cannot write
in re Nobody; nobody to narrate this
latter acknowledgement: the self that counts
words to a line, accountable survivor
pain-wedged, pinioned in the cleft trunk,
less petty than a sprite, poisonous as Ariel
to Prospero's own knowledge. In my room
a vase of peacock feathers. I will attempt
to describe them, as if for evidence
on which a life depends. Except for the eyes
they are threadbare: the threads hanging
from some luminate tough weed in February.
But those eyes—like a Greek letter,
omega, fossiled in an Indian shawl;
like a shaved cross-section of living tissue,
the edge metallic blue, the core of jet,
the white of the eye in fact closer to beige,
the whole encircled with a black-fringed green.
The peacock roosts alone on a Scots pine
at the garden end, in blustery twilight
his fulgent cloak a gathering of the dark,
the maharajah-bird that scavenges
close by the stone-troughed, stone-terraced, stone-ensurfed
Suffolk shoreline; at times displays his scream.

In Memoriam: Gillian Rose

1

I have a question to ask for the form's sake:
how that small happy boy in the seaside
photographs became the unstable man,
hobbyist of his own rage, engrafting it
on a stock of compliance, of hurt women.
You do not need to answer the question
or challenge imposture.
Whatever the protocol I should still construe.

2

There is a kind of sanity that hates weddings
but bears an intelligence of grief
in its own kind. There are achievements
that carry failure on their back, blindness
not as in Brueghel, but unfathomably
far-seeing.

3

Recap on words like compassion that I
never chanced in your living presence;
as empathy and empowerment.
I did not blunder into your room with flowers.
Despite the correct moves, you could have wiped me
in the championship finals of dislike.

4

Might you have responded to my question?
One will never know. You asked not to be
cheated of old age. No kidding, it is an
unlovely parley, although you
could have subdued it and set it to work,
met it without embracing. Edna
with her prosthetic jaw and nose
prevails over these exchanges.

5

Your anger against me would have been wrath
concerning the just city. Or poetry's
assumption of rule. Or its rôle
as wicked governor. This abdication
of self-censure indeed hauls it
within your long range of contempt,

6

unlike metaphysics which you had time for,
re-wedded to the city, a salutation
to Pallas, goddess of all polemics,
to Phocion's wife—who shall be nameless—
in Poussin's painting, gathering the disgraced
ashes of her husband. As you rightly said,
not some mere infinite love, a *finite act*
of political justice. Not many would see that.

7

If there's a healing of broken love it's not
as dyslexia's broken, learning to read signs.
In broken love you read the signs too late
although they are met with everywhere
like postcards of Manet and Monet, Van Gogh's shoes.
There are many rites exordinate to the occasion

8

though you have to choose one and get down to it—
it may involve grovelling or tearing of garments.
The just city is finally of some interest,
chiefly in the base senses of curiosity
and self-serving, if you understand me. You
do, of course, since I am using your three primers,

9

Mourning Becomes the Law, Love's Work, Paradiso:
a good legacy, which you should be proud of
except that pride is forever irrelevant
where you are now. So it continues,
the work, lurching on broken springs
or having to be dug out or jump-started
or welded together out of two wrecks
or donated to a good cause, like to the homeless

10

in the city that is not just, has never
known justice, except sporadically:
Solon, Phocion—and they gave him hemlock
and burned his body in an unhallowed place.
And his ashes were taken up and smuggled
into his own home, and buried beneath the hearth.

11

A familiar rare type of resistance
heroine, like that woman, is required by justice.
Whether the omens are propitious or unpropitious
the Lysander takes off, heads south, the Maquis
line out the chosen ground, the landing-strip,
with their brave vulnerable fires.

12

Sometimes the Gestapo are waiting, sometimes not,
and she gets clear. But the odds are heavy.
The odds are heavy-set against us all
though medics call the chances symbiosis
in their brusque insolent manner that denies
self-knowledge as the sufferer, her formal agon:
that word you chose to use, a standard term
but not despicable in context of *Love's Work*.

13

Poetry's its own agon that *allows us*
to recognize devastation as the rift
between power and powerlessness. But when I
say poetry I mean something impossible
to be described, except by adding lines
to lines that are sufficient as themselves.

14

Di-dum endures formally; and the pre-Socratics.
Phocion rests in his lost burial place.
Devastated is estuary; *devastation* remains
waste and shock. This ending is not the end,
more like the cleared spaces around St Paul's
and the gutted City after the fire-raid.
I find *love's work* a bleak ontology
to have to contemplate; it may be all we have.

Johannes Brahms, Opus 2

i

Oratory of those hammers: tenderness so defined.
Each phrase sounding its own future
resolution in opposition, discord in harmony

plus some other disporting of mastership.
Ponderable the élan and tensile bracing
with sorrow of acceptance

all-comporting; nothing that comes to grief.
Do not compound arrival with destiny
though here you could act so and be right.

Disposition of mind in the hands' posture.

ii

Or play off deportment into the found thing.
It will all go, the light clack of the keys
in the highest register, the incumbent sonorities

let us rehearse their passing, as Berkeley says
particles are units of the mind's energy:
in a while the body of our endurance

over and done with and still immortal
if we are that way inclined or otherwise
win cadence and closure.

In Memoriam: Aleksander Wat

O my brother, you have been well taken,
and by the writing hand most probably:
on photographs it looks to be the left,
the unlucky one. *Do nothing to revive me.*

Surrealism prescient of the real;
the unendurable to be assigned
no further, voice or no voice; funérailles,
songs of reft joy upon another planet.

Before Senility

dum possum volo

Intermezzo of sorts, something to do with gifts.
In plainer style, or sweeter, some figment
of gratitude and reconciliation
with the near things, with remnancy and love:

to measure the ownerless, worn, eighteenth-
century tombstones realigned like ashlar;
encompass the stark storm-severed head
of a sunflower blazing in mire of hail.

On Reading *The Essayes or Counsels, Civill and Morall*

I

So many had nothing; *we* have orchards
sometimes *ill-neighboured*, and are driven
to untimely harvest, simply to thwart thieves.
Our galleries may or may not be places
of seasonable resort.

2

Of Buildings and *Of Gardens* are themselves
exercises in prudence. *He that builds*
a fair house on an ill site doth commit
himself to prison. The sentences also
rise and fall.

3

There are *good whisperers* and *good magistrates*
by a noble collusion that is the style.
Even perjury and simony set forth
at a steady pace and arrive in time
for their host to receive them

4

with due courtesy and writs of attainder.
Of Prophecies is not beyond our scope
nor *Of Riches* our means. Is this Senecan?
Of the True Greatness of Kingdoms and Estates
is a major piece

5

whereas *Suspicion* is shortly dealt with.
What would men have? puts a radical question
as does the contest between wit and judgement.
Poverty is . . . tedious, and means chiefly
poverty of mind

6

that can accommodate what we would call
amplitude and quickness, which may be barren.
Religion, Matters of State, Great Persons
are to be spared jesting, *as is any case*
that deserves pity

7

though whether the dispossessed figure at all
is a question unasked at my lord's table.
There is much made of *precious ointment*
which is a potent magnanimity
that carries poison,

8

in my opinion, having read these things.
Dedications were tricky then; they're not now.
That's well worth an acknowledgement, a breather,
before the tide of *dark keeping*
sweeps us elsewhere

9

sputtering among the wreckage of late Demos.
So many had, and have, nothing; and Bacon
speaks of *privateness and retiring*. Consult
Of Judicature: the final book of Moses
is his landmark

10

and a good landmark, even: *the mislayer*
of a mere stone's to blame. So property
and equity are quits. My parents
never owned a house. Let it be said
that was their folly.

11

The poor are bunglers: my people, whom I
nonetheless honour, who bought no landmark
other than their graves. I wish I could keep
Baconian counsel, wish I could keep resentment
out of my voice.

In Memoriam: Ernst Barlach

I should have known Low German; perhaps
the closest measure of it is Black Country
to which the Scriptures were transposed by Kate Fletcher.
All the children uv Israel blartid fer Moses.
This has something of you, the carvings and bronzes,
the peasantry of the lower Elbe your inspiration.
A powerful rough language appropriate
to everything human and untutored,
such as my great grandmother would have spoken.
Except that for you there were the Gothic woodcarvers
and a landscape of burning potato-haulms,
a flatland to get lost in if you had the will.
My heart bleeds with grief but you give me strength
you carved in Low German for an *Ehrenmal*
or *Mahnmal* on which the Mother of God
is rayed round by seven swords that have the appearance
of stabbing her in the back. The vertical one
we call *crucifix* without too much straining
of faith or credulity. But the Low German
snapped at an angle is a right bugger.
Min Hart I think I can read, but the squinching
obscures things. Anyhow the War did for it: Kiel
was ill-used. And independent peasantry
is a myth, and *Artist Against the Third Reich*
something of a misnomer. You tried to buy time
and to stave off calamity as I would have done;
you were not Haeften nor could I have been.
A thick clahd cuvvud the mahntin fer six days
and then another forty and Moses was stuck in it
and came out with his face glowing and folk *wuz frit on 'im.*
And *glowery* is a mighty word with two meanings
if you crave ambiguity in plain speaking
as I do.

The Oath

(AFTER ANNE HÉBERT, 'LES OFFENSÉS')

By order of hunger the starving stood in line
by dint of wrath the traitors were arraigned
by virtue of conscience the judges came to trial
by scale of offence the injured lay accused
by score of wounds the crucified made their mark
the forlorn hope the final wretchedness
the dumb possessed the barricades en masse
their speechless cry so raggedly proclaimed
the Oath took arms against them street on street
its standards were the standard rods of charge
in lieu of words the one word fire
blazed from its heart

Coda

I

Shredded—my kite—in the myriad-snagged
crabapple crown, the cane cross-piece flailing;
a dark wind visible even deep in the hedge.
I knew then how much my eros
was emptiness, thorn-fixed by desolation,
as rain rode up Severn and we, on high ground
eastward, scarped and broke it, like some beleaguered
folk of the Heptarchy.

2

If it's the brunt of years and luck turned savage
this is our last call, difficult coda
to the facility, the bane of speech,
a taint of richesse in the haggard seasons,
withdrawing a Welsh iron-puddler's portion, his
penny a week insurance cum burial fund
cashing-in pain itself, stark induration,
something struck off, brought home, stuck on the mantle,

3

industry's knack, say, of bright Whitby jet,
randomness added to, the Family Bible
its own inventory. Egregious Randolph Ash,
Possession—the film—excited me, the sex,
those marked-up brooches, sombre aery genius
ours at a price. *Insuperable jokes*
as someone far off said, hilariously.
The things that strike us can be patented.

4

I add on oath (as prudent as you get)
that the Welsh puddler's my great grandfather,
from near Newtown, brought to the Black Country,
his house on *Furnace Row* stands in the census.
This is as formal as a curse or cry,
the verse I mean. Puddling's a way of life
and deadly in its kind, but more an art
than is some hammered threnos. Even so.

5

Write that I saw how much is gift-entailed,
great grandson, and son, of defeated men,
in my childhood, that is; even so I hope—
not believe, hope—our variously laboured
ways notwithstanding—we shall accountably
launch into death on a broad arc; our dark
abrupt spirit with fourth day constellations
that stood assembled to its first unknowing—

6

which is an abashed way invoking light,
the beatific vision, a species of heaven,
the presence of the first mover and all that,
great grandfather and Dante's *Paradiso*
understanding each other straight-on, to perfection.
I fear to wander in unbroken darkness
even with those I love. I know that sounds
a wicked thing to say.

Lyric Fragment

I hear an invisible
source of light skirling
off objects round about me—the granite portal,
women's hair also, and a deer's antlers.
In February a solitary oak leaf
dominates recognition. Are there
ancient coins wreathed with Medusa's head?

Nachwort

Sometime, with a near-helpless cry, I shall
wrench out of this. I don't much have
the patience, now, of the artificer
that so enthralls itself, impels
mass, energy, deep, the stubborn line,
the line that is that quickens to delay.

—Urge to unmake
all wrought finalities, become a babbler
in the crowd's face

Ludo

Epigraphs and Colophons
to
The Daybooks

1

We who are lovers through a grace of days
in diverse ways; who to variant clays
are self-adherent; and heirs apparent
to parent fears and fears recurrent:
how this preamble must resemble
tossed-out arrears,
and shail and wamble
and tossers' tremble,
fertile pessimism, one that yet waylays
generation and the jolly ramble of years.

2

These to praise, loners of immortal phase,
redressers, grace-givers.
Uphold. While tasers
stun. And the shouldheavers.
Shield-bestowers. Pax,
senex, for all your powers.

3

Cherished, they perish, our sad natures:
that girl whose features
floated off in the bath, the spool
of chemical
persistence under oath:

Break for syntax. Drop in semtex. Grin-tax
up and rising. Non-stop. Bitter Lenten cup.

4

Is this a stratum best unvisited?
Unwasted such a singular datum
had better be. Triangular bearings
bear on one point to an unmarked degree.
Reclaim a tight seam that might yet be
worked.
For so I am, unsarked, like with a blue scar
and a canary; a bled-for tattoo.
A maestro of the hands is not rare;
nor iron manias.
Rarer some ironies
and some brands of despair.

5

Miser Catulle. Spendthrift miser. Wiser Tully.
Spiel-tafel. Full fable of the belly. Cut cable . . .
Mind drift. Mend craft. Deemed folly. Shamed. Daft.

6

Medieval bones deep that city to disinter.
Splinter to enter. Veil of equity in poor state.
Mortal temple ample to commote fear.
Violence uncivil. The dead, the kept ones
who toll silence as to berate:

Reversed prayer made for non-payment they aver.
　　　　Rumor a maimed palindrome.
Malign lingam of lignum vitae; Vera ill-served.
Emerod-ridden rear end well-riddled by rod. And?
Viva revived. Review those long aggrieved.

7

Oratory demons orcs from my head,
lords and commons. Who casts rests indeed,
who the finest minister of tirades?
　　　　Propertius translates well
　　　　Hell and its properties;
Julia and her eye-patch among the shades.

Cynthia now no catch, wretched ruby ring
cracked from the pyre; soot-blacked upped finger.
It is moot claim whether there be desire
　　　　except in spirit.
　　　　Demerit and debt
answer no summons and possession goes spare.

8

He said, have babies without phobias?
Had I misheard, did I misinterpret
peregrinations of the word-spirit?
Etymology one of my hobbies;
rubber-necking in cinema lobbies
another. Misunderstood hyped merit
in for the Turner Prize and suchlike
acts of darkness, Orpheus, Persephone,
　　　　branded torchlike.

9

The old man composed his pools: sestinas
of cudgelled numbers. He won ten shillings,
I recall; but never those bright shiners
that would have gained us, briefly, top billings
in the Brummagem rags, with posh diners.
Scripture decrees all to their callings:
kickings, brayings, of Hegemony's ass
through the region of Balaam that is and
        that ever was.

10

   Triste lupus
   the 'sorrowful wolf'
   to wild no-hopers
   at brutish parse—
   let's count myself
   as of that clause—
   I dedicate
   to the inaccurate
god of system, to national
defence, and the irrational
rationale that spikes reason;
the barren in foison;
to the 'Tory hegemony',
banks that breed yet beg money.
   Turbulent John Skelton
   pray for us in meltdown,
   you with the language
   in that strong age
     of brigandage
     and foetor;
     interlocutor
     of *gentilnes*.
The Virgin would recognize
your laurel crown a prize
     wrought from distress.

11

Retune to tin quatrain and settle this
rattle-wise. No head smoking on rap.
Time to be held in trust as timed on tape.
Rhyme to these measures and proceed shaking.

12

Verdictives applied to void adjectives
          scooped by default.
Track to verdict, loop-loop cry signed edict.
          Who sustained
   brain-welt circuiting the occult?
          None undersigned.
Establish whiteboards as a bible
          Metsys-built.
Bible call inexhaustible
          to countdown, melt.

13

   Small steadfast throng
   go get it wrong.
   Sprung late among
          the Pieties

   Eudaemonia
   calls the money,
   Apollo's crony.
          Smiles pitiless

   their skin of song.
   Helpless, look, fing-
   er Marsyas strung,
          shitting ditties.

14

Economic laws survive their vio-
lation: thus Hirst in my birth-year. Pricy.
Better old Hirst than *Homage to Clio*?
Lord, let me know my end, is what I say
          sounding hellish,

somewhat unstable; for homiletics
ought not too readily engage metrics
with any audience; and the critics
          acting churlish.

Verse is change-ringing. *Economic laws*
survive their violation. Conceiving
laws of survival proves taxing and shows.
I know the argument backwards, grieving,
          but deemed bullish.

15

Waving her arms and hands at Easter mass,
  Christ's happy tictac
  Cash in the Attic
  appears hypnotic
or so I condescend to see pass.

Shall not embroider this a confession
  of ingratitude.
  It is merely snide
  and common; devoid
of what the clergy nickname compassion.

How shall I sing the Lord in this strange land?—
  if that is my brief
  which I doubt: a thief
  of others' belief.
A mercy almost the now-failing mind.

16

Use of the ampersand in thought-conveyance—
  some have deployed it—
I wish were not now in such abeyance.
Squats in verse a curse of stayed writ.
  Look to affiance.

  If strength were not fleeting
things would be worth a flyting at length
  & strength avoid it.

17

Break to the varied disciplines of light,
of good faith in politics, a dimension,
a value, equal to that of scansion.
Havel I have to thank for this insight

expressed as a vertical; not *upright*,
precisely; *vertical*; intersection
without disseverance, and without action
given over wholly to the distraught.

It is a good song and as such is taught
by tonic sol-fa in that singing school
the mastery of which requires a fool
to keep his head courting the king's daught-
  er.

18

How but in broken memory maintain
           time's unbroken skin?
                Intolerable
     much that passes for fable.
Recollect cane, cement, and balsa wood,
waxed paper, tissue, parts untimely glued.
            That homemade kite
            could glide and skate,
tugged hard and high, well-nigh invisible,
           racing with the reel;
           half across Wildmoor
                its shadow spoor
                before it fell.
                . . . . . .
           Pigeons lurch from the boughs
           like a gang of roughs.
     A small hawk hovers and swings
against the sun; transparent its wings
           or so they appear
           for an instant, sheer,
through the brain tricked by light
or visitation made of lost birthright.

19

What's here anarchic and libidinous
Shakespeare names *Will*; I have it from his pen—
more from his pen than I've had hot dinners.
Strip to foundation and begin again,
a few home truths said to abide in us;
this groaning is a groan of triumph then?
Magnificently cheated: what an air,
eh, Yeats, great double-breasted winter coat
           collared with fur!

20

Grief is everywhere; a terrorist cell
           either side of the wall,
                one might as well
                pick the short straw;
                it will not grow
with watching; arbitrarily though law
bends natural justice to accommodate will.

21

For want of text, recycle: *verse is change-*
ringing in tone-stung stinging stone towers,
blurring with other peals at extreme range,
consituate with raw wind-shifted showers,
signals at once familiar and strange—
as with the mobbing rooks, blast-anchored crows—
dinning at the core of an old silence
licensed to announce a new year, ordain
       time's happenstance.

22

These roses are convoluted lanterns,
especially gratifying: themselves
yet other; standards from the queen's gardens
       that some legend improves.

The wired pear tree I still associate
with hard sour fruit, I have not seen, now,
for sixty years that are as chalk on slate.
       Age no less keen now

confers its fullest preoccupation,
concentrates, thus: time, luminant details,
eddies of recall spinning on station
       as memory falls

into renewed exactions. Overhead,
its engine cut, the small yellow trainer
deploys in a stall, as they planned it would
       for the beginner.

23

However by these you call witnesses:
       how exactly
to your own measure, matter-of-factly,
       with politenesses
       circumspectly,
like watching the sycamore seeds at spin,
       if incorrectly
       they aeroplane.
How might this be wired to the declared
       with such detachment
       small wings of parchment
intimately cherished, some remnant spared?

24

Take nervous exactitude
    for a ride
and lose it in the poisoned wood;

a lucifer's jetting spark
    against dark-
    ness and shock

as in the old trench-system
    of the Somme,
    barrelling flame.

What must a code confer
    on conscript fear
    or minister

to, in gas mask, awkward,
    off the record,
    with stifled word?

    Whether staked wire
    abrupts or carrier
pigeons wheeling through fire;

      whether countermands
      unstain the hands;
      spare soul-divers the bends?

Type your answer
from *somewhere in France*, or
    some place fancier.

25

Creation is metamorphic not trans-
cryptic: *doth suffer a sea-change*
      take as instance.
It is not a matter of the glans,
        of becoming strange
while angels awkwardly upon pins
        dance;
and not simply exposure
of ethical matter to its own fissure
        under pressure;
nor activation of dead metaphor
to fabulate the gases of a star.
      It is not a stunt
      [*cetera desunt*]

26

Take the refrain;
put it through the filters again.
So much for perdition
granted us as a nation.
So much for the shadows
of live elms in meadows;
so much for the wild service tree
in the Forest of Wyre,
and the tricky deer;
the crouch-church of Kenelm,
the psalter to my psalm,
and knack of half-rhyme;
right love held so briefly,
to speak truthfully
of that righteous realm.

27

I cannot comprehend the situation
as I describe it;
let verse enrobe it
with lively fantasy of time and motion.

As to what finally might merit diction
I shall not here say,
to ensure privacy
for the sordid act of begetting fiction;

conceding as I do some self-contusion—
ah, the weak endings,
mute understandings,
forlorn pacts between compaction, diffusion.

28

If made martyr by art the more fool I:
whether to Baal, Moloch, or to the Logos
of *cutting-edge technology*. Truly
one is surrounded by rogues.
The cultic democratic élite,
here elegized,
paradox not oxymoron.
Don't they know there's a war on?
Hard-fought by some, the lost battles of Crete
unpraised, unprized.

29

Convicted of nothing whereby to dwell convinced,
nor by mere loathing abstracted from the sty;
nor by conformity to be advanced.
                    Get *enormity*
right here; further distress *careen*.
                    Where've you been?
Serve pagan poetry its fierce obscure grave pyre,
        curious lyre with Etruscan pottery.
                Mediocrity, though, of address
                rivalling neither bedazz
                nor wittery Della Cruscan.

30

Part-salvageable the dead sections, heaped
like Nash's *Totesmeer*; at shrewd angles.
Even as some by sod's law have escaped
play a dirge of sorts, Mr Bojangles,
and pitch it to me, type-cast to be typed,
while patience snarls and acceptance wrangles,
drawn to the edge of intolerance by
intolerable items that against
                    justice prance by.

31

How turbulent, then, the runic cross,
the dragon-clawed sword- or shield-boss,
the ornate vine stems to uncumber
of saints' entrails and obscene clamber,
the beacon drenched timber and clawed ember,
the dragon banished from its tarnished ness?

32

Supplicate for a super-injunction
                commanding sanction.
Whether this would terminate parody
                of Nobodaddy
                I cannot guess;
                though I confess
to having projected a confessing state;
hence my present embarrassment, pray note,
                lords of the press.

33

Gone from radar claim it by what you know.
Little blame to show how brand leader outshone.
Grand time for imagination only.
Nation-image draped fondly for certain bidder.
Gravely display—pull curtain—marge ration,
Dives-bar-Lazar bravely having it away.
Fix lame propeller for game gospeller;
powered by new buzzword bearings run hot.
            No swearing the fuzz words.
One may have stitched too much off a sow's ear.
Steer enclichéd pierrot towards peer riot.
Fabricate clued-in state ode before due date.
            Score-rate off wides?

34

The bayley berith the bell away
some might take for Christ's allegory,
            which it isn't.
      Fresh snow crimples the ground
      with thin wires of frail sound;
      among these a cock pheasant,
            inviting image,
            makes naive display
of bronzed crimson and green plumage.
The bayley berith the bell away.

35

Let it be spoken that a cosmic spring
has broken, spilling all to anarchy
untroubling to the consuls or the grand.
Why should the obvious go underground,
or have recourse to the absurd's far cry,
or take just measure with odd bits of string?

36

To make or withhold disclosure,
      heroic at pleasure:
      can technē be stoic,
            my treasure;
or as the toils of Arachnē
            to measure?

37

Set something here, footnote, bill of lading;
do not pretend to have been under fire.
      Do more towards the end
         you require
         least degrading.

38

Impecunious, read *The Letters of Junius*
      in a cheap edition
      for edification.
Address the coroner: I do not recognize
      myself in this gaze,
      the guise of a mourner.
Spurn deceptions. Establish the options.
      Give language a turn.

39

The cousins were distant by self-appointment,
      the lily, the rose, the rose I lay.
A high step-sided Austin saloon car
      with silverplated bonnet thermometer
         functioning beautifully
eased us down those slowly unwinding hills
away from Abberley and towards Tenbury Wells.
And through the glass window shines the sun
that has not moved though for us many times
      our time has run.

40

What is induction to the point of desire,
      soi-disant Herr?
Name to deter, to detect, redeem the Other,
      to defect or not bother.
      Who goes there?

41

Curt oblong section herewith conserves
befittingly, as this practice requires.
Here's to us, the grand notional juries:
cry equity for strong souls with weak nerves.

42

How many ogres
in *The Pilgrim's Progress?*

How come rightwisenesses still adhere to wrong;
is the secret so long sought pure rhyming slang?

Affix the label,
Neighbour Pliable.

Let us have right order and sacrament and song.

43

Whether we have Lollard ancestors
time in due season doubtless will recall,
visiting us upon poor denizens of hell,
primed with extrasensory transistors
to owre goostly comforte and proffite,

some scant mean between deprivation and surfeit.

44

The day-doused lamps, the chimmering lustres,
acquire incessant faint tremulous-
nesses of that cracked house
Poetry England.
Edward Thomas most ably has sensed these.
Visitations even on the brink of surcease
genius sequesters,
works on with, though neither bailed-out nor bank-loaned.

45

Meccano-made think tank;
quaint stereoscope drawn blank;
Goody Wan-eye, be still;
the dead past born to kill:
the clockwork bride and groom
wound up like an alarm,
Staffordshire group glue-bound;
the traitor's kiss disowned;
a Spitfire hewn from brass
of a spent shell-case;
crabapple kop kite-crowned;
talked-through the telling face.

46

To hold a word, a phrase,
in the cross-hairs
without firing,
is this wise?
The dead re-appearing
showing their scars
blindly; I am scared.
Look, their limbs wired
to explode
in shards of ode
fatal at forty paces
among other devices
too vile to describe
as when succubae disrobe.
Do not smile
at my simile.
You also are feckless.
You should all fuck less
and pray more. Climate
is now dynamite.
I checkmate my own moves
to cope with a quatrain
of metre uncertain
and rhyme claiming as proven what art disproves.

47

Saint Vigor, Saint Cassian,
of rigour and passion,
and you, Breton saints,
with Cornish transplants,
that few here have heard of,
spare us yet the hard proof
of belief:
as many believe
Gauguin was let thrive,
compounded with for a tonne of sin
because of Pont-Aven,
The Vision after the Sermon—
those sanctified dim women—
presented to the Church,
cast out of the church porch,
now consecrate
to our dumb commingling of salvation and fate.

48

Think what you will, poetry
serves to claim and maintain pedigree:
Henry Howard, Earl of Surrey,
        to his friend Wyatt.
And hauteur can cohabit with riot
as in Surrey's case is well proven.
Forgive true poets to seventy times seven
                I
              say
          I say I say

49

        Nigra sum,
I am swart but comely: O Jerusalem,
how they deprave you; as the psalms reel dumb
        gross canticum.

50

Well, yes; but don't go Consiliar on me.
Let things be, straightforwardly civil; none
of this blank *sub rosa, anonyme.*
        Give the dog a bone.
        I see you have done.

        This swan on its nest
        squalidly at rest.
I have no cause to urge as one possessed.
Who reads darkly scrapes the palimpsest.
Give me good reason why we are not dust.

51

By common deed of grace, come mystic marriage,
        Linnaeus
found in each calyx, bees' effleurage,
        sex genius

        (Saint Francis
        songs dances)

From both potencies I have long derived
contemplative joy; in return wish them
reciprocal fulfilment, to flourish stem
with stem, their sunning hymns well-hived.

52

De Lorris's garden
did not fade with the gardener.
Poetry, cheating, and forgiveness,
my three givens,
my thesis.
Ungird the loins,
mooncalf,
to make scions.
Chaucer's pardoner
was not, at the last, himself.

53

What they spur for tradition is novelty
of an ancient kind
to which you and I, dearest muse, fall casualty
as disinclined.
Let the word ride free to proclaim causality
barely defined.

54

Nonsense verses set down versus conscience.

55

Scribe of epochs,
zealous
to name or create
time
by marvellous
eclipses and tyrants;
add
aurochs
to autarchs;
bad
but amusing
Baron Ochs;
trust–abusing
Karl Fuchs;
elevate
regents and vicegerents
of rhyme.
Happy those without shame.

56

Let us here invoke Staffordware figures
of T. E. Hulme and Mosley, Staffordshire squires.
    I would enter a bid
  for both, though without likelihood
    of owning them,
    Mosley and *Hulme*:
  Hulme for his creed of primal sin,
argument more than faith; and Mosley
    as that homunculus or djinn
    in no shape alien
to bottled spells that England frowsily
simmered with, drowsed in its patent heart;
sweetness, venom, not to be told apart.

57

Apotheosis of old lags, new lords,
suits well the time: Irn-Bru and fine brandies.
Love your disgusting aggregate, grandees,
demotic psycho-strippers and prize bards.

Commanded to deliver the *Creweian*
I shall tell them as much
in irregular verse demonstrating odd touch:
impassively the rhyme staggers its ruin.

Robe as a stipendiary, a fool
domestic, of the great; arthritic bounder.
They will tear you (marvelling) asunder
bending neither a finger nor a rule.

58

Miss Madge
Titheradge
recited Noyes
on golden deeds,
atop a tank,
to the rapt heads
of civil estates;
girl employees
    from the War Savings Bank
in attendance
    with redemption's certificates
and real mud from France.

59

Allegory's always cold when you awake
in the small hours
everything fallen away
from the high stake
and you pay
irritably
for those soul-making tours
weathered to anecdote
not wholly invalid
as the confessions of an invalid
of note.

60

The upas tree in my garden
invites a show of repose—
it is a rented house
and willow, I think, rather than upas
the tree, young for its burden
of chiaroscuro ivy,
Ruskinian trouvé—
the summer solstice poised upon its scales:
something within the balance that repels.

61

The mortifications are the fortifications.

62

Intelligence, superb affront,
to the fore.
Every verb a gerund,
Carthage not even a mound,
delenda there the agenda.
Messenger, your errand?
Historian, mend account.
Itinerant rhetor,
the victor your suitor.

63

You *tuneful bells of Belgium*
that Fritz wrung *stumm*;
and gabled houses ruined
as old Fordie mourned
     in a good poem;
help me to work my feint
     of lament,
to strike home under
the barrage-like thunder
     of war's loom.

64

We who are lovers for so short a time
     and climbers and divers
     for whom clamours
     consummation of rhyme:
Fear was first to make gods. Display
     your wits
in a testudo of iron odds. Can't say,
     things interlodged, it's
     right to put away
     ludo.

The Daybooks

The Daybooks

Expostulations on the Volcano

Now there shall be a man cohered out of tumult and chaos—
WALT WHITMAN, 1855

Such a voice seemed to clown verse rather than read it.
KATE LECHMERE, of Ezra Pound, *c.*1914

I

How anachronistic you are, Uncle;
And with such huge teeth; and so humourless;
Those man-trap jaws and that steel monocle.
I am myself not camera-averse.

Who's the lay-figure? Did I augur one
Smelling of chewed lead pencils, lying scared
For first-aider Girl Guides to practise on?
Mysterious types, beauties no more despaired.

Gifts to those altars. Ye shall offer no
Strange incense-effect. Nor ponder rhyme late.
Tycho, true man of parts, well-coffered nose,
A sounder mountebank than false Hamlet.

Workout at such pitch comports the jimjams.
I offer evidence how wit prevails
On weakness for hysterical emblems,
Love's body broken-through with weeping nails;

Not that I mean my word: in truth my vow
Never naked before any creature,
Not omitting the two wives until now.
Better drama than in the theatre.

2

Doubtless this is to propel the commons
To somnolence. *Words, are you myths and like*
Unto the myrtles of the shades? Omens
Uttered by means of an antic stand-mike.

So to misspeak my friend Desnos, so there
To float equity for all that it's now worth
On the exchanges. Wreathed in waning ire
The Furies ramble through old groves of earth.

Count here a juggler and a fire-eater
Plus the man who claims a life-consulship
In *Qliphoth*, an abysmal repertoire
Of drunks' mugshots taken on a school trip.

Invention piques and spasms, I have urged,
Immoderately. Where stalk those grand odes
Elsewhere than to this head, the unreneged
Custos of inerrantly fatal brides?

Whoever licensed glory, I admit
It is not ours nor us. *Writ with a coal,*
A legend for the telling. No new writ
Swings exculpation or faxed burial.

3

But shall I *shit in my hat and clap it*
Atop my head, as in that old footage
Of well-plumed patronage, servile crap wit?
Senile adolescence trips my dotage.

Catastrophe is formal but chaos
Less so. I deserve to remember such
Apophthegms. Comedians play us
In the theatres of correct research

And passable providence. How wit tells,
Tries, the clamps of destiny. Why retype?
I have cribbed already for what avails
Against least odds, thwacking twi-coloured tape

To shreds of lamination. Let it go,
Including stage business. That remains
For someone's visitations; one not so
Conspired in lewd responses and refrains.

Face to the wall I remember hearing
Flung by reflex at the class idiot.
So trivial some things past despairing
Although some things past repairing are not.

4

The clockwork animal has broken down.
I would not now submit to repair it—
The parts of shame dejected as here shown;
Long-resonant voicebox to shagged parrot.

Massiv und haltbar Goethe's vertebrae
Put up first for remedial auction.
With relics of hot tar and cautery
The vulgar error of Heine's foreskin,

Again catalogued, makes precipitate
Time on the Bourse; bad time for diffidence,
Affective union of man and mate,
And all such usage, sacred dividends

In sealed encomia. Derive God's word
From coxcombs and dyed hair, spilt *encrier*.
Nothing in bonded fetish more absurd.
Shell-out intimacies for town-crier.

Vertebrae: those of Goethe's young mistress
Immortal. His metres, too, more driven
Than mine. Too much rove-over draws distress.
Heine had poor joy in getting even.

5

I have not cleared my language with myself
For ever. At pick-a-word per half hour
The snail and the tortoise feign disbelief;
Princess winds back her hair in the tower.

One line describes me; a new equation
Figures me nowhere. It can stand in place
For a thousand years' enduring fiction;
Even projected as neo-Nazi.

Here there's a faster-than-light particle
That can reveal the secret about us,
Irradiant: our inarticulate
Brethren delivered as golden statues.

Appropriately, more forms of art drop
Earthward like space-junk that has shed some weight
In transit of obstructive aether, snip
Meteorites, pin-wits inebriate.

Spur the nice constraints of rhyme-flagrantive.
Rhyme is itself re-ordering of will,
Directio voluntatis, a long dive
Heavenward; held finally to be still.

6

Stock measurer yew tree, the lowest branch
Brushing a rabbits' grotto; tireless
Its rooting catchment in the rotten clunch.
The old King's speech favoured our new wireless—

Not to remit, here, all it takes to rile me:
Mendicant parts of common accounting
In time defaulted and this uptight realm
Gone at the core. Pride's abdication's bunting

Banners of *Qliphoth* at half-mast, sunset
Close to four; children's Nativity pitched
Like a rehearsal for snow's pent onset;
A shadow of ourselves briskly enriched

In dramas unrehearsed because I dis-
invented one wedding-night, took to bed
Her speaking image framed to dumb ideas.
You my anchorite doll nastily stroked;

Shared misfunding a blur of the mystic
In landscape that seems largely withdrawn: tracks
Of small creatures become *esemplastic*
Power; starlings' multi-helical flocks.

7

Wildly unprecocious you could call us.
I know what law we broke and what endured.
Here I am an old man drawn salacious
To intimate half-offers then undared.

Still, at the Fairfield–Bournheath road junction,
The curved wall stands, its Home Guard rifle-vents
Happily preserved by late compunction,
By unforetold unfolding of intents.

Bifold authority more bifocal
Choosiness; no choice. But found at random
Along those Welsh borders thought magical
The plaster-flake remnants of some grand Doom,

In stark of which, demand stands shiftless. Words
Render us callous the fuller they ring;
Stagger the more clankingly untowards;
Hauled to finesse in all manner of wrong:

Which is how change finds for us, long-lost one.
Oratory is pleading but not pledge;
Such haphazard closures of misfortune
Played by commandment on mechanic stage.

8

Fantastic to be Lowry by proxy,
Confabulating him; to stand tongue-tied
In awe of yourself; to hold epoxy-
Resin postures rather than be thought dead;

To ape his helpless vamping and to fall,
Squab-faced amid Dollarton's tide-machine,
Among odd jetsam to posture and flail,
Stark in the shallows, laved with soapy brine.

Who has not totted his black bile, Consul,
Where *Qliphoth* is wet coal and gritstone setts,
Spackled and wintry with hoary moonspill?
As vile an intro as the spirit gets.

Matter stubborn to be legendary
In situ: I fear they are off the beam,
Those masters who could break and brand fury,
Turning things back upon themselves. For shame

Concordance at its best not better made
Than, picked from underlip, shreds of *Gold Flake*.
And I no smoker. Let it be; upgrade
Folie à deux to singular double-take.

9

How to detonate self without pressing
Charges, prestidigitator; to have
Countercharges levelled of cross-dressing;
To work up a defence that will not move:

For that is how it becomes. Since Scottish
Law is Roman Law, migrate to Scotland
Where they sentimentalize equities;
Case-constraints in Equity forgotten,

Re al-Megrahi (not a Scots clan name
Though some might suppose it is). We have long
Known sentimentality without claim.
Translate into Latin [|] justice its song.

Timeless things to be discarded with ease.
One rarely gives raw chance a smoother start.
The hands at the lapels, thus, to propose;
Assiduous the masters of report.

Justice is song where song is primitive
As with poetics. Elsewhere more complex
Dénouements, if folly can stay alive;
Innocence, if machination strum lax.

10

I have tasted in dreams; not your body
It is true; but so circumstanced; and wine
I have indeed tasted, in sleep's moody
Inconsistencies, scene bundled through scene:

Irrelevant, in that I do not take
To *Anima Mundi*; but the day's guilts
I do accept, ragged on sleep's hot spike;
Nothing of restitution; all defaults.

But some weirds also, as when I proposed
To you and another; was accepted
By both before the nightmare fell confused.
In nobler times that would have been kept hid

With the marmalades and peccadilloes
In some inner chamber of the Queen's Grace
To a lute's pimping twang; thence to fail us,
The queen dispatched, re-plastered your old face.

What is mannerism if I cannot
Release you from it; or hopeless credence;
The hapless connotations that denote
Elisions of choice and inadvertence?

II

If prayer now applicable, pray advise
Those who trip counsel; this is not their hour;
Not here to trash damnation's paradise,
Out-of-sync Dollarton on the north shore.

Attention: these fragments of fire and flood,
I cannot name you their price; iambics
Fretted with binder-twine, scrotted to blood,
Litter of dereliction and clam-bakes,

So you may think: I paint a site unseen,
The body here elsewhere, prone to abuse.
Within faint hail of the meridian
Late drastic shifts of continence unwise.

To angst and dolour each co-provider;
I wish he hadn't, I wish I hadn't,
Followed through to the lair of the Hydra;
A Herculean will but late adjunct.

Shall not venture what favours opportune
Settling of account with upstart greatness,
Its following, scant plaudits filed online,
Though early days would have joyed in mute guess.

12

Fights I should have forced with the school bully
But failed to, lacking both courage and skill,
Let me thrust against time like a fool; my
Bruised reinterpretation of Blake's mill.

Blake would have pummelled him without a thought
Wasted; as he had once tackled Voltaire,
Rousseau; with nonchalance resumed his coat,
Cynosure of maids' eyes in Golden Square.

Am I to be relieved by an image
As for a much-studied lameness all round,
I ask rhetorically; win damage-
Compensation, and vittles, and all found?

Skew me denial's face. For three public
Pronouncements in a year I am well paid,
Though less than a hacking thesp; the fabric
Of governance set up on the right road

With a flourish of changed hands. Adjectives
Demonstrate weakness; an early lesson
I did not draw from once-adjacent lives.
Let verbs excrete blood, voiding confession.

13

What am I hymning that is not absurd?
I have reworked the least of me twelve times
For Cabbalistic humours, for the dead,
Buoyed by the storm music from *Peter Grimes*;

Fancying myself as a storm-petrel
With excellent reflexes and at ease
In the burly element I patrol,
Tempted by instinct's sinew to be wise.

There would be scandal. Let me off my hook
Of retrospection; say I was not caught
By what I feared, one mere untimely look;
It is not nature's way to be distraught.

The secrets of creative elements
Are not creation; nor do they vault forth,
Loved-clown-like; but, to exorbitant wants,
Protract and retract themselves, mould *Qliphoth*.

As to these pots, frost-broken, white, exposed
Roots, tendrils, pebbles, in a mouldered cake,
Some would still argue: have the mass emprosed
For as long as deconstruction may take.

14

Posthumous retroactive vocations
Contriving bric-à-brac and *scarabrie*;
Voice-overs—Pindar and the Movietones—
Hart Crane shark-vetting with the Caribee:

A swing of fragile bullishness chimes well
With a hangman's bellrope and a clapper
Working at sonorities. I recall
Few poems, each a birthday in leap year;

Such their plight, imaginary, sub-leased,
Not yet disproved. Yeats's late lust-attacks,
Fantastical virginity mis-phased,
Share some features with my inscape-and-wax.

I do not think any more that wilful
Conjunctures are late virgins. I do not
Establish the recondite as Hill-school;
Have long endorsed folly, wisdom, misdoubt,

In well-essayed sort. Play up depression
As witness to some capital offence.
Dismiss the charge. The heart is in season
Too rarely; and too rarely our wits dance.

15

Clown Donatello? Screw in ant-honey?
Is *pretty haglike* to be got from books
Of rhetoric, assured antiphony?
It is some time, now, since I lost my looks.

What sub-type of hubris thus self-provokes
Only to while away the endocrine
Sipping on mingy leaves of artichokes—
Old-fashioned stamp hinges in fibre-green?

Plot to assure the products of your pen.
Demise is certain and yields poor cover.
Rimbaud lived a near-anonymous man.
Soberly dissect *le Bateau-Ivre*.

Tush! I have not taken a male lover
Since last we corresponded. Discredit
Is yet volatile. Nothing to move here,
Demonstration a prevailing habit.

Loining by Alma-Tadema: Dub it,
Thus to propose a frisson. Misrecall
Ardour. Supernumeraries applauded
Remaindering detritus of the Fall.

16

I desire you to make music for this,
Being outside the act; of course deny
Myself no end of musical far cries
And all the suppleness money can buy.

The lust for possession, which is my lust
For nothingness under an assumed name,
At odds with the jerked equities and just
Discriminations and natural shame,

Mistakes this breather for inspiration.
I will not nod upon what evidence
The holy rollers themselves rate Zion
Established in ecstatic carnal sense.

Far better to collapse here; like a bout
Of underage drinking for a sex-film
Overseen by a consenting adult.
Marat's snuff-tableau shown in its wax calm,

This is the commentary from hell I
Fear; though of more restricted a future
Than that voracious fable, the belly
As boss-man's pleb-defaming portraiture.

17

With crush-crease-curvet what am I about—
A squeezebox pirouetting in a busk?
This is not an incitement to riot
And not a lead-in to a precise masque.

Mercedes, fair name, I do not gamble
With what promotes first offer; nor impose
Lightweight chance upon the scales that tremble.
Finicky and yet unfastidious,

Satire's investment, as exclusive club
I would build up a little and sell on.
I fear my bitterness has become glib.
Help carry this painting to the *Salon*:

Jacob's repose at Shiloh—Ribera—
For which I modelled, launched upon its fame
The sleep of reason; you my co-bearer
Of ambitious merit, foot in the jamb.

The friends who found me, such I abandoned
Later, most shamefully. The text remains
As I will it to you, the busk re-boned,
The petty agents thrusting for their skins.

18

Firmin the Consul, Hart Crane the Merman,
Distinctive natural allies in play,
Both beyond much caring that such harmon-
y staggers tequila along the bay.

Work accretes art profoundly like coral
On frames of graph paper and litmus strips.
Nothing delegate is the clipped moral.
Eight lines forward without moving my lips

I shall colloquize with the unfallen,
Unbelieving; though with some help I could
Revamp the late prayer to penicillin
That would have saved my hearing as a child.

Ignorant's simples force complexity.
This is the way of things. Withdraw comment.
What is hexity to dyslexia,
Dispossession? Angry styles in ferment,

The system conceived-of spreads tone clusters
Rather than a progression of named chords.
Coral to be discarded—it fractures—
Is not the atoll that I cruise towards.

19

At Melville's Tomb is already written,
To my regret; *Qliphoth, the realm of rinds,*
Ditto; picked up, tattered and betrodden,
From a grand structure's shards and left-behinds.

The consul, Firmin; merman, bloated Crane,
Snag on a gyre, or vortex impounds them,
Vast brass Tibetan prayer-wheel a-strain.
Dead planets' congress in love confounds whom?

Of course I give my password to stringers
As foreign as myself. The body count
Becomes prodigious; guest malingerers
Grown chirpy on the mescal of the saint.

Qliphoth retorts upon the cabbalist
Nothing; to me nothing; yet does for both.
Dissection's wheeze sections the analyst.
The lampshade's mock death-rattle sears the moth.

Innocent tequila! Best call the spate.
Accuracy mourns. Decencies let run
In frantic scritchings of chalk across slate.
Your understanding of such things could stun.

20

The tooth-crown snapping loose on its firm pin—
Boredom and irritation—spit, turn back
To the *via dolorosa*: Firmin
Who broke himself with tequila and crack,

No, not crack. Abuse out of use. Moral
Grammar satisfies longing that's ill-met
Otherwise. Ramble into a quarrel
With a love of confracture and fine fret.

Henceforward I take the second person.
Bear with me, as your dentist used to say
Introducing the dribbly bits; for soon
You shall yourself jag painful memory.

Supposing a verdict pronounced, even
Pronounceable: *I think this man is dead*;
So much now subtracted from the given,
So much beyond yourself in your own head,

So tiresome having to bind, formally,
The broken tiers of living, strike-patterns.
Terror-smitten old age in bomb alley
Begs immortality's cloak of neutrons.

21

Playing our song as a presentiment
Fifty years ago would have meant something
To trail-blazers of Nepal. Sentiment
Is impatient, irascible; same thing.

Navel-gazing I dismiss though better
Suited to some odd-centred symmetries,
Lady of Mixed Perceptions. Your letter
Of credit I hid under the mattress

From whence it was removed, c/o the First
Catechumen; you absent at the time.
Ancient plectra. And now Damien Hirst
With Tracey Emin; pent internal rhyme.

These I nominate to primped devotion
Foresuffering with bells on in the heat,
One word to extrapolate time, motion,
Authoritative reason. Contemplate

Thought with economy and politic
Contrivance. This is no stay-in-the-car
Comedy show; nor, sacred, the Young Vic.
Observe, remnant romantic faith, your star.

22

Should I exchange forms with the Cabbalist,
His *Tree of Life*? If so could I transship
The *Ship of Death*, its Etruscan ballast,
To Lowry's ribs gibbs-whitened on the slip?

Mariners: a Study in Missing Reefs,
This they will discover late and publish
To the detriment of his weathered griefs;
His ravishing order re-establish.

Appointed vice-consul to the Seychelles
Someone entirely other; the beach hut
Encrusted with rococo of sea-shells,
Wading on stilts, recalcitrant, a squat.

Should you ask, I'd say we must fantasize
Forms of invention; at the ocean's verge
Stubborn each day, wide night, for fantasies,
Displacements, that to none but him emerge.

Still I would check my name if I were you.
We are not all we say when in receipt
Of others' takings as on Mount Meru;
Gold bullion debased, the silver clipt.

23

Interest, then, in what we are dealing,
The life-dealers? In or on? Keep the torch.
Confession best to be unrevealing
While well-rewarded. Ignorance no slouch.

If she can yet be summoned up, the Saint
Of Hazardings, of Desperate Causes,
Must be called upon; a job to acquaint
Her with input, powers and abuses

As currently encountered. To elope
Now could be fatal. But other options?
Where did you say—Haiti, Guadalupe?
At eighty I am low on prescriptions.

These are my priorities; they include
You. Grant *La Mordida* our sacred scroll,
Unscrolled, not helpful. But adore us nude.
This hulk is trembling to the ocean swell.

Having to reckon high the low demands
Of others puts a strain on reckoning.
Summon this same Virgin from faithful strands;
Or plough to meet her, the haze thickening.

24

Magistral art does well to encompass
Past warnings of its gifts: the narwhal-horned
Bull-browed killer-wave such inspired rumpus
I would not leave our chances long unmourned;

Though how to contrive the mourning *topoi*
Presents difficulties, is made a theme
Counterpointing itself, a humming top
I found recently in parallel time—

I would visit her there if I could think
Swiftly but swiftness prevents me. Return
All rhapsodes from their expeditious brink,
The *Stone Angel* to her rebellion.

Devise: the pull of monorhyme's arrear,
Postdate backward strategies, where nothing
But immortality's to overhear
The scrap of genius with scrapped plaything.

Discharge grieving from its valediction
Among equals, equals without solace
Yet without equal. It is bold fiction,
No tears coming in last of the old race.

25

Watching the small towns of Nepal come up
On plasma it is how Old London Bridge
Appears in the Shakespearean time warp.
(Fat man tips anarchy to the lean judge.)

Royal colours of dark natural wood
Regale poor shopfronts; the rivers plunge, flayed,
Vast pelts of ox-hide; self-devourers; brood;
A rainbow, suddenly, all there, arrayed.

The *right side of despair* is not the right
Segment of the brain; or perhaps it is.
The world without us reigns pre-Adamite.
Inept fine-judging flails weak rhapsodies,

Of which *Qliphoth*—Cabbalah's tree of life
Stood on its crown—is final judgement-place,
The *realm of rinds*, landfill of rotten grief,
A dereliction of love's artifice.

Would it help if I balanced on one hand,
My feet juggling the promotion package
Of weighted years, assisted by the band;
The grand vibes of Nepal crated backstage?

26

Skull of the Cyclops an elephant's skull,
Bone archway for the trunk burned single eye,
By luck, terror, and poetics to impel
Sympathetic blanched hagiography.

Creatures all-scales fated to blow conches
At the fête of Britannia: suppose
They had feelings. Others olive branches,
And still others oratorical prose,

Some of it in the form of armour. Grand
Consequences could impend such fractile
Chainlets demonstrating the resolved mind
In moral labour for an intact style.

There is a tensile music of order
I would have them hear—Penelope's gang
Of brokers, aspirants to her boudoir,
Such insolently grovelling *hauptklang*—

And it is very like the bent strung bow.
Colophon: thus far I have brought this Greek-
Contrived eulogy of the comic flaw;
Sad elephantine nuisance at the wake.

27

Compères, junkies, and chancers: a slipped phrase;
Camera angles not of importance;
Mud wrestlers—cubist in an early phase;
Imported waifs it cannot hurt to dance.

But, of these, it is simply the wording
I would have you remember; as various
Remember hearing at Covent Garden
Some late diva, stacking her arias

Of banishment and sickness and return.
Assemble at the Abbey for the vile
Apotheosis of Victor Carroon
Brought back from *Qliphoth* in primitive style

About the time of Stalin's death. You may
Not have signed-on for this. Remain happy.
I run together the hapless years, my
Mother trying *Californian Poppy*

At Woolworth's, her old coat of nigger-brown.
Declare my dating frustrate; as it was,
And to my grievous loss, where I was thrown.
Repetitiousness of things destroys pace.

28

Peacocks and prostitutes brought together
By Guardian; fair trade, I know desire
Thanks to your vision Mrs Anstruther.
Wheels and Butterflies, too, I much admire.

What so delights here is arbitrary;
A peacock's plumes that give me the glad eye.
Thunderous sunshine and rain weathery
Self-immolating cast as a red sky.

Thus when the verb wires notice to our lost
Acts I am with you (but not in writing);
Somewhere beyond this sentence act as ghost,
Touched by truth's language, frail forth-spiriting.

Order is not by book; my archival
Sorrow strewn about the point of impact;
Survivors' records, vested, corrival,
Though given out with a certain grim tact.

Why we lost each other you must propose
To hazard: a project not worth mocking
The heart for, mocked though it now appears. Whose
That gift of threnody made self-locking?

29

Magnolia, at high summer darkened,
Dully fulgent. As I search for emblems
I will cast about in my unreckoned
Capacity for inventing dumb games.

The right side of despair my making;
But what making? Neither opprobrium
Brought on nor fame upheld; nor a play-king
Paraded with proclamation of drum.

Some trolls explode while others turn to stone,
The things one hears! Do not fail rhetoric
Or what price fancy, what prize invention?
Take the Schlieffen Plan, take Count Metternich,

And lose them somewhere like wooden soldiers.
Sun is in my eyes, the magnolia
Darker because of it. The mind's elders
Loom familiar amid such foliage.

Who is to take or assail a verdict
No-one caught over the rage of ringdoves?
Susceptibility of worn tear-duct;
Rilke's eyeball on a thorn; the thing moves.

30

Mescal no hope mescaline; *the white alps*
In context of dream a sex-threnody.
Of one who compounded her lovers' whelps
Let it be said that she hurt nobody

Less than she maimed fancy. View the lovescape
Through a porthole-window in time. Fiction
Has numbered virtues through which to escape.
Shall we get at the truth by c-section

Even though this not our watch, señora?
Concentrate the attention on one tooth
Is good advice, knowledge fit to inure.
It was even so in our dead of youth;

Nor are we patently finished. *To get
On the right side of one's despair*: to me
An obvious conclusion; on target;
A broken consort of loves; a great tome.

Panta rhei, though I have not subscribed
You or myself into that flashy cruise.
You may think I have; but so much is cribbed;
So much conceived of dying to amuse.

31

So where was anywhere space for the pre-
Atom: out of which atoms exploded
Light from which dark matter is this debris?
Ignorance as grace wrongly decoded,

Where are we for the right turn? Vexed compass
I cannot bring to bear on the question;
Audenesque needling of self in the grim pass;
Nor tagged the gestures of restitution.

Survival-tracking. Do I rhyme *friends* : *fiends*
Anywhere in my posthumous *oeuvre*?
Such accidents are like getting the bends
From reckless ascent. Act the survivor.

What particles pass through the sieve—Pascal's—
Like stardust, minute fragments of God's scan,
Further reduced yet quivering the scales?
Very strange man, Auden, very strange man.

That all is wildly amiss since the first
Crack-up I accept; as scattered options,
Shiftiness of the moral life; cloudburst
Of stellar gas domestic eruptions.

32

Ships were lost in the St George's Channel,
Torpedoed, that is. My father survived
Through missing the leave-packet: annual
Narration well-handled and well received.

So, *black-and-tan man* is the dark mutter;
The step dance faltering. I'm out of sorts
With Irishry myself, for that matter.
But, no; he was innocent of their sports.

Ordered out of a Somme draft he was, too,
By brotherly intervention. Chance, luck,
Immeasurably moving; *déjà vu*
At his hazard I can prance on this deck,

But cannot here say what it is I mourn
In spite of him; or what would be entailed
By the unlooked for, scarce-greeted return;
All shames remitted, recompense withheld.

Sad jazz, are we alone? You taught me riffs
Though, by that time, I was a grandfather
And flugeler of old redundant griefs.
Your high trumpets caracol and feather.

33

As often as here named the veterans
Will weep, forever without alibi;
The age of Mars reborn as slow Saturn's;
Death here always unconstrained ad-libber

Of various outrage. I would parade
Chiefly my wits in semblance of honour
As though I had fought for something; were glad;
A visionary without retainer.

Speaking of blankness, this is why I build,
Submit myself to interrogation
For nothing; superannuation sold
To breed poppies for your toxic nation,

Mrs Anstruther. Why do you tease me
With celibate marriage, and yet for love
Of those in the wars? Sealed with blood plasma
I find this demanding and yet furtive.

Grief is about, though not the *mania
For solitude*, Pavese's contriving;
Nor yet Whitman's *woods of Virginia*,
Landscape drenched in eros, unforgiving.

34

Why you vexin' me so, bluesless Muzak,
With ripped-off solace? Give me back my speech;
There are annulments to be made: Woyzeck
Not a grand antihero; a dumb kvetch.

Difficult, all the dredged marvels of words
And without profit. Rake me my account;
I shall rebury it with due regards;
Knock you down Woyzeck as a lumpen saint;

Which is simple: *when did you last make it*,
A question I am here set up to flash
If and when I next encounter naked
Desires of my heart blowing on ash.

Not to be disclosed all I decoded
From Büchner's abrupt style, or from Pindar.
Who, of our youth, qualifies for ode-aid?
Centuries more of light from a blind star.

Whether to call paint-textures prurient
Or *klangfarben* intrusive, I am at
A loss to judge; or to fulfil my stint
As votive agent; or to disclaim that.

35

What flesh to be conjured up from spirit;
What flesh of spirit without instruments?
Granted the impediment declare it,
Tied-in with demands and counter-demands.

Is the intelligence you have heartfelt?
Does not maintain an answer. We are slow.
Hypocrisies bertbrechted and kurtweillt;
Off-key the blatant brasses blow us raw.

Show me how to stoop to your discretion
Edited-in. Some say the spirit lives
Best while embodied: the elect nation;
Transfigurations; have-nots have close shaves.

Things at their most intelligent broken
Across the line. Patents? If I had not
So ventured I would not so have spoken.
Always to wait and wait for the lead-note.

I am more short-tempered with mysteries
Than I have declared lately; freak desire
To go stately into those green pastures
And find you; all else found derisory.

36

Spads have their own advisers; bank Gnome-Rhônes;
The dogfights a spectacular peril;
Illyria peers skyward, dodges bones.
Death is a rich kid running things three-rail.

If there is a fatal message here I
Have not found it; but repaired ailerons.
Rhyme is the grand enforcer; casts hero,
Apes trim ungallants, picks off frailer ones.

Blown at a single breath the double fraud
Of the millennium and poetry.
As armed presages botch the Turin shroud
Al-ud-Din dispenses our common day.

Swear this Enigma: caca is hidden
Among the rotors. Why enlarge deceit?
Why the lame caesura and the sudden
Exposure, the distinguished counterfeit?

You have me at a disadvantage, soul
Split by high-frequency and ultrasound;
Truth in the detail I fail to recall;
Tactics I cannot get my head around.

37

Sharing with Jane Grey three words of Hebrew,
And she a clever slip and a good thing,
Knowing in Greek how to raise an eyebrow;
Intransigent, though, over the God-thing:

Excluded from typic power that is
Not potency but accumulation
Of attributes from unproven status,
A ministerial car on station

Like a frigate on station, a poor film
Nostalgicised. Is this about us, then?
Partly us; and partly about the realm.
Solved inner dialogue, dissolved question.

Plant non-evidence; take credit for it;
Love's innards trailed to the mob. Not Petrarch
Le viscere dell'amore. Merit
Where it is earned; words; industry's sweat-mark.

What if test-inspiration sites ground glass
In the gut; I intend no specimen
Of fecal blood to deplete our congress.
There are ranker demons who piss as men.

38

Not better drama than the theatre.
More Wycherley than Lowry at the last
Revived business: the creator-creature
Stands up to the *Bronze Horseman* and *Stone Guest*,

Conceiving music as Prokofiev
For Pollock's proscenium, sets hand-en-
twined lovers next the twin-headed club-knave;
Other postures—noble abandonment

With a parade of justice kept in stock;
Blok's puppet-booth, its fate-entoying strings,
Absurdly tragic and inspired to chic;
Dead empire ill-exhumed with all it brings,

Conveyed by beat. I imagine *five*: *four*,
Eleven: *four*, even; Diocletian
Attending Romeo; fine brazener
Of kind, triumphalist of the short span.

Indented for: a stanza on rollers
Already with its trade-accoutrements
In penny plain or with paintbox colours,
Illuminations for cancelled events.

39

Ye shall offer no strange incense thereon
Though strange enough Wat's cracked *pug-iron stove*,
Here with small adjustments: a gridiron,
Ingeniously a bed for aggrieved love.

Between a golden calf and a limbeck
I place my inventiveness; at salute
To Lowry, Wat, scribes of *Qliphoth's* psalm book;
This scarce-accessible; the plundered rite;

As I would try them, acting to rue this
For a late hazard much too early made.
Erudition no longer an issue,
Look under *Dada* on the dog's iPad

While I fiddle with line endings and brakes.
No cunning too basic, no oath too strange
For the disservices one undertakes.
Give me my medal for rhymed sabotage;

Claim catastrophe now as jubilee,
The chant at the core of things marginal.
Rappel à l'ordre cries *merde*, though ably
Restored the surrealist urinal.

40

I cannot judge how to retrieve our trade.
A million for my judgement; a trophy
Wife new-installed in Exhibition Glade.
East India men and the Grand Sophy,

Grandee John Dee, alchemical retorts'
Sulph'rous fogs over London: comic books'
Philosophy of craft delights all sorts,
Myself included, flailing these rude hooks

Of bespoke making. Perhaps I once col-
lected pearl buttons; certainly marbles
Strewn on the floor of Sylvester's dance school.
Swift's correspondence speaks well of rabbles;

Yet he's judged a moralist of stature;
And went mad with a kind of insane grief.
Stress is at the heart of architecture.
Swift struck himself a Latin epitaph

Many can quote in two tongues; few in Erse
I should imagine. Things get in the way:
Vanity, stupidity, and remorse;
And the unruly laws we must obey.

41

October's curt heatwave unseasonal—
Darkness draws early—becomes as Tuscan
Or Umbrian in shocking fashion. All
Senses on retarded alert; as, can

Animals comprehend death in their kind?
What homing draws us to such exile here?
The hyper-chirr of bats is wired for sound
In the void mastoid bone of my dead ear.

How to imagine imagination
When it briefs me apparitions like you?
What I have made you inscribe. Slow motion
Revival of action stalled at *take two*,

Marked for effort. I have miscarried us
Perhaps for the last stretch of common themes,
Signed immanations to kiss; wearied as
I am, counting on shot fingers and thumbs.

Battered for a siesta, poetry
Emotes for love and primes itself apart,
Exquisite throat, exquisite garottry.
Dogs can scent death: whimper, and rise a-start.

42

There is no choice of mercies; but what comes
Is grace; whatever's proportioned, not ours,
At the final tally of loves and crimes,
The crotty ashes that are *Whinney-moor's*,

Qliphoth, more like, for now. There is a space
And you fill it. It may make immortal
By some freak of persistence, like trench-lice.
Whatever's here measured does not total.

Do I give back-word, so, on my language?
True fright not solely in the making; right
Side of anything is how to engage.
Too many embarrassingly distraught

In this dire art that is more mud-suction
Than moral tenacity. Who would stall
Worse by writing-off poetic diction
In favour of penance-mad commonweal

Setting aside myself? There you have it.
Hope for no end of mastery to bear
Past the savage joy of crying *leave it*,
Renunciation's profited career.

43

Hold up to fresh light beginners' pencil;
Soft graphite neb's miniature finger nail;
Look to this stub worn down by brusque counsel.
Chartered my own mind to itself long-haul.

Buoyant trouvé discovers that he clowned
His verses rather than recited them.
I field urgent recall of things disowned
During birth; long-laboured rebutted theme.

Could one, in short, retract recompenses
Yet protract end-stopping? Edited thus,
No account taken of savage menses.
Unodoured my late-accredited muse.

I will not say I have discovered fate
In you; but something of a wild concept
Troubles me still, perceived in shadow-state.
That image declared itself while one slept?

It could be too much to swear to, but why
Swear? Act out the dénouement. It is ours,
Even with five failing senses at cry
Unanswering to the artificers.

44

Might find vocation in the *Liturgy*
of Chrysostom set by Gretchanínov.
Chalybeate water drunk as shit-purge, I
Rattle pages for news to complain of.

She said, *state lunches for late emperors*,
That ancient actress, of *I, Claudius*;
Her resonance better than Klemperer's;
No less striking than he on videos.

What you lose, or what might turn up again
In time for the next move, is not fatal,
Evidently not. Books ruined by rain,
The winter rose drawn to its last petal,

I exaggerate. Tell me what you hear.
Reversed bloodlines not world's worst circuitries
Impending. Téll me what does nót appear
And I will prophesy: expect fruit trees,

The large wild garden (all shall be bestowed;
For not death only waits there with your name
Upon it, mere accident overawed)
And into self-possession surely come.

45

It is All Souls' Eve and one damson tree
Stands as miser to its wiltering leaves.
The best of British, dumb-blind Samsonry,
Cleaves to those rots like rose-roots into graves.

Brisk wind off the Fens drags through evergreens,
Sets fruit trees to rapid, stiffish, motion;
More presences here sensed of the unseens,
The putting-by, pull of hibernation.

Qliphoth it is not: St Vigor's louvres
Visible now through stained autumnal mesh.
A commonplace of morning manoeuvres
Itself into such a splendour of trash

That I have come to stand at the house door,
Awkward with lame synergy, revelling.
Lawrence, who knew each creature by its spoor,
The dead by yet-tenacious hard dealing,

Vexed variously the spirit of place.
I name, according to drift's burden, grief
And things vestigial, like the gummy trace
Tugged from old damson bark, an amber quiff.

46

Too much too early. The model stitching
Snagged. Let us go over the books again.
No more than you can I defend stretching
The body at ransom to excite pain.

Nor do I propose faith as mock option,
Not even as fund forgotten many years
In lees-undrained ledgers; old corruption
Dragged out of close confinement by the hairs.

Could these excite some fit of celestial
Boffinry? And by whose intransigence
Would we go forward again from mis-trial
Still symbollocking in transit hence?

Nor would I convey you as anything
Other than the late Muse of Poetry,
Our love sealed with a grope and penny ring,
Though I have grown tired from your harlotry.

Back to the books. The lining of account.
I have few past convictions as their guest.
So soon, in this grand cycle of affront,
Draw to conclusion and the heart's arrest.

47

From lead to mercury the sky; bare trees,
Refined archaic leaf-patterns of slate
Against the sky-tone, veins to arteries:
Mid-November, correctile, intricate,

Under strange genial suns; at least two.
Mute acoustics of light to bring aligned.
Why should Rutland Water, unsung, not glow;
Undulant midland shires, the many-faned?

They have been too long reflective, I grant,
In a bent mirror of longing not theirs
At all; concave to convex or mere slant;
Staggering hermeneutics of arrears,

Barely wrought to fixed legacy. Finish
So; finish with this or that absurd grief
In resolution; fields under varnish
Of new-sliced red earth held cuttingly stiff.

Shall call this *Bacchanal for over-pre-
pared Piano*: nothing original;
Girt evanescent England, its display,
Whichever way I play it, not final.

48

Jacob wrestling with the angel one thing;
With a ladder another. If the late
Writings are about grace and self-loathing
Tick the box; if comedy is your fate

Know how it strikes you. All could be sudden
Master-erasure or slow consignment,
Brutish beholdings tamed and beholden,
Obscure heart-splinter fleshed as truth's figment:

Craft-ingrown lace-maker of blitzed Ypres
As it might be; fable could up its bid.
Not as gift the rigged target of prayers,
Parachute-harness hung, still crucified.

I should mutter you blanked out with the fall
As was expected; but that you are now
Master of the small bribes, theatrical
Posings, wills, worthless disclosures at law.

If *Cairncross*, say, was a *strange bitter man*
Who could have done untold harm but didn't
By weirdest chance, if the next letter can
Yield you top score, who shall go unpardoned?

49

Time and light move simultaneously
In either direction: such is my view
Based on a vision that came painlessly
And liquorless as mostly I am now.

I say *painlessly*; but there stands belief
With things densely familiar. Time, great
Laden shuttle reduced to its begriff,
In which you and I, love, rue with Wyatt,

Against the whinge of pulsars; a pressure
Unimaginable; here recognized
And with charts to prove them. I am less sure
Of other measures anarchs have devised.

Clue me as to how we are immortal
Yet again. Yet again impulsive flares
From lourd sophistry, of misrequital;
Much as this causeless spin our lords and heirs

Have not forefashioned. Must we end with him,
This mortifying old man, his bent wits,
With the slow-dying spiral of his rhyme;
And with whatever else in judgement sits?

50

Words now alms; as no more let deliver
Imagination the feeling knowledge
Of water, sensient as a retriever,
Nosing among reeds and Keatsian sedge.

Wombed urn-burial, grace-impacted mind:
What the soul may let rip with thereafter
Greek to me, disillusionment in kind,
Deprived since when of stinger and snifter,

Tit fresh from the shower, the telephone
Dancing, the gi'mel in its kinky boot;
Enticements of the foregone prize forgone,
Billed as for secrets kept of the squared root,

An altar's worth: ye shall offer no strange
Incense thereon. Keep the astringencies
For some lament wit may lately manage
To pen in time. Discourage late strangeness

Of purchase. Nothing now is going cheap.
We pay good money for the dead at war.
When all is said why should the gut not reap
Thy wants; with conscience, aching predator?

51

Crutches of rock and roll, he said. *Crutches*,
The Genesis man, his lame interview
Spun sprightly. Leave the subject in stitches.
Plain eulogy for what satire will show.

So what thus determines you physical
Mortal strength here to rib? State exception
Whatever the rule. Slap non-musical
Waste efflorescence above the rapt tune.

Fetish? You care now how twisted things are,
How flattened, how punctured, vowel music
Purchased online? Spieled *emptor* to beware.
Trick to be both consumer and quizzic-

al: I can sketch an idyllic rating,
Rich mellifluousness in pale packets.
Late exercise, strenuous begetting,
Not nearly the nookie that some luck gets.

Dawn here, with grey light through the ivy leaves
Pitting my window glass like large raindrops,
Qliphoth, the blank that such ennui conceives.
Eventually, rat-like, the brain stops.

52

Così fan tutte. Venusberg Music.
Bankers love Bayreuth better than Glyndebourne.
Probably untrue; and not amusing.
Whip me to the tin tube for a mindscan.

Why cannot you be wholly serious,
Uncle Matthew? I rather admire them,
Those well-spoken, pert, and imperious
Children contemptuous of such esteem.

Thinking is repetitious so invent:
Dark energy, the enigmatic pulse,
Begging a mystery not yet a stunt
Brews its own compound of soul and salsa.

Clinch this like changing gear into the truth
Position; though the road steers deceptive,
Or as the sight deceives, or perhaps both.
I am, as ever, free to make captive

The genius of language; leave betrayed.
Evidence shows that we are not alone.
I say let all be gainfully employed;
Old Mother Riley, infantile, egged on.

53

Sometime in the false future I shall use
Dark with excessive bright for epigraph.
Celebrity defines, annuls, the Muse.
Rhyme is insentient, sense a trophy,

And music the self-set, the final dance
Of refuge. How teasingly it is done
Before the dancer's serene countenance
Splits between quarter tone and quarter tone.

Recycling end-notes wills no lasting harm
To final judgement; wit is *up to here*
In old mischief; despondency caps fame;
The fuse must rehabilitate to fire.

No call here for *resurgam*, popular
Among the blitzed pieties; most likely
Anglo-Catholics of Stepney, Poplar,
Such places, who lit candles spikily

Fixing their contrived altars. The moment
Is gone, now, when I could have found her: draped
In plaster dust and asbestos room-rent;
Or someone else from tall fiction escaped.

54

Who sacrificed our young daughters to win
Compensation and our sons to gain time;
Whose loves were implicate with rites obscene,
Whose beauty was of light, angle, and frame:

How shall we expel a new birth? My age
Tells against me in a speech not my own
But familiar. Face raddled with rouge
Cast me as Quentin Crisp not as Timon;

A tenured special adviser to life.
Could have wished confirmation while all slept.
I would not curse to redefine belief,
Disfigure telling rhyme of the adept.

Calvinist-Papist, stuck with a basic
Flaw in deportment. Note: I am still owed
For the lost memory stick. *Take physic*,
Pomp, ill-rehearsed by voices well-endowed.

Grand zero wurlitzer tops all in this,
Its co-ordinates late Nemo's. No man's
Certitude my servitude. Nothingness
Mates infinity. There are no demons.

Liber Illustrium Virorum

To Alice Goodman

The End of Worship amongst men, is Power.
THOMAS HOBBES, *Leviathan*, Part II, chap. 31

he, vertue dead,
Revives;
ANDREW MARVELL, *A Poem upon the Death of O. C.*

Words like the locust-shells, moved by no inner being;
EZRA POUND, *Canto VII*

RESIGN RESIGN RESIGN T. S. ELIOT, *Coriolan*

I

Medusas, basilisks, dragons in fens,
Eternal in their demands. Dragon's teeth
I have learned use of; with Coriolan's
Obliviousness also a plundered myth;
Determination of necessity;
Past recklessness in bruised misreckoning;
That blazed Yeatsian thing
Of savage joy:
The reed lake; wintering
Wild geese a-clang.
Phenomenon darkens
The comprehension of its vanes,
Lividness in fettle. Something unclear
Scales the escarpment of this eightieth year,
Prays the child's terrified
Comfort of bed.
Who is best able to
Choose whom to fable to,
Horse away on a laugh,
Prance equity,
Appear both ends of the school photograph?

II

Reestimate a segment of terrain
In which it seems no-one has ever lived,
Riddled and worm-cast, photographed by plane.
Amidst all that Bill Williams survived
To teach us Latin, civilize the foul.
The Somme was in his blood, his blood the Somme's;
New voicing the old hymns;
Birthright hwyl
Preached us at ends of terms;
August his themes.
I cannot say whether
We choose ill, or if some other
Principality devotes a saving
Grace to predetermine well-deserving;
Whether some innate flaw
Was my shadow,
Stultified that boy's heart
By reconfirmed report
But to find rapt dismay
Becoming will
With which mere sweet possession could not play.

III

Embusquéd lazily heartland outgrown;
The pain too early and the pride too late;
The man's estate pre-squandered while half-known;
The poverty of things turned profligate;
Too well monotony too prompt to know;
Haphazard faith stranded en route at call.
How to say what befell
Within their law.
Say he was prone to squeal
Of things at school.
This is the turn, re-wind
Tautology so aptly twinned
More with embarrassment than shame. He cries
Kamarad to the charge of memories,
The dodgems' carnival
He rode not well;
Pathetic fortune spent
Within Sosostris' tent
With fresh unstigma'd hand
Unfurrowed brow.
Late ignorance squares up to comprehend.

IV

Salvation it was not; fierce regression
Returned him sulking to maternal wrath:
Volumnia Victrix at her station;
In all things living she was his death.
You said, 'when I saw you together I
Could have fled the concourse'. So much for that
Fifty Shilling new coat;
Virginity
Unblooded at first heat,
Stripped off, despite.
If you scrabble ahead
Roughly six decades you are heard.
The beauty of the thing all that it came with,
No mortgage needed and none blameworthy.
Aufidius meanwhile
Volscian style
Exultantly at ease,
No baggage and no *crise*,
Secure in self-keeping;
His weather-eye
Focused, his praetorians unsleeping.

V

Would as the would of will; would have: would have
His first love back for sure; would so break down
Marriages and liaisons; would behave
Worse than tyrannous lovers in fiction—
Not censored to hit off one or many.
How create sane expression, recommit
To reason in despite
Of such puny
Resource, poor sense, worse wit?
Compassionate
That wrench in reasoning,
Vertical order sent spinning.
Spill me no more metrical hierarchies,
Nor steer him with sermons towards darkness
Rebuffed: would not as will;
As probable
Consequence, conjunction
Of mere will with sanction.
He has read all your books
For my money
On cataclysm and its aftershocks.

VI

Such purity and sweetness of tone, that
Exquisite modulation: must I beg
The old twister's pardon for this late spate
Of malediction, stabbings infra dig
Into the weasand and underbelly,
Putting questions with stump ingratitude
As you but lately did
On the telly;
The bidders the outbid
For a signed nod?
A promptitude long sought
To squinny lust of the unbought
Grace of life miscalled—áh well!—bonuses
For known abuses, high-toned tonelessness.
Go bless the little ships,
The splendid chaps,
Brave Duke of York his men
Swept off by bursts of fun;
The nation in its loss
Horrent mêlée
About the tumuli of bard and boss.

VII

All that's here theatred can relocate.
I propose these overtures to my mind.
Carved gemstones are not an elaborate
Substitute, though beautiful in their kind.
So long as you are compos and scribing
Hazard is in game to its own hazard.
Fate not undispleasured
By much probing.
Chance lies multi-fissured
And life-assured.
But to say I digress
From my brief re the Universe
Is patently untrue—ungrund, urgrund.
I have played young Brand lately old Peer Gynt
In my time. Beware all
Who pick the Fool
To your Lear. You cannot
Bet your shirt on the Goat
As Dean Donne came aware
Late disrobing
To the chaste windings of the frost's attire.

VIII

Reintroduce us to good mother-wit;
We have been far too long estranged; take up
A grace of life discovered in its dirt;
Invention not still betting on old rope:
Charged for nature's chemicals refuel
With spirit. Bring false shame through its menses;
Submit to consensus
By the last call.
Witness Spinoza's lens
Define the ens.
I cannot set in mind,
However, any so unmanned
By women's tears to double jeopardy.
Again, I have not seen the leopard try
Its nerve at hunting-gait.
Intuit it.
Why not assume this pain
As positive to win,
Constriction sensed at large,
As poised for kill,
As from the pupae fragile wings emerge.

IX

No better than a brutish virgin boy
He could be cast as. Shakespeare's aim-to-please:
Someone as pander, someone's dirty joy,
Someone despoiler of festivities.
That may be travesty. I've not respread
The broadsheets lately. There's a mirthless sense
Goes against evidence.
And she is dead,
Coriolan's long-since
Bride of silence.
'No, I'm breaking in this
Mouth for a friend.' Resynthesize
Whatever stays the judgement, the dissent,
Sanctioning desire as unmisspent.
With top to tail wisdom
Shifting doomwise
So it prevails, the spin,
The desire to out-grin
Emulating desire
Beyond all need.
In Latium they will have got my wire.

X

Messenger Angel, bring me some new rule
That cannot be accommodated in,
By, office equipment. Blessedly rile
Those who commit to nothing not inane.
Who cares to whom or for what is given
The virtue of caring? Alienate
Commodity of State,
Squire of heaven.
Does my instruction grate
And shrill, my spite
Attract? Anathema
If I do not deploy this theme?
Overset straitly by rhetorical
Furor, the problem declared metrical,
Labile as blood pressure,
Await seizure.
Hard strophes high-taxed me
Long ere rage annexed me,
I confess sweat-streaming
And unshriven.
Strange rule this sentence of my own framing.

XI

Illiterate I would blaze myself the un-
tutored elect of language: it's that strong—
Stronger almost than Keats with his mute urn—
Nor needs identity so to belong.
The unreflective faces of rag dolls
Answered sage children. This is otherwise.
Possession by surprise
Surprise foretells:
The eloquent, because
The abrupt, Muse.
Aloof intuition
Imagine the situation.
True and false dittany: of one the right
Burning bush may be drawn; the oils ignite
As mantles of vapour
That disappear
Without harm to the plant,
Like the death of a saint
Or *The Golden Legend*
Or Sufic souls;
The severance of things with things conjoined.

XII

The magnolia, like a far rock face,
Pinkish white chalk scattered with juniper
Or other dark green shrub, sustains that splice
Even as filled perspectives reappear.
This is too much of a conceit, I think,
To show meditation tolerable
Other than as fable
At its own brink.
Now it becomes marble.
Seeing double,
Haggard solipsism
Finds this crammed tree a bright chasm
Presenting revelation its own faith
As what we are born to and draw as breath.
I cannot tempt how far
From right prayer
These occasions maintain
Meru, the saints' mountain:
The visionary scales,
The eyes that blink
Into such darkness when such light prevails.

XIII

The Brasschaffer Exchanges: let me set
These on the line; seeing indecorum
Jarring against the limits blindly met,
Propriety beset by gross alarum,
Stare down safe lubricities. Half-buried
Anachronism is not my worst fear,
Nor yet the Third World War,
Of fears serried:
Must read an orator
Again this year.
If study can repel
Enemies of the Commonweal
Let them take on my impassioned reading,
Circuits going down from overloading.
So much for that. Last stands
Attract young minds,
Distress one's friends, provoke
Obituary smoke,
The crookèd oblation,
Ill-laid, ill-fired,
Sprung in some despite of mired devotion.

XIV

Who said: *a perpetual . . . trumpeting*
And coming up to judgement? Who decreed
Language like that as close to a great thing
As you could get amid drool, cant, and screed?
Not Coriolan, not Aufidius,
Not either tribune, no sham soothsayer
Bound from Etruria
By singing bus;
No bum-forward liar
Tarred on his rail;
No senator on skids
With forced plebeian platitudes.
Name one who well might ill-become all these
Mystagogues of rival categories.
Something about the Fates'
Rule on status
Passionately desired.
Conclude such passion wired
By common artifice
Twixt him and us;
Self-served innumerate to his own price.

XV

As self-description *Three-legg'd Acrobat*
Has its attraction. I would be disarmed
Though I am not the judge. So much now set
In the sick-bed, the extremities warmed,
Even tripodic waddling could assault,
Thespianwise, the mood to let things lie.
Starveling temerity
With pegleg lilt,
Not in all charity
Th' authority
To commandeer report,
In kind, on the forgotten fart,
Nonetheless, in one sense, exhilarates
With the exhilaration of first hates
Carried now like a badge
Of pilgrimage.
The late work I find strange
To live with, like derange-
ment, the immune system
Thrown to a fault,
Triggered malfunction rocketing esteem.

XVI

Here is a curt new music to my ears
Though I have played it often. The cue-tip
Racked ramrod straight awaits its clued satrap;
The well-cuffed baize to ease and buff the spheres.
Shall you question me on this, Count Egmont?
Word no apology for the Logos
In respect of svelte rogues;
Contrived segment.
No upbraiding segués;
Chafed monologues.
Nothing I find less strange
Than the changelessness of all change;
Variety reset to monotone;
The heartline bleeping straight on heart-machine.
A tobacco auction
Redeems diction.
Saint-Pol-Roux rode other-
worldly vatic blather
Into acquitted voice.
Cumaean vent
Made restitution take up time and place.

XVII

Who could have turned instinct with inked in-
constancy: my Lord of Essex? Ralegh?
Allowing folly not a mortal sin
God has ripe ordering of unholy
Pride, Robin Leicester's; the younger Wyatt's
Cracked fun. Brightness panders, heads for the trough;
And the judges perch stiff
In those high hats;
And each indignant ruff
Sets the mouth off.
Here, lad, gie's a quick squint
Chortles some well-rounded young aunt.
Priceless quires on their own flames regatta'd;
Seldom mourned, rarely even regretted.
Crawl home; rise reconciled
To the Christ-child:
Jesuitical praise,
Agony of surprise,
Stricken into the dawn.
Spare me try-outs,
Racy motions, stuck Commedia clown.

XVIII

Experiments with range: Nelson's gunners
Skipped cannonballs across sea surfaces;
Smart calculation, frisking-onerous,
Smashed bones and brains, unclean orifices.
Naturally frank, liberal, and large
Says Bradley, yet another ranging shot
On Coriolan. Not
So much the rage.
We try to service what
Propels us hot
Into the body of
Words to be made ours: study of
Densities, ratios, opinions.
Into the bodies of companions
Seems a less vital form
Of thrusting harm,
These times. But all pulls wrong,
Velocities or string.
I strike mirrors as old.
This trickster age.
Barnes Wallis learned of bouncing spheres; was bold.

XIX

The Augsburger has it made. In theatre
The ineffective is a judged effect.
Even the vicious creature has stature,
Double alienation twinned in Brecht.
Someone hard-named it Shakespeare's only great
Political play. The process not done
With when sinners atone,
Damnation's treat.
Doubled-up, speechless, gone
Phut from the scene;
Thesis, antithesis,
Unsatisfied; nil catharsis.
Some take to Finis as a high plateau
Strewn with mute lay figures garbed for Pity.
More reaching than sorrow
Their sad error.
Practise music; it does
Not suffer our cracked woes;
No snarl-ups of the will
Such as create
Intolerable burdens reared on style.

XX

Dulle Griet no dancer. Who is now Bert
Brecht alias Brueghel? The godly haul
Harnessed like Mother Courage to her cart,
Death's energies diverting vglie Hel:
Intricate quick-committing pluck luck-like,
Due governance, process of intellect,
Outrageousness intact,
While regions quake,
The calyx from the bract,
Cause and effect,
The natures of base things
Grown loudly fanciful with wings,
Jarring the mind, leaving spirit ajar
Narrowly gaping against the dense air;
Nakedness as our deed
Of gift ill-bred;
Sentiment of closure
Guaranteed usura;
Indignation cast down,
The double take,
Skew-wiff the bloody head the paper crown.

XXI

My gracious silence—club-effrontery.
Pushes virtue its rebarbative style.
Best kept unattempted new century.
More vicious arrogances trade misrule.
Let us mount upon the back of events
To watch these follies pass as in review:
Machiavelli slow
To dodge attaints,
Unlucky dice, each throw
Against the raw-
Spent justice malenfamed.
Nor impounded judgement redeemed.
Charity for afters. Machiavelli
Found little mundane success, really.
A stickler but in vain,
Coriolan.
Punters proclaims our mode.
That these were such made odd
Paired generosi; poor
Butt of laments.
Timon here may set his transient spoor.

XXII

Menenius is one you can handle,
Work with; doubtless the common reaction;
Duplicitously direct, the swindle
Almost a pleasure, poetic diction
In busy prose. After that, horrid bung-
ling for a fact. Set-piece Aufidius
Is cut to the bias
Of king and thing.
Tribunes made to try us,
Our ideas—
Equity and labour,
The worthlessness of the rouble
Adding to our confusion. How to judge
This terrible one man who will not budge,
Laurels and lictors' wands,
Cadets, brass bands,
Notwithstanding; his pride
Re-engined to degrade,
In the worst inn's worst room,
Self-menacing,
Demanding of one last first voice acclaim.

XXIII

Menenius taps Liverpool City
Of Culture. Hawthorne, Melville, transients there.
Hawthorne promenaded obliquity;
Melville snapped-to its hollow quicklime flare
In a basement area; sufficient
To take the tide of living and dying;
His words odd, out-staying,
Unpatrician'd,
Sentiment-defying,
Not worth buying.
How would one factor his
Estimate of mock victories?
The *Melville Log* had registered the name—
Coriolan—once only. Beat a drum,
Call Little Dog Toby
To the lobby:
Hup-hup! apologies,
Rodomontade and lies,
Blazing high on belief.
Mass-auditioned
Voices of slaves grow fainter, drifting off.

XXIV

Plebs create soul music; he understood
Little of that; touched no instrument nor
Was touched; apart, that is, from a damned good
Tune or the tanned drums flexuring for war.
He did grand work with the early legions.
There was small time and less will for acting
One-to-one. Evicting
Sly foreigners
He was good. Compacting,
Analecting,
Others could do later.
He would have broken the guitar
Over the singer's head. I am working
Slowly through rubbled evidence, clerking,
Trying to understand
Things at his end.
From devious mores
Derive the glamorous
Culinary women;
My ignorance
Caught amid the soulful, the unhuman.

XXV

Conceivably Caliban—still avoid
Rhyming the names. Caliban patrician
Bye-blow of resentment hoi-polloi'd;
Set under bondage to no magician;
Yet an unholy brewing-up of toad
In the bowl of his skull. Fatality
At home, fatuity
Carried abroad,
Strutting impunity,
Scarred lenity.
Such whanging and whingeing
Unhinged, forever unhingeing
Good citizens' doors. Civilities nil
And all the dire arrogance of the fool
Cheap as trophies. Victrix
And dissectrix
Bestrides his harrowed corpse:
Volumnia, her troops
Heiling and goose-stepping—
Shrine of a god!—
This last fantasy replete with keeping.

XXVI

If Timon hot-bunked Coriolan his
Poet still could sing snug in the rôle. But
Through such history poets are zanies
Although their flatteries may be well put
In the style of something cadgily learned.
Change the tictac in this mad typewriter
And transcribe a letter
To one exurned
As perfumous matter,
Stinks' gazetteer.
Do not name him Orphée
(He who had willed nothing away
Save through excess of a reclamant love
For what he had lost and would again have).
This we speak of must be
Satiety
And run-down terminus,
Catchment's voided remains;
Perhaps Pasolini
His ashes dunned
For the redemption of some trashed ciné.

XXVII

Set you right there, blundering empathy;
As to move you to alarums or tears
I would not so hazard. Temper thy
Affliction with sights: those quick eye-repairs.
That guy was some tragedy of a fool
Broken from and into clashed malfeasance,
Saddest all self-treasons
Beyond the pale:
Lords, commons and paysans,
Lies and lesions;
Tribunes' ineptitude.
As to markets, bankrupts they bode.
Somewhat also of medals not disowned
In a half decent beggary; the bound
Memoirs of a campaign;
The Senate's vein
Pronounced questionable;
Preened statues unstable.
I would not now use this
Language at all.
Clapped indictments all ways he enthuses.

XXVIII

You would rehearse me if I stood my brief.
I beg no pride where pity overran.
True to such ingress runs a mortal thief;
False to conclusion breaks an iron man.
Legendary years before the City
Broke with its senses and blew the archive.
What will they next retrieve
From piety?
Contrivances with the sieve
Good riddling slave!
So to labour finesse
Of wit in terms gross and unwise;
So to be engineering trial
Of homage, disinheritance, travail.
Recompense me nothing
Pyrrhic plaything.
No nosce teipsum
Delivered as jetsam.
Patriot-patristics
Dead vanity.
Carthage disstructured by its own ballistics.

XXIX

Who is it who for vanity destroys
That city which built him? Or who would so
Spare it, since monumentally he buys
Off, costing life and honour: how could he?
Let us begin with the simplest questions
That cannot be answered; before the need
To challenge head to head
Horned suggestions
Or spill some young bull's blood
To whet the mood.
The contest is strophic,
Irrecoverably Orphic,
And poets both archaic and arcane,
Solon, Pindar, Hesiod, not triune
And but few of many,
Hegemony
Have censured and proclaimed;
Language no less redeemed
Recalcitrant polis;
Ancient fustians
Vaporized between the glittering poles.

XXX

Write until sickened: such the instruction
Like something snarled, at range, ex-Cerberus;
Nothing other-worldly; by refraction
The en-suite cracked, the stateroom barbarous
With hitherto unhung Caravaggios.
I could not say whether by sea or land
Be wary lest your mind
Set egregious
Standards most would rescind.
So let unwind
That skein of wit the head
Bears to be extended at need,
Filaments fresh-daubed with a white matter,
Capillaries of blood. Sign the letter
To the chief magistrate,
Pre-stamped post-date.
Compose yourself and soon
The unseen ink will run
To memento mori;
Handmade pages
Untouched by hand, dictates of Mercury.

XXXI

What they must have not what he yields in spite;
One foot of advance instantly a yard
Lost; embarrassed breathing not in dispute;
Mistaken as to others' strengths; absurd.
Ah! black svelted horse unfazed by black plume;
Step at a time seemliness to portray.
Grand late apostasy
Torched for the rhyme;
Present gored artery.
Contributory
Love held in pride of place,
Iphigeneia's sacrifice
Something given to art in summation.
Here and here trapped lewdness of vocation,
Such grunting and heaving
For conceiving
Merely to set sapphics
Beyond reproach; graphics
Of scabrous oathfest staid
By strict metrum;
Iphigeneia's scorn under the blade.

XXXII

Ars legendi: whether you are reading
Silently, o–u–t l–o–u–d, believe no legend
Less enigmatic—the state corpse bleeding,
Catastrophic darkness refulgent,
Composure's fragile citadel betrayed.
Common agitations have served us well,
Write-offs as they prevail,
Love-ins destroyed.
The Triumph of the Will
Unwilled recall.
Kurfürst Leviathan,
Weak celluloid sucked from the can.
Go for portraits as if caricatures,
Let us have selfmade greatness plucked by wires.
Must I confess that I'm
Partial to fame,
The grand puff and clatter
Of noble Herr Reuter
And all his sage minions,
The writs unstayed,
Endless submission of spiked opinions?

XXXIII

I buy terrific gyre that builds around
Jerusalem's golden axis to find strange;
That things more than familiar compound;
Apocalypse hung by a loose brass hinge.
Another stately pentameter bites
Its own genitals in audacious pique,
Applauded and risqué.
O timely Fates
Fortunate in your marque
And tenure track,
Leb wohl, selfsubsisting
Like something nuclear coasting
Patently and at purr in its own sphere,
Ride violence straitened to the grand phare.
What we have to hope I
Shall term *copy*
To proclaim objective
Free from life's abject dive,
Posterity's judgement.
As to lewd rites,
Úranus took palpable abridgement.

XXXIV

Of us the Jews, a crucified people,
Have washed their hands; and now as governors
Of Philistia see and speak double;
No more this time Jehovah's sojourners.
Where is Amos? Some Palestinian
Ventriloquizes plebeian complaint.
Let us trade compliant
Dominion.
Compassion has grown faint
From its long jaunt.
Young have aged, have grown dead,
In presence of *Hatikvah* played
Even more passionately than klezmer.
Sacrificial parades of blood plasma
Edify the Temple,
Set example:
See callow Bethlehem
And Jordan's garbled stream
As legends choked with wrongs;
Her onion
To which that crazed woman in frenzy clings.

XXXV

Commonplace hegemonies: everywhere
Dismantled hierarchies. They would do well
Recalling mock emissaries from Tyre.
Devotion self-vending the endless wall.
Not to update moral insanity
Boundaries, some might term lethal error.
Between skull and mirror
Of vanity
Habakkuk's pared career:
Find occult seer.
I would not rumour these
Confrontations mere mysteries,
Altars of Javeh blackened and sodden;
The vengeance machine riddling and ridden.
Isaac, sweet son and heir,
Call me Meier.
No evidence that psalms
Have cashed-in their spent claims,
Song-shrilling Deborah
Her annuity.
Moses' landmark rides massif of Torah.

XXXVI

Deconstruct the Flavian dynasty;
Judge them without prejudice to this time;
Deadly entertainment the prime estay;
Snuff ectoplasm spun meaty as game;
Poet Martial a satisfied client
And yet sardonic. Suetonius made
His sycophantic mode
Blood-compliant;
Shade spitted upon shade
To fix a god.
In sum the Flavians
Were impresarios, took pains,
Looted the world for each scenario,
And melted down the Golden Menorah,
Javeh's hulked ransom, from
Jerusalem.
Even Domitian
Was a worthy scion,
From whom we could take much
That's relevant
To have the oiled sphere spinning at our touch.

XXXVII

Those who go native in Gaddish places
Divert sots with the rôle of Semele.
Some in the unbreakable glass houses
Yet debouch wanton and unseemlily:
What they so snatch up the accountable
Jackal too lopes off with greasy and louche.
Top your pollute cache,
Beggared noble
Pestered by the farouche.
Art in its niche
Cannot have been safer.
Anyway, bring out the *Sepher*
Tephelim, slowly; soothe the awkward squad.
What disturbs fluency sticks, is my speed:
Some quantum of science,
Gas and ions,
That such compounds can make
Salvation by a fluke,
The chemistry of grace
Presentable:
These the elect, those others without trace.

XXXVIII

Gauche poet does right by wronged general:
There is a lilt to that, it takes the truth.
In part you're Cincinnatus or de Gaulle;
One or the other, less likely both;
Famed as a holding spirit in the breach;
Brave scar emblazoned through the palimpsest;
Some call to readjust
The Ides of March;
The mob ranged in its dust
Crying the cost:
The slow trajectory
Of peace imploding victory.
So to this grave, this avenue; you have
The verdured gods, the flood, the architrave;
A marbled floor through which
The light may glitch
And run like wax; here turn
A torso or an urn;
The painted shadow-keel,
The ceiling-arch
A pool of nymphs wherein you sway and reel.

XXXIX

Scotland takes Roman Law but sits to fail.
Equity is not compassion's squealer;
Lost virility of a cancer cell;
Teased gradations of financial pallor;
Nor even one of those portentous games
Shakespeare configures in his Problem Plays;
Though what the sly duke says
Of moral crimes,
Whose trespass and who pays—
Forfeited joys—
Works closer to the nub
Of justice than new gifts of gab.
I grant that we are mysteries; I grant
Metrum not tagged exempt from pride of cant;
Aniseed baits the lure;
But there is more;
And what is spoiled of just
Measure, verse must protest;
Be neither rare nor spare;
Make new *Cathay*s,
Confucian Odes; by hazard maintain care.

XL

Yeats—and yet again I fail to avoid
Him as my seamark—plotted some Roman
Fascisti-Shakescene but lost that bid:
Paudeen, some would say, hating the showman.
Coriolan best played in Afrikaans;
They were butchers and would understand him
And cheerfully brand him
Chief of their sons;
With diamonds blind him.
I commend rhyme
That pledged graceless MacBride
As one who stabbed the tender side
Of Britannia when she was busy
With many sore issues, perhaps dizzy
From Zulu blood-letting.
This voids vetting,
Stands primed for stout impress.
Mark rattle of duress,
Siren and omen-light.
So for my sins
I gut *The Washing of the Spears* by night.

XLI

Odourless sardine stone: advance your gift.
Proceed with many others. Jazz the star
Of the Nativity that does not shift
From where it stood like a gas-chandelier;
From whence it rose eventing through the zone.
The Magi take their moment, then aloof
As their own camels, hoof
And fly-whisk, gone.
New things rattle a gyre
Void of due care.
So with a well-contrived
Thread of myth with which I have lived
Long enough, I embroider my prayer
Of forgetfulness layer by layer;
Petition petition,
Cross of station;
A time-regifted graft,
A shambles to redraft
For purity and style
Which if well done
Draws desire its abnegation of will.

XLII

So wish to spell out speech I would bestow
In long lines halting near side of the grave's
Loquations. Or what have you. Metric law
More insistent such times than frustrate loves,
I would have the oddness of things ride rough
Over strangeness of grammar and high tone.
So to truth on the bone
For epitaph.
The ghosts' blood is in clone.
I so incline.
Mr Inflammable
Gass runs and is unshameable.
Did Agamemnon pitching it for calm
Sea, scavenging voyage, enrage a dream?
Sitting primed for new loss,
Oblivious
To long-spent exchanges
Between the phalanges,
What could be said? It is
Judgement enough:
Blackout and whiteout bred us prodigies.

XLIII

It is the simplest narrative that flies
Together in double chronology;
For that words are analogues of crisis;
Cross-stress and dissonance bind eulogy:
Obedience held axiomatic,
The circle is not squared by dividers.
Alert to confiders
Sane, erratic,
Weeping, some, of murders
Under orders:
He will not take as bought
Wehrmacht insignia so wrought;
Through which stress he has served his ritterkreuz
With oakleaves swords and diamonds. His cross—
Composite irony—
Faithless crony.
Fine-tuned as thinking man
Between *jawohl* and *nein*
Brings *mit Gottes Hilfe*
From the attic
Awkwardly, like tarnished wedding silver.

XLIV: To Tony Harrison

Correctly scotching the snake he's not yet
Convinced of his power. Heat gets to him.
Like manual dexterity his thought.
Commencing thus fifty-odd years on stream,
He does not know, but suspects, Poetry's
Commitment to his longterm welfare. He—
Brutal—expat fairy
Finely portrays.
Nigeria's dowry,
Fly-blown, gory,
He cannot reconcile
With lasting shreds of nuptial spiel
(Mouth silently). All art is self-defeat
Of choice. Screeds diatribes to confound that.
Igbo and Yoruba
Burnt to rubber
Promote Greek tragedy
In a new mode: i.e.
Okigbo, sold short, late
The Patria's
Bearing above itself its fallen state.

XLV: To Tony Harrison

Cato and Cato Street he equably
Resorts to. Substance for aspirations
Republican. But let us not squabble,
Animadvert, over our vile rations.
Believe he could have upstaged Lepidus
In the Triumvirate if allowed scope,
If in Eutopia
Three such leopards;
If in the isotope
A will to shape.
Grand baobab commonwealth
Proliferates by open stealth,
Balances on its arms, contortionist
Of virtù that from virtus strikes, is blest.
All these are to his mind
But one legend
With suckered analogues
Compounding their blind leagues.
I must forgive him much
That he confides,
My moral tightrope twanging at full stretch.

XLVI: To Tony Harrison

Queen not *fairy* tops protest. Poetic
Licence revoked. Say when. All are guilty.
Spent dedication leaves us neurotic;
No tax-free excuse in mortal frailty.
Look here, I declare we needs must labour
As odds are called. It is called getting on;
Pressing verb against noun,
Grand war-lubber,
Upending *tyrant's frown*;
Lovely rap-man!
So many our old hates
Preserved as photographic plates
From a swift exodus, a sluggish fame,
Or vice-versa, giving life to drama.
Not all there, but a glad
Going for gold;
Not a judgement at law;
Not a failed interview.
Parp parp, hear this: his Dutch
Reformed neighbour,
Freaked-out Peugeot, comes to drive him to Church.

XLVII

Suffer them lamenting to make return
On poor stocks of good will, scarves, ribands,
Anonymous scatterpelt ash enurn;
Grant to restored scavengers full stipends.
Whatever the stress you must build finely:
Commonwealth conned into Protectorate
For a poem of State;
Fame made meanly.
Urge no rhyme upon hate
For exeat;
More play upon our lives.
He, vertue dead, revives. Revives,
He revives, *dead vertue*, surely he does.
How many times has your luck come that close
On the scratch-card, only
Unfunnily
To grin back at you. *Mad
World my Masters* was said
Routinely when they were
As routinely
Strung up and gutted near a thoroughfare.

XLVIII

You feel the sea's lithe columns haul your legs
As for a hanged martyr giving slow birth;
The swimmer's mane confused with counter-swags
Of golden toffee roiling to enwreathe.
Be close-famed with the cognoscenti, proved
In strenuosities of nature's gift;
Kelp round the salted cleft;
The dealers moved
By talk of common craft
High-strung, bereft.
Appurtenanced, at play,
Dashing accessories of spray,
Beating the harpies off, Odysseus,
Born chancer twice-born, revelling duress:
How could you learn so much
And not be rich?
No torment pulls apart
Your bowels from your heart.
Spring-wrenched affront your day;
Copper-engraved
The calling card upon the silver tray.

XLIX

Granted bronze-locked *Head of an Idiot*
Self-critical stunt would some yet argue,
Emotional charge charged with dream riot?
Pass me please the new deluxe catalogue.
Nor would these of Gertler's *Merrygoround*
Think any less idly. Epic measure:
Marvell's head of Caesar
Might so be found.
The bloody eraser!
Merci, m'sieur.
Rubbed out the gifts of French
Genius, steady in front trench
And in the wasted charge; Neuville-St-Vaast
Huddled in the lee of Vimy's swiped crest.
Gertler the embusqué
Allowed risky.
Must hoard our scant heroes
Of art. Be serious,
Their spirit unspent. Twi-
natured gerund,
Fleshed magnolia, unfazed entity—

L

Unfazed entity to carry over
Anarchism and the Petrarchan ode
Not here as Yeats's *lover with lover*
Diminishing, conceivings that abrade
So much ingathered, how much introdden,
Wild geese's multitudinous complaint.
Even so compliant,
Darkness ridden
And the woods filled with scent,
And song so meant,
If I could break off here,
It would be something to inspire
Grief anciently enthroned as high courage;
Though such things with us now are wept slurrage,
It is yet difficult
To cry default:
Well-waged plea-bargaining.
Despair and again bring
The formless to order
As unbidden;
As with pre-contract paying for murder.

LI

As to flip furious from White Russians
To Auden's Fascist airman; swipe for luck
To a Johnny Depp character; sessions
With some once glamorous sad churl of rock:
Impossibles that beguile paradigm;
Triumph turned contest of ingratitude;
Pride without latitude
Trading stigma.
A covert self-hatred
Self-accoutred
Discredited to death.
Well vouched-for tribunes bidding worth
At a pound of flesh for gilt-faced silver;
Menenius, with a mite too clever
Diplomatic élan;
As by design
Spare my anatomy
The jests of Antium;
Flog me an antidote
To bitter phlegm
That will not bring the heart up through the throat.

LII

If I were to set my dreams in order,
What mésalliance with the job-market
You could subscribe me to; and what ordure;
The eternal squaddie with the shit-bucket
Which I never was to my shame; reading
The dead empiricists for fun. Why live
Sixty years your own slave,
Conscience-breeding
Without profit to sav-
our a last rave;
And at your own expense
Fulfil the time's improvidence
Without a moral honestly made yours
By insubordination to first fears;
Finding rejected love
Was yours to have
And not in dreams only.
Revise and greet wanly
With thankless doggerel
The air-treading
Crucifix-pose struck by that mousing owl.

LIII

From that which is not relevant we draw
Appropriate lessons. Celebrating
King James for its approval rating
Is not on. You smile as if I were slow.
Ranter Joe's my man in his marginal
Constituency of faith; though much good
May it do me. He stood
Original
Sin on its scurfy head;
Election's goad
Prodding salvation's way
As he bellowed *coal!* from his dray.
Unreceived in theme-park, folk museum—
How awkward there his presence, his *I am*—
He stands as when first roused
By God; though razed
Each nerve in his employ;
The status of his joy
Yielding no carbon date;
Unmenial
His hand upon the blank Mosaic slate.

LIV

Bless hierarchy, dismiss hegemony,
Thus I grind to conclusion. Politics
Make sensate the maligned and monstrous play—
Shakespeare's apprentices rattling their sticks,
The aristocrats as such, like driving
Out Huguenots or Lombards. Their brain-flux
Cloacal muck-fix, grex
Up and jiving,
Faex Romuli in Rex
Stultorum hoax.
Corporatist-popul-
ist Gresham's Law degrades People.
Hierarchy yet: Blake's lordly plates to *Job*
And he was a sworn Leveller. Brit mob
Not here to procreate
Noble feature.
Say I repeat myself,
Beleaguered better half.
No doubt even this *drame*
Bears retrieving.
Backlog of monsters for another time.

Oraclau

Oracles

Er Cof Am
Pryce Jukes, Llanllwchaiarn,
1826–1895

Gwared ni rhag aur a gemau a gwisgoedd moethus.
Gwared ni rhag celfyddyd er mwyn celfyddyd
A thrythyllwch er mwyn trythyllwch.
Gwared ni rhag Arglwyddi'r Angau.

PENNAR DAVIES

Hail universal Lord, be bounteous still
To give us onely good; and if the night
Have gathered aught of evil or conceald
Disperse it, as now light dispels the dark.

Paradise Lost v: 205–8

1

The rain passes, briefly the flags are lit
Blue-grey wimpling in the stolid puddles;
  And one's mind meddles and muddles
  Briefly also for joy of it.
   How the morning is made
Intimately surprised that I am glad
By scraps of immaterial parade:
The world much fabled to be what it is—
Radiant mica'd creatures drawn through stress.

2

And I must readdress my mind to such
Harrumphing of blown fabrics as though joy
  Were something sacrilegiously
  Met with; an unlost secret touch
   Brought back into desire;
And let the grand simplicities aspire:
The rowan strung with its bunchbeaded wire,
Orange-red sprags that the eyes rawly feel
So boisterous this air struck from the foel.

3

  Sometimes it is like changing gear
With effort; at times a flaccid landscape;
  Estuary, blind cwm, slack air;
Fields weft by complainant curlew and snipe,
  Indeterminate angry calls;
   Or as a storm cracks down
Ricochets and staggers against the walls
Where you are ill-domiciled and wanton
With grieving; yet does not jiggle a spoon.

4

Sound me afresh from these formalities
Will you: I am at the natures of things—
  Basic simple imaginings
  That become as psalms of degrees.
    They are vibrant again,
The bushes in their formal evergreen
Glittering as though closely sheared by rain.
It is not nothing having to make sense
Of moods that argue so with case and tense.

5

  By adoption to entertain
Rancours touching upon Welsh poetry
  Muttered like imprecations when
The struck match-head breaks off and sparks awry.
  Your rayed cloud, slate-slatted Moel,
    Your many shark-mouths blaze.
Irrational the mind purports your will,
Nails the nail of logic into its glass
For an ugly vanishing trick of craze.

6

Here, take your gift of angry fellowship.
Salute the bards—the prized effoliate
  Atavisms—who yet recite
  Pieties through contentious sleep:
    Choosing not to despise
Your graft that sullenly revivifies
Expired encomia to exequies:
Standing your call, re-opening your vein;
Wanting some better grace to entertain.

7

I scarcely trust what I could wish emerge
From such a wishful thinking towards grace—
 Reception being beyond place.
 In small sun the laurels wax large.
  Fatal heredity
These afternoons when rain-mist brings the sea
Closer to the grey house set in its vee
Between hills of coarse-clad conglomerate
Where twice-blossoming gorse abides its state.

8

As the hebog in these windy sessions
Bends the seasons' pace about its track-rod;
 As in westward place the black cloud
 Jettisons candescent lesions:
  So I make sign for all
Heartsignings; so eternity without fail
Will fail us subject also to our spoil;
As even the last paradox dissolves
Into a scheme of mist about our selves.

9

As found by Enoch such transcendent gibe
The mortal part of us who would believe
 In Bala set daughters of Eve
 Hosting that many-pinioned tribe
  Unsubdued by the grand
Bouts of theology to comprehend;
Each peacocking its eye of virile wound:
Shackled at licence, unrestrained, defiled.
Blind brothels in the wilderness unveiled.

10: *i.m. T. H. Parry-Williams*

The mountain ash, the rowan tree,
Turning a riot, most unlikely flesh,
  Erectile on the hazing sky
Its peaceful foliage instinct with clash:
  The pacifist in his own head
    Sees things past what they are,
Their heightened colour blood unpacified;
The hallowed conscience followed through despair
Put to the torch entangled with the wire.

11

In terms of grace and carnal loss
To come as near logic as is allowed
  The mathematics of the cross,
The hazel nut, the witness to it, flawed;
  A world weighed in the mystic's hand
    As if all weight were known;
As when redeemed the plummets reascend;
As when the rote investiture of dawn
Rays implicate with ruined darkness crown.

12: *Blodeuwedd, 1969*

Sad character re-rakes his jobbing fire
Woodenly while the camera bitches.
  The changeling tries his luck which is,
  Because he's Welsh, vain heart's desire.
    Being yourselves myth-fouled
Let village idiots taunt the mad scold—
Grin-bleating extras of a ratty world.
The misprised coalfields of Aberystwyth
Fuel fantasies you rise possessed with.

13: *near St Beuno's*

Despite the Commune something of a Red;
Lover of Wales, the pity of her wrath;
  Her language to be troubled with;
  Griefs propositioning her dead.
    Spiritual rhetor,
High Tory hiraeth, *seldomer heartsore*;
But knew his own mind, minding the ploughshare;
Knew his flinched heart hooked by the brute hebog;
Flint under the flensing beat, the havoc.

14

Distant rain-draped slate flanks gleam like late snow
At high summer as the sun parades them,
  Cloud intermittently shades them,
  As our eyes interpret shadow;
    And the sheep are angled
Against the field walls that are quartz-spangled;
Celin bushes with raw wool-sprouts tangled:
Shadow supplanting shadow, Eryri;
The eagle glinting to its lost eyrie.

15: *Ann Griffiths* (1)

  Intelligence new made of late
By paradox and oxymoron pressed;
  The world fast-held the soul's estate
Entailed; old weakness mightily confessed.
  Across the Berwyn she moves
    In penitential climb
Up to strange Bala with Dolanog's loves:
All things exalted and reduced to Him
For whom her careful ecstasies of rhyme.

16: *Ann Griffiths* (II)

Adam's sin within us a chasm; love
Cannot work his charm; one letter enough
  To let us live in a fat slough.
  Pilgrims to Mecca! As I live
    I am a living psalm.
That said—but what was said?—*Enthusiasm*
Yet lately lit, fire's held fiat; prism
Set to reconstitute the light about
Jerusalem: such facets I have cut.

17: *Ann Griffiths* (III)

  It is not the eternal rocks
Though these are rugged in truth, to which I
  Constate law. I did not bleed books.
There was dancing, fiddles, the tunes catchy.
  These have been put by; an elect
    Providence surprises
All question; revelation is exact;
Visitation presses. I make praises,
Joy suffering: the Word dies, arises.

18

  Lyric precision so long tried
So many ways; so much itself a trial;
  Disprody's rictus certified;
The courts of love eloquent in denial.
  Even in age no name equates
    With what love reads to harm;
Or what especial chill precipitates,
Proscribes this ash grove that with paler trim
Than oak or alder allocates its gleam.

19: *Fforest Fawr, c.1987—Innominata*

Not even now established the true odds;
I think of him, but in miniature.
  Collateral light, also *sphere*,
  Come to mind as rejected codes.
    What pitched us out of frame
No mystical abruptions across time
Can now revoke. Too bad for me and him.
Extraordinary the common lot
We here project, collateral or not.

20: *Ibid.*

  Let me propose even so his
Wholly inadequate beauty: you can-
    not well divide the obsequies
Across such closely riven refts of span.
  Let us also imagine that
    Intelligent journal
Wrought with true pain of contrived grief and hate,
More Pavese than Rimbaud's infernal
Provocations of alchemic-carnal.

21: *Ille respondet*

Which is where I leave things and have always
Left them, as ashes in the themes and seams,
  Desolation transpierced by names
  Strange, arbitrary: Ystradgynlais
  Because she was there and I not.
    All else indifferent;
Various other places are like that,
Imagination caged, locked in assent
To derelictions paid for at high rent.

22: *i.m. R. Williams Parry*

Irreversible is all likelihood
By what we tell of disaster; spirit
  Hairpins through bland brain; and hurt
  Turns Crown's evidence in a mood.
    I would not recommend
Reading your own foreboding to the end;
I cannot say where equity is found
But as dilated of us on repeal;
Just as the injustices of trial.

23: *Trevecca, 1752*

As from oracle to tabernacle
So to remove, so to embrace this Love
  Of which the death of friends no grave
  Is; to forbear, no miracle.
    As with natural Wales
Supernature's light steadily prevails,
The Christ compassionately shows his nails.
Where we have been, shall be, let not indite
The genius of carnal love in spite.

24: *Hermeneutics* (I)

Torquing upon hwyl, wrestling grammar,
Trusting as Jacob—*torque* to be defined—
  In our disorder here ordained;
  Necessity to unstammer;
    Salvation's first blind flight
Against the elements, creating sight
Creation's war of terror and delight:
Who, formerly malignant as our choice,
Fell in one root, recovered by one voice.

25: *Hermeneutics* (II)

Whereof we are begotten, made
Of such grace patron or parent even;
  Love our bespoken accolade;
Hell's easy road regraded hard to heaven:
  So perilous minute regard,
    Lost diamonds in sieves,
Despair dependent from the common cord:
None at first so thwarted as one who craves
Christ the satisfaction between the thieves.

26: *Hermeneutics* (III)

Great cats elide us in salutation.
Language mislabouring out of Egypt
  Who shall receive, or who decrypt
  Immanence its dark mutation,
    With ignorance brought forth,
With the attendant bloodiness of birth,
The after-nursing and the milk of wrath,
Stark tenderness, and (to the wits that care)
A thorn-head spitting in a cage of fire?

27: *The Dark is Rising, 2007*

Why is Dark to be fought again?
Light yet confused, right family of wrongs;
  A thesis trashed and in the bin
Too late where manifestly it belongs;
  Communal fantasy in hell;
    Child-soul shall endure it;
Utilities engulfed past power to tell;
Redemption known by an uncanny merit
Seventh sons of seventh sons inherit.

28

Alchemic-carnal, such the earth remains
In winter even while snow asperges
  From shaken branches, shows the ridges
  Fresh-configured, swept by shadow-vanes;
    And transience transpires
Intensely focused crowing atop spires
To what light is, a glaze between great flares;
The sun arraying in the brittle llyn
A limbeck of itself or of the moon.

29: *at Blaenau Ffestiniog*

Love-feasts greedy for crying; cold fuss
With texts that are pregnant; predestinate
  Judgement chalked on the local slate.
  The years faithless, industrious,
    Bring to begetting:
Where now the sun, moved to a late setting,
Works its profounder disrecreating;
And fading colour-schemes of daylight stripe
Mountains upholden in their static rip.

30: *Musick . . . the most divine striker of the sences*

How to give ending; clauses unpredicted
Of justice on yourself; move equity
  To self-loathing from self-pity,
  Recidivists. These indicted,
    Go for resurrection—
Dismaying resurrection—it is done:
Deployment as to servitude hard-won;
Blessing in marriage your daughter's daughter;
She may look back with love; not now, later.

31: *to Thomas Vaughan* (I)

Proclaim these bodies our joint avatar;
The metamorphics from loves long unmade;
  That, as I elegize, parade
  Brusquely: like a spectacular
    Comet, the rough crown a-roast,
Which, when the line of its horizon's crossed,
Blazes away, vanishes, is not lost.
Insensate even so, of no avail;
And darkness readjusted to our will.

32: *to Thomas Vaughan* (II)

I am not decrying the Trinity,
However, at this distance. Here one says
  Read Irenaeus on heresies.
  Yet sleep an hour: concinnity
    Lapsing, the closing-in,
Words at supper, the directive from John,
Do it quickly, agony of things known.
Thus to those maimed by Christ the Gnostics give
Signal powers, gifts you would not believe.

33: *to Thomas Vaughan* (III)

Though you do, of course; as necromonger
To Christian ethicks; your brother's muse,
  Stones to transfigure and transfuse;
  Brinksman he of God's anger;
    Grave stele that curses self—
Servus inutilis—in love's behalf,
Here by the Usk, set on its verdant shelf.
But make a prayer for *Amoret* who dies
Leaving us tears confused with pleasantries.

34: *to Thomas Vaughan* (IV)

What you must do, do now: His Word
Not denied. Degenerate papyrus
  Root of these woes, black as Nile mud,
As myrrh to zane-sophistry's dead tyros.
  I would not have us lost in search
    Not found with theorem;
Nor making much of little like a torch
Building loud shadows bracketing the tomb.
(None saw the seraph issuing therefrom.)

35: *to Thomas Vaughan* (V)

  Not as in spirit fled the Usk;
Embodiment of late the legal City.
  No cedar tree nor tamarisk.
That you should there labour with temerity
  I do not, under correction, doubt:
    Your Throne of Solomon
Hermeneutics dark with alchemic soot.
Momentous instauration—all is One.
But time has crossed its arrow on the stone.

36

Perturbèd: let me here compound
Gaia and Thea, once twinned, spherical
  Bodies, twins by each other bound,
Wire-balancing till, by sad miracle,
  Gaia absorbed Thea entire;
    Enhanced gravitation
Enabling her to gather atmosphere
Hence to support life. That immolation
I cannot conceive of without emotion.

37

She's invisible: yet it shows
As the imagination's antichthon;
  Spiritual all-but-perfect laws
With which dead Platonists enrobe the sun;
  Yet adjunct to what soon appears
    A different story
Hung with fatalities and malign shears;
With legends of abysmal injury
And with a weightless weight too great to carry.

38

If poetry is not protean-fast
Not indeed wedded—test its unbested odes
  Like espousals among the gods—
  To immortality. Recast,
    Is this a crossed question
Best rebutted at a lost bastion
Last unlost cantref of Taliesin,
Great princes of the word, those names that guard
The Seven Tines, worthy of fame's award?

39

Belatedly as killing time consider,
Of wasps and bees oracular, life's hurt;
  With salmon also a retort
  In kind, a species of rough rider
    Charging as charged to spawn.
Of consummated fulness to be drawn:
It was not there philosophy began.
It is not here the least matter for sorrow;
Or thinking worse or better of tomorrow.

40

The metaphysics of affinity
I find estranging: how one aura
  Blesses its type; the next, neuro-
  spasms terrific confound pity.
    Shall we or shall we not
Twig our natures—hazelrod on the spot—
Know ourselves spellbound in the vatic sport?
Deadly the aftershows of neurospasm;
Known for its touch of toxic waste the chrism.

41

Old affinity with metaphysics
Comes into question but of course the term
  Is questionable and does harm.
  Not metaphysics: try clavics,
    Indigent casuistry;
My neo-Welsh pleadings hung out to dry.
Best settle in with a good mystery.
I'd say that metaphysical acrostics,
Rightly taken, are as good as joss sticks.

42

  Clavics, the alchemy of keys:
As lacking something so I have made art—
  The management, the formalities,
Working a transmutation of report
  While here these orchards,
Late apple, moving deep-Octoberwards,
Remainder to the root; their last discards
That gather chilly dew before daybreak,
Not now for the near-dying wasps to wreck.

43

Among rough-spreeing gorse, now heather
Gives new life to the colours of mourning;
  Expansive its dense sojourning
  Illuminates the drab weather
    That sags in off the sea,
Snags on the headland's thorny armoury.
I write, as though for you, my memory
Of what memory was; take my confession
Simply rejoicing in this ample season.

44

I have written elsewhere of descending
Crankwise the crimp-cramped road to Telford's bridge,
  The rocks reddish, junked in the gorge,
  Reddish conifers with green standing.
    I can imagine Herr
Humperdinck in Betws but not Wagner,
Nor the Festspielhaus with its insignia,
Hansel und Gretel but not *Parsifal*;
Though brought with dwarf solemnity the Grail.

45: *i.m. R. Williams Parry*

Yes, we are done; and the great stone threatens.
Has it moved? Does it yet breathe? As crystal
  Each perception of our timed fall.
  Now neither fox nor hare outruns us.
    Imagine a black spark
Struck like a spore from metamorphing rock,
Friction of flawed eternity and luck;
Lost to an instant, scored, indemnified;
The falling of a pebble or a bird.

46

Panic gone goggle-eyed under that wave:
Have swum up, choked on water and phlegm,
  Sewage—a used apophthegm
  Bobs past—much nearer dead than alive.
    Cannot I smile and say
I will not come water-tempting today,
Shall sit at home minding my curds and whey,
Looking deep, re-costing the dome of Paul's
Clamped to the murderous tonnage of its bells?

47

Set down *Wilkins* on the coal industry
Of Wales: true sycophancy's highest note;
  Plethoric homage to Lord Bute
  Of Bute Dock fame. Pay and display
    Chopin's *Funeral March.*
Time to collude with your high-minded search
For nine-foot seams of Anger to strike rich.
As to maimed humble grandeur, Ford's *How Green
Was My Valley* drew that across the screen.

48: *Wilkins scripsit, 1888*

The reconcilement of these explosions
With a mysterious Providence, with God,
  Perplexes all good talk abroad
  Among the difficult persuasions.
    Thrust from the Avon's gorge
The mathematics of Brunel emerge
Into light's buffeting, the winds at large;
Those who do well engaging grief and grace
As grand suspensions meeting in mid-space.

49

Do not count me among deniers
Of tribute, precedency presiding,
  Faith's necessity's engineers,
Old expediencies colliding;
  Encouragement to live life well
    With the hurled cage, gaunt wheel—
A gesture there to things rhetorical,
Curial, even—coal the heroic song,
Yeomen-industrialists, their valleys wrung.

50

Most celebrated of the *three iron kings*
For whom these annals: Crawshay by name.
  Brave puddlers tug his car of flame!
  Upthrust and downthrust pistonings
    Rough ways for improvement;
Great horizontally-eccentric movement
Casting valleys beneath iron pavement;
The naked spoils of Aberdare and Merthyr
Dispatched dark regions far afield and farther.

51

Disorder cannot be brought to the point
Which is the point of disorder. Yet mourn
  Cymmer, Ferndale, Risca of no return,
  One dead unlucky at Abernant.
    Blood-intrigued Capital
Enriches some life forms with things fatal;
You could ink your hymn sheets with black spittle.
This is a strange country, the words foreign.
Give that clever child a half sovereign.

52

The Three Iron Kings is a Welsh legend,
I make it so. *Make me some iron teeth*
  Gags the game witch to the blacksmith.
  Fiercer than we could have imagined
    The golden cockerel
Cries from the confines of his manger-stall
At dawn to salute birth and betrayal;
Verging on the ambience of things holy
But fatalistic-sounding, melancholy.

53: *******

  It needs to be done and done with
The never undone. This cannot be Lourdes.
  Seepage and sliding. Pardon death
The unanimity of these arcades.
  O Lady of Fatima, speak,
    You could tell us something
For our redemption. The humble unmeek
Swept up by some postfacto land-reclaiming.
The Day of Judgement will do its flame-thing.

54: *Marwnad Saunders Lewis* (1)

Merthyr to Dowlais looks different now;
Though *milk of Lethe* remains our poison.
  Rebarbative verses, treason
  Against unconscionable law,
    How or if these recur
I cannot say since I cannot be sure.
Let us climb together across the spur
And you shall teach me how to be received
By people amongst whom I have not lived.

55: *Marwnad Saunders Lewis* (II)

If there is yet a thief of mind
Between Calvinist chapel and cloned cell,
  Let him give alms or grease my hand;
What is worth doing if we reckon well?
  Complicitous catch-as-catch-can
    Justice taken below,
Driven off afterwards in a plain van.
For all that I can say such things I saw
With fire and knives prepared, set to the show.

56: *Marwnad Saunders Lewis* (III)

As though of old the things but lately planned;
As if real war imbrued the theatres.
  Coriolanus in the Thirties
  Made nosebleeds with its brazen sound.
  Mechanics with a bit of string
    As though all rose inspired.
I would not say we are owed anything;
The final mysteries at length retired
Into themselves, and the First Circle squared.

57: *Marwnad Saunders Lewis* (IV)

Think Racine's too credible monsters, take
Here as read the anarch's rigid humours;
  The alexandrine's fatal hammers,
  Its triumphs like a frigid wake:
    Think here, heroic lies
That the Welsh squandered; and the hierarchies,
Redundant now, warped in familiar ways.
Belated laurels crowd this beaklike head
That bears too much; its litanies betrayed.

58: *i.m. Alfred Janes*

A match for immortality's mocked swank
Kardomah's giant sentinels of light
　Well armed with canons of their wit
　Amaze themselves. Sometimes I think
　　Your portrait of that boy
Finer than Augustus John's; the clay
Dub of a nose looking like Tycho Brahe,
Those belladonna eyes, huge-beyond-clear,
Small god so thundered-at, great child of fear.

59: *T. S. Eliot in Swansea, 1944*

Do not remind me here of rancour spent—
As Adams-ite hauteur, if in my cups—
　Men with white mufflers, coal-greased caps,
　Swansea-bound in crammed compartment
　　To a big football match,
Neither civility's nor salvation's catch.
The dove descending broke upon your watch.
I am requited merit past my earning.
Surer than grief this coenobitic mourning.

60: *Bethesda*

Brutish vanities take tameness on trust.
What wine of Cana? Whose the fatted calf?
　I, when I fear to bruit myself
　Rumours of imputation, must
　　Nominate Ignorance
In Bunyan, hiking his soul through trance
Of free election to the grand entrance,
To Heavensgate; from which he is cast down,
Partly a tragic figure, partly clown.

61: *Hunllef*

Disturbed, the waters of the moon descending
On Gwalia, make quagmires become lakes.
　Well-set windows blur with the shakes.
　All things in flux, yet attending.
　　The skies livid, the red
Holts hereabout stand derelict: for long-dead
Readers of Virgil and Dante the wood
Where their resplintering voices gather
To cry love's vengeance and to hate each other.

62: *Ty-tryst* (I)

　Visionary malfunction—Danton
Ghosting the retina but Tredegar
　No matrix of red convention
Neither was it late or soon Blake's Tyger—
　Yes of course I allude to Nye—
　　What is now proved was once
Conceived in *Imagination*'s third eye;
The ordering of the divine impotence
Countermanded by its desire to dance.

63: *Ty-tryst* (II)

　Would I call it betrayal?—Years
We were fleeced, dunked in poisons. The sheep's
　Backs many times pulled over their ears;
Slate tallies alone shelved in the widowed shops.
　Come, let us take to the mountain
　　Our learned freedom of mind,
Unassailable freedoms to maintain.
In the conflagration of rain and wind
We shall see further visions of the blind.

64: *Ty-tryst* (III)

What a gift! Who're you? they had asked,
Or more likely not. There is no story
   Attaching to this inquiry.
The way injury becomes ours but mocked.
   You can tell: look how lopsided
      This configuration.
No question that we are divinely guided
By what some are pleased to call inspiration,
Inert matter and to each his portion.

65: *Ty-tryst* (IV)

That was Nye's phrase for it, *inert matter*.
Having crawled once to a picked seam I call
   Malevolence the voice of coal,
   Squealing, grunting, groaning like water.
   How did any man twist away
      Soul-free from that shining,
Rise undamaged into the raw day
With his black minstrel's face absurdly grinning,
Travestied as was Jude that drôle of learning?

66: *Ty-tryst* (V)

Inert matter dug from beneath the nation:
   Polemics win through to good
Order. Speak so as to be understood.
   True love practises seduction,
   Acts to mirror new delighting
      In those joys we keep;
Our acts of love, intelligence and writing:
So with a dormant people roused from sleep.
Milton said that, not something God let slip.

67: *Ty-tryst* (VI)

Nye was born old and died young, but—grief!—
  He is ageless; the stone has him
As he the cloud. A huge burden of relief
  Shoulders here the atavism
  That modernity is; threatens
    Nothing on which it looks—
Skied recollection of Tredegar's tenets;
All that anima-animus provokes;
The awkward mating-signs chalked on the rocks.

68

I shall write you herein without warning
  Or compunction; as Lawrence did,
Though he to finest shades of discerning;
  I with acrylic and a tin lid.
  A gesture, this, to countenance your
    Contemptuous off-set
For what lies here divorced, without answer;
The vague companions, the never-met;
The Japanese instructions with the kit.

69

  Die with me, don't die on me. Whither
Will this darkness take us; as, between times,
  We are not known to each other?
Lie there; receive oblivious my arms.
  Difficulties reprise one's lot,
    Tragic misalliance;
Before us the tribunal we forgot.
There will be noising abroad our silence,
Laughter among the sentries' dalliance.

70

The new age—great things are toward,
Though anything less apocalyptic
　　It would be hard to put forward.
Sense meaninglessness in things cryptic.
　　As to whether e.g. we live
　　　Out of march with the times—
Fifth Monarchy men knew how to behave.
I envy them that and the grand paradigms
In vivid patterns coming off the looms.

71: *Bollingen, May 1958 (Afal du Brogŵyr)*

One is for case-notes balanced on the knee;
Two for the courtesies that fame dictates.
　　Chilled wavelets rattle from the *See*,
　　A bronze-trimmed door beguiles the Fates.
　　The black mandala out of Wales
　　　With anthrax in its seams—
As coverage of figured speech prevails—
Provokes the ruin of well-fathomed dreams,
Ruin more waste than was Jerusalem's.

72: *Afal du Brogŵyr* (i)

　　That mandala, stone-black apple
Made so by the charring of permafrost
　　Or the sun's giving up the ghost
Of its corona: so some people
　　Dismayed. Nonetheless who shall say
　　　Which of us claims the wrong
Side of the myth in this catastrophe;
Who to their own imperviousness belong;
Whose is the spirit moving that dead thing?

73: *Afal du Brogŵyr* (II)

Alchemical introversion
Patent as compost: sublimities aspire.
  Introfusion of vision:
Poetry of such corruption and fire
  Baking the lily in its dung.
    Improvident the prize.
Not everything is rotten in Carl Jung.
Save from mystique the ravaged mysteries.
Nor is it less than simple to be wise.

74: *Afal du Brogŵyr* (III)

Alchemy itself is the Black Sun,
Absorption of convulsion, the *nigredo*,
  The pitchblende of immortal sign.
Some will name it anathema. I do
  Acknowledge so in my own name.
    Where is the mystery?
We have eternity to judge of time.
Civilization is not hysteria.
At first and last the element of fire.

75

Find me a fence or a wall; I am angry
  At being made angry. I would
Nor run into any kind of danger
  Nor Pride perilous and manifold.
    The sixty-sixth sonnet
Is pertinent; let us dilate upon it:
How first to stab a clause then grin it
Though in hell; till like new Humpty Dumpty
We're back in one piece again but empty.

76

Tarnished with yellow underhang,
Still-canopied, autumnal trees stand by
  As I am passing. So with strong
Memories implanted to be flung away
  England gifts me her signed photo.
    From grab bag to dump bin
Where does the soul of mankind get to?
Wales: are you in happier condition—
I trust so—by grace of Original Sin?

77

Harmonious colours; dissonances
In miniature; percussive dancers;
  Rattling cadences, remembrancers,
  Mid-October, best of seasons,
    Zest for the finding flash
Fruit of the horse-chestnut, its whorled varnish,
Its crack too fresh for gloss to diminish
Like drying pebbles. As to belong here—
My presence to myself no stranger.

78

Shafting through the burst veins of this thing
Depleted it is hard to sound sober,
  More like a skidrow tomb-robber;
  Poor chantry-fane void of its king,
    Voided unfeigning Jude—
It was his conscientiousness that did
For him, as Charles Sorley pithily said
Before he too went down, pursuing duty,
To Fields of Lamentation without Pity.

79

Insofar as ambition guides heroes:
  I would not speak irreverence
Of Andromeda, meat for Perseus.
  Pick your own Listerine revenants
  Among many who swarm in theme-
    Possessed Britannia
Stuck with her tacky amalgam of blame.
I yield to none in confessional mania.
Watch this marathon *Caritas Nimia*.

80

In this moment dead leaves at the window
  Are lit, bearing the stooped sun's blazon,
Like roses or tulips in full season;
  Recrudescing the child's wonder
    At shapes of rubied glass
In the front window of a strange new house,
Gold toffee wrappers unwrapped on the bus;
All national flags; journeys without fear
Of reaching death's kingdom, there to disappear.

81

  Yet children greatly fear dying—
Am I going to die?—monotonous
  Cadences that she, defraying,
When you are very old, made to address,
    Inadequate, stricken.
Look the kaleidoscope holds rebroken
The mirrored particles to stick and quicken.
No tears for immolation: Eros
Our importunity assigns its rose.

82

You are unbalanced; you are un-
balanced by me; this is not equitable
  As that good man said. Disable
The unlucky projection if you can;
    Disable, disavow,
Whatever. *Mon cœur se recommande à vous.*
I recommend enigma for your vows,
Matter indifferent to rote and flanges
No matter what the meaning of exchange is.

83: *B. S. Johnson in Llanengan churchyard*

Female cats on heat act like manic stoats.
A heavy strange wind takes up position
  Without distracting from their motion.
  What has them has us in our coats.
    Fine word, *extremities*;
I half expected it would be thus.
Which animal has no known enemies?
I think you are hilarious. The wind
In the trees must be a snarling of mind.

84: *in Llanengan churchyard*

Are you good with dialogue? Monologue
Is the fatal prowess; those who fail,
  Monologuists whose fears prevail,
  Racers ahead constrained by drogue;
    Sad their embogged labours
Meant to disembogue in dredged harbours,
Self-wreckers of promise, murderers
In a word if it's a word we're after
And not near-unrecognizable laughter.

85: *at Gregynog*

Intimate Welsh landscape of disquiet:
Cold stings the sinuses; the synapses
  Something else, the brain's ellipses;
  Let this be, do not untie it:
    The snow birth-littered where
The lambs have dropped, immanent atmosphere
Of crystal haze, much like creation, pure
As I imagined it to be these times
Among the fresh erasures of old names.

86: *at Gregynog: i.m. B. S. Johnson*

Do not expect to find me at the gate
If there is a gate. You are my device
  To tell truth. I do not practise
  Empathy but commiserate
    Hapless recoveries
Of primal innocence among the groves.
Knowing the names of plants may well save us
And in some cases will attract money.
Put to invention invent haemony.

87

I can do ashes but not diamonds.
She has returned to tease me. I allow—
  I think I do—that to will flaw
  For the beauty of amends
    Is aestheticism,
Spiritual pride, a touch of s. m.
For the effete nervous system.
Returning on occasion she astounds.
I can do ashes but not diamonds.

88: *Welsh apocalypse* (I): *i.m. B. S. Johnson*

With one stroke to recoup the ante—
So to be grotesquely funereal—
  Generations thrive, are unreal,
  Cheering splash ghastly spumante
    To mark your self-trashed span
Like tracking the wreckage of a light plane
In virgin country; you a heavy man.
Spasmodic correlation between failure
And fatal triumph in a horrent milieu.

89: *Welsh apocalypse* (II)

Büchner and Blok excelled with puppet mime.
I am not one of those to whom meta-
  physics are mere suspect data
  Though the world's body takes up time.
    How the *Bells of Rhymney*,
Elementary cadences, unman me!
I spill you this for luck tame enemy
Hoping to cast you quick over my shoulder.
I must live well before I am much older.

90: *Welsh apocalypse* (III)

Meaning dramatic does not void traumatic—
Epicks indeed!—means nowhere confession
  Other than as abrupt lesion;
  Not a confusion of emetic
    With bromide. So surcease
Of grand faculty commands success.
Fit a new engine to the old carcass.
Drive it into the ground, the humously
Dank cofarwydd where dead dramas lie.

91: *Welsh apocalypse* (IV)

Lashings of fresh kelp lolloping ashore
Odorous brown iodine slime on rocks
  Where the striations reach in racks
  Superabundances all frore
   Of impoverishment
Tuned to some other frequency of intent
See the empty crab shells tossed cracked and rent
All things are, nothing is, to be saved
Dints of survival stutterings engraved.

92: *Welsh apocalypse* (V)

Apocalyptic ragbag of forms no sign
Of supernal insight. Could you fit *Y Ddraig*
  Goch on the old union flag
  Without ruining the design?
   I would not sacrifice
The Cross of St George merely to be nice.
Bungalow-burning work for the police.
Road-signs in Welsh even your Sais approves.
Tudur uchelgais raised our common spivs.

93: *Welsh apocalypse* (VI)

It becomes ever harder to desist
Having so failed to master a complex brief.
  Spillage balloons your handkerchief.
  I admit, I have not the least
   Idea what *sea-green*
Incorruptible means, knowing the man;
What ironies a-dribble from what pen—
Yes, *yes*, Carlyle, wife Welsh!—madness to drive
The swarming of my wits from hive to hive.

94: *Welsh apocalypse* (VII)

Well, to come clean, it makes me think of snot,
Knees thick with scab; trouserings pitiful,
  Voices pitched between jeer and wail.
  True Welsh, I would be monoglot—
    Was this great grandfather
Before he buckled with long labour,
Stooped to Black Country pidgin and palaver?
Leap to project mind as a great harp,
Frame of desire through the years' rake and warp.

95: *Welsh apocalypse* (VIII)

Babylon had science, cosmic mensuration,
Eternal predication, temporal flame
  Though you would not linger there to scheme
  Dream-protocols for a nation.
  Or would you dispute this
Polity independent of mathesis?
And yes the planets shall have their catharsis.
What mystic statics rule those spheres ordained
Beyond the revolutions of our kind.

96: *Welsh apocalypse* (IX)

Let us draw, there is time, the red dragon.
The implications of its stance eclipse
  Destiny in *Apocalypse*,
  Babylon-brawling Greek agon
    Which so aroused David
Herbert Lawrence with the perfervid
Symbols that he both hated and loved;
That he made his, that stand redeemed; redeem
Revivalism's alien cherubim.

97: *Welsh apocalypse* (x)

Again dusk-fallen snow ghosts its own twilight
Where the red dragon spat fire to the chapels,
  From the dark forge-heart wrought apostles,
  While in oak woods worlds fell too quiet:
    The semiologies
Derived of sensate destruction, Logos
To crucified slaves and all underdogs—
Familial language once, old Berwyn—
These even now leaping estranged let burn.

98: *Welsh apocalypse* (xi)

Pick from this rota here armed prophecies,
Certitudes of sex among the most common
  Mostly unjust to men and women
  Who in odd ways can become wise.
    The Shakespearean wheel(s)
Of fire must differ from Ezekiel's;
Anaximander's differ in turn (*Diels?*).
Lovers rewrote us, not with our consent,
Fell to confusions, rose to what we meant.

99: *Welsh apocalypse* (xii)

I have made up too much for my own good,
Read that how you will. My creatures compound me.
  I am less primed than you found me.
  True cherubim are a like brood
    To Nebuchadnezzar's
Many times heated furnaces of the stars.
Errors of attribution stalk the seers.
Justified Daniel holds in leading reins,
Invincible, and of the spirit, lions.

100: *Welsh apocalypse* (XIII)

I wish you could grasp things to your own hurt.
Regeneration is your tossed plaything.
  Very well, then; in Welsh; nothing
  Certain but what you can assert.
    So there—Y Ddraig Goch swipes
His tail of frenzy through Apocalypse
Creating mayhem among the Types.
Fire nervous, earth bilious, air sanguine:
Substitute for Swansea murals by Brangwyn.

101: *to Caradoc Evans*

Truly not really I re-wrote for you
Though not to you: cribbed saturnalia
  Of dead reckoning, its taglia
  E-bayed at more than a quote or two,
    Splashed on a computer-
Driven model of Skeffington's daughter,
Supplied with screw-cleaner and self-tutor;
Fictive reality, dead blood's impaction,
The stomach contents from truth's dissection.

102: *Dafydd y Garreg Wen* (I)

Cant about de Valera and Parnell
My model: had Lloyd George eaten the heart—
  Tough enough—of Aneurin Fardd,
  Performing the said funeral,
    Such the dire wizardry,
Subjecting a famed hwyl to hazardry,
Would truth have struck anyone as worth the try,
Devotion all set, false lover's beckoning
To assignation with the broken rung?

103: *Dafydd y Garreg Wen* (II)

Eaten Parnell's heart: messy and bloody.
Resurgent Wales gripes for its Easter Rising.
  Poetry has some teeth missing;
  Eulogy needing a body
    Fresher than Dic Penderyn's
Hanged for a crime some other man's despairing's.
Unfocused centre, stupefied at margins,
Merthyr was Peterloo doubly done over;
Justice that shambles, righteousness not clever.

104: *Dafydd y Garreg Wen* (III)

Had Parnell eaten Lloyd George's brains
He would be Emperor of Ireland, no man's
  Dead king of weeping and sermons,
  Whiskey vomited down the drains.
    Hard to hack away from
This obsessiveness of metre and rhyme.
Haunted imagination not yet crime,
Fumbling with time, for alternative
Sequences in which to find you and live.

105: *Dafydd y Garreg Wen* (IV)

Gene mutation more Ovid than Lamarck.
When Lloyd George died, gnawing at his fist,
  Lying out in a shell hole, gassed,
  Gwalia transmogrified from shock;
    And *Niobe all tears*
Could not then silence the inspired compères
Crowning his passion, their dead metaphors,
Nor match the pomp with which grand eisteddfodau
Chaired his gangrenous putrescent body.

106: *Dafydd y Garreg Wen* (v)

Switch to music: disc on spinner,
Needle of thorn; through hissing quaver
  Lloyd George's gift, a graced tenor,
Leaps to perform *The Wizard of Dwyfor*,
  Pitched on the honour of Wales
    His eminent domain.
How his fine visage resembles Kodaly's—
White lion-mane loved by young women:
With mystic preservation of the semen.

107: *Mercian Incursion*

Documenting his late life crisis
Demands its documentary. Fix poor
  Small catherine wheel to lav door—
  It sticks after the first fizzes
    From its touchy blue bum.
Fuse to Guy Fawkes' plumb pudding of a bomb;
Hitler's moustache a melting plastic comb.
Crib from *Saint's Day* John Whiting's crib from *Lear*,
Letter-slot mouth, flamed kitchen mop for hair.

108

Novembering Wales, the flooded meadows
Pewter, lead-sheeting, briefly highlighted;
  Grand sog of red woods gold-leaf-fretted;
  The road squeezed skywards from wrung Betws;
    Now the deep-held tremor
Of pelting gullies that are wisps in summer
Behind the stone house with the slate shimmer;
Again this homing, strangely-abrupt word,
Possessed domestication of your goad.

109

As misguided fidelity
You might weigh this in the balance of love.
  You have my lost ability
Demonstrated in the way that you drove
  Past Gwynedd's cloud-shouldering lakes,
    Alienate catchments,
Touching ever so lightly the brakes,
Cursing the Tudurs for Welsh bewitchments;
I bound by g-force to your attachments.

110

Look, I was never the boy Bryn
Born to advertise the golden era,
  Pantycelyn; no such fawn.
Your *ponderous Saturn* I much admire,
  Poet to poet. My mistake.
    Nor could I once arouse
Wales to your passion for repentance' sake.
Your Calvinisms gnaw me. I recuse.
I cannot field lost planets of repose.

111

It was Patmore's *perturbèd Úranus*
Set up that chime. I've shrunk susceptible
  To Cabbala, suchlike Bible
  Sortilèges; to sojourners
    Amid deep turbulence.
Draw me a prophet in his brutish trance
A universe or universes hence
And I shall check myself as to precision:
What breaks us here is backlash of pre-vision.

112

A gale from out of Ireland ploughs up rough
Cardigan Bay; a following splendid rain
  Beats us indoors to self-sustain
  With radio and *Telegraph*;
    With such types and shadows
As are my mind working its own midrash
From texts that any fool of the dead knows
And will expatiate on for a small payment
Of salt: perhaps my blood's fatal deployment.

113

Near-ragged syncopations drive my verse,
Like Hopkins and Pete Townshend I revere
  Purcell with his tone-haunted ear,
  Discordant harmony as praise,
    Passing notes rove-over
The hesitancies moving their fine lever.
Hopkins learned sprung rhythm thus: the shiver-
ing of Tate's trim couplets; *the Blessed Virgin's
Expostulation*'s transgressed safety-margins.

114

Too self-sublimed by far, Roy Siencyn!—
Much-pampered guest to your own venal host.
  Dover sole on the bone. I'd trust
  Myself to fillet that Penguin
    Purity and Danger
Without becoming a cracked fetish-monger.
Someone more isolated and stranger?
Poetic furor rates among the tamest.
Asperger wouldn't rhyme there; but would almost.

115

What will you give me to recount my losses
Now that I have come so far a loser?
  Here you riposte: *even so, far*
  Better known than J. C. Powys is
    Which is bloody shameful.
Let me edge off here, weeping, triumphal,
As full of poison as a bad clam-shell,
However grandly to proclaim John Cowper
Our buried giant of deep things improper.

116

Four-by-fours churn, headlights mattressy-springing,
Up from Llanfrothen, dire mis-sited ways.
  Mud flings royally; big-tyred sashays;
  Horns blart. No, by God, psalm-singing.
    Psalm-singing! I warned you
Against such ritterkinder—my candour
Spurned as glazed envy of you in demand; for
My pains now addressed like Pope's manservant
(*Letter to Arbuthnot*). And I the savant.

117

In spite I'd say you rule as vanity
That I my own anger and impatience
  Elevate to the *Twelve Stations*—
  Who's to say with impunity—
    A Rebours! *Salammbô*!—
Associate-Christ and young Rimbaud
In and out of Temple and Tombeau.
I stand, stump brûle-gueule stuck in obstinate jaw,
Coaxing that lame albatross to Aberffraw.

118

Eh bien, alors—pardonnez . . .? *Baudelaire*?
Flushed with remorse yet happy in depiction,
  Bending stiff rules by hard traction,
  I mate sobriety with délire
    Privy to alchemists,
Code-breakers ecstatic fired by weird trysts,
All saints on whose fierce faith the Church subsists;
Latinate syntax thrust on English grammar,
Not like your Welsh, now, all song and stammer.

119: *Hiraeth* (I)

I would do gratefully what others claim
They could not: relive my adolescence
  If I were granted a special licence
  To learn Welsh and love you. Great shame
    I cannot speak or sing
This language of my late awakening
Nor ask your pardon, Beloved, nor bring
You, my bride, into the feasting house
Of first desire, dazed by your wedding dress.

120: *Hiraeth* (II)

Tell me, what is mý sense of *abiding*.
Ah, love, are we to labour over these
  Mechanic etymologies
  Who encountered blank forbidding
    Before we gave much thought
To language—touching was vivid sight,
Our fingers talked, we were illiterate.
Abide does not hit home as does *inure*:
I who have swum in love-words shore to shore!

121: *Hiraeth* (III)

With the miscredence of the desperate
I would blow hot on any fancy and forge
  From which the myths emerge
  Though keeping separate
    Your myth and my version;
I owe you that much from our misprision.
Supra and *infra* chain us to this session:
Guilt in its medieval court desires
To judge by pain, hands grappled to the fires.

122: *Hiraeth* (IV)

I yet hear an unsecured door thudding
Elsewhere in the recesses of my head,
  Loose boxes for horses now dead.
  What brings this bride to her wedding;
    Why does she affront me
With steady reproach like Charlotte Brontë
Smiting hubris for gain at ten-and-twenty;
Bidding curt rule dash curvetting emotions,
Causing blindness to betoken impotence?

123: *Hiraeth* (V)

Things do not suit too well with allegory.
I do not feel emblematic or moral.
  Take up the cell-phone and quarrel.
  Let us donate this old story
    To the geriatric
Programme of the Poor Sisters of St Patrick.
If I can cap this it will be a hat trick.
I do not think that you have Alzheimer's.
I could still cut capers with naked screamers.

124: *Hiraeth* (VI)

Maes-y-mochin calls us on our hiraeth,
Held by joint patent, of which I largely speak;
  So that passion at length grows weak
  And strong memory wearieth,
    Never draining the pond
Of blood and bile from which gulped cries ascend.
A *Nemcon* of bright stupor seals the land
Of which our love was and is part-arrear.
I shall have us—vanishing—strike the air!

125

True, I do not speak truthfully; how could I?
We are a fiction even to ourselves.
  Grand anaesthetist twists his valves;
  Spirit trips loose from the body,
    Finds prose or vers libre,
Theatre projects of low calibre,
Dissertations on Capital and Labour;
Ignorance wallowing but timely whelped;
Wisdom torn from the cranks legless and scalped.

126

  Repeat after me the adage:
Christ descended into our suffering
  But not into crippling sad age;
Not to set disabilities chaffering
  More than serves common practice
    Inside the zones of pain.
Clap to my working forehead the bagged ice
While I struggle with interest and lien
Set on the loans of time still to obtain.

127: *Marwnad William Phylip,*
Hendre Fechan (I)

It is clear: you addressed the proud places
And thought, this is their hour, this dark mêlée.
Judgement may blaze but on Ultima Thule
　To the afterworld's high graces.
　　Not here an Abraham;
There is neither commanding angel nor ram;
No godlike extrication from that drama.
Welsh like Hebrew is a punning language.
Deaf, blind, the struggle we for so long wage.

128: *Marwnad William Phylip,*
Hendre Fechan (II)

If it was indeed you I encountered
In that graveyard, there is some more to say—
　I was seventeen, wrong destiny
　Losing her, now so long lamented:
　　If, then, Hendre Fechan
Upon which in ignorance I had broken
As in a ghost story by Arthur Machen
Let us, I beg, *shake hands across a void*
For grief long since forgotten or gainsaid.

129: *Marwnad William Phylip,*
Hendre Fechan (III)

　Get back your *beautiful right order*;
Patch together the ripped off *secret of song*;
　Englynion ground to dry powder,
Silver become the bullet to bite on;
　Harp in its fine tuning-place
　　Sounds these days archaic.
Do not turn on me that bewildered face.
I cast the shuttle from cynic to stoic.
The tragic mask sticks that I made as mock.

130: *Marwnad William Phylip,*
Hendre Fechan (IV)

Sit in this dark room and rehearse
Whatever may be your secret containment,
  Retainers of music my Muse
As one fair daughter of the king of Spain meant:
  Civility above civics;
    Ripe nutmegs, leaves of bay;
Music and faith consonant with our clavics,
The science to which Reuchlin held the key.
Let us rehearse further of the fourth day.

131

Eloquent zoom to mute minder.
Policy is at best necromancy,
  Felled angelism. Allow candour:
Why such indwelling mured with such vacancy?
  Snap, crack, go slates of sound building;
    Demon Asmodeus,
Champ of long-memoried sclerotic gelding:
Caradoc used him as he might use us.
In Pandemonium the winner's dais.

132

That was more sharply at odds than most
What's-their-names' lampooning of my People,
  Less than an ex-pew-lizard's boast
Corroborates the Sanhedrin of Chapel;
  The gaslight's grimy emissions;
    Songs of a high order
Held apart from Caradoc's wicked versions:
The taste of taint become delicious sordor,
The lilies grown to relish their bad odour.

133

Gets congested as you grind down—
The air, the pit, where lethal dust collects.
  You should not take on such projects,
You being *me*, *I*, the personal pronoun.
  Attention is a type of stupor
    I could almost believe,
Else merest hatred of virgin paper
Would not sustain obsession. While we live
You must be something that I do not have.

134

It is not long, not long to eternity,
This all-consuming perpetual stasis,
  This meeting of periphrasis
  With curt dismissal. Unity
    Much-loved for its own sake,
As of all things the very mould and make,
With our five wits will leave us for a joke.
(Good marriages are made by guardian
Spirits, whatever loves ourselves ordain.)

135

Politics well in hand when out of mind
Make a piston of stasis. I repeat
  Myself stiffly, stalled on the beat.
  I that was of your blood, say. And—
    Yes—I would dedicate
Mark's *Behemoth* to your affairs of state;
Danced with precise, bare, and percussive feet.
Regal torso Hobbes' cage of little men.
Too early dropped fatality in fun.

136: *Welsh apotheosis* (I)

Saunders, ye gods! Ambiguous as wrath
Necessarily is; eaten by rust
  When not oiled; works in art best
  Distanced: I argue *Behemoth*,
    Not Hobbes, Mark Morris's
Most austere political masterpiece—
I call it that; doubtless he disagrees—
Its *drums and tramplings* made without music.
Order Romantic and disorder Classic.

137: *Welsh apotheosis* (II)

  What is noble in us will rate
Though by default. We have not flung far—
  Three centuries of slurried spate—
From Llwyd (Morgan) and Powell (Vavasour).
  Come, now, I embarrass my riff:
    By *sceptre* let portend
Gwalia's fullest sovereignty in fief,
With her unrivalled language at command,
Freed from subservience yet freely bound.

138: *Welsh apotheosis* (III)

  Challenge to myself: *rehearse it dry*.
Custos, have your peace with strange decorum.
  Concede withdrawn diversity;
Remarkably few key-words fix a quorum.
  Be brief. Wales has gone to the drains
    Leached of her genius
For the spendthrifts of twenty taxing reigns;
Yet I would decline to labour *heinous*.
Patent figuration lifts plus from minus.

139: *Welsh apotheosis* (IV)

That this is so we owe to more
Than to indentured pun or quibble.
　There are pragmatics found as pure,
Conceivably, as Welsh of the Welsh Bible.
　Equity's tower-of-the-mill,
　　Hopkins' vales of Clwyd,
Of Elwy, always moving and still,
Cleave immortal under frail strains of cloud.
There is no grace of which all stand devoid.

140: *Welsh apotheosis* (V)

Meant to honour Morgan Llwyd
For the last haul, right as to Heavensgate
　Where matter is neither fluid,
Claggy, nor adamant in redeemed state.
　Pedantic I remain, great Sun
　　That fires my dullest scheme
Into determination and re-run.
Let those not necessarily grasped by fame
Till time's eclipse rage at their world pro tem.

141: *Welsh apotheosis* (VI)

Chemical-yellow the chapel glass
Works to acclimatize the Holy City:
　The pitch-pine pews are buffed dirty,
　Deacons succeed in the Welsh hiss;
　　Much else given over
To silicosis, fatal childbed fever;
The sinner's hope faithed in the final river.
Caradoc with his dudgeon and his spleen
Set the Mad Hatter up on Zion's throne.

142: *Welsh apotheosis* (VII)

Nothing on the statutory language test;
Little of *yr hen iaith* when all is said;
  No new blood for the moody Plaid;
  No time for blazing Calvinist,
    Gutted Popish martyr;
Nothing on Richard Burton, Polly Garter,
Nor on Uncle Owy and grapefruit starter,
Nor of Llansteffan where remain unspent
That tide's infoaming and that moon's ascent.

143: *Welsh apotheosis* (VIII)

Whether to blaze out—trumpets to Eryri—
Or to go down with final rampage—
  Why not (b)? This is the Ramp Age
  Yet all too often damp-fiery.
    Think, those entombing pits
Where, I suppose, the odd skeleton still squats,
Unreached these many thousand-and-one nights;
Fable or not it is unbearable.
Nye died of cancer, surprised-by, terrible.

144: *Welsh apotheosis* (IX)

Fantastic logic found unreason here—
Russell's North Wales, Betws, Portmeirion.
  Who now would thrust inquiry on
  Beyond necessity of desire?
    I would be named: so pledge
Me, language you old reprobate, my rage
Your own eccentric loves drawn from the edge;
Transfigure my proclaimed ineptitude:
Twice-born that virgin bridegroom and his bride.

THE DAYBOOKS IV

Clavics

To Chris and Christine Woodhead

Concord is conquer'd: In this Urne there lies
The Master of great Musick's mysteries,
And in it is a riddle like the *cause*:
Will. Lawes was slain by such whose *wills* were *laws*.

THOMAS JORDAN, 'An Epitaph on Mr. *Will. Laws* Batcheler
in Musick, who was mortally shot at the siege of *Westchester*'

1

Bring torch for Cabbalah brand new treatise,
Numerology also makes much sense,
      O *Astraea*!
      Watch us conform
      To the immense
      Lore, hypertense
      Attaching to the swarm-
      ing mass, the dense
Fluctuations of the materia
Out from which I shall be lucky to twitch
      Creative fire.
      See where who goes?
      Astraea, bitch! —
      Protean ditch
      Suffices what she does
      Returning rich
To the low threshold of contemplation
Her servile master subsisting on scraps
      Keeping station
As one still pursuing ethics perhaps.

Intensive prayer ís intensive care
    Herbert says. I take it stress marks
    Convey less care than flair
    Shewing the works
    As here
    But if
    Distressed attire
    Be mere affect of clef
Dump my clavic books in the mire
And yes bid me strut myself off a cliff.

2

As good epitaphs go Will Lawes is slain
Permit me, sire, is slain by such whose wills
                    Be laws. Again
                    Swift and neat hand
                    Notate the viols
                    Flexures of styles
                Extravagant command
                    Purposeful frills
What comes of the upthrust and downthrust pen
These fantasies constrained by their own strings
                    Narcissus then
                    Crowns fantasy
                    Feasts what feast brings
                    Imaginings
                Consort like winter sky
                    Drawn from the wings.
Jolt into the epilogue by your leave
As into a mixed skirmish, a rout,
                    Punched semibreve
Like fatal bullet through the fine slashed coat.

❖

Because metaphysic is what you will
                Marking time is not beating time,
                    The drummer's deathly trill.
                    The pale sun's rime.
                    The sill.
                    The sun
                In hefty climb
            Has but barely begun
            To spade its memorial theme.
No last retort from zero to countdown.

3

Cultic beyond reason that king-martyr.
He was a double-dealer, betrayed friends
        Without quarter.
        Parliament
        Waved its black wands;
        The deodands
      Of sick spittle and cant
        Stained the altar.
The grace of music is its dissonance
Unresolved beneath resolution
        Of flow and stance:
        Our epic work —
        Cadenced nation —
        Figuration
      Running staidly amok,
        Discord made dance.
I am conspired, thinking best of our selves;
Chronic self-willing that with Furor feints;
        Justice devolves;
Conjures disjunction into printers' founts.

Take the old issue with chromatic tunes,
  False relation, dishabitude
    Of polity, dead loans
      Anarchs beside
      Lost thrones
      A m e n d
      Our sovran maims.
    Be to love as well-found.
  Drive slow instauration of themes.
Grant fidelity to heterophones.

4

Making of mere brightness the air to tremble
So the sun's aurora in deep winter
         Spiders' bramble
         Blazing white floss
         Silent stentor! —
         No more amass
         Viscosity and dross
         At the centre:
The whole anatomy of heaven and earth
Shewn as the alchemists declare it
         Poised beyond wrath
         Resurrection
         Of skin and bone
         To dispirit . . .
         The day cuts a chill swath,
         Dark hunkers down.
I think we are past Epiphany now.
Earth billows on, its everlasting
         Shadow in tow
And we with it, fake shadows onward casting.

❖

Trust you to be a comic poet manqué
         Evidence too sweet to dismiss
         See above. Well, *thank* you!
         (Taking the piss,
         Turnkey?)
         Confess
         Melancholy
         A touch too much my thing.
         Erasmus, *In Praise of Folly*:
Grand antidote no substitute for bling.

5

Edgy, you say, cagy, strange edginess.
Check the electric circuits, you booby.
       Brushes a mess;
       Check them again;
       A fine hobby!
       Feeling clubby
     Largely eases the pain.
       Perish nobly.
Should benefit from this mixed blood and flame
Utterance known first to the haruspex
       And then to fame.
       Best are logged on
       By paradox
       As with drab sex
     By desire to have done
       Old meretrix.
Mystic emendation shall be called for;
Metaphysical intensifiers
       Well enrolled-for.
Not all the bad poets are bad liars.

❖

Revealed thus as a type of figured bass
   Enriched ad libitum by hand
     Of cute accompanist:
       Hear the quills click
        My son
        My son
       The strings are slack
     Will Lawes *is broke* at Chest-
er; Lycidas lies in the sand;
Both justified. England rides rich on loss.

6

The enabling reader, the recusant
At my fingertips, for whom I write well
Into my scant-
Extended age
This ritual
Taking its toll
Much like the saxifrage
Breaking a wall:
On her reciprocal being, regard
For decorum, I now dread to renege
A further word
So tenuous
The catalogue.
Heroic blague
Bequeaths us and our vows
Ardour toward.
Her I embolden, wife to Mallarmé.
Together we shall enrich the cortège
Pli selon pli
Mathematicall Roses yet the rage.

❖

Could be an emblem of some consequence
Without thinking. How to derive
Virtue from ponce to prince —
Virtù — and thrive
By glance:
Believe
The rhetoric
Or not; any archive
Will demonstrate a plethoric
Rigour of stock conservation you dunce.

7

All this fluther, this *dance, clarion*
Air! Let Him take us to Court, then, with chant
      Of plague-siren.
      So, we gambled
      And lost the rent;
      Improvident
      Touch up late-assembled
      Votives to taunt.
Nów say, times feed Time's hot narrative,
Frigid default in the cosmic system.
      King Rat goes live!
      Are you new here,
      As to esteem
      And sage custom;
      Secret and strange desire
      In the guest-room?
Fame, you're slow again; quick to be set up.
Lawes is dead, disagreeably shot up —
      Hard to believe —
A misencountered re-enactment troupe.

❖

False relation charged as with false report.
  This is scarcely a conundrum.
    Rule of two negatives
    Need not apply.
    Repute
    To suit
    Raw panoply.
  Even the tuner thrives.
Brrrm, are we, Lawes and *The Tin Drum*?
As cast (*supra*), let Him take us to Court.

8

Intuitive mathematics' reason —
Be so of that Grace and bleed into it:
        This phosphor-fruit
        Void of season
        Re-examine.
        I intuit,
      Lumen de Lumine,
        That you do not.
By this much I mean only mystical
And eccentric, though with centrist leanings.
        Sophistical
        Is in part truth
        Where part is all-
        Overing foil:
      Registered azimuth
        With trade shinings.
Would I were pardoned the effluent virus
Pardoned that sick programme of pregnant odes.
        Near admirers
Cope with our begging Nescafé and rides.

❖

You who have edited Ben Jonson's masques
    All credit to your endeavours.
     (*Coelum Britannicum*
      Is not Jonson's.)
       That said
       He had
      Many mansions
     Each with many a room.
   Nail this *Jonson Redivivus*
Eunomy leading on regal grotesques.

9

How far give attestation its free ride —
A fair question. Poetry is eccentric
       Labour of pride;
       Fixates power;
       Fixes mantric
       Pitch and con trick;
     Nor hewer nor drawer;
      Not romantic.
Claim that it rises to its own jerked bait
Cites polity its *raison* among such
       Affairs of State
       You, I, might name,
       Set within touch
       Of heightened speech
     In some awed interim.
       You believe that?
I remit your citations, Lord Apollo,
Bestower of conundrums. Try me: what
       Flex to allow
Fixing this swing-arm with its counterweight.

      ❖

Listen to and make music while you can
    Pray *Mater ora Filium*
     Cry *Spem in Alium*
      God is made man
       Choric
       Lyric
      Heaven receives
     Impartial these tributes.
    Creation call it that believes
Even to blasphemy in our ranged throats.

10

Dearly beloved, grasp these sureties:
Decrepit lies the world and all things fail,
Exact their toll;
The Judgement must
Make trial, trust
Late Dorothy's —
Doctor D. Bethurum's —
Lorn expertise
Locked in her *Sermo Lupi ad Anglos.*
Give the old lady her due, concurreth
Doctor Pangloss.
We shall have sums
Right hand and left.
Lovely the Dooms,
These flaky; those bereft
Franciscan hymns:
Why, then, did you not call me in the night
To click the christian latch else dying might
With exequies
Of troubled phoenix ashes flame too bright?

❖

New opinion on the rates of stall
Not forestalling major profits.
All hands to the lever.
Calculation
Too right
Of fraught
Animation.
Persistence however
May overhear Minor Prophets
Cry that the Mercy of Things is not well.

11

Thing not to do: sacrifice college plate
For siege money. Music enriches state
      Of art mayhem,
      England's toxic
      Moving waxwork
      Astride the flame.
    Our beauties are pox-sick
    And miscreate.
If you say so, distinguished Councillor.
Fratty Will Lawes rarely unperplexes.
      Dukes and doxies,
      Tew's shook pillar;
      Strafford and Laud
      Nodded to blood;
    A bereaved recompense
    By contrivance
Danced on its head. What does this do for you
In the guise of things, milord of Sorrow?
    Confer taxes
As *Coelum Britannicum* taxed Carew?

Felicitas to conceive happiness,
  To have been where we met our eyes,
    But aware of gender,
     Nor asunder:
      Shew fouls
      From those
     Bloody towels
    As bat-like embryos.
I have plumbed too much here to re-render.
Scrub yourself down from late lamented guys.

12

What constitutes Metaphysics: you are
A revived soul like the spirit of Donne?
Or none; or none
Too bright a light.
Yet you rally.
I thought you might.
Sadly and *hopefully*
Climb to our sight–
Zenith, broad Jupiter. Not to desire
Sentiment on such track is difficult.
My fault my fault.
Sense the next line
Strike to result
From the dull melt.
Eager and unbenign
The click, the cult.
Will it be like leaving tokens to hand:
Tapes, I mean, unburned CDs, chinograph
Pencils; enough
Funky confessions wiser not to send?

❖

I detect something false in that disquiet;
So let's mark time as it remains.
Fiction may find itself
C o m p a t i b l e
With truth
Like Ruth
In the Bible;
In a bright simple clef;
Sul ponte, bearing on the strains;
Break C minor to C major at LIGHT.

13

Concurring that the old man is in shock
Won't do; the shocked are rarely so brazen.
                Timed by Great Clock
                Lyric-loutish
                Plays of swineherds
                And severed heads;
            Buzzle of things ruttish
                And things weazen;
Verses metronome-safe to emote by;
Tuning to spirit voices for control.
                Nightmare of school:
                There stands the Greek
                Hypotenuse
                With its long nose,
            Ruminating in black,
                Moved remotely.
Guide, pray, the mentally disadvantaged
Safe to Urbino; Yeats and your author
                Photomontaged,
Graciously inclined each to the other.

❖

Bring out the laden cope each hypocrite
        Dante makes wear: convoluted
            Sentence go beg. Marceau
            Mimed himself stuck;
                The last
                Mask-twist
            Paste face a-lock
            Fatalism of farce.
        Give you first go, hell-rerouted
Light entertainers weighed with leaden wit.

14

Working divisions on a shift of line
Take it as a ground some worth debating
            Collocating
            As you find them
            Things to outshine
            Gold from the Rhine;
        May fortune attend them
            Scant words of mine.
Thus I foretold the grand Staffordshire hoard
Long since, without benefit of crystal,
            Went spare, unheard.
            Hullo, thistle,
            Silver-silk head,
            Gashed green-blue woad,
        Buoyant in old fallow,
            Watch by your dead.
Thus to relatinate Cranmer's commons,
Media vita — singing rings hollow —
            Still the summons:
We shall go down to bed with worm pillow.

                        ❖

Some super-charade of spirits and ghosts
    I heard the man say. Nabokov,
        To recall the topic.
            Dutifully
            It seems
            The screams
            Of butterfly,
        Moth, float through biopic
From his father's stretched mouth. *Book of
Changes*: outré silencings make ripostes.

15

Don't accost me here on anomalies —
Will Lawes auditioning for Ronnie Scott,
   Alto sax, lute —
   So he survives
   Demi-famous
   The rakish hat
  Musicianship that moves
   Oddly in state.
Why do you so plug *wit and drollery*?
Clop-clip-clop, ups with his troop to Chester
   Unmerrily
   To register,
   To be felled, *slain*,
   Etcetera;
  In what corpse-rift unknown;
   Riffraffed the day.
Lawes makes his way in grinding the textures
Of harmony; so I think, here's a mind
   Would have vexed yours
With late unharpied bounty wrought to find.

❖

What else here fit but mimicked *consort setts*
  Patterns that crown elaborate
  True deliberation
  Fantasies come
   At cost:
   At best
  In crossing rhyme
 Shake a crosspatched nation.
 Small chance factoring at such rate
Wrote finish to, not stasis of, regrets.

16

Between dissatisfaction and finish
Is where it goes wrong. Getting under way
      The things vanish
      Marvellously;
      Leave as coda
      Some form of code
    Like sonnets of Spanish
      Autocracy.
Yes, I heard her: *my self-abnegation*
And drug-taking. I am in my right mind
      Do you still find?
      So that I spell
      And keep station?
      Arrogation
    Of entitled travail
      Contempt of kind.
Ah, but the wound of love is never healed!
While male and female voices busk and thrill
      The air grows riled:
Insidious the epiphanic spill.

❖

As you were, exiting philosopher;
    Anything numen of desire
    And neurocratic hope.
      Pass angel. Trope
      Azured
      Lizard.
      Sealed inquiries
    Open to chimaeras
    And other energies. Attained
Absolute relativity of mind.

17

Iniquitous heart, submit no new plea
As if to retell mere nonsense incurred;
            Logorrhea,
            Venus' lard,
            The singer's mouth
            Emetic-scarred;
        Travestied love, botched youth;
            Patrocleia
It is the lying in wait that demeans
Sanity of mind; even the sane thought
            Distrait, distraught;
            Purposed victim.
            One's best assigns
            Hector Troy's plains.
        How to depict you — them —
            And blood and drought.
Bear with defoliate terrain, betray
Why one word follows another or how
            Your words toss prey
To their own orchidlike emollient jaw.

❖

I'll beat you down — on sentiment as well —
        Ah, taci ingiusto core,
        Heart of all opera
            Rising sing swell
                To home
                On fame
            To aggrandize,
        Ingrate, veritable
    Core, thy pulsings irritable
Gifts grantable yet out of hand mere prize.

18

Music cannot forever exhaust time.
Tell me what it is I labour around,
      If you have found —
      Chill me with style —
      Rhyming *Coelum*
      Britannicum
      Such riches to entail,
      Poenia crown'd
Through which her haire starts up like a furie.
Do not in any case mock invention
      That holds story
      To what it is:
      By contention
      Slight poetry
      Pitching inquietus
      To Usury.
Conclude: to wit, such lyric enrostered
With stage convention, swags and curlicues,
      Word unbested,
Enriched out of Britannia her woes.

Opera enjoys the nefarious
      As if innocently sublime
      Ingiusto core. Try
      Supplication
      Of throes.
      One does
      Confrontation
      Without oratory?
Ah, taci, taci! In the womb
I could perform some of these arias.

19

How may I differ thee from defeat? If
Intricacy is resistance, take heart:

The strings of strife
Work their measures
Part against part
Junctured in sport.
Thy muse is in the wars
And plague, and tort.

Do not tell me what I should let fly with
(Head up!) in this solemn musketry drill;

Primed with spry oath
For oath, off tar-
get and too shrill.
Wit shall prevail
Paradoxical, spoor-
ing its poor trail

Of delicacies rigged without desire
Apart from emulation: *Astraea*

Redux, one more

Late felicity in the prompt ashtray.

❖

Perhaps in these unequal measures time

Takes its stand for us; equable,
Music and polity
Agree dissent
More than
We can
Make of misspent
Taxing equality

In respect of love's poor stable.
False relation in music shadows rhyme.

20

Da capo — to give fantasy its head.
The eyes embrace us, *gravi e tardi*;
      A threnody
      Escapes the lips
      Moved in study.
      I have admired
    Dawkins's mortal quips
      As was required.
Straw men in flagrante folk-upbraided.
The champagne of St Pancras sits tight-wired.
      Truth is austere
      I do believe.
      No deception
      Proved by caption,
    There is none to deceive . . .
      O the entire
Universe of Fun has begun to run
Down. While the Goodwin Committee en fête
      Is to debate
To some acid cud the taste of ruin.

❖

Taci, ingiusto core! Not a hope.
    What is arrayed here sits engrained —
      No chip for excision —
      Such fine texture
      Of rage.
      Assuage
    Nothing. Text ire
    To a few whose mission —
Here inadequately maligned —
Prays for redemption of your horoscope.

21

Into life we fell by brute eviction:
What prize brutish joy; what price compunction?
      To feel by trust
      Most things ill-won,
      Ill-held; even
      Your perfection
    Gross in its mistiming.
      In the dead mist
The fleet sweeps past, *Invincible*, others,
Derfflinger, *Grosser Kurfürst*; it is a dream
      Of undreaming,
      Chaste, all weathers.
      The journal ends
      Here in its fronds;
    Oblivious the calm
      Jolt of a wave.
That is an odd world from which to derive
History and our craft not feel the helm.
      Forgo blaming
On the loss of Empire the spent compère.

❖

You look at the thing; you think, *Not today*.
  Inopportunist Mechanics
    Adjust it otherwise
      Write as on slate.
      Yet I'd
      Concede
    Sensing the bite
  From the deep-laden rise
Of the word my thrill; as sonics
Are to spheres where surely strange gods deploy.

22

Our children stepping backward through the years
As wrong-footed warriors, prophetic
        Of all arrears
        Nineteen sixteen
        Caught in static
        So what appears
      Blindly upon the screen
        Ghosting vatic
Outlines of projects for which these obliged
Mostly declaring good will with dissent
        To uncamouflaged
        Futurists yet
        As backward bent
        On advancement,
      Their own enfuried rote?
        O wronged extant
And still forgotten souls of the slain
Bowed to be made memorable by lot
        The evergreen
Processionals tarnish held on remote.

❖

Let them set aside ten minutes each way
    For public condolence, prayer
      By those who will not pray
        I nay-sayer
        You say.
        Well then
       Haul irony
      Upon its rack; refrain
    Clavics archaic iron key:
Splash blessings on dead in Afghanistan.

23

Plug in a dissonance to make them wince.
Density a workable element.
  Name-acclaim once
  Reclaimed ransom
  Truth from figment
  Picks its fragment.
  Somewhere such a kingdom
  Roughed assonance.
Judith of Bethulia's well wrested
Calm. How controverted we have become,
  Questor quested;
  Answerable;
  Outside the frame
  You can't draw from
  Old dense pin-stabbed Bible
  Unmolested.
Somewhere is sacramental belonging.
Here we find but banking with God's grammar
  Strung unstringing
Grace from chance, worked like a novice stammer.

❖

Democracy is a Potemkin fiction
  Anarchical Plutocracy
  Proliferates its gyre
  Photo-couvade:
    How could
    You? said
  Savage, like glad.
  More substance than we are?
Phantom-chasing Natocracy.
Have Rubens patent his prize depiction.

24

That this should resemble a consort book
Or a book of ayres, my mere maggotry-
      Begotten joke.
      Was Lawes a clown
      Of the outré?
      One can but try
    Mild fudging of renown-
      Idolatry.
Do not dredge something odd from Jung,
Unnamed interlocutor; my gift
      Music restrung
      To play the times;
      No better craft;
      Medusa's raft
    On a grim sea of slimes
      Rubbish adrift.
I am rummaging here for a ground bass
To sustain a passacaglia, misc. saint,
      Our grand foundress
Of all that works through mêlée its descant.

Calling to witness here the Winter Queen
    The text wavers for cogency
    On that remote screen.
      See, she is vexed.
      Wotton
      Spot on
    In this context:
    All lyric cries demean
Intricacy and urgency
The clouds not clouds of witness nor of scene.

25

The Dolphin may be spared: lost Book of Hours
This most tender of presentations bears:
        What the Lover's
        Burden proffers
        A cradled gift
        The hard to lift
      Soul of exacted Christ;
        His almagest.
Intercept: whý should áll nót be of some
Praeterient holding? All too abrupt-
      ly break for home.
        Unrest; at least
        No narcolept,
        I go in fear
      Of Death's greed for the breast.
        Is this so far
Departed New Age as to resuggest
Imbecility's fit raiment? But one
        Candle lit on
The well-iced birthday slab so be my guest.

               ❖

Luck of the age is lottery-pittance
    While there is a grand unwisdom
      Legislates stun-wisdom.
        Buy your quittance
         Absurd
         Last card
      Stamped with patience
    Although bad luck quizzdom
  Scores well enough if you buzz bomb
Some sorry target, game-show or frot-dance.

26

Alternative chronicity for this
Means our being the one flesh as flesh dies.
How this may have
Told us to grieve,
Mourn much as dread:
The Enigma's
Refusal to be read
By common eyes.
Alchemical desires: stars and stones,
Compassioning embraces — what disturbs,
Proliferates:
Poor recompense,
More nouns than verbs.
How spleen defines
An essence that conflates
The drift of sense.
Smudge-typed Admiralty communiqué
Pronouncing valediction: in dense skeins
Of frozen spray
Corvettes raw-reeving through Icelandic day.

❖

Touché — Archie Rice it should be but I've
Seen neither play nor film. Permit
Me stock adaptation
Of tradition
To touch
Was pitch;
Pre-coition
Secretly off ration.
Here you have me near as dammit
A *living voice* dead ringer for alive.

27

Though they would warn me against world's regret,
The Vaughan brothers, Lawes presumably,
      Calculably
      As I confess
      Bulk of my fears;
      Theirs maybe not:
    World in its rot; but Faith
      Their good habit.
Gravitation something on which to click,
The Philosopher's Stone or Lotto luck;
      Absence of sloth,
      Irrelevant
      Virtue, discount.
      Saint's bone. It may —
    Virtù from mother earth —
      Be alchemy,
Though not all who treadle are gold-spinners.
Tom Vaughan an alchemist of the Cross
      Would price earth-dross
Tax on such infinitude of sinners.

❖

Shadows long wintering beneath the flare —
  Welsh once told kinship back to ninth
    Degree, much less so now —
    Declare the moon's
      Power:
      Thrawer
    Of benisons
   Benisons may bestow,
  Stilly riding her obscured plinth
Supremely unresponsive but aware.

28

Unity of knowledge — consilience —
The phrasing cribbed for I have no Science:
> Here infinite
> Clavics make spin,
> Keyed-in, commote,
> Bees' element
Attuned, compassed, by scent-
> Colours and sun.
As to the ant when chance disturbs the State,
Divisions huge, minute, crude, delicate,
> Like egg-and-spoon
> White grub — rice grain —
> She works her reach
> With pitch and stretch,
Staithed in that giant crèche.
> No metaphor.
The butterflies, high flyers on high winds;
Invisible to us they plane and soar
> Beyond our minds'
Troubled conventioning and do not err.

❖

Stood with their martyr-king at Rowton Heath
> The Vaughan twins? Mêléeing big
> Scrap. Bonny there, Will Lawes
> Barneyed his death.
> No way
> Au fait
> How your rutter-
> kin dabbles in these shows.
It must have been like sticking pig.
Talk of closure keeps open the matter.

29

In place of percentage absolution
Proclaiming best-tried ark for the nation,
   Come Ash-Wednesday,
   Corpus Christi
   When the bands play,
   Smoke-hung feisty
  Catholic Lancashire,
    Cry *ah my dear!*
For the likes of Tom Navvies and Poor Clares;
Doctrine of the Immaculate Concept.
   Read back transcript
   Of earth's desires:
   Felix Randal
   Folk from Pendle
  That woman with the slop
   Pail on the step.
Wrath and wrathful compassion, so Dante
Stuck in the Epistle to Can Grande
   Virtues by will.
Without them let us call plunder Plenty.

      ❖

In strife of certitudes to be outstared.
 Let me urge for myself virtues
  Of the skald as hit-man
   Things narrow thus
   Chaos
   Or chess
   To harrow us
  Go swanning through skidpan
 As a freelance virtuoso
Other means of advancement undeclared.

30

Haul in circumstantial intelligence
As Thomists handle nous; still so moving.
     Radio-stars
     Rake to find sense,
     Track the immense
     Particulars.
     Make no-one's disproving
     Void evidence.
Right at the tether's end right to be free
Your centre ev'rywhere I cannot be:
     Fully constrained
     By hope, this lost
     Freedom of mind–
     Territory.
     Ease to my foul bargains;
     Grief and the rest.
Absolute for rage hold rage compliant
As Yeats, in his crazy-final refrains,
     Bowed defiant.
A sunny window-sill and a stone plant.

❖

Parasites essential to survivals.
     Such teaching I have well absorbed
     Long harbouring with grin
     Blithe enemy.
     He talks
     Well, Dawks,
     Casts bonhomie
     To all save Mortal Sin —
     Root-proclivity and morbid —
Parasites intolerant of rivals.

31

The morning stormie with rough scuds of cloud
And leaden light on meres that lie about.

A sharp coda
Could fashion this
As sorrow's mode
Lawes is a mod.
Pi-driven artifice,
Goe, bid them shoot.

Believe it: that there is cunning to twist
Wind's declination of the cypress tops,

You fantasist.
Set it down here
As one who copes
With frets and stops
And gutty strands and wire
And forlorn hopes.

But in the meantime legs flown and guts drawn.
I need there to be a noble cadence,

Default riddance.

Discard to the age trumpery's sword, crown.

Of sweete wel governed voices: shew how com-
prised my wraith's lament. Sing not touch.

What is exorbitant
Is the just price.
It could
Be mood,
Of mood's device,
And is here grave entente.

When all is played I would not vouch
That what was done tossed nothing to réclame.

32

In the substraction of my yeares, I said,
With teares . . . yet to begin anew, as now,
                    Tea leaves to read,
                    Foutred desire,
                    Nectars that gnaw
                    In the old craw;
                Even *Forgive me, Sire,*
                    Stolen, for show;
The hard drive of words broken, plagiarist
Of their demanding virtue, and even
                    Of my own wrist.
                    What possessives,
                    Self-pederast?
                    Crack up what ghost,
                Ghost-rhetor of suasives,
                    Of faithful rust,
That old bay-windowed frontage since torn down?
The Ivy-Church and the Castle of Yew
                    Some cosmic yaw
Preserves from desecration to renown.

❖

Entretiens, Will? Why such place of resort
        As the rue Cujas? Star-pockt night,
            Cloud-like interstices,
            Moon-monody
                (Desnos
                's Muse
                's threnody
            For love-deprived spaces)
        Long division never got right;
Lost childhood's cunning famed unkept report.

33

Torching Cabbalah not a fine refrain.
Set on the dais drudging Uccello's
    Cruel *Profan-*
    ation that smug
    Trim and callous
    Custom allows
    Best employ dialogue
    Views before vows:
O I will give you your profanation
Cries the man with his back to the black stake
    But a notion
    That I am not
    Here and awake
    To spit and crack
    Bonds my voice to my throat.
    Dance jumping jack.
How did I so incline to this subject?
Because aesthetics are an inclined plane.
    I would object
Mildly to seeing the object again.

❖

Metaphysical intensifiers
    Barely a paradox: they say
    Inessential repairs
    Would wouldn't they
    Cracked fliers
    Built kites
    Gave themselves airs
    Setting the laws to rights,
    Hazard's itinerants the stars.
Meritocrats are crap meteorites.

34

Very well: this shall redirect the pain;
May already have worked me towards paean.
       Nothing retrieves
       Precisely; but
       Lost spring of loves
       Turns things about.
     My! this lever is stiff.
       So true to life,
Madame Champignon; and such rhyme my scheme
To right a wrong reading. Sacrosanct faith,
       Give me your death
       So that I may
       Die briefed; drama
       Hep the nation;
     Contrive well! Fix supply.
       Take it away,
Your Grace, that folly be made a weird dream
Of salutation if not salvation,
       Constatation
Of the cross I woke myself falling from.

❖

Add, as I must, unstintings of applause
   To the divine head or foot. Cue
     Viols. They worked for Lear
       Antic-mannered
         Woe king
         Waking
      Rag-and-bannered.
   'He' asks, *Have you come far?*
 And we die on our feet, Will, die:
Signed at reveille the no-exit clause.

35

Negotiating let us note more games
In the cunning position. Fantasias
      For wired alarms;
      Alarmed Whitehall.
      Art is dis-ease
      Its business;
      And self-regard's punksoul
      Chaste to excess.
Will Lawes was slain by pot-shot and ill luck.
That is utterly different, pronounce
      From the grave. Quick-
      ly a conceit —
      All innocence —
      Awaits th'advance;
      Make steady its three feet,
      Musketeer-stance.
Look it up in *Pen and Sword* to be sure.
There is no come-back. Shall I not compound
      Bounty and ire,
Angelus Novus, eh, my backward friend?

Had you lived, Paris could yet have made you
    Squire exorbitant violins
      With extra-fleshier
      Foibles of grace.
      Ah, Will,
      What style,
      What fretty lace
     Late ruined in Cheshire!
    I too strut thus amid ruins,
Dogged by wild cadences that obeyed you.

36

Chester Play of the Deluge played again
But this time outside the city. I fear
   Will's put to pain
   For his trouble.
   Blame the Bible
   Or curse the year.
  Pin it all on Prynne's ear.
   Cut and quibble.
When have we ever not been in a mess?
I inquire of the winds and waters. They
   Slither and pass
   And reed-fossick.
   Such hauteurs gay
   Sent slaughter's way.
  Gaunt unwritten music
   Ripe now to play.
Strikes angular as in Dai Jones' woodcuts
For the pretty edition you once had
   Before the Flood.
A watery sun squats on the mud-flats.

❖

Do not presume on others' misfortunes.
 It is a bad trait. Difficult
  Not to take up and tweak
   Petty dramas?
   Plangent–
   Engined.
  Voice of the times,
 Treble about to break,
While Herrick's insidious lilt
Procures our late scenario's lute-tunes.

37

Music, you are the *absolute sole lord*
Crashaw names *love*. Add Sidney's own *striker*
      Of the senses
      And we're away.
      Add, a maker
      Up of discord
      And a demon to play;
      That but once *is*
Until the next time, which may not occur
But mostly does. The beauty of the thing
      As a black choir,
      In a high riff,
      With a silk thong,
      An undersong,
      And a mystical life,
      And a still tongue:
I need no loss adjuster to spin this
Strange kind of work. I am minded to claim
      Dark premises;
To ditch my new lover for you, old flame.

❖

At source now this would be a brutish cry.
    You imagine it simply waits
      Around in a thin rain
      For us to call,
      Do you?
      You do
      Not at all well
    Called upon to explain
    To the Queen and her Four Estates
Rare gifts unprized in garish Britishry.

38

Mannerism will yet save us. Baroque-
Magisterial. And shall wrest away
   My clique, your claque;
   Sustain a pride-
   Flecked shot array,
   Will's cavalry,
  The deep wound in the side,
   The feathered prey.
O we are too much cut from ambition.
His would have been a sorry appearance.
   Did the nation
   Project better
   Apparition?
   The Queen for France.
  Pig's blood and french letter
   Fables' portion.
Did you hear it thud, that grand mimicry
Of cavalier investment? Hark, whose brain
   Splashed abrupt cry?
True tears of lead scalding false tears of brine.

❖

Directly inclining an oblique king
 Is lobbyists' work not music-
  Theory promotion,
   Not even this.
   Too much
   Con-touch
  To harmonize
 Orphic inanition.
So, tell finesse to act basic.
Casket yet in place for lordly freaking.

39

Bull and Froberger I will not interpret
To your inattention. *Nor Lawes neither.*
My idiom
Happily set
In versing's room
Of home-and-realm.
Time, its leaden feather
Laid on bride, groom,
Gives me away to myself, a pity
So to flake out with eloquential fire.
Adversity
Is love's true squire
And armourer.
Tempted by rhyme
To deal this like a game
Change down a gear
He mutters, he feels the chassis shaking
Across the bad Caroline road surface.
Epoch-making
He rear-ends finally without surprise.

Standard discourse or variant welcome.
Audits reprise of monorhyme.
Uptake to be in shape-
Shifter programme:
Ripost-
ed jest,
Quarled epigram,
Weak emblematic type.
What blunt angle on what rote name?
Suchlike assaults not judged to be a crime.

40

Quasi-Shakespearean this play on *Will*
But I am down to the last variant
   Of that viol;
   Swift passing-notes
   Slow to invent
   In sweetened rant
  The bitterest rewrites,
   And slight and scant.
That will have them up and dancing? No doubt
Will's pleased to take his full measure of things
   While still afloat.
   Bobbing to rhyme
   Is good for him,
   Is it not? We
  Seemed to have turned weighty.
   Themed water wings
Thus made a fashion nobles emulate.
Mourning rare Lawes, grief-enscrolled business,
   Bravely refines
Music's harsh concord with the laws of state.

❖

(Shit) it can peg out, cathetered high art.
  At best now pitied by sporting
   Crites in his sot's whine.
   Pissmen of old,
   Recoup:
   New Hope
   Spews dissolved gold
  Vanities, yet divine,
 I do accept that; ribs hurting,
Sign-off the last sleeve-note; make to depart.

41

Rage will not assuage the instrumental
And timeless jury. Tall equitation
     In the front hall
     Of the nation.
     Interject here
     Chromatic grace-
    Notes; and barely retire;
     Take up true place
With paid assessors of much-prized fiction
And affordable truth; allegory's
     Defunct traction;
     The plaster ducks
     Of the Furies,
     Guy Fawkes's tyres;
    The seaside for two weeks'
     Compounded years:
None would then have proposed me the fine arc
So newly taken for justice. Flight path
     Collides with wraith.
Needle quivers. Waters thrust from the sac.

❖

After all, the shallow-leaded letters
   Rot among sodden marble chips
    The cracked vase is askew
     And holds nothing
      Except
      A zapt
     Stalk. Re-teething
    Weeds with no rose to shew
   Proclaim growth. Fatality grips
And is held. I am nailed by my fathers.

42

There is a noise in my head: the breaking
Of sequence. Have worked to repletion
     Not yet disgust.
     As ever cost-
     Estimates fall
     Short of cost. Still,
   Before sleep, on waking,
     Know the eyes bleed.
Undertaken for honouring the dead
From our nation. Fulfilled in a thrusting
     Forward of rhyme
     Upon a theme
     Long protesting
     Some lame notion
   I had and have: barely
     But entirely
Devoted to those I disregarded,
Who looked to me, then; and no more retain
     The common pain.
From gapped inscripts let them gape recorded.

❖

Trespass and consequence; misrequital;
  Lightly hidden lies equity.
   I shall not reveal how
    Much warmth was spent
     In ice
     Device.
   Are we slid cant
  Wishing to end well? Now
 Good occasion not to pity
Those so barely moved by such recital.

THE DAYBOOKS V

Odi Barbare

To Christopher Middleton and Marius Kociejowski

arma diu senior desueta trementibus aeuo
circumdat nequiquam umeris et inutile ferrum
cingitur ac densos fertur moriturus in hostis

Aeneid ii: 509–11

Are then humane mindes priviledg'd so meanly,
As that hatefull death can abridge them of powre,
With the voyce of truth to recorde to all worldes,
That we be her spoyles?

SIDNEY

I

If the soul so glares at annihilation,
Name despair one deviant path of wisdom;
Music steel-rimmed spectacles make as objects
    Claiming a victim:

Not moronic but a fell world of equals,
Things to fall for, deep in our study sessions,
Ready metered set to a mark perfection
    Staggers away from:

Anarchs' paradiso the infrastructure,
Luck permitting love and its grave verdictives.
Some have gone purblind and athwart our sensors,
    Broken not brain dead.

Ewig endurances, for good and all done,
Labour our survival and their reviving.
Nonsense too deep meaning a derogation.
    Torch not untimely.

Measure loss re-cadencing Sidney's sapphics
Not as words fall but as they rise to meaning.
Laurels withheld, fractured the noble column;
    Alien torsos

Too much gifted. Angular backlit miners'
Profiles. Build up roofing and side supports, quote
Axioms, blast access to unsuspected
    Caverns of fluorspar.

II

Like Carducci meant, barely more than rustic;
Not urbane, not welcomed the Aula Regis.
Rhetoric uptight, the morose consensus
    Freely enhanced. *I*

Hate barbarians taking a stab at meaning
Freaks elision. Tell those who move the circle:
Words that have clear biznis before the threshold
    Need not profane us.

Sacrificial oxen the gift of Virgil,
Ruminating white sacrificial oxen
Heaving lyre-pronged heads from hoof-podged Clitumnus,
    Suffer their garlands.

Rumpus, uncouth anacolutha, bullish
Metamorphs treading out a line, the luckless
Fetishizing blood of the lucky victims.
    Rote ruination:

Rimini marred, Pisa the slew of armies,
Apennine muscular brusque torrents voiding
Panzers Anzacs out of the rocky slurry
    Mud-wrestled corpses.

Virgil loves bees reads by the way as Plato
In the *Symposium* on immortal being.
What price this verdict to regrouping nature's
    Plenary sessions?

III

Wild desire far-conjured to be *black lightning*.
Take these strange-willed odes as of his clairvoyance;
Stilted offspring tripped by electric discharge
    Kicking themselves up;

Or as some tell Munchausen syndrome hauling
Self from grimpen by your own tight-stitched hairpiece.
Welcome lost brother of eternal credit
    (Knew you from Adam).

Something scarce-caught: instance we have abiding,
As with first love though there are other windows;
Infinite starlight yet a key to purpose
    Stark beyond hazard.

Tacitus self-willing the Imperator;
Trajan makes one template of definition;
Also holds clouds ropy and barred together
    Through which Jove blunders.

Truces, pacts, ruins, fix the pledge of stalling
Time. Advances made thus against infarction.
I would not have you in another time frame
    Raging your heart out;

Belting this tocsin better left imagined,
Metaphor's grand bell in its trope of towers
Out of temper—taking wild swings at people—
    Sullenly dumbed down.

IV

Have I cloned Horace or reduced myself to
Weeping plasma? Never again so rightly,
Not again those *marvellous early poems*
        Lately acknowledged.

How the sea–lightning with a flash at hazard
Cleft the lanterned yard into pelting angles.
Had we been there, had you then turned towards me,
        By this remembered . . .

Yo, my sad love, clad in our dark declensions;
Never once naked to the other given;
Honey, milk, spices, of that night forgathered
        Lost in summation;

Mirrors fading where the bright-brutish roses
Held themselves royally akin their nature.
Berkeley could have granted us our existence
        Had we but known him.

Still suffices language its constitution;
Solipsist somehow must acknowledge this. Not
Quite enough said when what was said is nothing
        Granted recital.

Here is my good voice; you may well remember
Making up such things. It is what I do. Hark,
Love, how cross-rhythms are at stake to purpose
        From the beginning.

V

I could not name Jericho what she stands for.
Call it stubborn harlotry, crass denial.
Let her walls tremble to the aggro trumpets
    Braying the mortar.

Hides from our eyes God in a certain placement,
Worries his self-satisfied bulk, the indis-
criminate vengeance of the Flood, and blithely
    Switches to Rainbow.

Ruach cried up but it is *racha* taunts me.
Earthly things fall back upon Sheol sometime.
How redeem live prophecies thence: good question
    Short of an answer

Nominating Israel here as rogue state.
So it must be justified though unwisely
Some slur Abram Chaldee; incorporate his
    Horror of darkness.

Striking praise songs Judith and Deborah planned
Plus the dancers. Prophecy's tunnel vision,
Full rendition zeroing lethal flashes,
    Children of Canaan.

Ruach cried up but it is *racha* haunts me.
Earthly things fall back upon Sheol sometime.
Best avoid Yahweh not to have Jehovah
    Riddle the whirlwind.

VI

I can hack most laureates' roster-homage,
Make a pranged voice nasal through ruptured matchbox;
Brief the act undangerously heroic;
        We will survive it.

This astounding people (Disraeli), their spears
Beating shield-hides murmuring high a basso,
Hive-like, buzzing rage, become torpor almost
        Blood self-enthralling.

Assegais whish-washed in the fleshy Empire
Jelk you inside out like a dumdum bullet;
Death by numbers, one-shot Martini-Henry
        Redhot on target.

Errant Chelmsford, yet if slow Pulleine then had
Ordered form square, he could have saved their breakfast,
Might have subscribed that long-abandoned letter
        Dead on the table.

Stand-to you viewers. Mark how Chard and Bromhead
There with plucked Hook posthumously ill-fictioned
And a Welsh Jew—Land of My Fathers bless them—
        Staggered the impi.

Though your own sapped psyche so courts retraction,
Soldiery's grand comedy plays to curtains.
Who denies this I would expect the Queen to
        Rise up and smite him.

VII

Call the soul's journey through the seven circuits
Furthest infestations of Cuban rumba.
What is far-fetched shores up the breaking cento
    But for a moment.

Far-fetched, high-priced, ever-dissembling Plato
Daring unloved truth by design Socratic;
Thing about caves, powers, inebriations:
    Man, who ya tellin?

Fly untasered, quasi-immortal spirit;
You shall go far, you may well meet McTaggart,
Certified immortal, with what awaits us
    Void of its terrors.

That I could wish this for his loves, for mine too,
Goes without saying though I here declare it.
Affirmations bought undisputed: not all
    Lie beyond question.

This abrupt, else how should I level with you,
Primitive heart-sight unself-stabilizing.
As for that justice to our selves observe these
    Hymns to Mathesis.

With the black disc perfect divine Apollo
Casts up his arms—O—at the moon's blind sev'rance
Light emergent stark from that occultation
    Uncatastrophic.

VIII

Ace of first blessings, Joachim Fiore
Everlasting timekeeper. Francis also,
Canny-handed terrible man with flowers
        Given to gospel:

Dominic self-hounding his instauration,
Acting Christ's cur clipping the moneyers' heels,
Though on whose say-so?—we are souls benighted.
        Pitch me *vox clamans*.

So to our vision at a price this temple
Dedication worthy if too abrupt bring,
Though to hog vile ways and procrast the tribute
        Twixt porch and altar:

Casting song's agon most unlike Assisi.
Granted effort let us imagine purpose,
Poverty married in the way conceit's made
        Hostage to metrum.

Loved that come-back; how well you speak out, padre:
Secular plaudits as the best-befitting!
Francis sings vacantly, his vocals faded
        Sweetly but somewhat.

Dominic's pledged though, as for Yeats von Hügel.
Dissertations answer to final conclave.
Bide me my pardon, enigmatic cadence
        Cracked and repaired thus.

IX

Granted our choice say it is Metaphysic.
Shales the tide backward where it paused self-gathered;
Mutterings endless the salt wound of Being
      Sutured by dolphins.

Hold in vision windbreaks and winter jasmine;
As for these eyes only by your responding
Whether some Welsh chine is to take its colour
      Into remembrance.

I cannot show you any further legend
Than of our marvellously entertaining
Chastity; our lives' instrumental voyage
      Winning remission.

When the hands touch trust me to apprehend this.
So young so untried it had best be instinct.
I should call impulse comprehension's talon.
      Well may it strike us

In effect here, now, far-off, predetermined;
Freely like mere providence. It is not our
Grief devalues clamant eternals. I am
      Sick of this dying

Time that bends so beautifully around things;
Justice named sum total of ev'ry virtue.
Mia cara, how well you held account of
      Seabird and shadow.

X

No, not wrong bride, wronged was the word first thought of.
Comedy's plight ready to corpse unbidden.
Scope for tragic himmelfarb, things by Fordie
    (Take *The Good Soldier*),

Meredith's prized watchmaker's monocle. True,
This is but how comedy piques narration;
Noble lives pre-eminently disordered.
      How do you read me?

So far so granting, as finesse of prankdom,
Incompatibilities new-devoted;
Gifts declaimed here, taxing prorata nuptials,
     Virginal, blindly.

Failing true faith yet one may have contrition.
It is your face, none other self about me;
Something registered in imagination
     Factored by edits.

How that elm heatstruck shall appear shade-wrangled;
Stay so ringdove; croon the horizon vaguer.
Lyric exstase traded against possessing.
     Spare me prediction;

Spare me long lifestyles of ungrieving godheads;
Eros no blessing nor the masque of Iris.
Where as time shakes down clarimote and sunfleck
     Choose to be lucky.

XI

Like a regal pardon begin the film now.
How pathetically the world is breathing,
Haunts with blue creased face unresponsive planets
      Cast for survival.

Recognition turning upon cognition,
Fictive played-out ghosts of the Leonati,
Passive agon gravity's apatheia
      Held by momentum.

Bifold lamentation embarked on lamely.
This is some doing, soul of late embarking.
Since I've used graph-paper, we may resolve these
      Things or again not.

Animation limning on film directly,
Synchronizing music as you were once taught—
Other self (Poland or the Czech Republic)—
      All that's beyond me.

Calculating ethos an occupation
Not for chemists nor for astronomers; for
Those behind state-theatre I would reckon,
      Hazards a-plenty.

Wise to have help. Where these ideas come from
Uranus knows or some erratic cyclic
State-of-art project with the radio-fields
      Draining hoped aeons.

XII

Extraordinary the common parley;
Reunited, endless the separation.
Tommy bronze-putteed in his place attendant
    Daubed with a green clay.

Signifiers casting small exhibitions,
Midday-lit moon stooping her own late relict;
Things else mildly brandish their presence, bugle
    Sounding the silence.

Pause in clock-time veterans who at call stand
Manifestly natty, well-hackled, their horse-
Collared poppies heaped on the barricaded
    Child-steps of mourning.

Theirs *the fourth dimension of understanding*—
Man who saw that signing his peace with otters.
Inconclusive what had been fought and died for
    In a far season.

Spurn day's arrow whatever god so bent you.
Morphic resonance in an instant self-found;
Being so bodied yet to have this glancing
    Apotheosis

As of bare hedges as of fields awash, light
Clouds I call grey-coppery early mornings
Fused with sun-shot fog and the grassblades crispy
    Barely-heard tinsel.

XIII

Boreal, light-loaded, incorrigible
Plutocratic anarchy breaks the archons.
Little praised here more adamantine than those
    Clapped into durance.

Herod rants; pageants on their wooden tractions
Cannot hold him. Now he is in the shambles,
Butchers Row. Come back, you old wakeman, watch us
    Cartwheel to ruin.

Terms at law viz *Tragedy Anticommons*:
Tudor statecraft sounds only half as stately.
Interludes they acted in fiery winter,
    Heywood and Medwall.

So then tell us, what inspiration sets I-
magination back on its heels of rancour?
Inner cells where rigged Politeia barters
    Cash-back rack-victims,

Shall they break us twice in unbroken cycle,
Lords of our time, losers of others' livings,
Negative life equity left our children
    With a bone ploughshare?

Who are these restless in the darkened kingdom?
Apprehension, memory, clamour spectral.
Turn in conned sleep, murmurous vexing nation,
    Now and regardless.

XIV

Integer vitae yet can't disembarrass,
Maugre your good self, from a span so meted.
How I thus brooded is this sum of wastage
    Lavished against time.

Rattus rattus feasts off bamboos that blossom
Broadly each half century, cosset black plague,
North or northeast India, some place far-trekked
    Draggle of beer cans.

Esperanto tract on the Lisbon earthquake.
Call for plain English or dub Latin endings.
Plug of three gems blind in the gravelled metrum,
    Rubied toad's canker.

Passiveness let gather that Graf von Moltke
Said by some pundits to have scuppered Schlieffen.
Tubular Bells, Liberty Ships faith-building
    Lindisfarne Gospels.

Who can dodge consequence is maestro. There goes
Africa's best promise of back-projection:
Dead balloonists over the Niger Delta
    Skywriting *Freedom*.

Right as you bear griefs you may here assuage them,
All in good faith, let me approve the prophets
Zephaniah, Benjamin Zephaniah,
    Sting singing Dowland.

XV

Glowing fresco journeys define our judgement
Who at leisure wander across the Magi
With their snoot slaves, haut heavy-lidded camels,
    Keeping the star straight.

Logics purport twisted to sport of purpose,
One dimension ruled out by deep perspective,
Lost equation mourned; our unequal shadow
    Blessing perfection.

Permutations wrung in excess of challenge
Let appeal now each too-aggrieving verdict;
In between sentences to find our freedom
    Given the finger.

Coleridge held Scotus from the Land of Logic,
Dreamed for him some sensual congress. Guiltless
We are not, if reparable the vision.
    So there you have me.

Solipsism which was once high-debated,
Bradley's lampblack scuttery gusts and spectral:
He might well tease anyone, edge salvation
    Over the marker.

Apt, grotesque, free-run predetermined spirit
Win mispride its eminent categories;
Fancying Pisa's decommissioned cages
    Ornate with vine stems.

XVI

Such egregious sponsors of fame, post-*Georgics*
All in line here. They should have known *Quaderni*
Stands as book six mastered and still replaying
    Gramsci in Hades.

What is progress asked Mussolini, not in
Those precise words, nor I would guess in earnest.
He had men well-stationed in laws attend him;
    Blooded the harrow.

Blazoned EP also sent in credentials.
I could hold sound arguments, credit bêtises,
Centos-worth late lyrical fine fiasco
    Clipped out of logic,

Found in error, forced to a substitution,
Do it smartly, blushing without self-pity.
Can you do that? Use a beginners' pencil's
    India-rubber?

Deem of laws excising the wicked poet.
Through which process, or by what form of trial,
Pound attained his rôle as the grillo's compère
    Preach at self-hazard.

Gramsci scribed his will as a dead man risen,
Veins of durance granted to certain spirits.
Cancel Hades; write *purgatorially*
    Tried the assayer.

XVII

Time now beating back more than it delivers.
We are in deeper than good will would take us;
Psychic cri goes critical as psychosis
        Gives with the motley.

Face of such woes grins elegiac triumph.
We are all born premature thing built bloody;
Nine months more might better equip this labour
        Strange to our bodies.

Labour that point, I would so have it carried.
You may well stumble and the act define you.
Something found there, rise up and be of substance,
        Splendida verba.

That we do gamble and that who accepts may
Call us on it: words as their own tribunal,
Stelae shown hallowed by the goddess Justice
        Thought but a fiction:

If so, fiction stands to the Troyan Virgil
Epic threnos crying inconstant tribute;
Snarled with more than common devotion; broken,
        Bloodied, bewailing.

Thus for Priam gorgeously shaken. As rage
So with age, both, wreathed in his spectral armour;
That the severed image defies extinction
        Gives me the shivers.

XVIII

Much too much flair crediting party favours;
We are not Israel nor a spillaged sheikhdom.
As for war-aid well I recall those fifty
    Spavined destroyers.

Cakewalk dancers gape-grinning nine days' wonder,
Not that I catch evidence they were ever
Cursed by rabid Yahweh's unplugged creation
    Foully befoundered.

Cold campagna, Tuscan, rain-lacerated.
Lacking combat readiness black detachments
Spent themselves downgraded to road repair gangs—
    Check against sources.

Ponderous with mortal fragilities, twitched
Sherman turrets cluttered by vineyard rubble.
Reconnoitre *poor* for a term of sorrows'
    Impedimenta,

As in *poor Karl* whichever side he fought for.
How to mark this simply by telling stories;
Better than where bloody arbitrement meets
    Raw arbitration?

Like a common amnesty fix affrontage
That the soldiers volley sky-tilting rifles;
That the high grave Fortresses yet may go down
    Trailing their long screams.

XIX

Carmen saeculare I might have called this;
Now am too far in. In a way much better
Done as not doting on mellifluousness.
      You know me better.

Must I conjure augur to rest with anger?
Give me plain text choruses, then, *The Suppliant
Women*. That will do very well for now, its
      Obvious music.

Ever grief concedes what was so makes distant.
Youngsters dead, dead city could not protect. Where
Hatred sleeps in peace let the dream decide its
      Live entertainment.

Had we stood poised briefly beneath the high roof,
Both in fleshed sequins, I with my Walt whiskers,
I could vaunt how leaping becomes incumbent
      Slow strangulation.

There is our message notwithstanding stout Hulme's
More heroic system, his *tragic values*.
Adequate sheer freethinking Tory spat felled—
      Grandslam Hun stunner.

Word tag world; trick how not to die encumbered,
Endlessly challenging immortal spirits;
Shock confession seeing how unremembrant
      Time shall avail us.

XX

Surely much moved, even by chance conjunction,
All declamatory emotion scoring,
Explications forming upon a process
    Metric makes gnomic.

At the book fair, having found *Phoenix*, looks up
Yet does not cry fire. On the convex skylight
Fat birds prom'nade possibly magnified but
    Fail to endow much.

Do but mark chances, how they mate procedure;
Noman crawls forth, bloodied, the trench in Homer;
We have seen transfixed by the arcs Mephisto's
    Mortified prowess.

Diligence too might be a shade alarmist
Exorcizing trouvailles, if festal-bonded
Fate's proceedings wrought, like the anvil chorus,
    Festspielhaus turnage.

Vulgar Corpus clock with its nasty locust
Sybaritic public consumption warrants,
Synchronization that replaces order
    Not for a second;

While in wintry Stockholm the sun rehearsing
Celebrates your golden hexameters, en-
dows my cricked sapphics with immeasurable
    Natural reason.

XXI

Land of Logic, self of illogic later;
Nor become sated with a bane of stricture;
Origen unmanned and the robot surgeon
　　　Twisting his lasers.

All in all V Mary did not enjoy great
Gabriel, although the tall wings inspired her
Welch ein gruss ist das as a quantum made in
　　　Time her condition.

Begging still her pardon I here accept all
Necessary mysteries, barring one sleight
Which I will not stomach for so it beggars
　　　Matrix of substance;

So to brand postures as to be unfearful.
Nothing burneth there but self will says Boehme.
Dante yet names Brutus Iscariot hell's
　　　Fecal impaction.

Forceps tease judgement to finesse with mercy.
Such the free topoi absolution's finis.
Count galactic neo-Averroism
　　　Ready for uplift.

Reconcile old failures to new assumptions;
Sacrifice won selfhood to that which makes us.
Total strangers think they are in our prayers,
　　　Can you believe it?

XXII

Time's remittance. Linacre, Lupset, Starkey,
Commonweal censors, not Utopians though
Men of More's circle. Woe my ploy of speaking,
        What have you wrought me?

So to claim these shards of a formal vantage,
Snapping back, wind-warping the daffodils' frame;
Whiteish new-drawn shreds of a grafted tenure
        Held to be forfeit

Then let go. Dorset, the striated cliffs of
Multicoloured sandstone and sand raw-weathered;
Pembrokeshire swaying on its rooted tide-wrack;
        Still life-befathomed

Anglian sea-beaches in winter strewn; bare
Midland acres haunted by blighted elm-wraiths;
Woods yet thriving lapped in an intricate still
        Tumult of ivy:

These to yield grudging as withholding plenty.
Name forbearance heir to some stricken dictum.
Here extend comb-rhombing, the Lenten prayer wheel's
        Turn of reprisal—

See above—retaxing the sullen cognate
Celibate nation far as faith will take it.
Infinite time (seemed) to rehearse at leisure
        Grasping our portion.

XXIII

Stranger these years, say you consented sleeping.
Even dead ears perk when the gist is this bad.
Peace to fierce claims; maybe there is a balm in
    Gilead, sister;

Something like; some trace that's more manna maybe;
No more no less common complaisance huddled;
Sign that one bleeds faith in symbolic numbers;
    Practise provision.

If this *soul*, much good may it do my phantom:
You who look not anyplace much for torment.
Nor I so like demi-divine Adonis
    Born of a myrrh tree.

Cradle-blessed lone children to twinned redemption,
Let me not fear saecular rites dismembered.
All to come, sweet mother of our redeemer
    Virgine bella.

You may be still waiting against the summons,
Something wrought more telling than melopoeia.
Thousand sighs turn graphite from such a patience,
    Ambered the thorn-ends.

Winter-clogged bushes as the sun arises,
Cresting those flash webs as they slant abristle,
Stipulate on-line resurrection. This clicks—
    Damn—is for ever.

XXIV

What is far hence led to the den of making
Moves unlike wildfire; not so simple-happy
Ploughman hammers ploughshare, his *durum dentem*
    Digging the *Georgics*.

Vision loads landscape, lauds Idoto Mater
Bearing up sacrally so graced with bodies,
Voids the challenge how far from Igboland great-
    Stallioned Argos.

Vehemencies minus the ripe arraignment
Clapper this art; taken to heart the fiction.
What are those harsh cryings astrew the marshes?
    Weep not to hear them.

Accolade Muses' dithyrambics far-fraught;
Borrowed labour ashen with sullen harrow;
Cruel past that Sidney and vesperal Tom
    Campion courted.

Put to claim, not otherwise vowed, the era.
What else here goes I am no Igbo wit well
Versed in Virgil, Pindar, Euripides, child-
    Hallowed Idoto.

Revelation blessed in its unforthcoming,
Closed with *tempus aedificandi tempus*
Destruendi, bringing discharge of measure,
    Blasting the home-straight.

XXV

Lovelace, there come difficult times between us,
Though in your place I cannot well imagine
Why I should not follow her chequered steps in-
      Out of the sunlight.

Candlelight here given the invocation,
Starlit even. Whatever else is silence
Gratiana somewhere still she is dancing
      Dancing⌢and⌢singing

Singing not her heart out beyond the fable,
Grand carotid arteries self-fulfilling.
How the blood's tempered in its modulation
      Balanced impulsive.

So are our storms trackered from solemn orbit,
Turbulence granted our sequestered sphere, now
Buffetted, now spun on an awl, now baffled,
      Wreathed in cloud-garlands.

Masques do so challenge and compose to labour;
Hers the masque-like venture, the scenes mechanic.
Stars have held being since creation's fourth day
      Turned to their music.

Noble her frame, troubling the fame we yield her;
All rites well done short of a consummation;
Treading down nothingness to ever-dealing
      Maker unmonstrant.

XXVI

Łodz: I've been there, done that. The vanished children.
Klezmer makes glad music at Lazarus' gate.
If as straggling voices the dead return now
    They have our number.

Breathing hard we wrestled asbestos brake-pads;
Luminously radioactive watches
Fizzled green plaque riding elastic wrist-bands;
    Glue smelt of peardrops.

Someone those taut days was predicting biros.
Not my blubbered Jewish pal, bright, a bully.
That we knew klezmer I much doubt, the *Wedding
    Dance for the Old Men.*

Time released me from him as I could not have.
Many then had foresight but I was not one.
Vital spinners counting, there's no subtraction
    Ever can oust them.

Odds are on pittance where redemption strands us,
Debts of those long-dead sparks of phantom brain cells.
Who's to dance *broyges tants* the dance of anger's
    Conciliation?

There is no known voice but a clarinet sounds
Almost human touting a melt to die for.
Hurl of things fastbound the last-known survivors'
    Wailed diminution.

XXVII

Breathe on my nesh eyes as upon a glass this
Something so exquisite I scarce can bear it.
I do not think solely I could have borne it
        If not for real.

Make estrangement all our desires that age so;
Perfect empowerment the imperfection;
How indemnify a degraded legend
        Lost to computing?

Contumacious that I am and that now, like
Poggio, I too much enjoy invective,
This for our good. So what you saw me turned on?
        Mind if I stress this?

Breathe on my nesh eyes, I am tired of sleeping.
Largo ma non troppo affettuoso
Well becomes fierce *Didone trionfante*;
        Lyric oblation

As fantastic here as in those odd films we
Watched, albeit singly, *The Tales of Hoffmann.*
What we must be not to be worked with mirrors,
        Hives of perspective.

Could I have found you in a film by Ophüls,
Silent resonances of glass configured,
Had I but struck us off *The Masque of Blackness*
        As it was playing.

XXVIII

Broken that first kiss by the race to shelter,
Scratchy brisk rain irritable as tinder;
Hearing light thrum faintly the chords of laurel
  Taller than we were.

Fear to have already the direst choosing,
Sixty years spent as by procrastination.
Answer one question, this is all I need, so
  Speeding denial.

Ancient question haunting the Platonist: can
Spirit ransom body, and if so could I
Rise again in presence of your devoting
  Sorrow to sorrow?

Quick, is love's truth seriously immortal?
Would you might think so and not be this other
Finally known only through affirmation's
  Failing induction.

What though, wedded, we would have had annulment's
Consummation early, and though in darkness
I could see that glimmerous rim of folly
  Lave our condition,

Had we not so stumbled on grace betimely
In that chanced day brief as the sun's arising
Preternaturally without a shadow
  Cast in its presence.

XXIX

Plug in random volts to precision's language;
There remains folly if you take my meaning.
Do you right now, face of tribunal, charged with
    Strict contrapunctus?

Senex Pound's here-valent refusals no more
Vanities than Plato's tendentious troping.
Soul's perusal, eyes of discernment long since
    Hazy in focus.

So much here well turned as to meaning *act now*,
Truth's uncomely witness in things most proper.
There are few that lucky; if you should count them
    Sign the occasion.

Briefed at hazard scamble the brittle crystal
Bough from saltmine Stendhal has made so much of.
Titan arum's rotten Sumatran splendour
    Passion of substance.

Silicon meltdowns freeze communication
Rabelais forecast in his mute phonetics.
Find poetics' entrails exposed as at the
    Pompidou Centre.

Reinstatement held to recuse this statement:
Ignorance, madness, being springs of action.
Cannot you hear yourself as I can saying
    Yes I would burn books?

XXX

Well so maybe Rembrandt's *The Polish Rider*
Probably not Polish, not Rembrandt even.
Pity each stricken reassignment, *Polska*
    Non Rediviva.

Right, if this be so, what would I inscribe else
Souls to God, bones cast to Cassino's keeping?
Casualty picks out our lives, and none more
    Sorry than I am.

Plucky short straw, how does one do it, die so,
Lie there, graces case-winged at blind disposal?
Purgatory's pain unimaginable
    Dante imagined.

Trust that signal luck is first blood in combat.
Things are not sold simple beyond the chaos.
Knock again, old embusqué sweat's confession,
    Not for the last time.

Shoddinesses, meanness of stock betrayal,
Must I pump more stresses as you command me?
Even so extortion demands one station
    Further than dying.

Multi-voiced rumours of the Cave confound us.
Name me one classic that can do them justice.
Round and round we go as in Gertler's painting
    Riding on seizure.

XXXI

Ghelderode's price here or the cost of Ensor.
Bloated Eros, your pain-extended body,
Jerked abroad scar-angry, a coarse cadaver
        Wired to a fine art.

Google my old blind of Platonics with Mc-
Taggart's mystic corpulence deemed endearing.
Sentiment grown wholly at one with logic,
        Durance feints passes.

Nobbled rhetor cleared but as aberration,
Scarcely gauge what skin I would have you shed here.
Rhetor not slave killer with net and trident
        Though it could well be.

So Petrarca, *prego Madonna prego*;
Wear dark glasses we must protect the sun. This
When in some sense naked desire's upon us
        Let us defer to.

Beggars' clay bowls ample for what was given;
I remember also Tagore's ecstatic
Mornings, all that rhapsody tuned by rapt strings,
        Shantineketan.

Given your pledge I would commute to service.
Vessels once fit only for salvage bear my,
Our, libations fructile towards the altar
        Stone of this strophe.

XXXII

Easter swoops down; flames and ejaculations
Sign in hazardous. I am good for nothing
Else these days than making of wings and altars
          Love's hieroglyphics:

Blowy fieldbanks haggarded with narcissi,
Fells that change colour as the sunlight strengthens.
Dread the now done with to be out of hearing.
          Endless field a'ves,

Mounds of slow build, flashers of brash arrival,
Telling what message if not resurrection,
Your squat upthrusts, cog-casquing dandelion,
          Serried in trespass.

Dead connections made to apotheosis,
Once our unaccountable visionary
Time is judged discounted way out of series,
          Marked down to error.

Not to charge gaunt seraph for vexed reception,
Rule of free will freedom irrevocable.
Watched salvation's voyager cone alighting
          Briefly on Pendle.

Cast in their own sakes, let be blackthorn, whitethorn,
Branches fisting twigtight new-knuckled well-stubbed
Starry!—Purcell's burgeoning bass chaconies
          Stressed and in order.

XXXIII

Girls who read too much shall decline stoop shouldered,
En plein air claustral; so their deaths mishandled,
Brought to bed finally; of love's castration
    Virgins defiant.

Unbeseemly, Fenimore Cooper's grandniece;
Death in Venice. Too lately shocked, a frantic
Henry James there dollied her logged ballooning
    Skirts in trashed water.

Mate these facets, there would have been no bridal.
Olives munitioning a trim estate, black
Figs that taste though faintly of anaesthetic
    Fleshed on your own tree.

What is set down duly to be imagined
Recollects itself a precise dry runner.
Who remarked that day on the vaporetto's
    Running behind time?

There are brief seasons to have things eternal;
Death your mentor. Amherst vociferously
Wrangles words down. Who is that stubborn spinster
    Hand to her throat lace?

Bounty postpartum as it were unwritten,
Rich in those others let me herewith cite you,
Sheathed in black pearls miscegenation brimming,
    Silvered, exultant.

XXXIV

Outmanoeuvered, why so exactly bond with
Things triumphal? I shall have more to say there.
Night is rising bringing a moon upon it
    Proper to omens.

If I do not mourn what is my rejoicing?
If I do not greatly lament him then whom?
Do the dead take innocence up by dying?
    Ask me another.

In the bunkers they are designing new towns:
Whisky flask here, so, on display the in-stock
Biscuit tin grandees with their wines and velvets;
    Finished by Christmas.

Forfeit your next leave if you cannot name them,
Legend-planted almost undreamt-of flowers
Leaching schlachtfelds, long-buried rust blotch-reddened,
    Strange to their species.

Masaryk, wizard, whom Kokoschka sainted,
Wish them not ill, heirs to misfestive folly.
Raised full glasses, broke them against the firestep,
    Dreading such children.

Given what credit can be held for valour,
Give no quarter. Paucity's commons granted
Heroes incumbent, so make miscreant lords
    Lords of creation.

XXXV

Conscript fathers, hell-bent from wars returning,
Ninety years gone here to redress the summons.
These were not nothing though you would not count on
    Teaspoons from Flanders.

Jokers' four black starshells to scatter *Cease Fire*;
Spectral bubbles bursting Cimmerian pitch;
Branded, quenchless, berthed-upon, sodden, minding,
    Sense-bereaved transports.

Whom should I feature in sick reparation:
Undeciphered vivid yet photophobic
Shattered ampullae minds reset as jigsawed
    Charity's option?

Into scrap language unpredicted landscape;
Passchendaele's chill mud at a gulp engorging
Men and redhot rashers of sizzling metal;
    Cheers of the Spartans.

Suppliants all. Shattered the virgin branches,
These so ancient latterly, trunks disrooted.
Chariots, no close ups and hope no bloody
    Wheels going backwards.

Fought to distraction, griefs the cult non-juring;
Due observance, hardwrought imaginations
Crying *O our great threnodist is dead no*
    Way he could swing it.

XXXVI

Righteousness self-wronging as if by edict.
Todesfuge not in your gift of proxy.
This as near murder as I mean to bring us,
        Rabbi of Hillel.

How such things bite home I shall re-examine;
Panzer newsreels vectoring shtetled Russia;
Every house ash, with the black-bricked chimneys
        Stiff as a forest.

Hopeless I vamp Hebrew and name the hidden
Name of God; arch characters moving much like
Tolle lege, pricking the Scroll. Thus *La'med*
        Late have I sought you,

Half-believing that, at the sound of Yiddish,
Klezmer or folk poetry, long demolished
Iron bridges clamped over backstreet inlets
        Tremor to footfalls.

Israel found in its goliath's armour,
Even such mystical transfiguration
(Terror's own concept parenthetical State
        Striking the instant).

Yes: that I mourn as now her wasted prophets,
Broken features mended in slack succession.
Lyric after lyric, I think I wrote these
        Or something like them.

XXXVII

Cromwell's axe-exeat exact yet not neat.
Wyatt slipped his luck to a falcon's shadow.
Witticisms' knell, you could say he hears it,
    Likely in earnest,

Through his own paean to the toppled column
Though Petrarca punned on that name more roundly.
Endless invention are you saying *why have*
    Endless invention?

Yeats with his clangour of despotic beauty,
Pound's destructive matrix, creative hatred,
Stevens circumstancing that blockish rider:
    Just as it takes them

On indictment; grunted our comprehension.
Time is not kept here for us; brands our making;
Shifts our closures; rotes a surveillance breved in
    Final graffiti

Though perhaps not then, even, making great sense.
Let the inconsistencies pull together,
Breakup being nerve of induction, both toc-
    cata and spieltrieb.

We will wing it, working through all the forms now,
Shedding excellencies like moulting angels:
Nitro Glisserinski the anarchist with
    Nitra his daughter.

XXXVIII

Versifier called to divine transmission,
Work your will but let there be no mistake here.
Courtesy fields Clarendon's *dirty people*,
        People of no name.

Moved to make protest I protest its presence:
Should have been mine, freely subvented cuts a
Tranche from ur-zeitgeist; you can quote me; file with
        Misattributions.

It is not entirely an understanding
Calls up potent, ill-endowed, medieval
Style: Fortuna bringing midwinter thunder's
        Luck to the hovels.

Have you not said somewhere within my speech-range
Fabulous sprite weds animality; long
Wounded our mundanities. What is best done
        Short of forgiveness

Spares acquittals gist of noncompensation.
Practical wisdom is a world unbridled.
What you damn well care then bestowing credence?
        What does it matter,

Beneficiary of what late bestowal,
One whose father, while he was yet afar off,
Ran, received him joyfully, who is nameless
        Given that greeting?

XXXIX

Exponential surplus of illth the actors,
As the days shorten through insidious summer,
Practise throat-cutting for the rites of Timon.
      Do you mean Titus?

No, I mean Timon the misanthropist who
Speaks his best, late, beautifully; exacting
Quivering cadences he brought so far, mis-
      spoken remembrance.

Generous small mouth is as if past praying;
Massive those turbines of a salt invective;
Could I so bear witness and yet survive the
      Rift of my chagrin.

Plutocratic anarchy call it, taxing
All that one has: things in themselves devoted;
Surging obsolescence (our battle cruisers
      Buried untimely);

Sentimentalities of splayed resistance,
Not of my making, fit for ravens' garbage;
Rhetoric, my indigent termination
      Rich once in Athens.

Things well laboured gaze us to subjugation,
Things that one hears of like the violinist's
Neck and chin bleeding from an all-extorting
      Final cadenza.

XL

Betws-y-Coed, dullish red glow Swiss-chasmed,
Myriad-black-faceted Blaenau gaping;
Senile grins, galls, humbles our greed. So fancy
         Senile in Bala?

Squatting Brummies' sullen mood synthesizers;
Adelina Patti who gargled Welsh airs;
Where should one brood *Parsifal* but in wild Wales?
         Sinister Grail-talk.

Your guess what twists us so rightwing and dotty.
Europe's secrets not safe with Sanskrit; even
Gwalia hostage to insatiable
         Swoln rhododendrons.

Goldengrove notebooks ripped for late bequeathing;
Dyscrasy Publike its own gifts to plunder;
Hazardings unscathed by the harsh alignments
         Made for survival.

Make believe Merz might be collage of rip-offs.
Bless the mute, parlous for our safe bestowings.
Meteor showers sign expropriation.
         Cypress's roof-tree:

Hendre Fechan, hearth of our hearts' indwelling,
Giving song hearth-room and the harp's thrilled diction,
Deep penillion woven to snow's curled measures
         Heard past unhearing.

XLI

God who holds our memories reft at pre-birth,
I would trust, intended their restitution.
Sense them sometimes vibrant in music's ratios
    Tighten the grammar.

Harry said once, one myth conceives a lifetime.
Long his own time-mythist, the seventeen arched
Accrington Town viaduct wired immortal
    Even in passing.

Lamentation's triumph, rejoicing Orpheus:
His detached head that can be tuned to pleasure.
Speculate these opera cast the shades by
    Lucent obstruction.

(Strange to each other in that intimacy
Purgatory, even, can learn to weep at.
Paolo I am not nor are you Francesca;
    No such temptation.)

This is no rare dogma confiding why such
Acts encrypt endings. Let us reap the darkness,
Take to ourselves limping Eurydice's cry
    New to abandon.

Lunar fallibilities, eyes adjusting;
I do not grasp half of what I would tell. No
Tragedy no triumph. A bulging moonface
    Tops the horizon.

XLII

Herein public dyscracy given notice
Not by mere non-jurors. Take Common Law Coke,
Held too great an oracle with the People.
   England could bear him.

Ignorance beats innocence through the checkpoint.
Many sit unsaved; should I claim exemption?
Many lose wagers with themselves as stake-out,
   Bugger *what fettle.*

Noble lines, pre-eminently disordered;
How the hierarchies overshot their runways.
I have had savant say *monarchical re-*
   public befell us.

Obligation's challenger unjust right, old
Triumph wired *no triumph no tragedy.* De-
mystification of our Lords and Commons
   Contra naturam.

I would not offload to malignant spheroids;
Fate v choice grudging, we persist and so on.
Uningratiatingly light revisits
   Rimming the re-scars.

Ancientry booms if you are Norfolk freehold:
Bracken-guarded airfields where now the pigeons
Ponderous, wingladen, in near-botched take-offs,
   Rattle the spinneys.

XLIII

Lucrative failing no poor oxymoron.
Gravely highlight solo polyphony, this
Shagged ur-pragmatism of standup comics
    Working rejection.

Not at all like self-harmers, much more like the
Scorpion Ibsen, my reputed master,
Plied with sick fruit there to transplant its venom;
    Each to his hobby.

Targeted late laurels, a full thesaurus,
Whom could you grudge crowned with essential honours?
Time's observance, high-wrought imagination's
    Body of nerve ends,

May appear humdrum till the planes touch combat:
Stand-in tall comrade siphons Fritz off your tail,
Vibrant fabrics twanging to fatal eye-flash
    Flamers of spirit.

Snap of our poised loves in the breaking consort,
Vibrancies signed for by archaic plectrum,
Hallelujah stripped off the strapping harp strings,
    Orpheus in passage.

What is *just reach* apropos just surviving?
Spell me war's haulage of forgotten ensigns;
Torque me Sopwith Camel around its prop-shaft
    Spinning the pilot.

XLIV

This had best be set as an intermezzo.
Prettily scarsilvered the cuffs that grow round
Stumps of lopped branches, that are seen in winter,
     Beauty inclement.

How to praise rightly or to prize you; even
Beg the folk verb *uncomfort*; none shall thee un-
comfort. As it might be in some sought language
     I should have known you.

Half-stripped altars, these I have troubled lately.
I would not quota to the lengths that some do,
Casting back light's verification darkly
     Into the spectrum.

Move the registrar, the domain eludes him.
Undisclosed clairvoyance of apperception
All around: church towers and silos catching
     Shafts of the broad day;

Mistletoe's globules and conglomerations
Sealing boughs waxen with rich-cupped meniscus;
Gilding bare orchards by the moon's endowment
     Even at sunrise.

Sacrosanct life which is so held in prospect,
Dispossessed inestimable regard, such
Years to accomplish sent astray one morning
     By misadventure.

XLV

Here at full noon only endormant cloudscapes,
Active curtailed nerves of the earth-scarps braded,
Flense of some late glacier's vanished keel yet
    Cutting between them.

Sunning, selfblazoned, the great gorse conclamant
Rakes and reivers barrens; rebuilds burnt acres.
What requires my heart to acclaim its own well
    Set in the vistas?

If on some raw tangent I yet outlive you,
Late eccentric (why must we seem so formal?),
Begging something you had once said, *old age is*
    Not for the squeamish.

Once and always this is the merest memo.
I do not see us reabsorbed in nature.
Would you start back if I revamped this saying
    Very well show me?

This is what I signed for—*musicien français*
But in English—as when that time-eliding
Brief rhapsodic lento begins Debussy's
    Cello Sonata.

Throps a buzzard, lazily photographs his
Aerial scenics. Be a fool and say so:
Adamantine age set to melt in flames of
    Absolute longing.

XLVI

Stayed with you know what, at the quired committal,
Catching that moment which defines the whole man.
Formidable then your disruptive tenor,
      Laughter presiding.

Sometime screen formalities best unscripted;
Valediction *cum privilegio*, his
Feces his worst enemy. Well you could not
      Lightly speak fairer.

Clapped with judged equals to defray the judgement,
On repeal *Cena de le Ceneri*. The
Feast of ashes some will cry cold-collated
      Talk of things flagrant.

Also in some deeper sense crafting us mute
(Not that black Esau shrinks like one belittled).
Shall true comics adequately return us
      Evil for evil?

Moving oddly as the procession takes them,
Fix one donor-gifted interpretation.
Something portrayed thus, discomposed the victor,
      Where is the trophy?

As to conception, what presaged this knowledge,
Made me so happy, or which cunning agent
Levered dire presswork seeding text with savage(d)
      Variant readings?

XLVII

Since by death came sexual death's erection,
Let the hung-up accolade just suffice it.
Do not now play too much for love the four-horned
    Lyre of betrayal.

Granted fiction's mark we can talk the truth out,
Metaphor's late wardrobe malfunction, granted
We admire its lustrous celebrity hair
    Given the treatment.

When affinities are released to strangeness,
I am not with you in this burthened fable.
Is it so well proven we fell together
    Into deployment,

Neither begging time off for erudition,
Doubting even where we should look for help, not
Mystical Strindberg not Kokoschka with *The*
    Nature of Visions?

Whose interstice is it admits the fine point?
Try that staunch wound-dresser, the wound itself, try
Mastering judgement when the highest prizes
    Fall to hysterics.

Poppies, root-torn, blaze into grand remonstrance:
That is nature reigning obliviously
Though not insentient and in place of labour—
    Ours—for survival.

XLVIII

But imagine, shall I, the mirror broken,
Treading slivers. Pray not to be a sophist.
Nor would you find dramatization fitting
      Such a persona

So to be whipped up out of wax and stylus.
Pardon affectation. The apparitions—
Paper lanterns, paper extinguishers, where
      Flame is observance—

Made by folly's competency imperilled.
Conjured shards dancing on the leather desktop,
Orpen's self portrait in the French hotel room
      Quizzing his helmet

(He was no war man) and the brandy bottle
Concentrated sluttish within reflection;
Peril implicate but not here intrusive.
      There will be shadows.

Granted they hold firm to eluding virtue
Codifications volunteer perspectives,
Mathematics' figures predestinated
      Infinite regress.

Something sprung here that you may yet recoil from.
Stick with hazardous enigmatic fractured
Metaphysics' laboured accommodation
      Unrecommended.

XLIX

Rapt elation made of a shuffled stepdance;
Duff bodhrán's bull measure on stinging denim;
Concertina doubling-up fiddles' dummy,
        Glasstight black porter.

Shall all there step back or aside from that stark
Ramified stomp, drunken intently sober,
Densely mortal so that there may outpace us
        Death to be honest.

Make reply, tell troping a trial motive;
Formal speech-urge narrative fed through symbol;
Scatheless grief, star dancer across crisp cinders,
        Leaping the mickey.

Let me hear praised eloquence better dispraised.
Stupefaction, show how the act creates us;
Draws to new cadence, though the news is ancient
        Lachrimae rerum.

Set to stand thus, so much now past achievement,
Unprocessioned, made in despite this measure.
What price whose dance? Would I had told you later,
        Language disturbs things;

Treats with faith found ⎸ not so much resurrection;
Adds salvation; chides us beyond all bearing,
Declaration opting its vicious solace
        Fatal in error.

L

Words of three, four, characters, five if reckless,
Serve to keep this stirring alchemic portent.
Union played for in the limbeck's furor,
    Spiritus mundi.

Here be force-fields not all the empyrean's;
Marvel how well primed virtuosos tally
Each with other, brush up from assignations'
    Precious detritus:

Stars are great souls, witnesses Origen. He
Draws them under manifold observation;
Enterprising hope of conception's odd births
    Cosmos-encompassed.

John upon Patmos, high on charts abysmal,
Quick with Torah, trasher of things Chaldean,
Well-endowed credence and with welcome bitters
    Brewing the Sabbath:

I would not plug chance its desire to fail us;
Maybe could hope some less-affronting emblem.
Many prime greetings from the nowise-threatened
    Ars moriendi.

Trials henceforth chiefly of petty spirits,
Smallish late sins mended. Communicate that,
Lord of Fearsome Aspect, as Dante signed his
    Terse apparition.

LI

Name as bond made free with, not franchised. You are?
Let this be, let error be (mine as surely
Willing) sacked self ill-rid of dire empathics
      Sounding corruption.

Arbitration, heard you say. *Arbitration*?
Arbitrage takes out what was ill-invested.
Dowell, Dobet, starkers their right proceeding.
      Get a good mantra.

Finally said, mine is the entertainment.
Charge you maintain justice not meretricious.
If we meet each other in Hell it's not hell.
      You here means him though.

Three stiffs go our separate ways profanely.
When did I last stagger resolved acquaintance?
Such a purgatorial reenactment—
      Fine, no reprisal.

Keep off all tauntings might provoke sad anger.
Pax poetics, murderous, peace-promoting.
What sustains itself by your own admission.
      Tradesmen trade entrance.

Milton spared, scarce heard in the City; Will Blake,
Artisan, broke, Hercules Buildings Lambeth;
Ruskin past master of the keys, his sweet swart
      Labour of Zion.

LII

Not faced death, not been there, not done with dying;
Proven things not salvageable like collage;
Work that takes intelligent patience, but no
      Time now for patience.

Nor Cassandra's only but Laocoön's
Bawling struck Troy barely retaining reason;
Stranded dead-pregnant in the ranks of civics'
      Obdurate clangour.

Any fragment serves for a token fragment.
Fix the new day squaring a cut-price flamen.
Nothing made so clear *per amica*—EI!—*si-*
      lentia lunae.

Time and crosswords, both, yield us topless towers.
Much have pondered, even considered saying,
Always some things human demand of us in-
      human poetics.

Set up quacks' hurdles for ourselves. Does that reft
Oak, at last, graft something to dying? Tolstoy's
Kind of gnomic questioning affirmation
      Like in that long film

That, I think, went on for too long. I woke up
During battles. Tell me a mystery, a
Tale of winter, so I shall love you wisely.
      Wisdom is fable.

THE DAYBOOKS VI

Al Tempo de' Tremuoti

To Michael and Alessandra Griffiths

e vidi il Tempo rimenar tal prede
de' nostri nomi ch'io gli ebbi per nulla . . .

1

A signal pre-election to free choice:
The mother's face foresuffering, the child
Big, almost unmanageably held,
Such attestation in God's passive voice.

The seraphs chime their wings of florid stance.
Things are as strange as need be, never rise
Up from this blur and cleave of centuries;
Grace condescending to things framed in chance.

Humility can afford the brutal
Splendiferousness of those Medici tombs.
Let the brain empty its own catacombs.
For love only one might hazard souls immortal.

Or in alert idleness build a tower
Of Fibonacci numbers where each term
Stands in its self-reflection as the sum
Of those two that precede it: the sunflower

Head is packed with them, and the pine cone,
Odd symmetries holding the mind at gaze
Unlike that solipsism of the maze
Circling the focus of self will alone.

2

Poetry, first born of curiosity,
As Vico says, daughter of Ignorance,
Something stupendous: a divining glance
Stuprate thereafter and void of pity.

The pregnant squalor beautifully told,
The odour now of primed incense, the stable
Of the nativity regrouped in marble,
Even the beastly dung made to shine gold.

Spirit affords matter; it is all one;
You cannot answer fór them. Matter, spirit.
No matter love's brought blindly to inherit
Its mutual sight, here, now, and as soon gone.

Infatuations exorcised too late,
The paradox, the furthest stretch of wrong,
Racked to salvation where it may belong;
Self-judgement judged to be extortionate.

Let her humility pardon the divine
Presumption. This is how it is put,
Presuming on the eloquently mute.
If there's redemption it could well be mine.

3

Eternity's beyond sense failing our cries
(Impacted lines the lives of rhetoric):
Particular instress each marked neural tic,
Tricks of bad light acclaimed epiphanies.

Proclivity attracts a hostile star.
I do not question this, taking as read
The absolute self-travestying of God.
A black madonna screws his avatar.

4

Begotten—and thrust out—with a last cry,
Straightforward anguish, complex the child of man,
Devastated, gobsmacked, over the moon,
Love misdirected to idolatry,

Desire to the miscalling of that word.
O endless tether, unexhausted grace
Found at Assisi or some other place,
Nor made by our credulities absurd.

5

Litter of many Maries in their grame,
Rid of all afterbirths, the mortal toss,
The dirt out of the crib, that firstling loss
So masterfully complicit with our shame.

Painful to write. Painful obscenity
Of the Imagination sensing an entire
Paraclete-rote, earthed its arch-vestal fire,
Venture and vesture of the harlot city.

The Fibonacci shall transform the Cave.
Practise dispassion. I do not believe
Those theologians know what they have.
The Word begets us crying *Fuck!* and *Ave!*

6

Orders of anarchy: what dead Beckett calls
The *Providential fulcrum*. For a joke.
In so far as jokes held to his turn, took
Hold in the dying matter of his cells.

Blank chatterers enriched him. Despair drives
Every which-way. (That apprentice-piece—
Dante and Vico—its inflated price.)
So many of us, fools of our own lives.

7

Darkness is greying as the birds begin
To air their quarrels. *Petra im Rosenhag*
Enters my thoughts unbidden, though I beg
Often enough the pain that I am in

To cease being a pain and more resemble
Some wayward art dense with transparencies,
Petra im Rosenhag, while here it is
Still early light and the light curtains tremble.

8

A genealogy of song: each flaw
Mastered in its own making, to-and-from
The rites of Venus and of Chrysostom.
Happy conjunction for a lyric flow.

Astronomy, astrology, flare in our grasp;
Teologia orfica holds audiences.
The world will die, an ancient cosmos dances,
Unity, duality, riding the cusp,

Lustrum to lustrum, ignorance unforbidding.
Dantean a two-euro. It is not
That we thrive otherwise than by det-
ritus of detritus, further reading.

Suffice the Fall, *pace* those Orphic meadows.
Each mystic good teased out from forfeit. Buy
Some nobler self; invoke ventriloquy.
Plato yet shines, Ficino shadows us.

9

A big tide tilts its camber to the shore
By Orford Ness and the Martello towers;
The sun at random harping with rayed showers;
Curt emanations brief us to endure.

But not that, not that ever again, my love;
Not ever again that dire unconsummate
Business of ours. Poetics tell our fate
The way your fingers picked the thread from a glove.

10

Augustine, Khlebnikov, parting the Red Sea.
New time upleaping to a double wand.
Gehenna shown to be the Promised Land.
Salvation re-rehearsed futurity.

Nihilation of all negatives; hierarchies
Of abandon; polarities annulled;
Syntax delivered and a world respelled;
Anarchy riding it with firecrackers.

The strain is terrible, change will barely keep.
Let Augustine be, and with him the inspired
Self-destitution of the zeal-impaired.
Beneath the *Soliloquia* flails our sleep;

The oracles that Khlebnikov sang his muse:
Whether the gravitational
Mass of Ur-Asia is more than notional;
Whether gravity itself is time's curse;

The constitution of all graphics; what form
Redemption takes, in and around nature.
The *King of Time*, his *radio of the future*,
Our entrée to the sacral, *bim-bam-bom*.

11

I too have been in Tuscany, have stood
Outside the house where Machiavelli wrote
Il Principe and donned his robes of court,
Abrupt with machinations and the good.

Without a crib I'm lost. Best to conjecture
He was a moderate and pious man
Pitched to a world made machiavellian.
I think I comprehend trajectory.

Seneca resonates also around thrones.
While Petrarch's *Love* clangs her triumphal car.
Probe old-new life, oölite and nenuphar.
But say the dread of hell is in our bones.

12

Long before Arno sludge a fouled cleansing.
Donatello made me think Scriptural
In situ: Habakkuk barely raptural,
His stock of prophecy, the stone sensing

Itself maltreated, slain into magnitude.
A prince of God, dole-featured Habakkuk,
Pondering his extraction from the block,
The garb shit-coloured and the head nude.

Here, without warning, meet a half-crazed
Asceticism that imputes its right,
That knows itself abhorrent to our sight,
Sparing no grief for wisdom, but apprised:

The lures of Babylon inure its tongue,
Mouthing the old exordium with new cause,
The laboured wrath that battens on our ease,
Disfiguring beauty it is stood among:

Christ thrashing money-changers from their stalls
Derives his blood. Indeed, the New Zion
Empowers such protestation's ancient kin
And sets the prophet up, stark in its halls.

13

Believe the act of sculpting was itself
Blasphemy, judged by Mosaic law.
Habakkuk judged the blasphemies he saw
As Moses had destroyed the golden calf.

We must pray to be formal: it will serve
Such realism, nerves in the stone skin.
Donatello's guilt, far other than guilt-spin,
Existential before time's pitch and curve.

Whether such figures were conceived in wrath
Or calculation hardly now appears:
Mystical rapture of the engineers,
Divine abstention showing itself as breath.

14

More images at random: this one might
Be late October, a tide smouldering
Back under the wind; a wildering
Of soughed reeds inland combs the light.

Bearing thought is not easy, a destruction
Innate to our substance. Keats' verse letter
To John Reynolds catches against the matter.
More often than not, though, we're blest in fiction,

Turning to fiction to absolve what's true.
And, in between, something, a mood, a fetch—
Melancholy remembrance is it?—which
One great pastoral fancier offers rue.

Imagination, I could give you a name.
It would be hers. What follows I left blank
For several days though desperate to think—
The reeds wind-chivvied, the mud-creeks aflame.

15

Fixed and unfixed time: the endurance of dreams;
Light bending gravity. We shall emerge
Younger than we are now and see the verge
Of first love steadying beyond the farms.

And, down by Pepperwood also, time's haze
Lifting from the tall bracken; something solved
Between us and us two truly beselved.
What did we guess to measure such a prize?

16

I have forgotten who it was supplied
Motus in fine velocior. Movement
Is swifter at the end. Whereby a moment
Inbreathes eternity. But who has died?

As we alone first guessed, velocity
Is itself spirit. Chance to be annulled
Way out beyond Plotinus: self-propelled
The Fibonacci zeroing as they

17

Imagination bringing me your bride:
The *Chamber-Idyll* that configures nothing
I cannot denude further; its reclothing
Always this graphic absence at my side.

How fine they are, the things of grossest hurt—
Coleridge enraptured by his grief would find
In this no more than love in its right mind;
The consummation held and set apart.

18

I can tell you this, though; Poetry's not
Imitation. Parallel worlds may better—
Discontinuities—matter ignites matter—
The mutual abruption: such our thought,

Workable grammar matching thrust to shove.
Syntax as coitus. Call Original Sin
Freedom being what it is (not Wittgenstein
Though something like him). Under and above,

Scattering bright (Donne). Angels and nematodes.
Even if in sex only, one can say
I will and yet my will does not obey.
Augustine's not all right stuck in his codes.

19

There are things here I wish I had not said
Or thought, even. A mythist and so loath
To grasp as real the otherness of breath
I am an old blasphemer and afraid;

Intractability of happenstance
Reduced to final supplication: Mary
Mediatrix, absolve my word-memory
Uprisen in this late self-hallowing trance.

20

The truth—said someone—is a different realm,
Or words to that effect. If this be so
What constitution are they subject to,
And are they judged by theorem or psalm?

Why do I write in front of witnesses?
Show me who else does. Nor is there any pledge
Held sacred at vocabulary's edge,
Nor life governed by mastery of stresses.

21

Quomodo sedet sola civitas—
How Dante loads that cry with glory's toll,
The death of Beatrice, the City's shell,
Zion among its mounds its cavities.

Quomodo sedet—Vulgate Jeremiah.
Donatello also díd hím: savage twin turn,
Damning the tyrants with its mud-mouthed grin,
God's grandeur custody of the pariah.

Gramsci read Dante by the maestro's laws
In carcere, letting the grammar work
His own redemption out of grief and shock;
Fascisti justice like the harpy's claws.

Hail, noblest of feasts, ours at the last day!
Our fetters are struck off, the charged ions
That held us | now as nothing to the aeons.
Even so transfigured our captivity.

22

Donatello's Habakkuk I'd say was wrought
From legends of lost Dante among the folk;
Back of beyond hill-villagers' dread mock,
Old evil eye whatever the glare caught.

As for myself I think I must have dreamed
The fresco of Dante's features, much decayed;
Salts from congested corpse-warrens had flayed
Pigments and plaster both; wiped out the damned.

I think it wíll be ¦ ancient and terrible
Just as the rabbis prayed, *then let him come*
But let me not be living at that time;
Full turnout for the Apocalyptic Bible.

Something still unbetokened, the first star,
Re-born, of the Nativity: Dante's course
Not being Gramsci's—Gramsci's being worse—
The ends of justice being what they are.

23

Alabaster or limewood. See, the dead
Christ like a weary lover in the lap
Of Magdalen, her hand under his nape.
Mortality the burden scarcely shed,

Necessity by miracle made choice,
Perfected here the medium of trial;
The burden of redemption our denial.
Hear how a line lies so lightly on the voice.

24

Of course rage narrows: no enemy
Contracted to formalities. Depletion
Of forces incommensurate with creation.
Conservat omnia turned anomy:

The poet-lawgivers, Solon, Confucius.
Pound with his rectitude and epic blague
Mascot of the reactionary league.
Yeats noble in his grandiose confusions.

Time grants free arbitration for such errors;
Taking from each but giving some their due;
Rebuking and correcting (it's not true
That the Annunciation was worked with mirrors).

We should have been together in the House
On the Fontanka; should have known Mandelstam,
Pushkin and Blok, Akhmatova's mute *Poem*,
Before their worlds collapsed into applause.

25

That wind's heard everywhere—so Pasternak—
Buffeting the Big House, the carriage-ride,
Trees dashed by rain, his poetry—the *'Third*
Book'—*death itself.* A paean for dead Blok.

Blok hailed that storm, its power to overthrow.
He knew in it the coming Nemesis
He so desired and feared and made his verses
Anticipate always with triumphant awe.

26

Across fields where the rye's been whirried down
The horizon's rim stands threatening, abrupt,
Streaked with red as a reaper's skin's raw-striped,
Such consanguinity impels the dawn.

Nature these days, so beautiful, unstable,
Like omens to the state, infects our mood:
Water, iron and rust, a taste like blood,
The river and the swamp, impending fable.

Blok is himself and us, our zigzag courses,
Persistent yet as changeable as weather;
Or as folk still remember his grandfather,
Old Jacobin, the carriage with six horses,

Mad jockey for postilion, the wind
Racing against him on his native heath,
His spirit plain to see, transparent truth,
The grandson holding with him, mind with mind.

Such is the climate that had penetrated
Blok's inmost self in those still-earliest years,
As in the run of things, that now appears
Uncanny gifts at once so free, so fated.

27

So, out of night and chaos, the Latin orator
Addressing himself as to our plight: 'I came
Already late to the benightedness of Rome.'
Yes, true: the nadir, the declining star.

But you watched, rather, the dire grandeur;
Well-steaded, even as you bade farewell
To what had been; saw from the Capitol
The forms of livid glory that would endure.

When the world is in travail he is fortunate
Whose words register | áll that is visited;
A various discourse ranged in that one head;
For such exalted counsels he is not too late;

Nor you, Tyutchev, held by your own words.
Many go crazed on portents; you had mastered
What is immortal ín them, the unwasted;
In spite of, and already with, the gods.

28

Who shall survive and be fêted? Who be judged
Surplus to demand? Speak, sycophants.
Pushkin was overridden by events.
Your dissertations thrive magistral-lodged.

Blok stood impervious to threat or bribe;
One prophet not employed in bearing down
From Sinai the dictator's words of stone.
He gave no law to any client-tribe;

Envisioning his Rus as sacred ground,
Denied by protocols and commissars,
Silenced amid the brazening, the roars
Unending. And obliviously crowned.

29

Some in the stagnant time, that second serfdom,
Had lost all sense of whence they came or how.
We are less fortunate. The lots we drew
Teach us our inexorable freedom:

War hails the masses to their lonely doom.
These fated years; this glare of smelting: now
We see, nor am I blind to what I show,
A multitude, the one delirium.

Birds of ill omen, ravens, their black fiefdom,
Above these wastes appropriately soar.
Our words are dying. Hearts laid bare with sorrow
Some few may hope to find a Heavenly Kingdom.

30

When—if—you brood: how our days are numbered
And also fleeting, and are stalled in dread,
Borne down by introspection, lift your head
And count these graves, Siena's dead unnumbered.

You may well ask, where are the eternal shades?
I answer, here. The Sibylline mouthings
For all their frenzy utter some true things,
Christ's resurrection, his harrowing of the shades.

Bear with what you are given. Given stone,
The sculptor's chisel is our soothsayer.
Live your life well, even when every prayer,
Every prediction, has been turned to stone.

There is such life forgathered on these tombs:
A boy depicted with a bird, a flower.
Here, with his documents, a man of power.
A senex here, crutch-lurching to the tomb.

My soul, be still, even as you strive and love;
Neither urge onward nor yet hold me back.
It will come soon enough, that stark
Encounter ⏐ with the certainty of love.

31

Not much escapes our consoles of attaint
A question, then: did Blok on his one journey
Through Italy, discover in Siena
Lorenzetti's fresco of *Good Government*?

How poets and painters agree the state
Between them, with their images that chime
Like a reflected starscape, is sublime.
Only the duffers are importunate.

Ecco, where some went holy and depraved,
The mystics' void, the dense heresiarchs,
The antimatter of the hierarchies,
The thing abandoned there to be believed.

Ecco, then, the *Commedia*, its vast
Cycles of cosmic howlers: the Guelf
City discarding viciously of itself—
The damned imploded from that civic waste.

Donatello, come back! Say all's forgiven.
Habakkuk, stay put; though I have raked your scroll
For what it will not bear. Ezekiel
Would stay me many years, my bones unshriven.

32

We should talk I suppose about storm
Surges and music. Gets more difficult.
Beauty stemming from the aboriginal fault.
Tardi e gravi in the dolorous room.

Whatever—the harshest—conclusion. Yeats
Writing *The Words Upon the Window-pane*
From rage and pity, Swift and the world's bane,
The heroic mind maddened by its defeats—

Hester Van Homrigh and her beggared womb.
I'll grant you *Anger of the Annunciation.*
The jagged clamour's classical striation.
A clinching eloquence our mouths gone dumb.

33

I have outlived Yeats now. The old man hád
Seen something, well, rhetorically tenable
Between the huge vortex and the little stable,
High tide, tempest, the raging Herod,

Innocents everywhere. The foul Troubles
Mock-countenanced with a Fool's ranty head,
Spurts of *jus primae noctis* . . . Also did
Marching songs for Bluto's blue-chinned rabbles.

Whatever wisdom he wón | róde on the verb:
Slouches—'The Second Coming'—is one such,
The mayhem of his visionary lech
Reduced to tragic grammar, self's recurb.

Reason for writing: to hear a voice cry
Rise and walk, familiar alien call,
With its own absolute pitch, its own fall.
Freedom to fall is our stability.

34

I have read *The King of the Great Clock Tower*,
Dwarf Noh play, séance voiced by drum and gong;
With bonuses of supernatural song;
Uncanny joy delivered on the hour

Like something brutish, relish of foul weather;
Verdictives are the stamp of strategy
Or the unprincipled acting-up, cagy;
Or the state's mystic marriage to the Other:

Something conclusive heard over the wire.
The rhetorics of closure claim their place—
The grand style bayed into so tight a space,
A word the final creature of desire.

35

It's a wild question whether we had or have
A nation disproportionately imagined
Like Pakistan today, its founder margined,
Or Gandhi's India which could never thrive:

Or like the States whose written constitution
Glossed those issues of the people's will
That Whitman brought his commons to fulfil:
Or de Gaulle's France with Péguy out of action:

Ireland as Paddy Pearse conceived of it,
And Yeats projected in that noble coinage,
A dream thrust spinning into our own age
Fanatical and ignorant of profit:

And our late Civill warre: stylish abuse
Like Hobbes on Anarchy, so beautiful
It makes you want to laugh and do things well;
Clarendon's love of Falkland and his House.

Transgression is transition via the world:
The claims of order, lyrical, severe,
Immediacy of right judgement—*here, and here*—
Delivered to the weltering manifold.

And some will fáll | oút of the hands of God.
And others not. Yet others wanly fade
With their own time immoderately made;
Love's truth still unconfigured to accord.

Our greatness is in showing how things go
And stand revealed. The impetus of quantum
Physics may have inspired this phantom.
Mandelstam said we should read Dante so.

36

Throughout her childhood years in Umbria
Brightness shone from the mists, like intimations
Of what is now upon her. In their stations
The roses wore, and wear, the light's penumbra,

A light trembling with bells. So she embroiders
At a small frame, a silk coronet.
Her girl companions are not as quiet;
They are bold, their glances do not avoid ours.

The artist watches, hidden in his fame.
His brush moves—now we shall see it all!—
Crimson clashing with the gold of the wall.
She is held—this turbulence, does it bear a name?

It is a seraph armed with a tall reed
Or perhaps a lily: the paint has darkened
Somewhat since this glory first awakened.
He stoops towards her; fearful, she snaps a thread.

Thus he makes salutation, works possession,
Building his still tabernacle of vibrant wings
Above them both. And now he croons and sings—
(Ah, love! I show the mastery of this passion)—

Dazed, torn, with incredulity and belief,
'Who am I to bear this?' Braids tumble.
She touches her breast; the fingers tremble,
Her lips, with unattributable grief.

Over them, strangely, an heraldic beast,
A griffin rampant, stares out across its prey,
A cruelty of self-will in this display:
Imbrued with fallen nature, some patron's crest.

It is enough. I hear a voice repeat
'Behold the handmaid of the Lord.' In Luke's
Gospel she says this. Our salvation takes.
'Profani procul ite'—it is I who say it.

37

Ars poetica: thís must be seen as.
Strange not to have noticed sooner. Before
Proceeding we shall reassemble here,
Without dramatics, operatic *scenas*.

I have just watched one of the smallest hawks
Rest for a moment in a wittering garden.
This always-noticing becomes a burden
Like childhood's penance of long Sunday walks;

Childhood, so naturally endowed with scheming.
Three dragonflies arrive, stropping the air
As though they've just been hatched, begun to whirr.
We must be moral, thoúgh I prefer dreaming.

Rimbaud snubbed fame; adept so many ways,
Like exploration, making money, lying;
His poetry left for dead but never dying.
Let's drudge like Hesiod in *Works and Days*,

Or delve; or bring the bull among the herd.
Mandelstam and Rimbaud one should try
To emulate: linguistic alchemy,
Vicarious redemption by the word:

Physicists also, such as Schrödinger
Who'd read the mystics. *Brilliant only child.*
The particle in its magnetic field,
Atman to Brahman, void of love or anger:

He saved those for poor poems and young girls.
And yet of course his universe is lovely
In its conception, sinless and behovely,
Who, to find silence, plugged his ears with pearls.

38

SATOR AREPO TENET OPERA ROTAS
Between front and reverse there may be space,
Miraculously, for a moment's peace.
Best if you don't speak Latin, you're not Brutus.

Tic-tac Firenze welcomed its black flood.
Blok loathed the place, would not have wept for it.
Montale, jobless, sweated the War out;
Dallapiccola, eating his bitter bread

At Fiesole gripped by the War's fifth winter,
Pen-sprigged his diary naming Webern *master*,
Integrity competing with disaster,
A long-dead farce; not one to disinter.

Turn and turn about, they fill the quotas.
Not all are here and there's no end of staring:
A simple faith subscribed to frigid daring;
Un-invoiced for false teeth, old stiffnecked photos.

39

Ravenna, this was your doing: when you buried
All those ephemeral things. They have gone deep.
You are yourself like a great child asleep,
Ravenna. Even eternity is tired.

Slaves, through these gates, no longer heave and sway
The monstrous toppling luxuries; the blaze
Of mural gilding in the basilicas
Is turning ashen as day follows day.

They too are gone, the plangent obsequies;
The moisture weeps. In the sarcophagi
Where local saints and great empresses lie,
The walls are scabbed with clinging verdigris.

The sea long-since withdrawn, only a surge
Of roses breaks upon the ramparts now;
Presume Theodoric and his dreams that grow
Could be held still beneath these words of charge.

Galla Placidia's black-blazing eyes, her voice,
Remain immured: yet at a breath, a start,
Of their awakening the stones would part,
Those riven centuries: blood, fire and grace.

Here are old gardens, rubbish under vines;
And all who tended them have gone to ground.
The tomb-inscriptions live and re-resound,
Embronzed as trumpets their imperious lines.

Sometimes at night, as though he had no grave,
The shade of Dante stands, affronts the gloom,
And gives account of all the time to come,
Predicting a New Life: that life we have.

40

Not much Italian, as this must show.
Best with the visuals, an *autoscatto*
Stuck in a folder. The Gabinetto
Vieusseux, Firenze, knows about Time's maw

Sotto parole tacite, the odd guests
Among the echo-chambers. Fraught with tact
The forms of patronage and interdict;
Sedately whetted by polite requests.

Indignity is the grave of love—that grave
Heaped in the archive I've been brought to browse,
Make conjuration with, until they close;
So fierce upon me this old Guelf enclave,

Via de' Tornabuoni, the hotels
With lifts that tremble, slow in their dispatch;
The heavy doors, the functionary-watch,
A wealth secreted, shops like citadels.

Quomodo sedet sola civitas
Means, whatsoever, ever to commute
Through Love's exchanges, never the same lute;
Archaic lore, the proud civilities

So natural to some, as of their being,
That Dante must have had despite his wrath,
Wearing his shoes thin on the exiles' path;
The self self-knowing in the Other-seeing.

These metaphysics blind you suddenly
With recognition. If there's to be a course
I cannot stay it or again rehearse
Those chances that first linger and then fly.

Blok's an idealist of things too real
To be endured: for him Italia cast
Intricate tyrannies as a glory past;
Ravenna ravaged yet still bountiful.

But Donatello's great self-standing
Figure of Habakkuk's best left alone.
It almost justifies what we have done;
Bears in its lonely filth our common ending

Without compunction, with impunity.
Back at the Gabinetto, closure, smiles.
Do not abjure the craft of shifting styles;
Nor, into private grief, impugn the City.

41

The world-Serpent changes his skin; we live
On a scrap of the old skin—Arsenio
To his lost Clizia. *Così son io.*
It's just the way Italians survive,

A cynicism that's not his but mine.
They have a wrought resilience like stoics
Beyond the pull even of mock heroics—
Arsenio's poems. Taken line by line

He might, with Feste, call the mind an opal;
But his is more an animus downplayed;
A sober opulence, a light delayed,
Comes iridescent between him and people.

Suppose that in the sun it scintillates,
Multi-faceted snakeskin; she might wear
Tokens to pledge what had befallen her:
The task of living at his visions' gates.

Failure or not, a stillness of commotion
Seems to ordain it with authority:
A love dispersed into disparity,
Privacy subject to so much privation,

Endurance toleration of affect.
Of power, her attribute, the Muse was brought
Hardly to speak, as one too dearly bought;
Impassioned with him, straightly circumspect.

42

Telling his stout lethargic recklessness
Flared by her jewels famously not rare
Amber and coral earrings—fringe attire—
Bracelets of silver, garnet necklaces

To which a vivid fable find attached
(Plucked from a train window and last seen
A tracer-streak of red caught against green)
The Vixen's trail, this, earthy and far-fetched

But of the legend with his solitudes,
That in the mind the redefining moment
Is for the poem what grace is to tórment.
How to expound it in less glowing words?

Six Variants on Montale, 'Il gallo cedrone'

43 (a)

Snapshot—that—the snapped shot. You foundered,
Who had been ponderous; echo a travesty
Of a mating-call, that 'guttural retching cry'.
Desperately sheltering, I too am plundered.

Capercailzie—'largest European grouse'—
Rare even in Andorra, to élitist taste.
We're broken, though, to stew and sink as waste;
Or so I ponder, making Earth's mulch my muse.

My wing-root's a smashed bone; as slowly
As you attempted it my crippled flight
Flails blindly to the wall. Therefore, this sight—
Blood-feathered tatters on a frost-bound holly.

That stately fracas after the year's turn;
Startling, those fragile eggs. The sticky-buds
Erupt like larvae; a god among his gods
Went down into the earth to be re-born.

43 (b)

Someone back there's no crackshot: you have crashed
Though I still hear your voice come bubbling up
Out of the black-red mulch, the primal soup.
Well, I'm ditched with you, being scorched and mashed.

Pain cries to cliché. Simply, it would be better
To live at hazard, even with your wings' traction—
Short ugly flight at most—an interjection—
Than feast these crusted flames' abysmal matter.

I hug your death in closest metaphor.
Mý breast's shot through beneath your clod of wings;
We break on stone in our blind staggerings;
Our strewn feathers, the ilex in its frore.

Erogenous magma!—see what you make of us:
The matings, nestings, clutch of precious eggs;
The new life festers with the old year's dregs,
The self-insemination dubbed as Jove's.

43 (c)

Black-red engulfs you now, shot-stricken bulk;
I catch your cry, the tumbling-over-plume,
Earth swirling, or the cloud, to primal grume
Where I as much as yoú flail. Of your ilk,

I struggle to impáct your pain. Although,
Like me, nó great athlete, better gone
Vanishing on the wings that staunchly shone
Than plunge into this fire-and-water slough.

So much is repetition; by the end
How much evasive, self-illusory!
How much ís mine, your last-ditch-heave to fly;
Stripped plumage on the holly's icy rind?

An old year dies; its death will disappear.
Birth-wet, cocoon-like breaking of the bud;
Grouse-eggs ground-laid, the scufflings near the brood:
Full of his jollities, our Jupiter.

43 (d)

After the shock, the outrage, you descend
(As we'd prefer, with injured dignity.
Afraid not; there's a flap, you sprawl to die.)
I from my gutter miserably attend.

'Aiuto!'—to interpret sigh or croak—
Rarer apotheosis, wind and sun,
Than here where your own body-sewers run,
Piled post-diluvian like other muck.

I've chest-pains—empathy's been oversold—
Still I feel fór you, that obtruded wing
Sore-travailed by its flail-and-spigotting.
The ilex, its dark splendour, shuttered, cold,

Memorializes nothing that we are . . .
The new nests, their fresh-offered sacrifice;
Maggots'-milk tackiness, the very lice
Enraptured at the flesh that crowds to war.

43 (e)

After the spraddle of the shots you fell,
Spasm and rattle in the dulling body.
I had not thought death could be so untidy.
My indeterminate self your self at call.

Dying cries out: any old death preferred
To this corruption; wind and sun are sweet;
Or pray to be dissolved and to forget
The primal smegma that our blood is, charred.

I feel in mý breast where the lethal flak,
Striking a wing-root, hurls your body round
As on a pivot, staggering to ground.
The frost-lit ilex does not lose a flake.

Spring-strut of victory; eggs that frailly hatch
Or spill an ichor; the perennials
Compound with horny buds your darkling spoils,
You are this buried god, who wake and stretch.

43 (f)

I shall now say: after the shot you screeched,
Your voice recoiled, rejected by the rich
Black and red 'salmi', procreative ditch,
Where I too crouch, in joint-distress, unscratched,

Deeper than empathy, knowing you—creature—
Your being of air. And now what magma
Swallows us at the kill, mud like phlegm
Plugged in the throat of the creator-fire

That, even so, doés for us. Your hurt is mine
I shall insist, and my flesh-floundering plight
Your frantic one-winged beating to gain height.
Hoar-frost encrusts the holly leaves like brine.

Effective too the way the year comes round,
Matings, buddings, fatal shows of birth;
You, I, the dead, enlivening the dead earth,
A god new-roused, fecundity his wound.

44

Capercailzie makes its 'retching' call
In Scots—no, Gaelic! So *aiuto*'s cut.
Strange if we'd spied Arsenio with the shoot,
Gun broken at the breech, a dog at heel—

Conspicuous pose in photos from *The Field*
Of Chamberlain and Halifax, the day's bag,
Around the time that we surrendered Prague.
Class petulance like virtue, well annealed.

In Scotia as in Austria or Andorra
Gallo cedrone wears the season's crown,
Minding its own passions, portly, grown
Succulent upon sweet alpine flora.

45

Arsenio, let us put this joke to bed.
Grouse-shoot turned crazy. But not you. We work,
Think nobly of the soul though mired in dreck.
Malvolio was late sprung, as privy-mad

As I have been; the angry pact of writing
Imagined here: our pilgrimage toward
The lost benevolent City many-towered
Where swallows weave and loop, at last alighting.

46: *i.m. Irma Brandeis*

Always new trees astonish—carob, aloe,
Blue-wenned fig, the trim and proper lemon,
The wild laurel rendering things trans-human.
Or think of *Resurrection*: that by Piero,

This by Bellini who saw Christ in hím.
Else I'm a closet-gnostic, misinterpret
Resurrection as rebirth of Spirit—
Montale likewise, who drew flesh through scrim.

Emblematic landscape moves at rest
In transformation: ever that meek vulture
Stuck with his thoughts above the Sepulture.
Composure says, this Light is its own guest

As here defined, replete of its outpouring,
Allows all accidentals in their frame;
is to becoming what long-since became,
Grants mystics their eternities adoring;

Does not commit, nor yet retract, the fire;
Neither discounts whatever destiny
Adjusts the spider to the zizzing fly,
Spiels us to fragments, leaves self-will entire.

Look, Clizia, look up! Hic signum est.
See where you are, and háve been all this while.
Age, death, upon us in a gathering file.
Strangely unwounded is our risen Christ.

47

Blok was all fatalism. Like a lamb.
Legend his reality a myth.
The force of things explodes the mystic wraith,
Beautiful Lady meets assassin's bomb.

Montale went much otherwise; he held
Myth in parentheses within the act
(This being poetry, love, their non-neglect)
Some other failure to beget a child.

I ha'e forekent ye! O I ha'e forekent—
MacDiarmid's chanter in *A Drunk Man Looks*
Translating something etiolate of Blok's.
A ghost of vision there, improvident,

No providence on call, nothing on oath
Even before we met or ever knew
The price extorted for what gifts allow,
Our long-drawn attestation of love's wrath.

In absence of possession many thole
And are discountenanced. So, with the *Phaedrus*,
One falls to brooding that the wings of *Eros*
Attach themselves so ardently to the soul

By undeclared desire to lash its pain;
The soul already ardent in its kind,
Encountering no such spectres-that-attend
As Dante met with on the monstrous plain.

48

I do not think that it will be a fribble,
The rabbis' prophecy, *He shall arrive*
And they be lucky who no longer live.
The naked spine of my disjointed Bible,

Threats to be reconciled with some Redeemer
If that were possible. *Götterdämmerung*
Was, is, gross; and there are *Judgements* hung
Across Europe, having survived the War

In ways not known to Jews and gipsy-stock.
Art is impregnable in what it claims,
Consoles itself while children curl in flames.
I could not say what registers the shock:

Perhaps nothing; perhaps the *Pietà*;
Or Donatello's Magdalen—calloused body
And withered mouth, lost teeth; a dried-up *wadi*
Might hold such remnants of things left to die:

Piero's or Bellini's *Resurrection*,
A barely-noticed miracle sustained
As the new blessing of all things by kind,
His risen light no less our light's refraction.

Or bet that little demon *Amor-Atys*
Impersonates the feral ghosts unborn,
Tarred embryos mismatched with those who mourn,
In the foundations of Millennial cities.

49

Why does this never falter? I say we múst
Túrn and be broken, even as metre holds—
Let's mean by that, *progresses* and *enfolds*—
Moving the syntax to a form of trust.

Fragile erratic medium and predator;
Thróugh-flurried pitches that can be received
As a year's gathering, as bees are hived:
Hear me my own willing self-auditor:

Tenebrae sopra Gesualdo, grief
To be solaced by, the ritornelli
Muttering between takes of deep and shrilly-
Resonant voices in concordant strife.

O vos omnes qui transitis per viam
Attendite et videte si est dolor.
Most flagellations are a buzz of squalor.
Scored Gesualdo writhes his joy of them.

50

And still there's more to it, the yielded phrase
Glad in its tessitura though the screed
Itself is lamentation, perhaps dread.
The words feel nothing and will not refuse

Hot stuff out of the shambles and the trench—
Sicut dolor meus, how to trim it;
Excessus mentis knowing its own limit.
And all this while a sorrow none can staunch:

The dark side of our minds in flames of music.
'Chanced-on survivors heard it as a *weird*
Organ-like sound, long-held dissonant chord',
Wreak-blast of synaesthesia, shriek-mosaic.

51

Not Moloch but that infant deity
Amor-Atys, he of the *laughing fierce*
Destruction that Yeats courted in high verse,
Such rhetoric proclaimed as his plain duty.

Imagine, if you will, Germania's night,
Her panoplies of fire topped by roast cloud
While Amor-Atys runs in molten lead;
And the clawed corpses' puppetry's a fright

Whirled in deep shelters when the air combusts—
Conglomerate agonies to crisp and boil,
A single cry transfixed, inaudible,
God time-expired amid galactic dusts.

52

Estimation crowns us its darling kings
Of necromancy. Chandrasekhar
On Eddington: *Let's see how high we soar*
Before the sun melts the wax from our wings.

Irony fails; the Logos put to shifts.
We? We are stalled, observe some feeble
Antinomy becoming its own double.
Lumen obscurum wrought of our best crafts.

A pristine comet its unfathomed orbit
Rakes into vision a rejoicing span,
Lifts its tail of detritus like a mane.
Theology keeps watch from ancient habit.

53

Ephemerality working against time.
Funded and tended it is the Sienese
Triumph of civics appointing the wise men.
That pilgrimage enjoys its little drama,

Its fixed dimensions. Here the doing-word
Is wield. They yield to their own magic; snow-
Bonfired the brust star that stands at show
Hosting the well-marked shepherds in their ward

Whatever happens. I can barely talk
Through our necessity, our fearfulness
Outlined with rage. There are the ox and ass
Companionably breathing, a lit balk,

Shrewd tyranny suspenseful of alarms,
Godhead self-scanted; judged as answerable,
Justice and Mercy, ever the unstable,
A secular preponderance of forms.

The place of sacrifice ordained as bargain,
The nuptial mysteries of those unwed
Aptly consenting, with an end bestowed
Some painter reaches out for. So begin.

54

They change perspective as in a deep mirror,
My wise men: Mandelstam who visited
Dante like an angel in his head;
Seraphic Blok born-again commissar;

Musorgsky rapt in some strange providence,
Pushkin's, Gogol's, treading with precision,
As music does, even a Fool's vision
Or dances *for the drunk Ukrainians*—

Missed from this scene but not extraneous
To what's contained: epiphanies and fools,
Sight, smells, of prisons, duomos, hospitals,
Bloodless nativity, the blood that's Siena's

Still to be brought upon us by this trek.
The grand providers, beings of high order,
Perfume things with their spiced unworldly odour;
The ox's horn scratches the ass's neck.

Woe to the great Doctors: the Immaculate
Conception of our sane and mortal Mary—
Hers in her mother Anna—a fine theory;
The bond between God and our flesh traduced by that.

55

Donatello's measured disturbance, pain
For the most part. Woe indeed to the great Doctors,
Divinity with the immaculate vectors,
Humankind everywhere, its tiresome stain.

One might try ecstasy: those unruly
Women, angular struck maenad-motion—
Di Giorgio's chased bronze *Lamentation*
At the Foot of the Cross; *nello stilo*

Burlesco, say, dancing with grief.
Deny yourself and swear that we became
Of the true faith the better to blaspheme.
The wastage of it all judders belief.

56

Emerald, ruby, sapphire, beryllium.
Here has come an end; and there is nothing
To hinder our salvation save self-loathing.
State which of the above is not a gem.

Or show how wronged things naturally come right
For someone's sake; cite the discovery
Proclaimed in *ode four* of the *Convivio*:
As water in a sphere concentrates light

And therefore heat, the converse of a prism,
So is love's agency, if so it move:
A burning-glass the clarity we have;
No virtue lost to our own protoplasm

Or riddled by *corruption of the air*.
As well decree the periodic table
Of chemical elements a mystic babble:
Her beauty is thy worth's accreditor.

57

Time being exponential, tenuate, dense,
In which death hits on most against their will;
The sun's incessant raging to be still;
Christ's tears effluvia that no art would cleanse:

Petrucci speaks, *I govern day by day;*
The age is stronger than our minds; his guest,
Terse Machiavelli, courteous at best:
Virtù not virtue's prized economy.

Mark how that Scythian shepherd screwed the law:
Death to those who piss in streams, on ashes,
Or terrified him with their photo-flashes,
Fell to their knees in the stale-bloodied straw.

Go back of choice. Petrucci said, *I rule*
Hour by hour, the paper-scuttering winds
Enroiled with dragons in scrolled mappamonds.
Blind beggar rides lame beggar the last mile.

58

Though Marx had said, man is *the sovereign*
Of circumstance, those fatalistic tyrants
Engage me most—Petrucci, aspirants
Bound to their plunder, arbitrary men,

By their own violence made circumspect,
Their faith-bedevilled centuries, the trials,
Assassinations, amnesties, espials;
Italia split all ways. Rich, derelict,

The *City of Good Governance* at odds
With its own governors; the commonplace
Misappropriations beyond trace,
Brawls, barratry, blind ambuscades on roads.

Tremuoti—earthquakes—a rare aurora
Flame-wraps the night skies over Austria.
History's progress via hysteria,
The ragged march, rote-brokerage of war.

59

An axe-blade resonates; the echo spurs—
Valley of Arno, aery campaniles!
Up from Firenze's falling and climbing bells
Some far-discerned gold-haloed vision nears:

Angelico, young, perched on tall Fiesole,
Hears the axe trill and thock, as I do, now;
Gazes across Firenze's worldly show:
Immortal child unsevered from things holy.

60

Blok's verdict on the age, austere and scabrous,
Was much like Dante's, at whose tomb he kept
Vigil for Europe, in twinned prescience rapt.
His verse, when not marmoreal, tenebrous,

Per umbram, with spondaic sequestry,
As, for a time, Virgil made credible:
The half-choked fulminations of the Sibyl,
The dull forboded ghosts of Italy

Hexametered into their formal coign.
Blok dreamed enlightenment, wrote from despair
Sibylline leaves candescent without air,
Flocculent treasure squandered, not in vain.

61

No question the elect are the saved remnant—
Vera Ierusalem—long since destroyed—
Old superstition neither raked nor ploughed.
Impacted salt, brick, jackals' tenement,

Avail the still too mortal Christ his stour.
Look, he is betrayed, the soldiers, they
Have come with torches though it is broad day.
Darkness crowds hard upon them for their hour.

62

Germania rapta, or, indeed, Private Jones:
Britannia and Germania Embracing,
Long-buried eros part resurfacing,
And Mr Tod's terrible house of bones.

A shrapnel-splintered steeple struck by light,
Equivalent to a high trumpet call
Held over muted strings, the pastoral
Sweep of a nation blessed in sound and sight.

63

Not wholly innocent Piero gave new grace
To the young subaltern dozing at the vault,
Something between penance and fresh default;
Christ miming resurrection in our space,

Concatenation of left knee, right arm,
Each limb drawn chilly from the stiff ascent;
A tenderness of luminous assent
Still-rising colours on the clouds affirm.

Seismic researches may unearth a cure
For epilepsy, it has been predicted.
Such is the leitmotiv of the afflicted,
These curious serrations deep and dure.

Or like a tranche cut from a crown of thorn
Or as cartoon fur with shot voltage through it,
Fit iconography for us distraught.
Bellini's Christ ecstatically upborne;

The force of levitation its own calm,
That graceful fauna, the scant passers-by,
Glow with intransitive intensity,
Edict and verdict reft and risen from.

64

Set to arpeggionize on death's bearing
Tremors of our first selves, a mute film score
Timed to a millisecond and to spare;
Accuracy at that pitch acutely wearing.

Dull these reflections: Arsenio's
Lamp-black, composure's revenants that ply
Effusive through self-sealing mercury.
Riffling plumes in the unstrung pianos:

Cling as we may, honestly, misguerdon
Sad fantasies, fit ending we make so,
Among our *sortilegi*, to and fro,
Questing and frustrate through the midnight garden.

65

Ars moriendi, ars poetica,
Entwined within thy love, grave Industry;
If I unleashed my dreams what words would fly!
Erotic honey's late erotica,

The wireless, mingled drone and susurration,
Heard up through floorboards in a cold house
By a child disciplined to its malaise;
Who in late life fixates a foreign station;

Whose clockwork toys had flints to make them spark;
Who saw the last British dirigible
Plunge towards Beauvais her fiery double.
Pitched safe on Ararat his flying ark.

66

Let your eye in ⎮ under the cello's bridge
Bow's early Bomberg's edgy cubism
Acuity of pitch processing spasm
Desire's infinitude sheared at that edge:

Crafting—say *weft*—the soul in selving kind
And of remembrances to disencumber
The heart's finally ineffectual chamber
Old age bewailing its lost *wunderkind*.

Music at last must die; such was our error
Angelus novus and the supernovae
Rage like stars in a stiff silent movie:
Your hidden God still to be found in Torah.

Not that it finishes us, the violence
Of sudden death the arbitrary
Becoming freedom by eternal nature
One to one the torch of misalliance

Body-tagged spirit mutual disaffection
Fidelity's safe-keeping, whether or not
Judged by such evidence as we were brought
The prophets then walked free of miscorrection.

67

Not nearly done. Sea-buckthorn is our stay.
Mars' glowering light burns to the dereliction-
Deliverance that some nominate *election*,
Some *aboriginal calamity*.

When Venus is alert in her sky-quarter
Turn your immoderate eyes where she hangs low
As seeking resolution by her law;
Treading delicately—blood of the satyr—

Syntax of hebetude contracts its reign.
She looks toward us; intricately simple
Her complex assignations. In the temple
I cannot say if Mars approves his sign;

Nor better grasp at destinies decreed
By stiff Mantuan *labor* of intent,
The fatal bifurcations provident.
In Stygian rumour yet those voices bleed.

68

Ravenna, Rimini, the Malatestas,
And the much-vested copia of rhyme
Turning a paradox on its réclame.
What a drag they are, the real imposters,

All these material lords of no avail.
Would you accept that, in the late
Democracies, solipsism is fate;
In an old city-state, hieratic will?

Evens we lose: plague, earthquakes, the jihad;
The torture-cells crowding the baptistry;
The lust to build imperiously to destroy;
Possessed Salome spliffs on Jokanaan's head,

He was so lucky. This, her studio pose,
Struck for the golden mediocrities.
Phyllis brought Aristotle to his knees,
Wisdom hag-ridden, piggish, comatose.

69: *i.m. R. B. Kitaj*

Describe you, how? Drawing a parabola
Consummately, as with Giotto's circle,
Whereby the loop describes its miracle;
Let us invoke that and your Cábbalah:

As of your suddenly ageing; and the bit
Where you imitate Sickert, pursing over food
With the slack nausea of an invalid,
Lips' bow recently broken, poorly reset,

As happens with age and grief—*a language
Of anger and distress*: how to augment
Intelligence with this mere idiot pigment,
The common *techne* that our wits engage

Even when they engage nothing. I know
That for you Donatello is grand guest-
Master of things constrained into the wrist:
Mass, void, stress, torsion, stone that can grow

The more it is cut back; impassive grip
Of passioning subdued, the calloused hand,
Much-prized aloofness, the self-jealous mind,
And youth ejaculating like a whip.

70: *i.m. R. B. Kitaj*

Sandra as Shekhinah, the divine being
Conceived as a woman, conceivably
Saying *I am that I am*, no love put by,
Phenomenally present, seraph's wing

Or spectral bush burning like brandy-wine.
Connubial with death, dazed ravisher
Stung by her yet-ravishing shock of hair;
Pencil across the paper coarse and fine.

71: *i.m. R. B. Kitaj*

Surge of the blood, massy, pre-coital;
And Patmore's hegemonics never curbed
Our dark proclivities, *like a perturbed
Moon of Uranus*, obscurely fatal.

Shrill contestation fractures factory glass.
The *O* precisely silent: who first ground
A future for industrial diamond?
The old man—what has brought him to this pass?

Ezekiel's boneyards rummaged by the gusts.
The rabbis gnaw their thumbs, *let him appear*
But let me not be living in that hour.
Your mercy is upon us, Lord of Hosts.

72

Throw me a scruple could you for my care
And I will speak. When Pound said *I cannot*
Make it cohere, his burden was the poet
Primus inter pares, shrunk vatic fire;

But also the spent paterfamilias
Feckless with wife, daughter, de facto son;
Unfaithful to the vows of humbler men,
Their telling gods, guardians of families.

My mind yet goes about to comprehend
How patience may be obduracy, muteness,
A body burning off the mind's witness,
All but last oracles gone from that mind.

I wish these were enough: late-vision-guided
Hermits embracing, a nativity
Scene by Sassetta, floating on gravity
Siena's towers rose-light-enfiladed.

Wind glintering like mica, far things glow,
Atollite portas!—O my spirit!—
We are what we are, self-disinherit
Most that's incumbent ón us to bestow.

73

Death and the Etruscans: Lawrence, perhaps
Yeats, who corrected proofs as they lay dying,
Dilate their spirits. Too much envying
Consumes the heart, yet fumes in that eclipse.

Nerofumo tropes dead mirrors, tantric,
Smearing everything, the soul so well
Extemporising between cell and cell,
Corpsing itself against inerrant metric.

74

Come le coturnici—the rock partridge
Crauckles its self-keeping, its own host,
Where we sometime alighted, tempest-cast;
Princely relief, a dukedom's entourage;

Comedy where redemptive joys ran riot
In the great houses of Illyria,
On seacoasts of Bohemia and Tyre.
Timon's misanthropy enjoyed its root.

Can empathy be taught, what should one ask?—
For, speaking tropically, too much our calm
Is of the lugworm and rock-boring clam;
Too skewed for charity Assisi's mask.

Who even dead hath yet his mind entire—
Blessed apotheosis of mishap,
Less empathy than grace. Clizia, look up!
Fa di clarità l'aer tremare.

75

Visiting England in the off-season,
For so I insist it was, Montale
Wrote enigmatically about Ely
Cathedral; a depressed man's orison.

(After solemn pianoforte *intrada*
The high tenor glissade, unaccompanied
Cadenza of distress, *wehklagelied*
For love requited, gone to decrepitude.)

And the pitched wind rattles Ely's lantern,
As I suppose it, running straight and raw
In from the North Sea, raking the dyked flow,
Reed-light upscouring from sogged Wicken Fen.

76: *to Hugh Maxton*

Purgatorial spirits: those who, Yeats says,
Dance to escape realities of flame
By denying they dream
(Not to give that much credence to his plays).

Courage by rite and rote: beyond question
Bring back citations, flags, and to their duty
Boy soldiers and caulked whisky-mystics. *Dirty*
People of no name redeem fame's bastion.

Brittle flâneur drops by at the Post Office,
Enscrolls himself—let me believe—who later,
Sidneian, gives away his cup of water.
Cuchulain farts blood from each orifice.

Say I invest things heavily in lieu.
Had I read you earlier I might have
Cast my words differently towards the grave.
Let stand these lurching paradigms to view.

77

Subject to late conditions, Morcom's *second*
Death is for me complicitous to mourn—
It happened when I was four—
Nerving into exposure Turing's mind,

Its paradox, determinate free will,
Cracked. Eddington had gifted him; it shows:
Molecular systems pitching their tone-rows,
Immortal spirit scurrying through that mill . . .

Eventually it is gone, love's will to hope
The still-adored, still-unrequiting muse
Stays active-passive in the universe:
The Clock House tower and its telescope

That I remember seeing from the road
A place as mythic as the sullen coast
Montale peopled with his father's ghost;
My father waiting on the Colonel's nod.

78

Everywhere, now, I find Italian
Is looking good—I write elliptically
Aldilà not *ladida*, red lily.
Reception into new life scarcely begun

To weigh its language: nothing yet condemns
The first perception as it is in Eden,
Transparency of things not yet forbidden.
Beyond the gate a block of towering hymns

To Cybele (is she orgies, or cities?).
So, how far is it true that *La Bufera*
E Altro brings to an end its era?
Set my words down, among the amenities

And triage. This is her doing: Vixen,
Our poet's other lady; she of the window
(Per diventare una leggenda)
Put to rejoice libido like an ex-nun:

Venereal wounds for which no use of martyrs—
Don't interrupt me here, let me recall
First kissing you, our lips still in their shell—
Crudel Amor! Take pity from your creatures.

Thinking of language incapacitates
It in some great measure. The axioms
Of mathematics rest on their void looms.
Lords of *Usura*, look to your estates.

79: *i.m. Alberto de Lacerda*

Against the odds I here become a gambler
On final justice. I had relegated
You, as I have others less ill-fated.
What honest scribe is not a knee-trembler

With our vile solace the consensual word?
My private ignorance might have predicted
These mortal scraps of paper, rage-evicted;
Your *sortes*, your *satura*. Could scarce afford

Not to. Is silence natural? To write
Obsessively can seem so. Suffer prayer.
Your exit that humiliating door.
To hostile London I submit no wreath.

80

Black puddle crudely flares its mutant eye.
The word is generation, *Anima*
Mundi itself being the dynamo.
The toad unreels her fabulous progeny.

Earth, best-rhymed original alchemist,
Proclaims *the very natural true sperm*
Of the great world. Charged thus to procreant Adam
My fecund winter glitters its verbed crest.

81: *1961, Between the Cherubim*

Tygers brush their compunction, sad drummer.
Our beat so to be beaten. Coventry's
Unlaunched Odeon hangs in its gantries.
Remind me, now, who died that November.

Off-rhyme a law to itself. Nonsense. It
Serves a turn, impales my comedians
Of tragic rigor with their weak grins.
I had not forgotten that death. Hence wit.

There is no true feeling without structure.
This may have been disputed. I recall
Nothing from that tagged year I would wish ill.
Viewed through communal smoke a bad picture.

If we had birth it roared at discretion
Of my wise child: a challenge to my theme
So well served by the dealers of mis-fame.
This hiss of truth within thick air's secretion

I owe him for his love. And fabulous
Music probably there was; and justice
In fair measure; as ever malpractice,
The trash of time cemented into fables.

82: *i.m. R. B. Kitaj*

Writing as now, numbly, to release feeling
And in a sense perplexed that my mind does
Things which amaze me even in its chaos,
Brute Actuality ever the unfailing—

People get by these days without the *lira*—
I wax rhetorical: for is it not
The governance of ourselves we are about,
Professed San Miniato? The *gira-*

sole stands a head taller than I am.
Poetics is a cross with all its stations;
My theme in these intemperate devotions
Intemperate devotion to my theme.

Indifferently thumbed, Vasari lives.
Pound's unread works we'd place among the best
Witnesses to that century of the lost,
Irrevocably at call, damned with those evils.

Be mindful how the evidence is put
Each time the City with a buzz of bronze
Belies the gospels — saint-struck Firenze;
The Baptistry so full it should be shut.

I think I know your humours. I confess
I have not visited Urbino—your
Uccello-mob destroying the Jew's door;
The little girl snucked in her mother's dress.

The freedom of this world inclines to fate
And we are not immune. Detritus
Of tragic closure claims its theatres;
As Dante's lost affiances new-met.

83

A se stesso, still too much the groper
Of late appetencies; and again you think
That's how it will be and *Christ, the stink!*
Memory and imagination both improper.

Beautiful, disagreeable, gold-grey
Unhurried carp, with rubbery mouths, that wend
Gobbing and pocking through the laden pond
Where the grand lilies, held at anchor, splay . . .

Difficult to attune as meditation—
The old woman abruptly so: *I feel
Sixteen still, but with something terrible.*
Voices of varying petulance and pain

That speak more to themselves than us;
Prolixities with which the mind performs
As if it stalked itself through the bare rooms
Seeking estrangement of its power to bless.

84: *Preghiera a ——*

I have ridden out one cosmos already,
Manner of speaking. The metaphysical
End of desire is always to be real;
The word and world well-met and going steady.

If this not possible, trick is to renew
Batteries of arcane matter: fatalism
For one; the labyrinth or chasm
Of language. Tedium can be made to glow.

Comes real at last only renunciation.
I am before that, inadequately tired;
What has been taken remains unrestored.
Each word excruciate in its computation.

Command I spit upon clay to obtain merit—
For what remains to us in the great set
Book of the People that is not escheat?—
Who once could beget love but could not bear it.

85

As we by others' judgement fall interdict
Whose powers extend even to the least
Coherent particle of the eucharist;
As Golem whirr-clanks to some monstrous final act;

As old Saturn, rough Mars, wield cosmic grudges,
Out of the cognates of dense time arisen,
With that *perturbèd moon of Úranus*,
Smash at the Tempio and Pisa's bridges,

Aggrieve old Baedeker. Rose and elephant
At Rimini; much like the dollar clef
That once redeemed us, S-and-I enscarf
Their pagan vows, baptized, paneloquent,

Determinism being the soul at play
In one of many of its crucial stations:
Unaccountable the life of nations.
Distinguish *satis* from *satiety*.

86

Strapped for cash I'm seeking—*bloody foreigners!*—
Time to unmake my golem. Those Jews were
Reckless with prophecy, snatching it from fire.
I can see parchment shrivelling at the corners,

Hebrew that might read *Lilith* black and writhing.
Ash pricks under the forefinger. Habakkuk,
Donatello's great side-kick, welcome back.
That epiphanic moment like the day-spring

I owe you and of course him: Firenze,
Duomo museum, unknown, half-expected;
A pleb's face by some angel interjected;
Imagining God's word in a gaunt frenzy . . .

Rosenberg entrenched, the last self-portraits,
Isaac, not Julius, jutting underlip,
Steel helmeted, his gear in sorry shape,
Butt for the regimental anti-Semites.

Alienated majesty applicable.
The grime, this always working to perfect
That which by nature must remain imperfect.
Clear vindication of prophetic scribble.

87: *on the Marriage of a Virgin*

Of density of being; of otherness;
That Eros alone, and rightly understood,
As some so marvellously have, his blood
Realigns with ours; his casual largess

Pragmatically acquired; of us apart
And part of us; as philosophical
Logic for the utterly naked soul;
Disorder's foil to some well-measured art.

Metabolism reassumes its tissue
Affronting us—with what—with sixty
Fixed years astonished by their fixity?
Not that I move them, speaking of you so,

Of the glory you were; begging words fetter
Their born eloquence, to bear *the heavy,*
The rinded, moon, sullen above your journey.
Not Eros the face, now, belovèd, but Ishtar.

Sei Madrigali

To PMH

88 (a)

Is it not strange that thou shouldst weep? So gravid
The sweetest song a burdening: the six
Metamorphoses, of violence and sex,
The sensuous oboe touched by sensual Ovid.

Pan pipes, the syrinx, the Orphic lyre;
The waters of the mere, reedy and full;
Poignant the false-relationed madrigal;
The hunter poised, the watcher with the lure.

88 (b)

The heron's flight out of the reeds is laggard
Yet still it climbs. You could have watched its slow
Navigation of the risen dawn,
Its neck drawn back, prehensilely long-legged,

But you were probably asleep, and I
Display too late my early grief. Too late
Pinions of holding lift and agitate.
The heron crests its high-reared heronry.

88 (c)

This keeping of delight makes to its strath.
As we must know it, the *perturbèd moon*
Which is the singular being and yet none
And of the sexual will its grief its graith,

Suffuses, broadens, rouses to subside.
Here too the archaic and reflective swan
Ploughs through its image before setting down.
The river-margins brim with each new tide.

88 (d)

So, solace without respite, as when, cour-
sing through the ear, Italian lute-songs
With preciosities pluck at the heart-strings,
Thy studied dissonance, *crudel Amor*.

Caccini's *Amarilli* I would play
At school assemblies, a scuffed seventy-eight
Bucking the needle, churning sweet disquiet.
Our loves are dying, we have had our day.

88 (e)

What would I have us do, enshrine Sosostris'
Aria from that fey *Midsummer Marriage*,
Joyous transcendent threnos before mere age,
All-mastering strings quelling things queer, disastrous?

Somewhere within the extravagant gauche plot
Is our true-plight, misfathomed, salutation.
If we should labour back against time's motion
Still distant are those lovers we were not.

88 (f)

What I have so invoked for us is true
As invocation. The Fibonacci range
Of numbers is a constant, like Stonehenge.
Like Ovid's book of changes to construe.

I can see someone walking there, a girl,
And she is you, old love. Edging the meadow
The may-tree is all light and all shadow.
Coming and going are the things eternal.

89

Yet more parading: Zoppo's moronic
Christ, Mantegna's plump sweaty St Mark
Weakly sensual at his grieving mouth;
The plunging of high bells heterochronic.

Let them create; let rouse the lyric men
And tetchy vitalists who have a cause
To argue, casuistical, crowd-wise;
Give cinquecento sciolists a run,

Give credits to the radiophonic workshop,
Eleusinian mysteries, Crab Nebula,
I-Ching and this choice Christian fabula,
With much else that we ignorantly worship,

Jarred round thy sainted streets, Londinium:
The Jewish chanteuse pitching through disgrace
Her lovely deep harsh register of voice,
Her grand self-maimings, whence and why they come.

Let fall how in furore we are scion
To the engorging cosmic synchrony
That draws more than our moon; a soundless cry
Sounding Andromeda and stark Orion.

90

Spewed-out hermeneutic, something the puppy
Chewed at—your wife's stick of mascara
And you stare horrified at the massacre—
Syntax magisterial, the wit stroppy.

My thoughts on plutocratic anarchy
Settle for grandeur and attend the sound
That trumpets of Siena can command;
My marked-up texts of the *Monarchia*.

Equity, most burdensome of powers,
Keeps time in riddles. Think of *nerofumo*
As satisfaction for black infamy
Evicted from the city via the sewers.

Everything that is not God is tourism,
Dante so nearly said. Let us secede
Even from your prophecies, pitiless Dada,
And from you also, antic Futurism;

Reluctant, immolate this photograph
Out of which the young Tristan Tzara
Stares like the mute assassin of a Tsar.
The aerobatic flame melting its trophy.

91

I am not good for much, the dour *Convivio*
No more my thing than Piero's Hercules,
Club-bollocky, with extroverted thews.
Wherefore, desiring now to make provision,

Suddenly the entire structure implodes.
The comedian's impudence towards the play
(Kafka) not altogether tragedy;
Survivors too, the stubborn palinodes.

First love is shattered, to be saved by luck,
Fidelity, whichever is the stronger.
Show me my bride and let me bring her
To Kiriath-sepher, City of the Book.

92: *to Alexander Goehr*

Had I wrought well this work might best attune
To *Arianna* after Monteverdi.
Without presuming on your parody;
As, where the gods descending to commune

Or stand aloof, or lie darkmans with mortals,
Inextricate the matter of their lives,
Ondriven by the bare recitatives;
Arias of grand abandon at the portals

Draw the inordinate *sub judice*.
These scrannel cornets, opulent trombones
Imitate sweetly-blarting megaphones.
Their blaze of rapture without prejudice

To mere palatial light, the candelabra
Feasting on nameless elements of air;
Theseus having slain the Minotaur,
Hiss of misprision striking like a cobra.

93

Stella maris, then, as she abides
The call to predicate her antichthon
A world hypostatized against-upon.
Salvation dips below the lunar tides.

O you who do not tremble to drink gold,
Aurum potabile of the alchemists,
The earth still magical, its veins and schists
None of the many mansions yet withheld:

What energy so urged the telegraph
As wealth of curiosity? My God,
You drive relentlessly the soul toward
Intelligence of the elect, though not enough.

Stupefied is your wisdom. Even
Septem Sermones ad Mortuos—Jung—
Hyperbolic, tortuous, unstrung,
I would subscribe to in despite of heaven.

Such troubling of the senses I recall,
Such red as when a singular, fissured, rose
Turbined the still air to equipose,
No colour more unearthly or more real.

94

Be mindful how much good derives from her.
Da lei, from her, from Justice. In Siena
Expect only the Virgin, *gratia plena*,
To be more lauded. And enjoy your summer.

The glory of poetry is that it is solemn,
Racked with anarchic laughter. Genius
Thriving on various expediences,
Like Petrarch's shattered and sustaining column,

Transforms bare reflex into rhapsody.
While we await death's distribution Liszt
Reprogrammes Dante as God's pianist
Playing like lightning through the infernal sky.

I am finished. I have done with golem
And dybbuk; the Cábbalah vortexed,
To my own purpose, far from the Urtext.
Megalomania is not a problem

Though other things are. Forcing this verse
Apart is like forcing apart hemispheres
In an experiment with air-pressures.
Arno forcing Ghiberti's doors was worse.

But there I rest my case. Vico knew neither
Neptune nor Úranus. Eddington, paranoid,
With darkening brilliance informed the Void
Of his conclusion; took God for his great Other.

We will get there, finding old Henry Moore's
Inexplicable jumps explicable
Additions to the Fibonnaci Table;
Reality itself grounded in our metaphors.

95

Reality so made: it is like fiction;
Like Brunelleschi's dome proportionate
Both to the thrustings of the city-state
And to the golden straddler, his perfection:

Quattrocento masters knowing them-
selves imbued practitioners of their scope
In fallen matter, in the mundane scape,
The bode of majesty their signal theme:

Donatello himself many times over
Master of the resources: Virgin, Babe,
Playing nosy-on-facy. So, what scribe
Or what Evangel, seeking things to discover,

Took such enraptured gazers for God's plight?—
They speak of what we are. Shagged Abraham
Self-thrusting from the knife, the trammelled arm;
John's head plumb on a platter, seem just right.

Judith feels Holofernes by the hair,
Wafting that scimitar, a broody look,
Taking her time, a murder for the book.
A picnic party addled by slurp-beer

The Apostles grunt and twitch, each as they're strewn;
How would you step among them? A courtyard,
Contorted accusation, Pilate's guard
Poising their torsos as they leer and fawn.

Perhaps not Donatello; one stands bemused.
That much would be in keeping. Error is,
And is endemic, and speaks mysteries;
Yahweh himself not wholly disabused

Of procreation. Time is the demiurge
For which our impotence cannot atone.
Nothing so fatal as creation's clone.
The stars asunder, gibbering, on the verge

ACKNOWLEDGEMENTS

COVER IMAGE

Oskar Kokoschka, 'Loreley', oil on canvas, Tate Gallery, London (© Fondation Oskar Kokoschka, Vevey, 2013, ProLitteris/DACS, 2013).

EPIGRAPHS

The lines from Psalm 98 in the King James Version, the rights of which are vested in the Crown, are reproduced by permission of the Crown's Patentee, Cambridge University Press.

The extract from Ezra Pound *Ta Hio: The Great Learning of Confucius* (New Directions Pamphlets, No 4, 1938; © Ezra Pound, 1938) is reproduced by permission of New Directions Publishing Corp.

POEMS

The texts of the poems that appear in *Collected Poems* (Penguin, 1985; © Geoffrey Hill, 1985) and in *Selected Poems* (Penguin, 2006; © Geoffrey Hill, 2006) are reprinted by permission of Penguin Books Ltd. The texts of the poems that appear in *Without Title* (Penguin/Yale, 2006; © Geoffrey Hill, 2006) and *A Treatise of Civil Power* (Penguin/Yale, 2007; © Geoffrey Hill; 2007) are reprinted by permission of Penguin Books Ltd and Yale University Press.

We have made every effort to trace and contact copyright holders. The publisher, if notified of errors or omissions, will rectify them at the earliest opportunity.

MERCIAN HYMNS

The epigraph by C. H. Sisson may be found in *The Avoidance of Literature*, ed. Michael Schmidt (Manchester, 1978) p. 202. (It was previously printed privately in Sisson's *Essays* of 1967.)

TENEBRAE

The epigraph by Sidney Keyes comes from 'Sour Land' (1940).

The epigraphs to 'The Pentecost Castle' are taken from *The Letters of W. B. Yeats*, ed. Allan Wade (London, 1954), p. 810 and Simone Weil, *First and Last Notebooks*, trans. Richard Rees (Oxford, 1970), p. 284. The epigraph to 'Tenebrae' is from Imogen Holst, *The Music of Gustav Holst*, 2nd edn (Oxford, 1968), p. 88.

Spanish and German poems have provided points of departure for several poems in this book. 'The Pentecost Castle' is particularly indebted to J. M. Cohen, *The Penguin Book of Spanish Verse*. The final sonnet of 'Lachrimae' is a free version of a sonnet by Lope de Vega (Cohen, p. 247), and the second sonnet of 'An Apology for the Revival of

Christian Architecture in England' is an imitation of a sonnet by L. L. de Argensola (Cohen, p. 202). 'Two Chorale-Preludes' includes a few phrases freely translated from two poems in Paul Celan's *Die Niemandsrose*: 'Eis, Eden' and 'Kermorvan'.

THE MYSTERY OF THE CHARITY OF CHARLES PÉGUY

The epigraph by Charles Péguy, from *Notre Jeunesse* (1909), can be found in *Basic Verities*, trans. Ann and Julian Green (New York, 1943), p. 102.

CANAAN

The sources of the epigraphs are, in order of appearance:

'Scenes with Harlequins': Avril Pyman, *The Life of Aleksandr Blok*, 2 vols (Oxford, 1979–80), vol. 1, p. 275 and vol. 2, p. 365.

'De Jure Belli ac Pacis', Part II: Ger van Roon, *Neuordnung im Widerstand* (Munich, 1967), commenting on a letter of von Haeften, 23 December 1938. Part VI: the Easter hymn by Luther ('Christ lag in Todesbanden') set by Bach in BWV 4. Part VIII: *Aufstand des Gewissens: Der militärische Widerstand gegen Hitler und das NS-Regime, 1933–1945* (Herford, 1984), p. 183.

'Sorrel': John Amphlett and Carleton Rea, *The Botany of Worcestershire* (Birmingham, 1909), p. 317.

'Churchill's Funeral', Part I: Jerrold Northrop Moore, *Edward Elgar: A Creative Life* (Oxford, 1984), p. 342, quoting a note by Elgar on the original inspiration for his *Cockaigne*. Part II: John Ruskin, *Unto This Last* (1862), 'Preface'. Part III: William Blake, *Milton* 44:34–5. Part V: William Blake, *Jerusalem* 31:17–18.

'To John Constable': the epitaph placed by John Constable on his wife's tomb in Hampstead churchyard.

'Psalms of Assize': John Colet's marginalia to the *Epistolae* of Marsilio Ficino, as transcribed by Sears Jayne, *John Colet and Marsilio Ficino* (Oxford, 1963).

SPEECH! SPEECH!

The fragment from Ennius, *Annals* is numbered 451 in Skutsch's edition. The epigraph by Günter Grass is the final line of 'Die Schule der Tenöre', in *Die Vorzüge der Windhühner* (Berlin, 1956).

SCENES FROM COMUS

The epigraph from Kafka is taken from *The Blue Octavo Notebooks*, ed. Max Brod, trans. Ernst Kaiser and Eithne Wilkins (Cambridge, MA, 1981), p. 26.

WITHOUT TITLE

The quotation from Bradley appears in *Essays on Truth and Reality* (Oxford, 1914), p. 10, n. 1, and the passage from Emerson in the lecture 'The Transcendentalist'.

The epigraph to 'Improvisations for Jimi Hendrix' comes from the lyrics to Hendrix's song 'The Wind Cries Mary'. The first line of Hart Crane's 'Reply' serves as the epigraph to 'Improvisations for Hart Crane'.

'The Storm' is a translation of 'La Bufera' by Eugenio Montale (© Arnoldo Mondadori Editore, Milan).

PINDARICS

Pindarics 30 includes a free imitation of some lines from André Frénaud, 'Le Beau Voyage', *Les Rois-Mages* (Pierre Seghers, 1943).

A TREATISE OF CIVIL POWER

Lines 7–8 of 'In Memoriam: Ernst Barlach' are from a letter by Barlach cited in Carl Dietrich Carls, *Ernst Barlach* (New York, 1969), p. 55. Other quotations in this poem are from Kate Fletcher, *The Old Testament in the Dialect of the Black Country*, Part 1 (Tipton, 1979).

'The Oath' is a free imitation of 'Les Offensés', found in Anne Hébert, *La Jour n'a d'égal que la nuit* (Boréal, Montreal, 1992).

EXPOSTULATIONS ON THE VOLCANO

The quotation from Whitman appears in the preface to the 1855 *Leaves of Grass*. Kate Lechmere is quoted in Alun R. Jones, *The Life and Opinions of T. E. Hulme* (London, 1960), p. 123.

ORACLAU | ORACLES

The lines from Pennar Davies are quoted in *Triskel Two: Essays on Welsh and Anglo-Welsh Literature*, ed. Sam Adams and Gwilym Rees Hughes (Llandybie, 1973), p. 126.

AL TEMPO DE' TREMUOTI

The title alludes to Francesco di Giorgio's painted book-cover of the Sienese Biccherna records, which depicts the Virgin of the Earthquake (1467–8). The epigraph is taken from Petrarch's 'Triumphus Temporis', ll. 130–1.

Russian and Italian poems have provided points of departure for several poems in this book. Sections 25, 26, and 28 are very free imitations, with transpositions and other liberties, of Pasternak's 'The Wind (Four Fragments about Blok)', as translated in Dimitri Obolensky, *The Penguin Book of Russian Verse* (1965), pp. 343–7. Section 27 imitates Tyutchev's 'Cicero' (Obolensky, pp. 131–2). Sections 29, 30, 36, and 39 freely rewrite and adapt poems found in *Aleksandr Blok: The Journey to Italy*, trans. Lucy E. Vogel (Ithaca, NY, 1973). The six 'variants' of section 43 respond to Eugenio Montale, 'The Capercaillie', in *The Storm and Other Things*, trans. William Arrowsmith (New York, 1985), p. 135.

INDEX OF TITLES

INDEX OF FIRST LINES